"A comprehensive and entertaining guide to get through both common and very difficult financial problems in second marriages. Great material. I give it a strong recommendation."

—*Henry K. Hebeler, retired President of Boeing Aerospace, former V. P. of Planning at Boeing. Author of J. K. Lasser's* **Your Winning Retirement Plan.**

"Two thumbs-up. The chapter on prenuptial agreements is incredible. The storyline is addictive. I not only enthusiastically recommend *Money and Marriage Two*, but will provide a copy to all of my clients contemplating a second marriage."

—*Jonathan R. Levine, Esq., Atlanta, Chairperson, ABA Sub-Committee on Family Law Litigation.*

"An extremely insightful and practical primer that is a must read for those contemplating their second marriage commitment."

—*John C. Mayoue, Esq., Family Law Attorney, Atlanta. Author of* **Competing Interests in Family Law: Legal Rights and Duties of Third Parties, Spouses, and Significant Others.**

"Love may be better the second time around, but will your finances be? Jon Fitzpatrick tackles the legal and financial complexities of a second marriage and lays out all you need to know to get your financial life in order. Follow your heart to happiness, but follow this book to financial well-being."

—*Don Phillips, Managing Director, Morningstar, Inc.*

"Love and legal strategy are strange but necessary bedfellows in second marriages. This enjoyable read takes difficult subjects for couples to discuss and provides clever tools for smart and painless planning."

—*Marna S. Tucker, Family Law Attorney; Trustee, National Women's Law Center; First Woman President of District of Columbia Bar.*

Money and Marriage Two

Money and Marriage Two

A Narrative Guide to Financial, Estate, and
Retirement Planning in a Second Marriage

By:

Jon Fitzpatrick, JD, CFP®
Attorney-at-Law

Forewords By:
Elaine E. Bedel, CFP®
and
Professor Lawrence W. Waggoner

iUniverse, Inc.
New York   Lincoln   Shanghai

Money and Marriage Two
A Narrative Guide to Financial, Estate,
and Retirement Planning in a Second Marriage

iUniverse, Inc.

For information address:
iUniverse, Inc.
2021 Pine Lake Road, Suite 100
Lincoln, NE 68512
www.iuniverse.com

ISBN: 0-595-31047-8

Printed in the United States of America

This is dedicated to Roxanne, and our children, Catherine, Laura, Susan, Kate, George, Jim, and Mary, all of whom have suffered and then dealt with loss due to either death or divorce—and especially to Roxanne, my wife and best friend, my teammate in a second marriage. Without her love, support, and inspiration, this adventure in learning would have remained but an idea.

Contents

Acknowledgements

Money and Marriage Two combines two complementary channels of communication under one cover: legal and financial concepts are first offered with a sweetener, in story form; they are also offered as a text, albeit one with an agenda—the author's effort to reduce large concepts to useful tools for couples in a second or subsequent marriage.

The classroom storyline portion of the book is fiction: it was written for fun, and to flavor a ten-course offering of ideas with the spice of dialogue, character, humor, and romance. For their reading of the storyline, and for their range of helpful comments, I thank my daughter, Catherine E. Drake, MBA, CFA, and my fellow Elsa Jane Carroll high school English student, now a New York-Washington lawyer, Stuart D. Root, Esq. They both sampled the novella portion before it left the kitchen.

On the text side, the work of countless experts, past and present, forms the backdrop of this particular shaping of legal and financial canons; I am humbly indebted to that body of experts. Also, for reviewing the text material, but not to shift responsibility (for all errors and omissions are mine alone), I am deeply grateful to the following group of practicing professionals for their time, effort, and expertise in helping to strengthen selected portions of the Reading Notes:

David F. Allen, Esq.—*Spousal Elections, Estate Planning*

Adjunct Professor Joyce E. Barrett, Esq.—*Prenuptial Agreements*

B. Richard Bodwell—*Life Insurance*

James G. Dickinson, Esq.—*Estate Planning*

Professor Louis B. Geneva, J.D., L.L.M.—*Estate Planning*

Thomas A. Gillen—*Investments, Retirement Planning*

Gary C. Haas, Esq.—*Intestate Succession, Wills, Trusts*

Edward R. Horejs, Jr., Esq.—*Property Ownership and Transfer*

David Carroll Johnson, Esq.—*Community Property*

James B. Krost, CLU, ChFC—*Life Insurance, Disability Insurance, Annuities*

John H. Mannen, CFP®, ChFC, CLU—*Financial Planning, Life Insurance, Retirement Planning*

Kenneth E. Pike—*Life Insurance, Annuities*

Renée G. Schettine, Esq.—*Medicaid, Medicare*

John R. Skala, Sr., LUTCF—*Property, Casualty, Liability Insurance, Life Insurance, Annuities*

Howard A. Slater, MBA, CMFC, ChFC—*Financial Planning, Investments, Retirement Planning*

Jeffry L. Weiler, Esq.—*Spousal Elections*

Leon A. Weiss, Esq.—*Probate, Will Contest, Trust Contest*

In addition, I want to thank John S. Seich, Esq., estate, trust, and tax lawyer, and my colleague at McCarthy, Lebit, Crystal & Liffman Co., L.P.A., Cleveland, for his thoughtful review and ongoing support.

Henry K. Hebeler, author and retirement expert, provided valuable suggestions based upon his research and experience, and he together with mutual fund authority Don Phillips, Managing Director of Morningstar, Inc., and three nationally known family law attorneys were kind enough to read selected portions of the manuscript and give their endorsements. I thank each of them. The attorneys are: Jonathan R. Levine, Esq., Levine & Smith, Atlanta; John C. Mayoue, Esq., Warner, Mayoue, Bates, Nolan & Collar, P.C., Atlanta; and Marna S. Tucker, Esq., Feldesman, Tucker, Leifer, Fidell, LLP, Washington, D.C.

For their help with intellectual property matters, I thank Robert V. Vickers, Esq., for registration of the Money and Marriage Two ® mark, and Deborah A. Wilcox, Esq., for her review of the manuscript and resource materials.

I also thank Debra H. Victor for the tireless application of her expert word processing skills, and Linnea M. Hoffman for her careful reading with *Strunk & White* at hand. Their help was continuous and indispensable. Thanks as well to William and Allison Reker for formatting the final text, and a special "thank you" to Eric Shapiro, my editor/proofreader at iUniverse, for his great care and professionalism.

My stepson-in-law, Mark W. Rominger, of Little Black Dog Designs Inc., Indianapolis, Indiana, is to be credited with the book cover design and the WWW.MONEYANDMARRIAGETWO.COM webpage. Thank you, Mark, for adding your considerable talents. Thanks, too, to Amy Castelli, Castelli Media Group, and Michael W. Carlton, Carlton Associates, Inc., for their marketing ideas.

Finally, it is with deep gratitude that I thank Professor Lawrence W. Waggoner, Lewis M. Simes Professor of Law at the University of Michigan, and Elaine E. Bedel CFP®, President of Bedel Financial Consulting Inc., for reviewing the manuscript, for their expert advice, and for their generous comments in the Forewords.

Financial Planning Professional Foreword

Entering into a second binding relationship should be a wonderful time of your life, but along with it will come the need to make choices and compromises. *Money and Marriage Two* will help you identify those decisions and the potential solutions that can keep your relationship on track.

Money and Marriage Two does an excellent job of explaining financial strategies and the potential impact of those strategies on your personal situation. The world of finance is becoming more complex. Before anyone can make a decision to take an action, he/she needs to have an understanding of the potential outcome.

In a storybook format, *Money and Marriage Two* is able to communicate many of the issues that couples entering into a second marriage must face. You will become enthralled and perhaps identify with the real life situations that unfold for each of the characters. The Reading Notes that accompany each of the chapters will give you a start to understanding the tools and techniques that you should consider or that a financial planner, estate planning attorney, or other professional may recommend for your situation.

Elaine E. Bedel, CFP®

- President, Bedel Financial Consulting, Inc., Indianapolis;
- Chairperson 2002, Certified Financial Planner Board of Governors;
- Member 2003-2003 Schwab Institutional Advisory Board;
- Named by *Financial Planning* Magazine (January 2003) as **one of five "Movers and Shakers" leading the planning profession**;
- Consistently named to the **National Top Financial Advisors** list published by *Worth Magazine*, 1994 to 2002;
- Featured as one of the **100 Great Financial Planners from Coast to Coast**, Published by *Mutual Funds Magazine*, October 2001/September 2002;
- Featured as one of the **150 Best Financial Advisors for Doctors**, *Medical Economics*, December 2002;
- Named on the list of **Bloomberg's Top Wealth Managers**, July/August 2002.

Estate Planning Expert Foreword

Remarriage has become common across society. Remarriages confront the parties and their families with a host of emotional and financial problems and potential conflicts that do not burden first marriages. Second marriages themselves take a variety of forms, but they all involve the family and legal version of mergers and acquisitions. Consider these typical cases:

- The second marriage occurring later in life, when a widow and widower decide to formalize a romance. These remarriages typically involve partners with grown children from their earlier long-term marriages. These second marriages will not produce children of their own, but the newlyweds' existing children might or might not rejoice at the prospect of mom or dad getting married again. As Jane Bryant Quinn noted in her book *Making the Most of Your Money*, "[When older people remarry,] your friends will be enchanted. But don't be surprised if your children aren't. It's usually not the 'pater' they worry about, but the patrimony."

- The second marriage occurring relatively early in adulthood following a divorce by one or both parties. These remarriages might or might not involve young children from the first marriage(s). These second marriages are also likely to produce children of their own.

- The second marriage occurring in mid-life for one or both parties, when the children of the prior marriage(s) are in their late teens or early adulthood. These second marriages might or might not produce children of their own.

There is no doubt that a self-help book devoted to financial and estate planning is of much interest to remarried partners, but can such a book be interesting? Jon Fitzpatrick has made his book interesting. This is no ordinary non-fiction book. Jon has come up with a unique way of presenting his material: as fiction. The setting for his novel is an adult course conducted at night in a local high school. His players are a couple of lawyers who teach the course and the students in the class. Each chapter addresses the classroom topic for that evening. The dialogue reveals the human story of each student. The result is a fascinating look into the lives and emotions of the characters as they learn about the financial and estate planning problems they face and how they might handle them.

Jon comes to his topic from personal and professional experience—as a lawyer for current or soon-to-be participants in a second marriage and as a participant in a second marriage of his own. He is to be congratulated on writing this book, which should be of use, interest, and comfort to those contemplating or experiencing Marriage Two.

Lawrence W. Waggoner

Lewis M. Simes Professor of Law, University of Michigan;

Reporter, Restatement (Third) of Property (Wills and Other Donative Transfers);

Director of Research, Joint Editorial Board for Uniform Trust and Estate Acts.

Introduction

The Stepfamily Association of America (WWW.STEPFAM.ORG) estimates that about 43 percent of all marriages are remarriages for at least one of the adults, about 65 percent of remarriages involve children from a prior marriage, and about 60 percent of remarriages end in divorce.

As you know, money is an issue in any marriage, especially so in a second or subsequent marriage. But money issues can be negotiated, and help is available. This book is about law, marriage, and money. It is written for you if you are remarried, contemplating remarriage, and/or have children from a prior marriage, and want help negotiating the money issues that can further your marriage while financially protecting yourself and your children.

Most of you may have first married between the ages of eighteen and twenty-six, and your marriage may have lasted for two, five, fifteen, twenty-five, thirty-five, or more years. You will have been through many financial trials with your former spouse and to this day may bear economic scars from a marriage ended by death or divorce. There will be emotional scars, too. For some, lives have been destroyed, while for others, though their lives are rebuilt, the lost dreams never go away.

Against this background you bring your prior marriage, together with your personal history, your beliefs, your values, and your friends and family—children, parents, and siblings—to a second or subsequent marriage. You also bring your financial resources, assets, career, and income. There may be debts or other financial obligations, too. Your situation is unique, and yet part of a common experience. You are a marital veteran, now married to another veteran. Together, you have created a new reality…familiar…but different. Together, your hope is to mold two personalities into a new union—with a new pledge to live together as one, until death do you part.

Nevertheless, human nature is human nature, and economic fundamentals do not change—there will be financial issues, both old and new. Although you have an opportunity for a better life, the potential for discord is real. But fear not—things can be worked out. You already have the basic ingredients to solve those problems: experience and maturity are on your side. So are your love and need for each other.

It is my hope that this book will give you guidance as well as a better awareness and understanding of the financial issues involved. The paradigm presented is one of fairness, but no punches are pulled: extreme positions can be taken, so the other side is shown as well. You need factual information in order to be fully informed, to be aware, and to reach a fair accord. An accord that is right for both of you.

The information is presented in the form of a story. An adult education class held over eleven evenings at a local high school is the setting. Although the story is designed to lay bare the financial issues that can arise in a second or subsequent marriage, it is also a story of human relationships, human frailty, romance, and love.

Our instructors are two attorneys from a downtown firm, Bob Bedar and Ted Thresher. The book you hold in your hand is based upon a recording of their class discussions, along with the Reading Notes that were assigned reading for each class. Six people signed up for the course; three women and three men. Anne, a widow with a daughter in college, is remarried. Betty, divorced with two grown children, is also remarried. Cris, divorced with a young son, is about to become engaged. Dan, a 70-year-old recent widower with two children, is now seeing someone. Ernie is divorced and remarried, with four children from his prior marriage. Frank is a young bigamist. His first spouse lives eighty miles away.

Bob Bedar, our lead instructor, is forty-eight years old, married for twenty-three years, and the father of two teenagers. As you will see, he is a compassionate person. As a young man he studied for the religious life, but later began teaching and coaching at the high school level. With help from his wife Liz, he eventually went to law school and pursued a career in estate planning.

Ted Thresher, Bob's assistant, is five years younger, and started out as a squad leader in the U.S. Army. As a young sergeant he trained and disciplined new volunteers to be soldiers. After a failed marriage of ten years he left the service and earned his formal education the hard way, including night law school. His former wife would say he is slightly ajar. He specializes in litigation and divorce.

In approaching a subject as diverse yet interrelated as this, I am reminded of my experience of taking dancing lessons during the period between my own divorce and remarriage. Every lesson involved five different dances: foxtrot, waltz, cha-cha, swing, and a fifth one I have blocked from memory. Each dance seemed to work well enough in its own little lesson compartment. Nevertheless, after nearly a year of lessons, I still had trouble when they changed the music between one dance and another. To top it off, to add a country-western touch, I took clog dancing—but was only able to follow the clitter-clatter steps until the music started. Then it all went haywire, so to speak.

So it is with this book. Each subject covered might seem simple enough. But the subjects and situations covered here are discussed by fictional characters. Real life is more complex. For example, each state has its own statutory and judge-made case law. And the law is not static; it changes and evolves. In addition, federal law supersedes state law in some matters. Finally, you, the reader, with your relationships, your finances, and your circumstances, are unique. For all these reasons it is imperative that you consult with your professional advisor(s) before taking action regarding any issue raised here. While this book discusses key issues and imparts information, the resolution of your own particular issues must be accomplished with the help of your attorney, your financial planner, and your tax, investment, and other advisors as needed.

You may want to consult WWW.MONEYANDMARRIAGETWO.COM for current information, and as a resource guide to professional advisors in your state. You can contact me through the same web site.

Jon Fitzpatrick, Esq.
Chagrin Falls, Ohio

February 14, 2004

Chapter One

Financial, Estate, and Retirement Planning

Ted stands in back loosening his tie as he watches the six students filter into the classroom one by one. Each stakes out a spot. Three are up and to his left, near the windows, one over by the door, the other two up from the door man, near the blackboard. His eyes touch on one of the women right away, then the other two. The first, in just eleven weeks, will change his life forever.

The six are uneasy with the high school setting and the newness of each other. Ted shares the feeling. He hasn't been in a high school in 25 years. Some things have changed; other things are the same. Varnished hardwood floors and bolted down wooden desks are just a memory, at least at Hunter-Wilson High. The floors are now neutral gray tile, easily mopped; the desks are lightweight moveable aluminum frames with dark blue plastic seats and backs and large mauve writing surfaces. They have wire containers attached under the seats for books. The rest of the room is familiar: teacher's desk up front near the windows, blackboards behind the teacher's desk, and blackboards on the side away from the windows. Except the blackboards are now slick, white erasable boards. Words of admonition and academic encouragement top the white blackboards. Ted ponders the scene and reminds himself that he isn't still in high school; he isn't here against his will. He looks to the windows and wishes he could open them to feel the balmy September evening air, but he can't. They are sealed. Taking his seat, he looks around at the others, glad that Bob has the lead tonight. His thoughts shift to the front of the room.

Bob, who has caught Ted's glance, surveys the group and organizes his notes. Only three men and three women. Well, they would certainly get to know each other.

"Good evening. It's seven o'clock, so let's get started. I'm Bob Bedar, an estate planning attorney with Holcomb, Schmidt, Williams & Temple. My partner there is Ted Thresher, a litigation and divorce attorney with our firm.

"I see you have our outline and Reading Notes for the eleven sessions. It's important that you read each week's material *before* coming to class in order to get the most out of our discussions. I know you didn't get a chance to review the materials for tonight, so we'll let you do that a little later. If you need to get a drink or use the facilities, there's a water fountain, snack machines, and restrooms just down the hall. Feel free to come and go; we'll be informal here, bring a snack and soft drink if you want.

"Okay, let's get started now by going around the room and introducing ourselves. Give us your name and tell us why you're taking this course. What's your main concern? Why are you here?" With a nod, Bob pointed to the gentleman who had been the first to arrive but had sat toward the back, near the door.

Frank cleared his throat and eased his hands into a clasp behind his head. He hadn't expected this. "My name is Frank," he said, still clearing his throat, "I'm in building material sales…cover Northern Ohio and Western Pennsylvania. I'm here because my wife and I…might be getting separated. I need to know about some of this."

Ted, with the eyes and ears of a litigator, sensed the man was lying and looked quickly at Bob. Bob either hadn't picked it up or chose to ignore it. He moved on.

"Okay, and you," Bob nodded to the thirty-five to fortyish pretty brunette with the tortoise shell reading glasses and navy suit sitting up front to Bob's right, by the first window.

Frank interrupted, "I just want to be fair."

"Okay, that's fine," Bob said with a smile and nodded again to the pretty brunette.

"My name is Cris, spelled C-R-I-S. I'm divorced with a 10-year-old boy, and I sell real estate for a living. I'm planning to remarry soon and want to know if I should have a prenuptial agreement."

"Very good question. Some people want them, some don't. We'll talk about prenuptial agreements in our third session. Have you read anything on the subject?"

"Not yet."

"That's something I always recommend. I don't recommend doing the agreement yourself…there are too many pitfalls…but I think it's a good idea to get some background on a subject like that before you see an attorney. It can help you to ask the right questions. Then let the attorney be responsible for drafting what you want." Cris nodded her agreement. Bob then pointed to the older gentlemen over by the blackboard, two seats up from Frank.

"I'm Dan, retired 3 years ago. I lost my wife last year and have started seeing a woman my wife and I used to know. I was wondering how to own things and share expenses if we get married."

"Important question. We talk about property ownership next week. It's the foundation for a lot of what we cover in this course; it has estate planning implications. In the chapter on financial planning we talk about sharing expenses. There are a lot of issues. In your case I would guess that education expenses for children wouldn't be an issue, but health care and retirement income might be."

"Right," Dan answered. Dan had arrived early and taken a seat on the side by the blackboard so that his good ear, the left one, would be open to the instructor and the class.

Bob then pointed with a nod to the trim, honey blonde in front of Dan. Mid-forties, he guessed. Attractive.

"My name is Anne. I'm a homemaker. My first husband died 5 years ago. We had one child, and she's in college. I remarried 2 years ago, but I'm concerned about retirement…and what to do if Hank should die."

"Yes…of course and we will cover both of those issues pretty well in the weeks ahead. Does Hank have a retirement plan at work?"

"I think he has a plan with his company, but we haven't really talked about it; he's the only employee."

"Communication about money is hard sometimes, especially in a second or subsequent marriage. We also talk about that in the financial planning chapter. Incidentally, I'll use the terms 'second marriage' and 'second or subsequent marriage' interchangeably. The same ideas apply to both…you'll know what I mean."

"Do you want to be next?" Bob chuckled as he pointed to the woman to his right in the flowered dress and tennis shoes, fifties, waving her hand and anxious to speak. She sat by the windows behind Cris.

"Yes, I don't want my things going to my husband's new wife if I die. I saw that happen to my friend. My name's Betty. I'm a homemaker too."

"Are you in a second marriage, Betty?"

"Yes, I divorced my first husband years ago. He drank. We had two kids. They're off and married now, and I'm married again myself. This one doesn't drink much."

"And you want to make sure your kids get your personal things; jewelry, family heirlooms, and so on?"

"Yes, I do."

"All right, we will certainly talk about that and what you can do. Personal effects generate strong emotions, and it's good to have a plan. There will be your things you want your children to have, things your husband wants for his children, and there will be things you bought since you were married. It's good to have a plan in place."

"We have some ideas for you later on in your Reading Notes," Ted added from the back of the room.

"You're next," Bob said, smiling at the middle-aged gentleman in the blue blazer and open collar who was sitting two seats behind Betty.

"My name is Ernie. I'm in corporate accounting. I have four children from my first marriage. The biggest thing is my wife already had a house when we got married. I moved in with her."

"And is that a problem?"

"Well, it's been an adjustment; let me put it that way."

"Yes, it is," Bob agreed in softened tone to Ernie, "and we'll get into several aspects of that. There are emotional issues as well as financial ones. Does she still have children at home?"

"Yes, two girls, 15 and 17; they'll be going to college soon."

"And are there savings for that?"

"Not much."

"And your children?"

"They're not with us. It's more of a financial thing now than an emotional thing," Ernie said.

"Okay, we'll cover the finances pretty well here; we'll have some ideas for you."

"So," Bob smiled looking over the small class, "we have a lot to talk about. We've heard concerns about *treating a spouse with fairness*, about *ownership of property between spouses*, about *sharing expenses*, about *prenuptial agreements*, about *living in the other's house*, about *protecting jewelry and family possessions*, about *college expenses*, about *retirement*, and about *death of a spouse*. We'll be covering all of these matters in the weeks ahead. Also, in our last class, week eleven, I'll ask you to discuss your main concern again in light of what you've learned in the course. Or, if you prefer, you can discuss any other issue you've learned about. We'll have a little show and tell in our eleventh session. You can even bring your spouse if you want.

"For tonight though, let's get a basic idea of what we mean when we talk about financial, estate, and retirement planning. And let's see if we can get an idea of how each of these might be different in a second or subsequent marriage.

"But first, I want to give you a sketch of my background, and Ted's background, and a brief outline of the course. Then we'll take a fifteen-minute break to give you a chance to look at your Reading Notes for tonight."

The six looked from one instructor to the other as Bob ran through a verbal resume of his and Ted's background, education, and experience. Hard to tell what they thought, but at least they would know they had qualified instructors. He told them of his years at John Carroll University and Case-Western Reserve University Law School. He gave them an idea of his role as the lead estate planning attorney within a diverse twenty-five person law firm. Ted's military service and education, and his work as a litigation and divorce attorney, were sketched out. Bob mentioned Ted's experience in the insurance and investment field while Ted was getting his law degree. He concluded his remarks by drawing their attention to the course outline, and the class listened with interest as Bob gave them a short overview of what they would be covering. When he finished, he asked if there were any questions. Frank asked if there would be any tests. The answer was no. Anne asked if the course would be useful for people that were married more than two times. The answer was yes; the same principles would apply. They then took a fifteen-minute break.

Bob and Ted walked down the hall, leaving the class to read the Notes for Chapter One. "What do you think?" Ted asked.

"It's not the turnout we wanted, but they seem like a good group. You never know, maybe we'll get some work out of this, maybe not."

"It was a lot to put together for six people," Ted said as he stopped at the water fountain for a drink.

"It was," Bob agreed. "Especially for you, with your schedule. But we'll use this material again. We're really just getting started. I'd like to do another one in the spring. Word will get around; a lot of people need this. We'll keep the ad going, and we'll get bigger groups as we go along. I see this as a new specialty for the firm, especially for you and me." Ted wasn't so sure. He wasn't sure he could be a personal planner, or even wanted to be. He was a litigator.

Bob got a drink of water, they chatted for a few minutes about the new associate at the office (she seemed like a go-getter…but who would she work for?), and then they returned to the classroom. Bob made some notes in his outline for the night, and Ted sat in the back leafing through interrogatories he had to answer the next day. He had decided not to say anything about his instinctive reaction to Frank.

"Okay, let's get started," Bob said at the end of the fifteen minutes. "First, what is financial planning?"

"Yes, Frank, what is financial planning?"

"It's having a plastic card with you when you go out to dinner."

"Right on…but then what?"

"Well the Notes lay it out like this: At the high end, for well-to-do people, it's probably insurance planning, tax planning, and investment planning, but a narrow approach might be to plan for one thing, like saving for college, or retirement."

"That's good. Anything else? Yes, Ernie?"

"Broader financial planning would include all a person's goals and how to achieve them. It's a comprehensive financial plan for the rest of your life."

"Yes…good…and comprehensive financial planning would include tax planning, insurance, investments, retirement planning, and estate planning. But how might these differ for you in a second marriage?"

Cris's hand went up first. "You might have different ideas of what you want to do. That's why I want to learn about a prenuptial agreement."

"You mean different ideas than your second husband?"

"Yes."

"That's true, but also you might be a different person, at say 40, than you were at age 25, for example."

"The real stickler," Ted added from the back, "is control of the money."

"That can be an issue," Bob agreed. "And your Notes raise other financial planning issues that we'll be covering in the weeks ahead, such as housing."

"All right, what about estate planning?" Bob asked. "Just what is estate planning?"

"It's planning where you want your money to go when you die," Betty volunteered.

"I agree," Bob said. "And that will be our focus. But we should be aware that it's really more. As a part of comprehensive financial planning, estate planning includes building an estate and managing it efficiently once it's built. It includes investment management, insurance planning, and tax planning. The primary purpose of building and maintaining an estate is to provide financial security for yourself and your family. But sometimes it's an ego thing too," he said, remembering his first estate planning client, a real estate developer. "Nevertheless, for this course, Betty is right. We'll concentrate on where your property goes when you die. In a nutshell, estate planning will help you get your property where you want it to go, and do so in a cost effective way."

"And don't forget the state," Ted added. "State law provides an estate plan for you if you don't have one. It even overrides your estate plan in some cases where you *do* have one."

"That's right," Bob nodded, "and we'll get into all of that.

"For tonight though, can anyone tell me just how estate planning might differ in a second marriage?"

Anne raised her hand. "In your first marriage you both usually plan to leave everything to your children. In a second marriage, you probably have different children."

"Right," Bob agreed, "and that is often the problem." He took a half-step back, hesitating, then said, "I think it's important for you to know early in this course that, without planning, all of your assets, everything you've worked for and saved for during your lifetime, even assets you inherited from your parents, could wind up with your spouse's children after you're gone. It's something we'll talk about in detail in the weeks ahead, but you need to be aware of it as we go along."

"You may *want* to leave something to your stepchildren, but let it be your conscious decision," Ted said. "I've seen some *egregious* situations," he added, stretching out the big word to impress the group. "I mean I've seen some surviving spouses' who inherited everything and then changed their wills within weeks to leave it all to their own children."

"What can I do to prevent that?" Anne asked, turning to Ted.

"We'll give you some ideas for protecting your children," Bob said to Anne. "There can be a happy medium here."

"Bob's a reconciler," Ted said, smiling at Bob. "All for one and one for all. I, on the other hand, will be your advocate; I'll talk about ways to get more to *your* kids if you want to. Maybe you've earned that right over the years, or maybe your kids need it more. I figure that protecting your kids is a major reason you're taking this course."

"Okay, okay," Bob said, laughing at Ted's theatrical intensity, "we'll get into all of that later. For now, though, what about retirement planning?" He smiled at Ted and shook his head. Ted loves a good fight. That's why he's a litigator. He loves to stir the pot, get people agitated. But he was right in a way. People should know all sides. They were, after all, lawyers, not judges. He would make his case for harmony and fairness. Let Ted be the devil's advocate.

Bob then looked to Ernie. "Do you really need to plan for retirement? Doesn't it just happen?" he asked.

"It probably does just happen for a lot of people," Ernie said, "but you should at least try to plan ahead…years ahead…and save for it."

"Agreed," Bob said, "and why is that so critical? After all, you probably have your house, Social Security, Medicare, and some kind of pension or 401(k) benefits anyway."

"Well, you don't know how long you might live, for one thing," Ernie replied, "and the cost-of-living will probably go up…and you might be living on a fixed income when you retire, and who knows about Social Security and 401(k) plans these days."

"All right, and what effect does being in a second marriage have on all of that?" Bob asked. Silence followed.

"Well," he continued, "let me give you just one hypothetical example that could affect not only your retirement plan, but your estate plan as well. Let's say the day comes when your spouse has to go into a nursing home and will be there for years…at $50,000, $70,000, $90,000 a year. Let's say it will use up all of his or her assets. Where does that leave you?"

"You would still have your own assets," Betty stated.

"Would you?" Bob asked. "For how long? Our Medicaid laws severely limit the assets the other spouse can keep and pass on." The group was silent.

"That's a tough issue for any couple…especially one in a second marriage," Ted said from the back, "but we'll have some ideas for you."

"Okay," Bob said, "that gives us something to think about as we go along. Now, I would like to shift gears for a few minutes.

"First, the premise of the course is that each of us wants love and financial security. That's our base line. Second, my bias, as Ted indicated, is one of fairness…What is the right thing to do? With that in mind, my approach through all this will be the approach taken by Stephen R. Covey in his book, *The Seven Habits of Highly Effective People*. I would strongly encourage you to get that book and use it as supplemental reading for this course.

"So, to sum it up, here's my thesis: You've made a commitment to your new spouse, a loving partner in a trusting, confidential relationship, and you will be happier, and better off financially, emotionally, and spiritually if you work through these issues together fairly, in support of each other first, and then worry about taking care of your children second. I hope to make that case in the weeks ahead.

"Ted, as you know, has a different take on all of this, and I will let him speak for himself."

Ted strode to the front of the room. He's raw boned, but rather good-looking, Anne thought, and he has a twinkle.

Ted opened his arms wide to the class. "I wish everyone loved each other all the time," he said. "But, as the saying goes, shtick happens. I'm a divorce lawyer. Been through a failed marriage myself. I see my role here as an advocate…someone to help you protect yourself and your children. As I see it, you have an even greater responsibility to protect yourself and your children first. I'll be giving you some ideas along those lines. Remember, a lot of second marriages don't last…and blood is blood. That's equally true even if you stay together…but I'll leave it at that for now. It's something to think about."

"So," Bob said, "we'll give you our different views as we go along. Ted has his take on all of this, and I have mine. Some of it you'll get from your Reading Notes and some of it you'll get from our class discussions…so read your Notes and come to class. Taken together, we hope to give you the tools you need to make the right decisions."

"Those Reading Notes look pretty heavy," Frank said.

"They can be scanned, read, or studied with a highlighter," Ted answered. "Take what you want…use them to ask questions."

"Alright," Bob continued as Frank fanned through the Reading Notes, "to finish up, let me say something about advisors. As you can see, this whole subject covers a broad range, including legal matters, insurance, money management, taxes, and much more. You might think this is a do-it-yourself project, but you would be well advised to use qualified professionals to help you.

"Advisors you may want to consider include an attorney, a financial planner, an investment advisor, an accountant, an insurance agent, and a trust officer. You have to pick and choose your advisors. In theory, advisors should work together as a team for your benefit, but many times one or the other wants to be in control. Don't let that happen. You have to stay in control.

"That said, let me suggest this: Today, financial planning is a profession, meaning there is a code of ethics and both academic and practice standards to be met…so, if you can find the right one, have a professional financial planner be the quarterback of your team. But you'll also need an estate planning attorney, someone who can handle these same issues. You may actually need a firm where you can draw on different talents. And speaking of attorneys, let me read you something from our firm's estate planning newsletter. Actually I wrote it," he said, making a face…

> Lawyers come from diverse backgrounds. One may have majored in engineering, music, or biology, while another was in sales or had an interest in history, English, economics or accounting. They brought their diversity, their 3.0+ grade point averages and their high Law School Admission Test scores to law school where they experienced a culture shock not unlike entry into the military service. They came to learn the law. What they learned instead was how to analyze legal problems. They learned a thought process designed to teach them how to think like lawyers. They learned in a competitive mold, under pressure, using case law as a vehicle. Then, after graduation and passing the bar exam, the new lawyer will often coordinate his or her legal education with a prior field of interest…for beneath that mantle of gray flannel there still beats the heart of an engineer, an accountant, an historian, a salesman, or a business major.

"In other words, lawyers are people with special talents, training, and interests, and an estate planning attorney has the talents, training, and interests you want. In addition to estate planning, he or she can be a good sounding board for a second opinion on most matters we cover here. Pick one that's right for you, one you're comfortable with.

"And," Bob added, surveying the group, "that goes with equal force in choosing a financial planner. Chances are she or he came to financial planning from somewhere else. So look for background, professional credentials, integrity, experience, and service. Finally, I suggest that you work with your financial planner on the same basis you work with your attorney, and that's on a fee basis. In other words, buy your products such as mutual funds, insurance, or annuities from someone else. That way you can get an unbiased professional opinion from your financial planner. If you do wind up buying products from your financial planner, however, and that *could* be the right thing for you to do in your situation, then let your estate planning attorney be the quarterback of your team. But regardless of who you have for a quarterback, always remember that you're the captain! This is your team…stay in control. Any questions on any of this?" he asked, gathering his notes. There were none. "Okay, see you next week."

Bob and Ted lingered for a few minutes and fielded afterthought questions from Cris and Ernie. The attorneys agreed that the class had gone well. Ted asked about Bob's reaction to Frank and found it to be the same as his. They left with a handshake and pats on the back, then headed for their cars; Bob the new metallic-beige Chrysler 300, in need of a wash, and Ted the two-year-old shiny black Chevy Blazer. As he pulled out of the parking lot, Ted noticed the silver slice of a first quarter moon on the rise. Still time to make a stop.

A quarter-mile from the school, Bob eased through the traffic light onto Chagrin Boulevard and headed home to Liz and the girls. The girls would be busy with homework, or be on the phone. Liz would catch him up on her day, and they would watch the 10:00 news together before going to bed. He had earlier decided to grab a bite to eat at his desk before class rather than wait until 9:00 to eat. It was better for Liz, too. It also gave him a chance to input his time sheets into the computer. He shared every other lawyer's aversion to timekeeping and billing, but it was the crux of doing business. Ted was a bit luckier that way; some of his cases were on a contingent fee basis. Ted was always on the lookout for a good contingent fee case. If he knew Ted, Ted was on his way to Johnny Malloy's right now, or on his way to shoot a game of pool and have a brewski at the Old Valley Tavern. You never knew where you might pick up a good case. Bob had suggested he join a country club, but Ted wasn't into that. He liked to hang out with his old buddies. Bob had been at it longer, though, and well understood firm policy as enunciated by its top tiger: You eat what you kill. He had joined the downtown Rotary Club 10 years ago to meet people, and he was still active in the Greater Cleveland Growth Association. He also had Liz to generate some good estate planning contacts through her volunteer work. Those contacts, together with his own client base built over 19 years of practice, and referrals from other members of the firm, meant that he didn't need to prospect any more. Still, this course would be fun. It would be good for Ted, too. He knew that Ted hated to go straight home to an empty apartment.

Chapter Two

Property Ownership and Transfer

Anne sits without a stir waiting for class to begin. Ted, up front, is pacing behind the desk, stopping at times to review his notes. To Anne he looks like someone you might date at college but not rush home to mom and dad. Maybe someone from the State University, even a townie. Wonder what he's like, she muses…different, for sure.

Anne was raised in Shaker Heights, daughter of a bank manager at the largest bank in Northern Ohio. Her parents had aspirations for her and her brother, and both attended private schools through grade twelve. Anne then went to Denison University in rural mid-Ohio with her parents hoping that she might meet a premed student. Maybe the son of a doctor.

Denison was idyllic. The Vietnam War was over and college life had returned to its former self: an oasis for learning and social growth. Anne did well in both courts. She majored in Sociology with a minor in Psychology, improved her tennis game, and was vice-president of her sorority. She didn't connect with the envisioned premed student, but her stature on campus jumped sharply when she was nominated for Homecoming Queen in her senior year. She blamed politics for the runner-up finish and wanted to enter the Miss Ohio Contest to prove a point. (Her parents refused to approve, and she dropped the idea along with her mother's pet project, piano training—a talent that might have taken her beyond the Miss Ohio Contest.)

That homecoming weekend, her best friend and sorority sister's brother, a grad student at Ohio State, visited campus. Anne and Tim began a dating marathon that would end two years later at St. Mark's Church with Anne, a smiling and happy vision in white, on her proud father's arm.

They settled in Tim's hometown, the Village of Hudson, and he became an executive in Human Resources, first with Goodyear and then with TRW. A year after the wedding, Anne had a baby girl, Terry, and she in time, like her father, attended public school in Hudson. The marriage lasted for 17 years until Tim's sudden death on the tennis court. His partner said he was rushing the net and just collapsed while making a shot.

Anne and Terry were devastated: Anne angry; Terry bereft at the loss of her father. The two were not left without sustenance, however. Tim, at his father-in-law's urging, had established a trust at the bank with a $10 deposit and a $750,000 life insurance policy. That, together with Tim's insurance from work, gave them $900,000, a sum that the bank trust officer assured them he could grow.

Three years after Tim died, with Terry off at her mother's alma mater, Anne married Hank, a never-before married businessman—a distributor—whom she'd met at the tennis club. Hank traveled a lot but made good money. He wasn't a doctor, Anne mused, but he was a guy she could have brought home from college.

"Good evening everyone," Ted said, interrupting her thoughts. "Bob is running late with a client meeting, so I'll get us started. Tonight we talk about property: the ownership of property and the transfer of property.

"First, and forgive this little speech but I think it's important, the private ownership and control of property in this country is central to our way of life, to our economy, and to our personal security. Not too many years ago we pushed the Indians off their land. They didn't own little plots in the suburbs; they shared the forest and the open range. We came in and pushed them out. We surveyed the land, marked it, fenced it, claimed it, took title to it, lived off it, and then passed it on to our children. We took it because we wanted it. We disinherited another's child to benefit our own. Think about that. Some of us carry that same idea into our homes and marriages today. Within lawful limits we are free to disinherit our loved ones, or our loved ones' loved ones. Within lawful limits we are free to transfer our property...and in many cases our spouses' property...to whomever we please. That's a powerful thing. Property is power! In a second marriage, with children from the first, you have to balance your power, your legal rights, your heart, and your sense of justice with the wisdom of an ancient Jewish king. It ain't easy, folks. End of speech."

Anne looked around the room, "Wish Bob could have heard that," she said.

"Well, I wouldn't want a senior partner to see me as anything but a warrior."

"Do you like divorce work?"

"It's what I do...but I also take a long weekend every other month."

"It's a burnout job, isn't it!"

"Do I look burned out?" Ted asked, winking and effecting a false macho-man pose to draw a laugh, which it did.

"Now, to get back on track," he said, "land is an *estate* in the classic sense that it has value, it supports our families, and it can be passed on to support the next generation. But in this day and age we have many types of property that can do the same thing; not only ranches or farms, but business interests, securities, bank accounts, and so on. They all have value, can support us in our old age, and can be passed on to our children.

"In addition, some of us have cyberspace property, intellectual property rights that have, despite all the failures, created enormous wealth. I mean patents, trademarks, and copyrights tied to technology, software, and the Internet. Anyone here in that situation?…If so, see me after class." Ted caught the quick smile from Anne. She's way more than attractive, he thought, with her below-the-shoulder natural honey blonde hair and quiet energy…her dark eyes sparkling like diamond shards. Pausing, he turned back to his notes. "Although few of us have Internet property rights, most of us do have career related property rights. Group life insurance and 401(k) benefits would be examples. It's not exactly high-flying stock options, but it's what we've got.

"Also, our career itself has value, although it's not property in the usual sense. Nevertheless, it may be our most valuable asset: the license to practice medicine or law, for example, or having a job using our degree in math, physics, or engineering. In a similar vein, our career may be built upon our smile, personality, creativity, hard work, or sales ability. It may also be based upon contacts and relationships. None of these personal attributes are property in the sense that they can be transferred, but they still have value…they too can generate income."

"If I can add to that," Bob said from a back seat he had just slipped into, "typical property values are not determined by our emotional state, or attitude, or motivation. But our emotional state, attitude, and motivation can determine the value of our career property."

"Agreed," Ted nodded with a smile. "A career is warm blooded, property is not. Do you want to take it, Bob?"

"No, you go ahead. I may have a comment or two at the end." They had prepared the course so that either of them could take any session; they never knew when one would be delayed or absent for some reason or another.

Bob sat observing the class from the back…getting an impression of the group…connecting names with people. He was not hard on people, yet his initial reaction to Betty, the mid-fifties remarried divorcee, was mixed…on the disheveled side, but she seemed fun, a free spirit. Anne, on the other hand, the remarried widow, probably still in her forties, was very attractive, blonde, trim, well dressed with a light touch of expensive jewelry. You could tell she was not shy about making eye contact with men. Ted had her rapt attention. Cris, the about-to-be-engaged divorcee, late thirties, smart, pretty, professional, looked as if she liked to be in charge.

The men, too, seemed an odd mix; he would have to get to know them. Ernie, the guy who was concerned about the house he was in, looked like a regular down-the-middle sort with a few remarriage adjustment problems: lost his house in a divorce, not the king of the castle anymore, some wounded pride, searching for an anchor. Tough at age 50, or probably any age, Bob thought. Dan, the widower, looked to be in his sixties or so. The guy was in good shape, took care of himself, probably having home-cooked meals delivered to his door. But there was a sadness in him that food wouldn't cure. At times he seemed interested, engaged in the class, but at other times it seemed as if the fire had gone out. Maybe it was the hour. But what was he doing here anyway? Frank, the one who said he was concerned about fairness, was a puzzle. He said he was in sales, yet something was amiss. If Ted thought he was lying, then he was lying. It seemed that way to Bob, too. Strange. He looked to be in his early thirties. Plenty young enough to make a go of it. But, if he had a family, kids from a first marriage, college, it wouldn't be easy.

Bob then let his thoughts drift back to the meeting he had just left. How could a 45-year-old with 50 percent of a business, and a growing family, not even have a will? It was beyond him. If the guy died right now it would be a mess. The kids would own part of the house…his wife couldn't sell it without a guardian ad litem being appointed by the probate court to represent the 10-and 12-year-olds…and his business partner would have some new shareholders demanding dividends. But that was only part of it. There would be unnecessary estate taxes as well. Once the client saw the problem, he wanted to sign something right then and there to fix it…he was flying to Mexico in two days! But it would take two or three weeks, on the fast track, to put things together for him. A corporate buy-sell agreement was needed, along with wills, trusts, powers-of-attorney, and more. What can you do? He was coming in for a quick-fix will tomorrow afternoon; a safety net hung with clothespins. Bob shook his head and returned his attention to Ted who was leading up to a question for the group.

"So, having read your Notes for this chapter," Ted said, "answer me this. Let's say you own a lot of jewelry. The jewelry is so valuable you seldom wear it. You keep it in a sealed envelope in a safe deposit box at the bank, intending that some-day it will go to your daughter. But you want someone on the box with you…so you and your second husband sign for the box; he keeps some old coins there. Now you die. Who gets your jewelry?"

"I have that very situation," Betty spoke up, "but I have a will, and it says my daughter gets my jewelry."

"Ah," Ted said, exchanging a glance with Bob, "but what does your contract say?"

"What contract?"

"Your rental contract, your lease agreement with the bank," Ted replied.

"I don't know," Betty answered, "but my will says my jewelry goes to my daughter, Sissy. Baker—that's my husband—Baker didn't buy that jewelry."

"Okay, here's the point," Ted said, turning away from Betty and suddenly realizing that he sounded like Ross Perot. "When you rent a safe deposit box you sign a lease with the bank. When two or more people sign the lease, it raises a question as to who owns the contents of the box. The bank doesn't want to get into the middle of that question, so the lease will typically provide for you to sign up as either *tenants-in-common* or as *joint-tenants with right of survivorship*. You have to read the agreement and understand those terms. I cited the *Steinhauser* case for you in your Table of Cases. Under that decision, Betty, your husband would get the jewelry if you signed up for the box as joint-tenants with right of survivorship. Of course, if that's the case, he may give the jewelry to your daughter anyway. If not, your executor may have to litigate, file suit."

"But Baker's my executor."

"Do you know how you own the box?" Ted asked.

"No," Betty said, "but I'll find out tomorrow." Ted looked to Bob. Point made.

People can fool you, Bob thought. Who would have guessed that Betty, with hair that hadn't seen a comb or brush all day, would have a box of valuable jewelry? Of course, who knows if it's valuable or not. Sounds like it's valuable to her, though.

"All right, here's another case," Ted said.

"Can Baker get my jewelry?" Betty interrupted.

"We can't give you specific legal advice in this course," Ted said. Of all the cases they might get, he thought, it had to be something like this…a costume jewelry in a safe deposit box case…with everyone fighting!

"You need to get a copy of your lease," Bob said. "If you don't understand it, take it to your attorney or talk with the bank's legal department."

"Why don't you just get your own safe deposit box?" Cris said, looking to Ted as she advised Betty.

"I think I will," replied Betty.

"Okay, here's another case," Ted said, with a nod of approval to Cris.

"Let's say your aged father told you and your brother that he was leaving each of you $50,000 under his will. The two $50,000s are in separate accounts at his bank. You and your brother both live at a distance, so your father confirmed all this to you in a letter.

"But your stepmother was concerned about someone being able to pay your father's bills if he got sick. So, with your father in tow, they went to the bank and added her name to the accounts as joint-tenants with right of survivorship. Six months later your father died. The question is, what happens to the two 'joint-tenants with right of survivorship' accounts: do they belong to your stepmother as the surviving joint-tenant, or do they belong to you and your brother?"

"Since the father went to the bank and added his wife's name, didn't he really *intend* for his wife to have the money?" Dan asked.

"Who knows for sure?" Ted answered. "He probably just added his wife to the accounts as a convenience to pay the bills. The kids lived across the country."

"Then I think it should go to the kids," Anne said, lowering a hand to the desk as if it were a gavel.

"Sorry," Ted said, a little surprised upon seeing sharpness in those lovely eyes. "But under the *Wright* case cited in your Table of Cases, it goes to the stepmother."

"That's not fair," Anne said, showing pique but knowing the result wouldn't change.

"Well," Ted said, "the courts in this state just got frustrated hearing cases involving joint and survivorship accounts and trying to determine the intent of a dead person. So, the *Wright* case established the rule in Ohio that the opening of a joint and survivorship account…in the absence of fraud, duress, undue influence or lack of capacity…is conclusive proof of intent to transfer the balance remaining in the account at death to the survivor. In short, if it says 'joint and survivor', it goes to the survivor. If it doesn't say 'joint and survivor', it's part of the decedent's estate."

"That's the law in this state right now," Bob added, "and not everyone is happy with it. But all the states wrestle with this problem, and if you move to another state you could get a different result. For instance, in Illinois, in the *Savage* case, a joint and survivor account between a father and a daughter was deemed to be a convenience account and was eventually shared by all his children."

"That's right, and here's a variation on the same theme," Ted said, looking up from his notes to Bob, and then making brief eye contact with Cris.

"Say instead of the father changing his accounts to joint-tenants with right of survivorship, say he had left them alone but had given his wife…I'll call her Hilda…say he had given Hilda a power-of-attorney?"

"What's that?" Betty asked.

"It's a writing that authorizes another person to do certain things for you, such as write checks for you, do your banking, sell your assets, and so on. It's usually a broad grant of authority, but it could be limited, too. In any case, you authorize another person to act for you, as your agent, your so-called attorney-in-fact."

"It's still your money, isn't it?" Ernie asked. "That person can't use it for himself can he?"

"Right, that's the idea anyway," Ted answered. "The attorney-in-fact is accountable for his or her actions to the principal, the person giving the power.

"So, let's say," Ted continued, "that the father gave his wife Hilda a power-of-attorney for those bank accounts with the understanding that she could use the funds to pay his bills if needed. Let's say further that Hilda used the power-of-attorney to withdraw money from the accounts, and say she used the money to set up a 'joint-tenants with right of survivorship' account with your father."

"Did the father sign the signature card for the new account?" Frank asked from the back.

"Yes," Ted answered, "she had him in tow at the bank."

"Then what happened?" Dan asked.

"Well, Hilda thought they needed a new car, so she bought one out of the joint account."

"Whose name?" Dan asked.

"Her own," Ted replied.

"What kind of car?" Frank chortled.

"Hope it was a Caddy," Betty answered.

"So what happened?" Dan asked.

"Well, as you might guess, the father died."

"Who gets the Caddy?" Betty asked, looking around.

"Well first, the *Wright* case, assuming no fraud or undue influence, et cetera, says that Hilda, as the survivor, gets the balance in the joint account," Ted answered. "But another case, *Thompson*, cited in your Table, says the Caddy belongs to the father's estate. *Thompson* provided that the funds in a joint account with right of survivorship belong, in the absence of clear and convincing evidence otherwise, to the one who contributed them, *as long as he is living*. Only upon his death do they belong to the survivor. In other words, she took the money out during his lifetime so it was his Cadillac."

"The living part makes sense," Ernie said, "but it still seems like the money should have gone to the kids when he died. I mean, how do you know he wasn't subject to some kind of influence, or how do you know that he really understood what he was doing?"

"Good question," Ted answered. "And we'll address that in our class on wills. Something for you to think about. For tonight, though, we need to cover some other property items.

"One of those items is a different type of bank account," Ted continued. "It's called a payable on death account, or P.O.D. account. With a P.O.D. account you can name a beneficiary to receive the account upon your death. While you live it's your money; when you die it goes to your beneficiary. In the case we just discussed, the father could have named the wife or the kids as his P.O.D. beneficiary. It's very straight forward.

"Any questions on that?" Ted asked. "Yes, Frank?"

"So if the accounts were P.O.D. accounts, they would not have gone to the kids under the father's will?"

"Right, they would have gone to whoever was the P.O.D. beneficiary, be it the kids or his wife."

"With a P.O.D. account, could Hilda still have bought the Caddy using the power of attorney?" Ernie asked.

"Yes," Ted answered, "but the same rules apply; it would have remained his Caddy unless he intended a gift to her.

"Okay," Ted said, moving back to his notes, "I want to cover a few real estate matters now."

"Before we go on," Cris said, leaning forward in her seat, "do these same rules apply to securities? For example, a mutual fund or a stock brokerage account?"

"Generally yes," Ted answered, noting how sharp she was. Too bad she was in a relationship. "You can have a joint-tenants with right of survivorship mutual fund, or stock brokerage account, or an individual stock or bond in joint and survivor form. With securities, though, the P.O.D. owner/beneficiary arrangement is usually called T.O.D.….Transfer on Death. Same idea."

"Thanks," Cris said. She moved slightly in her seat, thinking of her own situation, and then glanced over at Anne, wondering if Anne got the point: the father could have had P.O.D. or T.O.D. accounts for the kids, and his wife could have had a power-of-attorney as a convenience to pay the bills.

"Deeds," Ted repeated to the class. "You will see in your Notes that the ownership of real estate falls into categories similar to the ownership of bank accounts or stocks or bonds. You can own real estate in your own name, or in co-ownership form with one or more others…with or without a survivorship feature…and, in some states, you can name a T.O.D. beneficiary on the deed to receive the property upon your death."

"What's T.O.D. again?" Frank asked.

"Transfer on Death. It's a way to transfer real estate when you die without having it be subject to the rules and delays of probate."

"Going back to the last case," Ernie began, "could the father, on his own, have made those bank accounts payable to his kids?"

"Yes," Ted answered.

"Could he have done the same thing with the house?" Ernie asked.

Ted exchanged a glance with Bob: "No," he answered, moving away from his desk toward a relieved Ernie. "He couldn't have given clear title, at least not in this state. Not yet, anyway. Real estate is different in that the spouse of the owner must sign the deed along with the owner. It's a carryover from feudal days when wealth was largely in the land you owned and a husband couldn't sell or transfer his lands without his wife's consent. It was a protection for her, called dower rights. For men it's called curtesy. If you're married, your spouse must sign the deed when you sell or transfer real estate, at least right now in Ohio. That applies whether you own it individually or as joint-tenants."

"What if she forged his signature?" Anne asked with an impish smile.

"That would take some help, some complicity," Ted answered. "Remember, a deed is notarized, and in some states witnessed. In some of those states the notary can be one of the witnesses, but in others the notary must be another person. So it would take some doing.

"But," Ted continued, "let me give you this hypothetical case. Say the wife owns a house and she and her new husband agree that it should be in joint and survivor form. He tells her he'll take care of it. Unbeknownst to her, he wants to get a large loan from the bank, but the bank, of course, wants security for the loan. To make a long story short, he takes her to the bank to get the new deed witnessed and notarized. But along with the joint-tenants with right of survivorship deed is a mortgage deed. In the mix of conversation and papers, she signs both deeds."

"What's a mortgage deed?" Anne asked.

"It's a deed back to the lender in case the borrower defaults on the loan," Ted answered. "It's a lien against the property. It's security for the loan."

"She didn't understand what she was doing?" Frank asked.

"Nope...nope...nope..." Ted answered. "Paperwork and legal matters were confusing to her. She trusted her husband, and, in the mix of chitter-chatter about the weather in Florida and this year's vacation, she signed both deeds, properly witnessed and notarized."

"So, the husband got money from the bank and the bank had a lien on her house," Betty snapped.

"Right," Ted said, feeling her sting...the messenger's reward.

"Now, we have two more deeds to do," he said after a short pause, smirking at his own whimsy. "I said you could own real estate as co-owner with one or more others, with or without a survivorship feature. We have talked about the usual form of joint-tenants with right of survivorship where the property is owned outright by the survivor, or survivors, upon the death of one. But another form of survivorship deed is only available to a husband and wife, and it provides protection against creditors. It's called tenancy-by-the-entirety, or estates-by-the-entirety, and it's only available in some states. If you and your spouse want to have a survivorship deed, it's the way to go—if it's available."

"Like Florida," Bob added from the back.

"Right.

"Now, be aware that the most common form of real estate co-ownership does *not* involve survivorship," Ted said. He looked up from his notes and was again drawn into brief eye contact with Cris. "Unless the deed says 'with right of survivorship', or 'survivorship', or 'remainder to the survivor', or otherwise makes it clear that the surviving co-owner is to own the entire property upon the death of the other," he continued, "it's not a survivorship deed."

"What is it?" Anne asked.

"It's called tenants-in-common," Ted answered as he strolled her way. "It's the most common form of co-ownership for real estate. Tenants-in-common means each person owns a fractional part of the real estate but has the use of all of it. Upon the death of one, that one's interest passes to his or her heirs, or beneficiary, or trust, depending on how ownership was indicated on the deed. It doesn't go automatically to the other co-owner as in a survivorship deed."

"So," Ernie said, "each person owns half the real estate, live or die."

"Correct," Ted answered, "assuming there are two people and they are 50-50 owners. They could own it 75-25, or any other way. And there could be three or more co-owners in whatever percentages they choose. But yes, the point is that each one owns part of it, live or die."

"How do you tell the difference between a survivor deed and this kind?" Betty asked.

"This kind, a tenants-in-common deed, doesn't say anything about survivorship," Ted answered. "It would typically just say *John Doe and Mary Doe, husband and wife*. Period. Or *John Smith and Mary Smith and their heirs*. Period. Nothing about survivorship."

Ernie interrupted. "Going back to that scene where they signed the deed at the bank, if that had been a tenants-in-common deed, would the husband have owned half the house right then, live or die?"

"Yes," Ted answered.

"But what if she said she didn't understand what was happening?" Anne asked.

"Tough case when only one of the two is mistaken and didn't understand," Ted answered.

"But what about fraud?" Anne asked.

"Tough case," Ted answered.

"Bastard," Betty muttered. Everyone chuckled but Ernie, whose thoughts were elsewhere at the moment.

"Those are the main points I wanted to cover tonight," Ted said, "but I know Bob has a few comments. Do you want to take it now?"

"Yes, for just a few minutes," Bob said, walking to the front.

"I want to make sure you know that life insurance policies, annuities, and IRA accounts are also forms of intangible personal property. We will talk more about them, and their application in a second or subsequent marriage, when we get to insurance and estate planning. They operate like P.O.D. accounts in that you can name a beneficiary to receive the proceeds upon death. Benefits paid to a named beneficiary, an individual or a trust for example, do not go through probate. As the owner, you can name anyone you want as the beneficiary; you don't have to name your spouse, although community property laws, and certain other states' laws, do alter that to protect a spouse. We'll see in Chapter Nine that, in certain states, a surviving spouse may be able through the probate process to get more of the proceeds than you intended. These are the so-called 'augmented estate' states that have adopted that aspect of the Uniform Probate Code. Most states, like Ohio, have not taken that approach. In this state, and in most states, you can name anyone the beneficiary and have it stand."

"What about company retirement plans like pensions and 401(k) plans?" Frank asked.

"Okay, that's different," Bob said. "That's an example of where federal law controls. The Employee Retirement Income Security Act, or ERISA, as modified by the Retirement Equity Act, or REA, provides spousal protections; the law requires that the spouse of the employee be the beneficiary of an annuity unless the employee elects out and names someone else the beneficiary, and the spouse consents to those decisions. Also, as I said, your choice of IRA beneficiary may be altered in 'augmented estate' states, meaning that by state law your spouse may share an IRA you intended for your children."

"Doesn't that cut down what you can do in a second marriage?" Ernie asked.

"It does, but that's where a prenuptial agreement…with follow-up after you're married…can be a big help. For example, you can both agree to name your kids as your 401(k) or IRA beneficiaries as part of the prenup, and then you formalize that with spousal consent right after the marriage."

"Is that before or after you cut the cake?" Betty muttered.

"Maybe they slip the forms under your plate," Frank whispered back.

"Need a lawyer for a bridesmaid," Betty snorted.

"Now a similar idea," Bob went on, "is where you own assets in trust. You could be trustee of your own trust, for example, or maybe your adult child is your trustee. Either way, you have a lot of control and estate planning flexibility in a second or subsequent marriage. But again, a surviving spouse may be able to change your plan after-the-fact in some states. We'll get into that in the last weeks of the course."

"What's the general idea?" Frank asked. "Are they afraid you won't do right by your wife?"

"They want to make sure a surviving spouse gets a fair share of your whole asset picture, not just a share of what goes through probate. There are lots of ways to avoid probate," Bob answered.

"But only a few states do that, you say? It's pretty screwy if you ask me," Frank said. "I'd move."

"Some states give you latitude," Bob said. "You still have latitude here.

"For tonight, I just want you to be aware of the different types of property and some of the issues related to transfer of ownership. You can transfer ownership of assets to or from your own trust, for example, but you can't transfer ownership of your IRA or 401(k) accounts, at least not without first taking the money out and paying taxes, even a 10 percent penalty in most cases if you're under the age of 59 and a half.

"Another important asset for some," Bob continued, noting Anne's growing disinterest, "is stock ownership in a closely-held corporation, maybe a family business. The other shareholders, whether it's your father, your sister, or a business associate, typically don't want your spouse to take over your shares if you die, or if you get a divorce. So…what can you do in advance?"

"Have a prenuptial agreement," Dan answered.

"Right, and what else?"

"Can't you have a buy-sell agreement?" Ernie asked.

"You can, and should," Bob agreed. "The corporation, or the other shareholders, can have the option—or be required—to buy your shares upon your death; they can also buy them if the shares fall into someone else's hands, such as a former spouse or a creditor. There's usually life insurance to back up the agreement in case of death and to help fund a living buyout."

"So the wife is cut out of the business," Cris said.

"Or the husband, to be politically correct," Frank chirped.

"Right," Bob smiled, "but the estate gets cash and that's a good result for everyone. The cash can be invested in a diversified portfolio of securities, and the family isn't stuck with just one investment…shares of a closely-held company. Equally important, the company can operate without interference from an outside party."

"Now she's an outside party," Betty muttered.

"As long as it's a fair price," Ted said from the back.

"That's the idea, and that's all I wanted to touch on tonight," Bob said, putting his notes aside. "Any questions?"

"What's a fair price?" Anne asked, now interested.

"That's the big question," Bob answered. "And it's a question the business owners can best answer for themselves in a buy-sell agreement. It can be a serious problem if they don't. I included a checklist in the back of your materials, Appendix G I think, that I use in my own practice to help answer that question. But it's as much art as science; you'd be wise to use a valuation expert in most cases. Even then experts can differ, and sometimes the court has to get involved when there's a death or divorce. It gets messy."

"I had another question," Cris said, half raising her hand, making sure Anne was finished.

"Shoot," Bob said.

"In our Notes, it talked about an apartment building owned by two partners. Can you talk about that as it relates to a couple in a second marriage? For instance, if one of the partners died, what would his wife get and what would his children from his first marriage get?"

"Good question. It depends on a lot of things, though, such as whether or not he had a prenuptial agreement. Also, as we mentioned in your Notes, it could depend on what state he lived in. If he lived in a community property state, for instance, where half of the property acquired during the marriage belongs to the surviving spouse (but it's treated as his separate property if he had it before they married) it's one thing. But if he lived in an augmented estate state where a calculation is made based on the couple's total assets, or if he lived in a state like this, a common law separate property state, it's another thing.

"Assuming he lived here, and assuming it was a regular general partnership, the partnership, as such, would be dissolved and his interest, or the buy-sell price of his interest, would become part of his estate. Maybe there's a will, maybe not. Maybe there's a buy-sell agreement, maybe not. The wife and the children would get whatever they were entitled to from the estate."

"If he wanted to block his wife from getting that asset he could have owned it in a limited partnership," Ted added.

"How so," Cris asked, turning to Ted.

"In a limited partnership he could have someone else, a brother or his son for example, carry on as a general partner—the one with management control—and he could have left a limited partnership interest to his wife. All she'd have is a right to whatever the general partner paid out each year, if anything. Maybe nothing. Zippo. It's a great tool, as Bob well knows."

"Putting it into an irrevocable trust would be another idea," Bob said. "But on that note, I'd like to wrap it up for tonight. I don't want to get into the whole asset protection game this early in the course.

"So, to summarize, we've laid a foundation tonight that we can build on in the weeks ahead. You may want to refer back to your property Notes from time to time. There are also gift aspects to some of the transfers we discussed, and you need to be aware of that. There's no gift tax problem with spouse to spouse lifetime transfers, but there could be if you transfer property to someone else; for example, there is a tax issue if you put real estate into joint and survivor form with your child. Get tax counsel before you do something like that.

"Finally, I'll tie in property ownership and transfer issues in the weeks ahead with the idea of mutual support. As we'll see, property issues crop up in every session of the course, and my goal is to have you and your spouse use your property to take care of each other."

"And I want you to know how to take care of yourself," Ted said from the back.

"That's important too," Bob added. "We'll see that in the next chapter when we discuss prenuptial agreements.

"So, thank you for your attention and we'll see you next week. Enjoy the rest of this beautiful evening; the days are getting shorter."

"Boy," Frank said, getting up, "you need a Philadelphia lawyer to figure this out."

"Yeah," Betty laughed, pulling her book bag from under her desk. "Maybe I should get me one." She gave Frank a wink and headed for the door, looking for a place to deposit her empty Dr. Pepper can.

The whole group, including Ted and Bob, filtered out of the building into the warm night air. It was 8:30, and Bob was glad that the traffic on Jefferson Street was light; he looked forward to getting home. Ted said he had to stop at the laundromat on his way home.

As Cris and Anne strolled across the parking lot toward their cars, Anne glanced sideways to Cris and said, "Ted's kind of cute, don't you think?"

"Yes, in a rough sort of way. But I think his bark is worse than his bite. He's actually shy one-on-one. I was surprised."

"You're seeing Ted?" Anne exclaimed.

"No, no, we just ran into each other last week at an open house and wound up having something to eat."

"Dinner?" Anne asked.

"A glass of merlot and hors d'oeuvre's," Cris answered over her shoulder as she unlocked her small black Mercedes.

"Oh," Anne said, turning toward her own car, plunging a hand into her purse, fumbling for her keys.

Chapter Three

Prenuptial Agreements

Frank looks at his Notes for the night, waiting for class to begin. Anne, up front, is chatting with Bob and Ted. "Nuptial," he repeats to himself. It sounds so innocent, so good, so pink and blue mixed together, so happy. But then there is the word "agreement," a formal coming together, so negotiated, so compromised, so *legal*. You give up some things in the hope of getting others. Money.

He'd made his own agreements, he thought, and was happy with two women, until now. He really didn't want to get a divorce; Sally didn't deserve that. It had just happened with Marcie. The chemistry was immediate…and intense. No one's fault. Then it was marry her or lose her, for she had another guy. A real Catch-22. They were married out of state six weeks later. Life is messy. But living on the edge made it into a game, and he has benefits few enjoy. Sally and Marcie are different: different looks, different laughs, they like different things. They are as different as Madonna and Linda Ronstadt. Sally is comfortable, but with Marcie he keeps his edge. And then there are the two boys, little Frankie, fifteen months, and Samson (really Samuel) after her seldom seen father, just two months. The boys are growing and changing every week; Sally has her hands full, especially when he's on the road. But now Marcie wants a baby. It's getting complicated. The challenge is to make it work, if it can work. If it doesn't, he'd have nothing. Or maybe jail. Nah, not likely, he thought.

Frank continued to think about his predicament and the possibility of maintaining two families. He thought of little Frankie and Samson. He wanted them to have a better start in life than he'd had, though some of his troubles, he knew, were of his own making. He'd been a show-off as a kid, always vying for attention, often in trouble at home or school; his mother couldn't control him, except with a belt. It was either the belt or "wait until your father gets home." A few years later, the summer after he finished high school, his father pushed him out of the house after a fight about the hours he kept. Frank wouldn't go back, and he had no money for college. He lived in old Mrs. Bender's basement for 3 years and managed to cover his food, gas, and car insurance with assorted jobs, including that of hod carrier for a bricklayer. Through the bricklayer, he got an inside sales job with a building material supply company—a job that had led, four years later, to his current sales position. But now there was a possibility he'd lose his job; his sales were down, he'd lost two key accounts to mergers this year. The atmosphere at the company was changing, too; the new sales manager was leaning hard on him. It can't go on like this, he thought. He had to figure something out. At least Marcie has a good job. But Sally has never worked, except as a waitress. She needs to get some computer skills or something, and lose a few pounds.

The sound of an approaching siren broke into his thoughts. He watched the red, blue, and white lights of an EMS vehicle flash past the rain-spattered windows. Frank then looked at the other men in the room: Ernie and Dan, Ted and Bob. He imagined their dull, secure lives, and then concentrated on the two who might have some answers for him.

Bob and Ted were standing together by the desk, chatting before class. Frank noted that Bob was in decent shape, but he would have to watch his weight. A very genuine guy. Not an insincere bone in his body. And he had a sense of humor, too. Yet there he was, wearing brown shoes with a blue suit. He needed some help. Either that or it was a weak protest. Who knows? The other guy, Ted, was taller, leaner, tougher looking, definitely in good shape. The sound of Bob's raised voice interrupted his thoughts.

"Anne just made a comment that we should all hear. Let's start with that," Bob said, nodding to Anne.

"Well, I just don't know how people can deal with this," Anne began. "They fall in love and are engaged to be married. Then along with this they have to write things down about money and property and who gets what and when. It just seems like they're saying they don't trust each other."

"You bet," Betty said, lifting a diet Pepsi from her bag.

"I mean, shouldn't marriage be based on trust?" Anne asked.

"Shtick happens," Ted said without smiling.

"So, you mean if I'm going to get married, my husband-to-be and I go to a lawyer and he gives us a contract to sign? That doesn't sound like much fun," she said, finishing her comment with a sideways glance at Cris.

"Actually, there should be two lawyers," Bob said. "Each party should be represented by his or her own attorney. If they used the same attorney, there would be a conflict of interest. One attorney shouldn't represent both."

"So you double the cost and have two lawyers arguing with each other even before you get married," Frank said. "What does that do for anyone?"

"Well, the cost isn't doubled," Bob replied, not wanting to sound defensive.

"It's a cost of doing business," Ted injected with a quick power-smile to Frank. "As to lawyers arguing, I've found little of that in practice. The lawyers need to protect their client's interests, but at the same time they want to facilitate the transaction." The word *transaction* sounded hard on all ears, including Bob's.

"The lawyers are sensitive to the situation," Bob said. "But they will usually raise issues that the couple hasn't thought of, and that can lead to some discussion, some give and take, but things usually get worked out."

"Better sooner than later," Betty said.

"But what if hurt feelings or hard feelings develop?" Anne asked. "Or distrust?"

"Better sooner than later," chirped Betty as she gave Anne an all-knowing look.

"Those things can lead to marital problems," Anne said. "They can carryover and crop-up later."

"They can indeed," Ted responded. "But no pain, no gain."

"What Ted means," Bob said, moving away from the desk, "is it can be difficult at times for some couples to work these things out, but there are important benefits."

"It could also be that age and life experience are factors," Dan said, looking from Bob to Anne. "And kids too," he added with raised eyebrows. "I know my friend and I have only been dating a few months; we're just enjoying each other's company, but already my kids are bringing it up. Get a prenup dad, they tell me. Got to do a prenup. Heck, I don't know what they're so worried about. They're both doing pretty well. But they seem mighty worried."

"In a case like that," Bob said, "one of the biggest benefits can be peace and harmony within the family. With a prenup your children may be more accepting of your new friend. They may not feel so threatened."

"We'll see," Dan replied with a quick glance across the room to Cris.

"Also," Ted added, stopping on his way to the back, "you might want your kids to be represented by their own lawyer and have them be parties to the agreement. It could save some grief later."

"That sounds complicated," Cris said.

"It could be," Ted said. "In fact, if the kids refer their dad to a lawyer, there's a question as to who the lawyer represents…the kids or the dad. Who's the client? Each party should have his own lawyer."

"Now it's three lawyers," Frank mumbled.

"Maybe four," Betty said.

"In most cases, you can stick with just two lawyers," Bob said. "In effect, the kids are beneficiaries of their parent's agreement; they can enforce it later if they have to."

"If there's anything left," Betty said.

"Well, if that's the concern, the parents could set assets aside in an irrevocable trust for the kids' benefit before marriage, or as part of the agreement," Bob said.

"I didn't realize it could be so complicated," Cris said.

"In most cases, it's not," Bob said, not wanting to get too far afield.

"It gets complicated when big money is involved," Ted said. "You can get into estate and gift tax issues, and transfer of wealth issues. Most cases aren't that involved."

"I agree," Bob added.

"But even in smaller cases," Ernie said, "it seems you could have complications…like housing, for instance. The Notes mentioned housing as one thing that could be covered in a prenuptial agreement. Could you talk about that?"

"Sure, that's the issue you mentioned at our first meeting, isn't it?"

"Yes."

"But you don't have a prenuptial agreement, do you?"

"No."

"Okay, well, housing is certainly something that can be dealt with in the agreement. You can agree on ownership, upkeep, mortgage payments, additions, improvements, and so on. The big rub comes when the homeowner dies. Where does that leave the surviving spouse, and where does that leave the homeowner's kids?"

"Where *does* it leave everyone?" Cris asked. "What if my new spouse owns the house and dies?"

"You can anticipate that in your agreement," Bob answered. "Ernie, you don't have an agreement, but here are a few things you could have done that Cris can still do.

"A prenup can provide a life estate to the surviving spouse so that if the homeowner dies, the other spouse can stay in the house as long as he or she lives, or, if it applies, until he or she remarries."

"I'd want him out then," Betty said, shaking her head.

"But what about his kids?" Cris asked.

"In that case, they wait their turn," Bob answered. "They wait for their stepparent to die."

Betty again shook her head.

"What if I want to sell the house?" Cris asked.

"It depends on your agreement," Ted answered from the back. "The proceeds could go into another house, or maybe you get the income from the invested proceeds, or maybe the proceeds go to the kids at that point. It depends on what you work out."

"How do you protect all that to make sure it happens?" Ernie asked.

"You can put the house into a trust," Bob answered.

"Or the kids could have a lien on the house," Ted added.

"It does get complicated," Dan said, wondering what his two sons would want. He didn't want to shortchange them, but he would also have a new wife to consider. Put a lien on the house? How would that work?

"Well, that gives you some ideas," Bob concluded. "There are income, estate, and gift tax issues involved as well, but they will only be a real concern in larger cases."

"Couldn't life insurance solve some of these problems?" Frank asked.

"You're right about that," Bob answered. "If you can afford it and can get it, life insurance can solve a lot of problems. We'll talk more about that in Chapters Six and Ten."

"The kids get the house and the spouse gets the insurance," Frank said.

"Or vice versa," Ted added. "As you'll see in the weeks ahead, the policyowner can change the beneficiary of life insurance, but he can't change the surviving spouse's legal right to stay at least temporarily in the house. You have to look at all sides of that issue…who should get the insurance and who should get other assets."

"And all of that can be handled in a prenuptial agreement," Bob added.

"Now let's look at some other issues," Bob said, moving back toward the desk.

"Can I ask a question?" Frank said, waving his hand slowly like a pendulum anchored to the desk by his elbow. "I read the Notes on this: Do people really get into all that nitty-gritty stuff? No offense, but you lawyers would blow people apart with all those questions."

"Well," Bob said, with a glance to Ted, now changing colors, "the Notes cover a broad landscape. You would pick those issues that were important to you, such as protecting a closely-held business, and make sure they were covered. Other things might be accepted as being the nature of the beast. Those things, the things that weren't important to you, like being executor of the other's estate perhaps, would get glossed over in the interest of harmony."

"So you don't necessarily go into all the stuff you mentioned?"

"They're not all dealt with to the same degree, but you should be aware of them, be aware of what you're not going to make an issue of. At this point, people want protection, or they want to realize certain expectations; they don't want to blow up the relationship. They work it out."

"And how do the lawyers help?"

"We explain and negotiate the legal issues, hopefully in human terms," Bob answered with quiet emphasis, noting that Ted had settled down, glad he hadn't gotten up to defend his Notes, or the entire legal profession. "And let me just add this: it's a good idea for a couple to go through that checklist before they get married anyway, even if they don't do a prenup. It could save a lot of trouble later…especially if there's a business involved."

"Better to get it on the table," Betty said.

"Right," Bob agreed, wanting to move on.

"Okay," he said, "one more issue I just want to mention again in passing, and then we'll look at some cases. That issue, once again, is retirement plan benefits. We talked about it last week, and we'll talk more about it later, but I want to mention it now because it should be dealt with in the prenup, even though, arguably, an agreement made in the prenup related to qualified plan benefits may not be enforceable. Make sense?"

"No," Anne said, "what do you mean?"

"The Employee Retirement Income Security Act, ERISA, and the Retirement Equity Act, REA, say your spouse is the beneficiary of your qualified retirement plan benefits. So you have to already be married before you can elect to have someone other than your spouse as your ERISA plan beneficiary...such as the beneficiary of your 401(k) plan...and your spouse must consent *while you're married.* That's federal law, and it supercedes the state law that would govern your prenup.

"So," Bob continued, "if your spouse agreed in the prenup that your children could be your 401(k) beneficiary, and then refused to consent to it after you were married, you would have a devil of a time trying to enforce the prenuptial agreement on that point. That's why you want to get the consent taken care of soon after you're married."

"While the glow is fresh," Betty said.

"Right," Bob laughed.

"Okay," he continued, "let's look at some prenup cases now. We'll talk more about retirement benefits later.

"Here's a question: Do you think a wife should be limited to a given property division upon divorce if she agreed to that division earlier in a prenuptial agreement? Say a couple married in 1968 and then divorced after 14 years of marriage due to his alleged misconduct."

"I'll bet it was alleged," Betty muttered.

"Assume that they had signed a prenuptial agreement and at that time his assets were $550,000. Assume that she had very little in assets. Further, assume they had agreed that upon divorce they would split the proceeds from the sale of the house and she would be paid $200 a month as alimony for 10 years. Finally, assume that by the time of the divorce in 1982, his assets had grown to $8,000,000 and his net worth to $6,000,000."

"Whoa," Betty said, rolling her eyes.

"You can now, of course, assume that she claimed the growth in assets happened during the marriage and that she should share in that growth. She said the property settlement, whereby she would only get half the value of the house, was unfair. What say you?"

"I agree with her," Betty answered quickly, before anyone else could jump in. "They were married; she contributed to his success; she helped make it happen. $8,000,000? Whoa."

"What about the $200 a month alimony for 10 years?" Bob asked.

"That's ridiculous," Betty answered with a steady gaze.

"Well, that is the *Gross* case cited in your Table of Cases. The court agreed with you in part and disagreed with you in part. The court upheld the original property settlement but not the alimony provision. It said the property settlement was freely entered into at the time of the agreement and should be upheld. It said a perfect or equal division of marital property is not required. Incidentally, *Gross* followed the lead of the watershed *Posner* case out of Florida. As to the alimony provision, however, the court in *Gross* said that it could work a hardship on her, after her opulent standard of living, to have to live on $200 a month."

"Couldn't get her nails done for that," Betty chipped in with a knowing look toward Anne. "And why didn't they throw the whole agreement out? Given his *alleged* misconduct, we can imagine he didn't even keep his most sacred marital agreement."

"In this case," Ted answered, "the parties didn't make misconduct part of their prenuptial agreement, and without an express provision to that effect the court wouldn't set the agreement aside."

"You know," Cris finally said, "it just doesn't seem fair. Maybe the court did require support payments that would enable her to maintain her standard of living, but that's not the same as her having control of half the money. Just look at the inflation we had during their 14-year marriage," she added. "That was the Nixon to Ford to Carter to Reagan era. Her monthly support payments would have bought less and less every year."

"She could have gone into court and had her alimony payments increased," Ted answered.

"Yes, but what a pain," Cris responded. "If she had her own assets, she could invest them and be on her own."

"This is interesting," Dan said, looking from Cris to Ted. "There are lots of unknowns. If she had the assets but didn't know much about investing, a drop in the stock market could wipe her out. Look at 1973-1974, or 1987, or 2000-2002. Or what if a bad-apple investment guy got hold of her?"

"Boy, do you need sensitivity training," Betty muttered.

"Here's another thing," Cris said, ignoring both comments. "If the court wanted to increase her alimony, or support, or whatever it's called, because she had acquired an opulent lifestyle, what would they have done if she had been a frugal little housewife? Kept her at $200 a month because that's all she needed?"

"These are good questions," Bob said, acknowledging both Cris and Dan's comments. "In fact, there was a strong dissenting opinion in this case that would have supported a division of the property. The court was divided 4-3, and the minority opinion made the point you just made. In fact, there are other cases in other states that would support the idea of a division of property. And, of course, if this had been a community property state it would have been a very different ballgame."

"Well, what about that," Frank said, perking up in his seat. "How would you know all that, and what if you move to another state?"

"The answer to both questions is to see an attorney," Ted answered from the back. "We can only hope to make you aware of the issue."

"That's right," Bob said as he went back to his notes. "That's all we can do here. Now, let's look at another case decided two years later by the same court that decided *Gross*, except this was a divorce case that *didn't* involve a prenuptial agreement. The question again relates to a division of property. Here it involves the marital home. In this case, the *Worthington* case, the husband had owned farm property before the marriage and had built the marital home on the farm property, completing it after the marriage. He was a career employee with Proctor and Gamble and was covered by its pension plan. His wife was Korean born, spoke broken English, and had little education. She was a homemaker. The judge, based upon the facts of this case, and using his judicial discretion to achieve a fair and equitable division of marital property, awarded her a share of the total assets, including the appreciation that had taken place over the years in the value of the farm and house."

"The significance of this," Ted interjected from his seat, "is that the court took a non-marital asset, that is the farm and the house that he owned as his separate property before the marriage, and treated it as a marital asset; the court divided its appreciation in value from the time of the marriage until the divorce."

"That's right," Bob said, putting down his notes to discuss the case, "and it was a 6-1 decision. The court said that where significant marital funds and labor are expended to improve and maintain non-marital property, its appreciation in value is a marital asset."

"Do you think the court was bending over backwards just to help a disadvantaged wife in this case?" Ernie asked.

"That's probably true," Bob replied, "but the importance of the case is that not one judge disagreed with the idea that the wife should share in the increased value of the property attributed to the *maintenance and improvements* made during the marriage. Then, maybe to help her out, the court went beyond that. She was credited with appreciation of the whole property, not just the part that related to maintenance and improvements during the marriage."

"Isn't that the opposite of what the same court said in the *Gross* case?" Cris asked. "In *Gross*, the wife didn't get a share of the increased property value, but in *Worthington*, she did."

"True," Ted answered. "The difference is that *Gross* involved a prenuptial agreement, a *contract* made before marriage, and the *Worthington* case did not. The court upheld the contract in *Gross*; it didn't have to in *Worthington*. But, in addition to that, if the court had broken through the prenuptial agreement in

Gross—a divorce case—to give the wife a share of his $6,000,000 net worth, it might have opened the door to doing the same thing in a case of death instead of divorce. And remember, the original use of prenuptial agreements was to preserve your property for your children upon your death, and to keep it from your new spouse. The court didn't want to endanger that with *Gross*."

"I agree with that," Bob said. "*Gross* preserved tradition and existing law."

Ernie, pondering what he had just heard, tuned out further discussion about the difficulty the court sometimes had in deciding a case fairly, on its own facts, in light of prior decisions and public policy considerations. Ernie wondered about the *Worthington* case and his own situation. He was putting money into his wife Jennie's house, new driveway, painting, paper, carpeting, furnace, and mortgage payments, but he didn't own the house—she did. Would he get anything out of it? He didn't have a prenuptial agreement, so he wouldn't be hurt by that. But he wasn't an uneducated immigrant, either. Of course, he also didn't want a divorce. He was concerned, though, by the prospects of old age. He didn't have a whole lot left after his divorce. Would he have enough to live on? And what about his kids? He wanted to leave them something, but he was putting a lot of his money into this house. Still, he had to live somewhere. And he loved Jennie. Life with Jennie was good.

"Let's look now at the *Hook* case," Bob was saying. Ernie returned his attention to the moment.

"They could have preserved his property in *Worthington* and still let her share the growth," Betty muttered.

Bob picked up his notes from the desk as Ted, walking up the aisle, smiled across the room to Anne.

"In *Hook*, the court said, 'Although the provision made for the intended wife in a prenuptial contract is wholly disproportionate, she will be bound by voluntarily entering into the contract after full disclosure or with full knowledge.'" With a wave of his notes to dispel any doubt, Bob summarized the law: "The key in this state is full disclosure or otherwise full knowledge of the other's assets. If you have that going into the prenuptial agreement, along with other factors, the separation of property between you and your spouse will be upheld by the court upon the death of either of you. Appreciation or no appreciation."

"And that assumes," Ted added, "the other factors we stated in your Notes, such as it being your voluntary act, free of coercion, fraud, duress and so on, and it being fair and reasonable at the time you sign the agreement, given your particular facts and circumstances."

"That sounds like there's still some wiggle room," Anne said to Ted with a little wiggle.

"Some," he agreed, "but you're getting the flavor of it."

Yum, Anne thought to herself, crossing her knees and smoothing her hair with a delicate hand.

"In the *Eule* case," Bob was saying, "the wife was married six times and the husband was married nine times. They were married to each other three times."

"Whoa," Betty muttered while rolling her eyes at Dan and stamping her foot lightly, "way to go." Dan turned to the front, not wanting to encourage her.

"For their third wedding, they signed a prenuptial agreement immediately before the ceremony, which incidentally took place the day after her prior marriage ended with a Mr. Goulding, whom she had married twice."

"It's nice they had someone to turn to," Frank said with a wink to Betty, who acknowledged his sarcasm with a quiet chuckle.

"This third get-together with Eule lasted only fifty-four days."

"Whoa," Betty said.

"Without spending a lot of time on it ourselves," Bob continued, "one of the issues in the case was this: before she signed the agreement with Eule, she took her settlement proceeds from Goulding, gave them to her brother to hold in trust for her Goulding children, and then didn't disclose those assets to Eule before signing the prenuptial agreement. She tried to hide those assets."

"Maybe she knew something," Betty said.

"Is there much fraud involved in these agreements?" Ernie asked.

"Can't say," Ted answered. "A successful fraud wouldn't be discovered."

"The point you want to remember," Bob added, "is that there should be no fraud. This is a marriage; it's based on good faith.

"Nevertheless, one case does come to mind," Bob said. "In that one, the husband, near the end of his life, transferred assets to his sons as a gift, and the transfers were found to be *so* unreasonable in amount that they undermined the wife's financial position. They were found to be fraudulent and in violation of the couple's prenuptial agreement. That's the *Dubin* case. A more typical case seems to be where the prenuptial agreement is signed within a short time of the wedding, and questions later arise as to full disclosure or coercion or duress under the circumstances. But even then, the particular facts will determine the outcome.

"In the *Juhasz* case," Bob continued, "the wife had limited knowledge of the English language, and the prenuptial agreement was explained to her by the husband's attorney, through an interpreter, over a strudel dinner she prepared for them all before the wedding. The court later favored her challenge of the agreement."

"A strudel dinner," Betty repeated, shaking her head.

"In *Fletcher*, both parties were represented by different lawyers, but the lawyers were from the same law firm…the firm that had represented each of them in prior divorces. The agreement was presented to the woman just before the wedding. When the marriage ended 7 years later, she challenged the prenuptial agreement on the grounds of coercion and lack of a meaningful opportunity to consult with separate legal counsel. She lost in a 4-3 decision. There was a forceful minority opinion, but she still lost."

"The minority thought she got a raw deal," Ted said. "Same firm representing both sides."

"In the *Troha* case," Bob continued, "the wife's attack on the prenuptial agreement was defeated in a 7-0 decision. In that case, she was found to have had substantial assets of her own before the agreement was signed, and she also had business experience. The court noted, as an aside, that he had died while they were on a European vacation and she, after notifying his children and shipping him back, had just continued her vacation for four more months."

"Probably had a Eurorail pass," Betty said under her breath.

"Well, it's 8:30 and time to wrap it up," Bob said to the class as he glanced at the round clock on the back wall; so different from the schoolroom clock he remembered from high school. "By necessity, we've only highlighted some of the issues that can arise in this area. Our look at cases was limited, but we gave you a sample of the kinds of problems that can arise."

"Let me add one thing," Ted said. "I've done a lot of these and this is the best way you can protect yourself and your kids. So protect your assets and your income: Do a prenup before you get married."

"But none of us did that," Anne said.

"And that's the reason for this course," Ted answered, "that's what it's all about from now on."

"Even so," Bob interjected, "a prenup doesn't relieve you from needing to support each other. And that, to me, is the heart of the matter; it's the heart of the marriage and should be the heart of your planning."

"But what I get out of this," Cris said, "is that these agreements aren't always enforceable. That troubles me."

"Well," Bob responded, "if properly done, with proper legal safeguards, they can be relied upon to protect your property. In short, the property you bring to the marriage is generally what you or your heirs can expect to take out upon death or divorce, and the same for your spouse. That's the usual setting and it usually work. Some of the cases we looked at tonight lacked the proper legal safeguards."

"So you're confident these work," Cris said.

"I'm confident they *can* work," Bob answered. "Be aware, though, that the legal safeguards can vary from state to state; they're different in California or Wisconsin, for example, than they are here or in Pennsylvania. And also be aware that, beyond what we talked about, the parties can make other commitments in the agreement. For example, one can agree to make a substantial gift to the other, either outright or in trust, or buy a life insurance policy for the benefit of the other, or make the other the beneficiary of an existing insurance policy or investment account. There are lots of things that might be done, depending on the circumstances."

"I'd like to find out more about this," Cris said.

"Well, Ted can help you there," Bob said. "Our emphasis in this course is on second or subsequent marriages where there is no prenuptial agreement. But, as I said, some of the issues we will discuss in the weeks ahead apply even if you have a prenuptial agreement."

"What about agreements made after you're married?" Frank asked as Bob opened his briefcase and slid his notes into a leather pocket that held his Palm pilot and financial calculator.

"You can have post-nuptial agreements relating to property in a number of states, namely the community property states and states adopting the Uniform Probate Code," Bob said, "but not here in Ohio. Here, the only post-nuptial agreement that's recognized is a Separation Agreement whereby you and your spouse separate and no longer have marital relations. In that case, you can have an agreement that divides your property and deals with the issues of spousal support and child support. The Separation Agreement can then be submitted to the court in an action for divorce or dissolution of marriage. Beyond that," Bob said, continuing to gather his papers from the desk, "you can only have financial agreements within the marriage for personal or tax reasons…nothing that would be binding on death or divorce."

"Maybe they're afraid of pillow-talk agreements," Frank said, getting up to follow the others as they left the room.

"You're probably right," Bob said, shaking his head, wishing he had caught Ted for a minute before he left. "But times are changing, and we may see a time when post-marital agreements, done with the same safeguards as prenuptial agreements, and done fairly, would be enforceable as to property divisions upon death or divorce. Don't look for it soon, though."

"Thanks," Frank said as he and Bob started out of the room.

Outside, Anne caught up with the tall figure striding across the darkened parking lot. "Ted, could you walk me to my car? There's something I want to talk to you about."

"Sure. Which way?"

"Ted! Don't be so hard to get. You know my car."

Chapter Four

Financial Planning

The Copper Grille is tucked into a little cove at the strip mall on Wheeler Road; they say it serves the best scampies between New York and Chicago. Ted and Anne have been nestled over a small table there for the past two hours; the conversation has come easily. They like each other, are charmed by each other. Her honey-blonde hair, now cut shoulder-length, shines in the light of a candle. Her dark eyes are warm, alive with interest and curiosity. She smiles with her full attention on him.

"Anne, it's been very nice, great in fact…but where are we going…?"

"I don't know, but it is nice isn't it? I've enjoyed this time with you, Ted. And my scampies were delicious. I hope we can do this again."

"Anne, I'd love to, but I'm not comfortable with it…You're married, you know."

"Yes,…but don't you ever get lonely Ted…just want to talk with someone? I know I do."

"Yes, sometimes."

"Don't you want a friend? It seems like people ought to be able to be friends, don't you think?"

"I don't know if I can be just friends with you, Anne."

She smiled warmly and extended her hand across the table. "Would you like to do this again, Ted?"

"Yes…I would. It's been very nice…great in fact." He didn't know what else to say. He smiled, warmed by the touch of her hand lingering in his.

They left the restaurant and walked to her car. "Why don't you go ahead, Ted. I'll follow along and come to class a few minutes later."

"Okay, you know the way from here?"

"Yes, but I'll keep an eye on you anyway." They stood by her car for a long moment, looking at each other in silence, then she gave him a hug. He squeezed her to himself, reluctant to let go. It was the beginning of October; change was in the air.

Ted left the parking lot and drove the Blazer across town and out toward the school. He would have to hurry a little so he could get there and take a look at his notes before class. "Love Me Tender" eased from his special back speakers. His thoughts were on Anne; she was a puzzle, complex, but very lovely. Complexity, at this point in his life, he did not need. But he still felt the hug, felt drawn, felt her need…and his own. She said she was lonely. He knew that meant trouble; what was her husband like? Ted drove on with a feeling of apprehension, yet also excitement, knowing he would see her again—and wanting to see her again.

He walked into the classroom, conferred for a moment with Bob, and then took a seat in the back. This was Bob's session. Anne came in and walked to her front seat; Ted's eyes followed her up the aisle. He stirred in his seat and then looked at Bob's outline as he began the class.

"Good evening again," Bob began, noticing that only Betty and Frank were looking at him. "Tonight we talk about financial planning; I hope you had a chance to review your Reading Notes and give some thought to your own financial planning issues.

"Here's one that I want you to consider," Bob said, surveying the small class, hoping this would shock-start them.

"By law, a husband has a duty to support his wife, so long as he is able. By law, a wife has a duty to support her husband, so long as she is able. In fact, by law, each may compel the other to contribute to his or her support if needed. Now, take that a step further," he said, noting that he had the attention of every person in the room. "Not only can one spouse compel the other to contribute to his or her support, but the *state* can compel the same thing. Just think about that. The state can compel you to support your spouse."

Maybe, maybe not, Frank thought to himself.

"What about a prenuptial agreement?" Dan interrupted.

"Remember, a prenuptial agreement is intended to control the distribution of property upon the death of one, or upon the couple's divorce. It doesn't control issues of fundamental support. Society has an interest in seeing that married people support each other.

"This raises the planning issue I brought up in our first class," Bob went on. "Society can enforce spousal support through the Medicaid rules, as well as time-honored court orders for support. I just want you to be aware of the Medicaid problem. It's very real as it relates to planning in a second or subsequent marriage. We'll go into that in more detail in the weeks ahead, but let's move on for now. Let's hear about your own financial planning issues."

"It stinks," Betty announced from her seat behind Cris. Cris shuttered. Why had she taken this seat? Now, due to classroom protocol, she was stuck with it.

"Why do you say that?" Bob asked.

"I hate budgets. I used to do all that. I'd list all our expenses and keep a record. I hated it."

"I understand," Bob responded with genuine empathy. "We all hate budgets. We hate them so much we don't even call them budgets anymore. We call them Cash Management Statements."

"I like that," Anne said, looking over to Betty.

"I don't even balance my checkbook anymore," Betty muttered.

Bob ignored the comment, assuming it to be true, and moved over toward Anne. "When we use the term 'cash management' we feel we're in control. And that's important. We want to feel that we control our money. We don't want to feel controlled by a budget."

"I like that," Betty interjected.

"Of course you do," Bob said, "of course you do. We all want to be in control. Look, you don't need to get hung-up on this. Just take your checkbook, look at the last 2 years, see what you're spending, and sketch out your expenses under two headings: fixed and variable. What can't you control as a practical matter, in the near term at least, and what can you control. The whole idea is to get control, to see what you need and what you don't need, to see what is fixed and what can be changed.

"So sketch out a Cash Management Statement that covers your fixed expenses and helps you control your variable, discretionary expenses. Leave yourself some flexibility. Don't be so tight and rigid that you just have to break out of it, like going off a diet. Be realistic. There will be unexpected expenses, and you also need room for entertainment, some fun money. You have to be sensible…controlled but flexible, if you know what I mean. The important thing is to see where you can free up some cash for longer-term goals like education of children, or money for your retirement. Your Cash Management Statement will help you move steadily in that direction."

"I liken it to time management," Ted added from the back of the room. "You have to decide what's most important to you…set priorities. You only have so many hours in a day; you have to decide what you want to achieve. You set goals and then allocate time to achieve them. That means you have to channel your energies, use your discretionary time, or in this case, use your discretionary money, to achieve your goals."

Ted was now on his feet, moving halfway up the aisle. "In time management, you free up time by dropping unimportant matters, and by delegating certain things to others. Here you discover money by dropping unimportant things, things that don't really matter."

"I tried to drop smoking," Betty said. "After a while, it finally worked."

"Ted has a good analogy," Bob said from the front. "That's a very good analogy. You'll find time management ideas, along with other life-changing ideas, in *Seven Habits of Highly Effective People*, the book I mentioned for supplemental reading."

"This is really about life planning," Ted added. "Money is an important part of it. What we're trying to do here is solve money problems so you can get to what matters most in life: your relationship with your spouse and children, and your personal growth." Ted returned to his seat, and one person in particular began to see a different side of him. Betty tucked the thought away for future reference.

"Okay, let me just summarize a few points," Bob said. "First, you want to set goals and write them down. Check your Reading Notes on this. Second, do a Cash Management Statement just like we talked about. Third, analyze where you can squeeze out some money to put toward your goals. Fourth, get help from financial planning software or from a web site or a financial planner."

"Which do you recommend?" Cris asked.

"I like a combination," Bob answered. "I like to see a person reach out on his or her own first—to a book, or to a course, or through the computer, or to all three. This is an education process; it makes you think, you learn from it. Learning about it will help you maintain control when you do engage a financial planner, which I also recommend. Having a financial planner is like having a coach. You will improve your game with a coach."

"What about someone like me?" Betty asked. "I get lost in all this. It makes me dizzy. I don't even balance my checkbook."

"Then you need to get help. You can at least set goals. Then have someone go through your checkbook for you and develop a Cash Management Statement. *Then* get professional help."

"I suppose that costs money."

"I suppose," Bob replied.

"You forgot one thing, though," Betty smiled.

"What's that?"

"You could increase your income, heh, heh."

"Right-a-roni. Certainly true for some, but not all."

Bob glanced at his notes and said, "You can get a good overview of the financial planning process at 'WWW.CFP.NET.' Click on 'learn about financial planning.' Take a look at that before you start.

"Now, I want to cover some specific things tonight; they relate to the education of children, housing, and sharing of living expenses. We'll cover retirement planning, estate planning, investments, and other matters in the weeks ahead.

"Education of children: Let's look at that first. And here I'm talking about college or vocational education beyond high school. The question is, who should pay for it in a second or subsequent marriage and how much will it cost?

"Let me first answer part of that myself. Tuition cost can vary all over the lot, as you know. Vocational school is one thing; a private liberal arts college is another. Then there is room, board, and transportation. The child might live at home or across the country, even across the ocean. Costs can climb faster than smoke. But costs can be softened by grants, scholarships, and student loans. And, of course, the child can contribute his or her earnings from part-time work and summer jobs.

"But," Bob said, looking at Dan, "we may still be left with a sizable bill. The question is, who should pay for it?"

"The child's biological parents," Dan answered.

"Even if it's a second marriage?" Cris asked. "And the mother can't afford it?" It was a rhetorical question, but its message carried across the room.

"What about the child's father?" Anne asked Cris.

"Right," Bob interjected before Cris could respond, "let's look at that from two angles. First, assume the child's father is still living; assume the parents are divorced. Does that father have an obligation to pay for his child's higher education?"

"I think so," Anne said.

"Maybe the father can't afford it," Ernie said.

"Ted, you want to add something?" Bob asked. Ted had inched up the aisle and stood by the blackboard.

"Yes, the divorced father may or may not have a legal obligation here; you have to look at the divorce decree and the parties' Separation Agreement as part of the divorce. Did it address this issue? Did the father make a commitment?"

"Even if he did," Ernie said, "what if things change?"

"He has a moral obligation," Anne said.

Bob was looking at Anne as she spoke. He noticed a spark in those dark eyes, now changed from the ones that had flattered him only moments before.

"Go back to their Separation Agreement," Ted emphasized again. "Was a commitment made? If so, can you enforce it as a practical matter? That's your point, Ernie. If a commitment was made then, yes, there is a moral obligation, and yes, there is a legal obligation, and yes, you can take him to court to enforce the decree. But as a practical matter you may not get anything. He may not have the money. I say he; it could be she. Shtick happens. He could be a deadbeat."

Ernie sat staring straight ahead.

"So," Bob picked up, "can we say that whether or not a child of a divorced couple receives an education beyond high school depends…one way or another…on the child and the child's biological parents…throwing in whatever financial aid they might get? Does that sound right?"

"It's fine with me," Anne answered.

"I agree," Dan said, looking from Bob to Cris.

"Well," Cris said, "I think you have a new situation. Say the mother has custody of the child and say the mother remarries. Now you have a new family unit; the child has a stepfather. Hopefully this is a loving, supportive relationship with the new husband loving the child's mother and loving the child. He wants them to be happy, and the mother's happiness is tied to her child's happiness. She wants her child to go to college…and what if the child has his heart set on a particular college? Maybe the biological father just isn't involved. Why shouldn't his stepfather contribute to his education? They're a new family now."

"That's a good point, too," Bob said, "and every situation is different. Anyone have another thought?"

"I do," Ernie said. "Maybe the stepfather has a tough time making ends meet. I think if the child wants to go to college, the child needs to figure out a way. Where there's a will there's a way. And the child should look to his own father and mother if he needs help. Otherwise, the stepfather is going to feel like a failure if he can't do it all, and it's not even his responsibility."

Bob nodded. "Any other comments?"

Dan half raised his hand. "The stepfather might also feel that he's paid his dues, or is still paying them. He's educated his own children, or might still have to for that matter. He also might need to save for his retirement. Who's going to take care of him?"

"Good question," Bob said. "These are all good points and the solution won't be the same for everyone. Adjustments may have to be made. You may have to lower your expectations. For some couples, there won't be enough money to go around. For others, it's a matter of figuring out how to share the cost, and that goes to the whole question we're dealing with here."

"'Preservation or self-preservation?'" Betty said. "That is the question."

"And we hope the answer is both," Bob answered.

"But let me change the situation now. Say instead of a divorce, we have a widow who has remarried, and she has children from her first marriage. They also want an education. How does that change things?"

"I think it makes my point even more," Cris offered. "It's a new family unit. The new husband is even more involved. Where is the child to look? This is the person the child's mother has brought into his life. He needs to be a real stepfather. They're a new family; they're in it together."

The room was silent for a moment until Bob asked, "Any other thoughts?"

"It's the same situation except the real father isn't there," Frank said.

"He's there in a lot of ways," Anne said, looking at Frank as if he were a child.

"That could be a whole new problem then," Frank said, returning her look.

"There are emotional issues in either case, death or divorce," Bob said. "They're real and they underlie the financial issues. Nevertheless, people have to go on; they have to muddle through. The question here, assuming death of a spouse, is who should bear the cost of educating the deceased spouse's child?"

"I still think the child's biological parents," Dan said. "The child's father, assuming it was the father who died, could have had life insurance or provided other means for the education of his children."

"That's true in some cases," Bob answered.

"If he did, that should solve the problem," Frank said, with a smirk not seen by Anne.

"I agree," Anne said. "If the father provided adequately for his child, those funds should be used for the child's college education."

"There's still the matter of bonding," Cris said. "If the stepfather contributes to the child's education, that's a bonding thing between them, and it bonds the mother, too. They're a family. He's assuming a role in the family. And one more thing," Cris said, "and then I'll shut up. The mother will feel vulnerable after the death of her husband. The financial help of her new husband in the education of her children is bound to give her a sense of security. She can save her own money for the future. That would be a bonding thing too, I should think."

"That wasn't my situation," Anne said, "but I think that would be true. It would be for me."

"Making a family out of your relationship is the important thing," Cris added.

"That's fine if the new guy can afford it," Dan said, "but he may have his own financial problems, or his own kids, or his own old age, to think about. Hopefully they can bond over something besides money."

"I agree," Ernie said. "Divorce can wipe you out. Maybe he needs a chance to recoup and start over. And don't forget: he needs to feel bonded, too. He's part of this family."

"Just whose family is it anyway?" Betty cracked.

"Every situation is different," Bob said. "And the roles could be reversed. Dan is right: it could be the husband's child who needs education money. Also, a lot depends on the age, sex, and personalities of the children. The stepparent may have been part of their lives since they were very young, or maybe not. And, just what is the financial arrangement of the new couple? Is it open, mutual, and supportive? Or is it separate, private, and secretive? What is their attitude toward money? How were they raised? What was their first marriage like? The only thing you can do is try to be fair, try to understand, try to be supportive. You have to work it out. And Cris's point is well taken. You want to come through these issues as a loving and supportive family. That's what it's all about. That's what I see this course to be all about."

"Thank you," Cris said. "I realize each one has needs, but closeness and togetherness are what really matter."

"We all want that," Dan said. "I know children have needs, but adults have needs too. Like Ernie said, the new husband may be starting over. Or in my case, I'm not working anymore. I live on a fixed income."

"The children come first," Cris said in a low voice.

"Show me the money, baby," was said in an even lower voice. Ted chuckled to himself and shook his head. Betty was something else.

"In our case," Bob said, "hopefully the deceased father provided enough of an estate to educate his children. If not, there may be financial aid available, or the child may be able to help out. The mother and stepfather can contribute based upon what makes sense all around. But they do have their own needs, their own financial security issues, and their own relationship to consider. They have to muddle through. As Cris said, you want to come through as a family. Again, take a look at *Seven Habits*.

"But let's move on. There's another subject I want to cover, and that's the subject of housing."

"Every king needs his castle," Betty announced.

"Or every queen her nest," Anne said.

"Well, that's often the underlying emotion," Bob said.

"Before you leave education," Frank said, leaning back with hands clasped behind his head, "how do you know how much to save every month…say your kid is 2 years old and you need the money in 16 years, and then you have another one coming along a year later, and another 2 years after that?"

"We've listed several excellent web sites in your Notes," Bob answered. "They will be helpful, and your financial planner can also help you with that. The gist of it is to figure the cost of college now, inflate that number into the future, and then calculate the monthly savings you need—assuming a certain rate of return on your money—to accumulate that future sum. You do that for each child. We'll look at the methodology more closely when we get to retirement planning. It's the same concept; in either case, you're saving to accumulate a future sum of money."

"Thanks," Frank said, "I'll check the web sites."

"You didn't mention saving for a daughter's wedding, but that could be something too," Anne said.

"You're right," Bob agreed.

"Okay, let's look now at three housing situations: she moves into his place, he moves into her place, or they move into a new place.

"Ideally, they might move into a new place; it's neutral territory for both of them, or so it would appear. There are still questions of title to the property, who puts up the money, who is paying the mortgage, and who all is living there. So, as you can see, there are issues to be smoothed out even with a neutral site. The resolution of those issues will depend on the people involved. Of course that's also true in the other situations, but they might be resolved more easily with a neutral location: a new home for both."

"Let me inject a thought here," Ted said from the back. "If the couple selects a new location, a fresh place for both of them, chances are they're both contributing to it. They'll often have a 50-50 interest in the house, or condo, or whatever. They may also cover the rest of their housing costs 50-50."

"I think that's true in many cases," Bob added, "but it depends on what they bring to the marriage, and it also ties in with their retirement planning and estate planning. There are any number of possible scenarios, and a big factor is whether they stay in the same general location or move completely away…to another state, for example. But I agree with Ted; if it's a new place, chances are they both contribute to it.

"Another possibility is that she moves into his place," Bob continued. "That doesn't happen very often."

"Because he doesn't get the house," Ernie said.

"Even if he did, it's not her nest," Anne offered.

"That's right," Bob agreed. "It could happen if he has a place of his own and she doesn't. But it's not likely to happen if his place was the home of his first wife."

"It could happen if he's a bit older and has moved into a new condo," Dan said.

"It could," Anne agreed. "But you can bet there will be new furniture and decorating. She'll redo it."

"If she has children, that will be a factor too," Cris added.

"That's a big factor," Bob agreed. "If he has a house and she doesn't, they might live at his place, or, for a lot of reasons, he might sell it and buy a new place. In that event, he might own it and pay the upkeep, as he did for his old place, or they might share it one way or another."

"They might also be renters," Frank said. "Not everyone is a homeowner."

"They could be renters," Bob agreed. "If they rent, they just need to decide how to share the rent.

"Now let's look at a common situation," Bob continued as he put down his notes. "Very often the new husband moves into his wife's house. That can happen for a number of reasons. One is, in a divorce, the wife might have gotten the house as part of the settlement. The flip side, as Ernie indicated, is the husband has lost a house. Another reason is that if her first husband died, she may still be living in their house. And, if she has children still at home, she usually wants to provide as much security and stability for them as possible. That often means staying in the family home."

"That was certainly my case," Anne said.

"Mine too," Cris added.

"It was my case too," Ernie said, "or I should say my wife's case. She got the house and custody of the kids."

"And how is it going for all of you?" Bob asked.

"I'm not remarried yet," Cris said. "I'm still trying to work all this out. That's why I'm here."

"In my case, when I remarried, it was tough at first," Ernie said. "It was tough for all of us. But thank God she has good kids. They couldn't be better. I know of other couples where the whole thing came apart over the kids…drinking, drugs, cars, rebellion, discipline, all that stuff."

"You're lucky," Ted said.

"You really are," Frank added, "but why do I get the feeling there's more to this?"

"Yeah, well, the financial part, but it's hard to talk about. I mean, she had a house and I didn't, so I moved in with her. She was great, and so were the kids. But I've paid the mortgage and our mutual expenses over the years, helped with improvements and done the upkeep, but I don't have anything to show for it."

"Didn't she help with some of it?" Frank asked.

"Yeah, some of the improvements," Ernie answered.

"Cripes, what-a-ya cryin' about?" Frank muttered to himself.

"Are you worried about it?" Anne asked.

"Yeah, I don't feel like a homeowner. Truth be told, I'm *not* a homeowner. I've paid out a lot of money, but I don't have the security of owning a home."

"Are you afraid she'll throw you out?" Frank asked.

"Maybe."

"Then see your lawyer," Ted said.

"I wouldn't throw you out," Betty said.

"Are you happy?" Cris asked.

"Yes, I am happy."

"Do you feel bonded?" Cris asked. "Do you feel you're part of a family?"

"Yeah, I do," Ernie answered, straightening in his seat, "but I'd be happier if I had something to show for the money I've spent—some security."

"Your marriage is an investment," Cris said. "I'm sure she won't throw you out."

"Is there something else here?" Frank asked. "Is there a control problem? Do you feel like you're not the man of the house?"

Ernie stammered for a moment, put on the spot, then said: "It's not my house."

"Money talks," Frank muttered.

"You guys and your control," Betty said, "stay loose…we're not going to dump you." All eyes turned to Betty, the diet Coke, the uncombed hair, the tent dress and tennis shoes. She smiled back a confident smile.

"Does it bother you Ernie?" Ted asked. "I think it would bother me."

"Yeah, sometimes."

"Every king needs his castle," Betty said, looking to Bob.

"That's true," Bob said. "Divorce can tear things up financially and emotionally. You had an anchor before…now it's gone."

"You just have a new anchor," Betty said.

"The women lose the most," Cris said. "They're the ones hit the hardest. But it sounds like you have a home, Ernie, and love, even if you don't own the house."

"I do," Ernie answered.

"I bet you have your own chair," Betty chortled.

"Yes, I do," Ernie said with a chuckle, "yes I do. I'm really a lucky duck. But home equity would be good."

"And more control," Frank added.

"Yeah, that too," Ernie agreed.

"A controlling duck," Betty said. "That's all we need."

Ted had moved up the aisle, so Bob extended an open hand in his direction, inviting Ted's comment.

"I just want to say one thing, and I say this as a generic comment, not a personal one to anyone here. When a guy moves into his new wife's house, he's expected to carry his fair share of the load, one way or another. I mean, he buys half the house or he puts an addition onto it or he pays the mortgage or he pays the taxes, utilities, and insurance, or he mows the lawn or whatever. I would just say this to him: Put your tools where you want them, hang your pictures, set up your speakers, get your chair up in front of that TV, and be at home. It's your home too."

"A regular Archie Bunker," Betty mumbled.

"Not really," Ted answered. "It all depends on how you go about it. But this *is* a marriage, after all. It's not a boarding house."

"She may want to keep things as they were; she may be sheltering her children," Anne said. "It's not easy bringing a strange man into a home with children. The children have to come first."

"I understand," Ted answered. "And if he's the right kind of guy, he can handle that. I'm just saying there has to be a balance. The guy needs to feel at home."

"It's a tough problem," Bob said. "The reality is we have limited resources, and, at the same time, housing issues touch deep emotions. We have a house one day and it's gone the next. Things can get turned upside-down. Egos get bruised. But we have to adjust, make choices, turn our egos in a new direction, and move on. All in all, it sounds like you've made good choices, Ernie. And control or no control, you don't look emasculated to me! It looks like you can handle yourself. Right?"

"Well, yeah, it's just that sometimes you feel like a man without a country, especially during the early years. You lose your history, you know."

"These *are* emotional issues," Bob agreed, "especially when it comes to housing, and especially around the holidays. And it's true, you do lose your history. You just have to concentrate on building a new life."

"Your spouse is in much the same boat," Anne said. "It's not easy for her either. But I think you should share your history and traditions with each other, especially holiday traditions."

"I don't mean to be a wet blanket," Dan said, "and I understand that history is important, but a guy like Ernie, and like me for that matter, still has to think about the future, about retirement and old age. He could wind up with nothing, and that's not fair. What if she dies, or what if she does throw him out when he's 75 and snores a lot?"

"He won't have to live on the streets," Cris said with a smile that repressed a laugh.

"You never know," Dan said.

"Well, I hear all of this," Frank said, looking from Ernie to Bob to Dan, "but the way I look at it is: if a guy marries my wife, if I die, or if I'm divorced, I think he should take care of her, period. If he's not prepared to do that, he shouldn't marry her in the first place."

Cris turned and smiled with approval. Don't look at me, honey, Frank thought, I've got two already.

"I can see that," Ernie said. "That's fine if you've got a lot of money, which I don't. But, at the same time, I do have a loving wife and family. Without that, I'd be out there running around, getting old in a hurry." He started to say something else, but stopped himself.

"I can just see you running around…" Betty said, laughing, then cutting it short, seeing that Ernie wasn't listening anymore.

He sat staring straight ahead at the blackboard; Bob was a shadow moving across his thoughts; Ernie looked like a man who had just lost a six-round fight and was now adding to the damage. Why had he talked so much? What was he doing? He slumped back in his seat. He knew Frank thought he was a wimp. But Frank was a punk. The hell with Frank. Ernie wished he could leave, bolt out the door right now and get to a meeting; AA and the support group he had there were his lifeline, his religion.

He thought of the car accident 10 years ago this month; he'd skidded through the stop sign at Broad and Henry, hit the white econovan broadside. Serious injuries to the other driver. She lived, but Ernie had nearly died. Within a year, he had lost his job, his savings, his house, and his family. AA and a welcoming evangelical church saved him. He met Jennie at the church, thank God. They were married two years later. Her little family took him in; Jennie and the two girls, Beth and Amy, then ten and eight, and though he couldn't replace the husband

and father they'd lost, they shared their love with him. He knew he was loved, and there was no other feeling that good. He felt secure, yet he was insecure. He'd been loved before and had screwed it up, lost it. And money was a worry. He couldn't do it all; he couldn't pay the bills, educate the girls, and save enough to buy into the house. And what of his own poor kids, the casualties of divorce? He didn't see much of them, but he loved them; he was sorry he had disappointed them. Only one of the four had gone to college, and that one had done it on his own. More failure as a father. And what *about* retirement?

Ernie hitched himself up in his seat. He wished he'd kept his mouth shut. Why had he opened up to these people? *I must look like a fool.* When this class ended, that would be it: he was out of here…didn't have to see them again.

But then he thought of Jennie, and her love, and of the time when he first felt the love of a Higher Power. It had been 5 years now; it happened as Ernie was driving to an early morning business meeting, so early that it was dark and no other cars were on the road. He had been troubled and frustrated and wrangling with problems that he seemed powerless to solve. Suddenly, out of the dark, a lighted cross came at him quickly, then flashed by! He saw as it passed that it was a school bus from a rural bible school, and it had a cross of lights on the grill. Coincidence? He didn't think so. A feeling of peace swept over him. He felt like a schoolchild at his desk who had been unable to work the assignment, when the teacher, who had been watching, stopped at his side, put her hand on his shoulder, and smiled her love. It would be all right. It didn't matter if he solved the problem. He was loved anyway. It was all about feeling loved; that was all that mattered. He had never felt more secure.

Warmed by the memory, Ernie removed his glasses for a moment and set them on the desk. Why should he care what these people think? It didn't matter. What he really needed to do was sit down with Jennie and talk about all this. And he should look for a better paying job. He could be a comptroller for a mid-size company. That would pay more than that staff accounting job of his.

As Ernie put his glasses back on and returned to the moment, people were laughing at something Dan had just said.

"I hate to end it here," Bob smiled at Dan, "but we have to wrap it up. I want to thank you for sharing with us, Ernie. That kind of honesty takes courage. I hope we can continue with that. We all have something to contribute, and we can learn from each other. Thank you again.

"And that brings me to my final topic for tonight: sharing living expenses. For background on this, and home finance and budgeting in general, read *For Richer, Not Poorer* by Ruth L. Hayden. Also, for breakthrough ideas about budgeting based on your deepest values, see David Bach's book, *Smart Couples Finish Rich*. And for an inspiring get-out-of-debt story, and practical ideas about debt management, see

Dave Ramsey's book, *Financial Peace Revisited*. You'll get lots of good ideas there, so I won't belabor them here. Our emphasis in this course is on how you and your spouse in a second or subsequent marriage share the burden of your mutual support. In the end, it's something you have to work out yourselves, and hopefully you're married to a team player...whether you each contribute 50-50 or contribute based on income or whatever. I think a sense of fairness and mutual comfort will dictate how you share general, and even extraordinary, living expenses, and also how you share income tax issues. But you have to communicate with each other and reach an understanding. You can't have one who by temperament or design just can't deal with it...one who stonewalls the other. You need to know what to expect.

"For more good background, read *Couples & Money* by Victoria Felton-Collins. She's a psychologist and a Certified Financial Planner, and she traces these money management issues to their emotional roots: freedom, security, power, and love. She contends that one or another is a prime mover for each of us.

"And that's my final comment," Bob said, glancing at the clock. "Good communication. I know Liz and I still have to work on that even after twenty-three years. I would just say that if you talk with each other, you can work it out. Start with deep empathetic listening, because that leads to understanding."

"And understanding leads to wisdom, and wisdom leads to problem solving," Ted said with open arms to Bob, "but I'm a litigator!"

"And I'm a counselor," Bob said, "and my interest is in strengthening the marriage."

"I think we need good counselors." Anne smiled at Bob.

"Okay, see you next week," Bob said with a blush, hoping it didn't show.

"We need good litigators too," Anne whispered to Ted on her way out.

As the group walked out of the building and down the worn steps to the parking lot, Cris and Dan caught hold of Ernie, spoke a few words of appreciation, and walked him to his car, a year-old silver Corvette; his single extravagance. "See you next week," Ernie said as they parted.

Chapter Five

Investments

Ted lay on his bunk thinking about the previous night: the storm, the woman, what was said. He wanted a cigarette for the first time in years and was glad he didn't have a match.

They had met at the Southeast Mall and driven for an hour to Joey's, up along the lake, for pasta. He remembered every detail: the stem of his wine glass, the table cloth, her hair, her perfume, her warmth, her beige silk blouse, the ring on her finger.

Dinner was leisure itself; they savored the food, the wine, their togetherness. The place was not crowded; the waitress let them be. The talk concerned themselves—growing up, parents, places they had lived in and visited. They laughed together and shared their lives. They spoke of how they seemed to connect so quickly, so easily and naturally.

When they left, they ran through the rain to his Blazer and got inside, laughing and just a little wet. The man who had been at the bar hurried under a black umbrella to his nearby car. The rain increased as Ted pulled from the parking lot and turned onto the two-lane macadam road that went along the lake and then cut inland. It was safe and cozy inside against the strong winds. The rain beat down on them as trees along the road bent with the sudden near gale force. Lightning struck all around, lighting up the night with flickering pictures of the passing houses, trees, and fields. Anne wanted to snuggle closer to him but was blocked by the console between the bucket seats. "Not like high school," he said, referring to the barrier between them. She laughed and said how romantic it was. He reached his arm around her, caressed her hair. They drove on in contented silence.

There were few cars on the road, and only occasionally did he see one behind them, always at a distance. They were happy yet anticipated the loss that separation would bring. She talked about her marriage, her husband's travels, her sense of loneliness. They both felt the intimacy of the moment and hated to see it end.

Ted's headlights found the cutoff road as the storm lessened, and they were soon up to speed on the main highway. A short time later, they reached the mall and talked a little longer in the misty light of the parking lot before he escorted her to her metallic blue BMW 330 Ci convertible and watched it cross the glistening black acres and disappear behind the darkened stores. It was midnight. There was only one car left in the lot when he headed home.

Ted knew he should get up and get going, but he lay there listening to soft jazz on 91.5 and stared at the ceiling. He thought about this developing relationship with Anne; not what it meant for the future, but what it meant for right now, the excitement they both felt. The pure discovery of each other added to the excitement, as did the need to be careful. But the essence, he knew, wasn't love; it was a chemistry that could carry them to a land where they should not go, even though they were tempted. They were becoming enveloped in each other's thoughts, and they craved connections to keep the current flowing. She more than he. Ted tucked that insight into a recess of his mind, the part where he suppressed all the things wrong with the relationship, the part kept captive by squads of hormones. It was there, in that cell, that he kept his worries about what it all meant, about commitment, about right and wrong, about her husband, about the future. Closer to the surface, battling their way out, were worries about discovery, about emotional dependence, about loss.

He had been naturally dependent upon his mother and lost her when he was 12. His father was seldom seen thereafter—career Air Force, married to the controls of a B-52 at forty thousand feet, a fading vapor. Raised by grandparents who tried to be parents, Ted was loved, it seemed, more out of duty than nature. He lessened his dependence on them over the next 4 years and then, at 16, gave it all to an auburn-haired girl he met in study hall, a girl he soon loved with an intensity he had never known, but now, years later, feared. It lasted 2 years before she broke his heart.

Ted took his broken heart on the road and enlisted at age 18. Basic training, advanced infantry, airborne, unit assignments, Germany, Korea, Panama, Alaska, Ft. Stewart, Ft. Bragg, finally to Ft. Knox as a hardened Sergeant to take baggy pants boys and train them to be disciples of discipline.

Along the way, he met and married Cindy, and again gave his heart away. But she was one who had known others before and, he learned, since. His first reaction was to keep his shaky core, and his anger, in an ordered place with a safe outlet: the army, a life he knew and trusted. But that changed one night, and the marriage ended in a web of lies about a big-eared second lieutenant at Ft. Knox. Serving out the balance of his time, Ted collected his pay and headed home at age 30 to a new life, the life of a college freshman at Kent State University.

He went straight through Kent in 3 years, did well enough as a business student, then went straight through a 4-year night program at Cleveland-Marshall College of Law. He worked days in insurance and investments, a mix of sales and sales support, and learned the language of finance. At 37, he joined Holcomb, Schmidt, Williams & Temple and was thrown in to sink or swim as a litigator. He thrived on it, especially at first. The law gave him a hammer and he used it.

Ted's thoughts drifted back to the moment, to the course he was teaching with Bob, and then to Anne and last night. Where was this going? He didn't know. He only knew he was now running late and had to hustle. His feet hit the floor, and he closed the drawer where he kept an unopened pack of Marlboro's. Time to get ready for the troops.

Ted had come home early to prepare for class; it was his session tonight; Bob had to meet a client in St. Louis. He got ready quickly and left, thinking about Bob as he drove to school. Bob would be upset about this thing with Anne. Bob would be clear about the need to break it off, citing ethics, professionalism, firm image, the attorney-client relationship. But Anne wasn't a client; this was an adult education class. Bob would see it otherwise. Bob didn't have to know.

Ted started the class right on time. Everyone was there; funny how they always took the same seats. Anne gave him a warm smile. "Good evening," he began, "Bob's out of town, so I'm it for tonight. Actually, this was planned to be my session anyway. Bob will be back in two weeks to talk about retirement planning. I'm scheduled to handle investments tonight and insurance next week.

"First, are there any questions from last week about financial planning? No? You all understand it? That's good." It takes time to warm up, he thought, time for them to shift gears from their various worries to the subject at hand.

"All right, to start with tonight, I want to give you a few thoughts about investing that are not covered in your Reading Notes.

"You can look at investing as basically preserving and enhancing your net worth, increasing the spread between your assets and your liabilities. In doing that, you first need a defensive strategy to protect your assets from loss…including insurable losses such as health, life, disability, property, casualty, and liability losses. For instance, an automobile accident could wipe you out because of a hospitalization or disability or because you didn't have enough liability insurance. In each case, you could lose your entire investment portfolio."

"Bummer," Betty said.

Ernie shifted in his seat.

"Having an emergency fund is another basic defensive strategy. You have to expect some bumps in the road, medical expenses, furnace replacement, job loss, etc. For that reason, experts advise having three to six months worth of living expenses in a reserve account. From another standpoint, an investment portfolio standpoint, a reserve of two to four years worth of living expenses is recession insurance; it should get you through most bad market cycles."

"Saving like that can be hard to do," Cris said, "especially when you're young. Just getting out of debt can be tough, almost impossible sometimes."

"I know," Ted agreed. "I've been there. You have to take it one step at a time and just tough it out. Start building that reserve in a cookie jar if you have to. It starts with a state of mind, a commitment to survive.

"In addition," Ted continued, wondering if Cris was that down and out (she didn't look it), "your Notes discussed diversification of investments. Diversification is needed in order to minimize the chance that a large loss in any given investment could seriously hurt your overall portfolio. That, too, is a basic defensive strategy. There's safety in owning a cross section of different kinds of securities."

"Like owning different kinds of mutual funds?" Frank asked.

"That's one way," Ted agreed.

"Then you need an offensive strategy to add to your net worth in the face of taxes and inflation. Needless to say, you, your health, and your career are the basis of your offense. You're the income generator. You need to take care of yourself physically, mentally, and emotionally. You also need to take care of your career, your job. You have to work at it, keep up-to-date…that's an investment. For most of you, your job is the basis of your financial security, and the fringe benefits from your job are the core of your health insurance, life insurance, disability insurance, and retirement programs. It's what you build on, that and your marriage. Your marriage is an investment, too. You know and I know that it's not easy finding the right balance for all of this: for your job, for your marriage, for your family, and for yourself. It's a real challenge."

Cris, in particular, was paying close attention, wondering about her own single parent issues and how they might change with marriage. Casey came first with his schedule of school activities, one leading to another: from baseball, to soccer, to basketball, to spring sports, with an overlay of his beloved guitar lessons, not to mention activities with friends. But she also had a competitive sales job, the house, the dog, meals, and her own needs. Add to this a new husband and stepfather. Would it all work? She wondered…hoping it would, thinking it would.

"Your home equity and your retirement plans are next," Ted was saying. "These are your bedrock investments. You want to get that house paid for and get those tax-deferred retirement accounts built up…contribute to that 401(k), contribute to that ROTH IRA.

"Then the real challenge of saving and investment begins. You need to have commitment and persistence to pass up current consumption in favor of investment. If you have that, the battle is half won. The rest is a matter of knowing your tolerance for risk, choosing the right asset allocation strategy, and then selecting good long-term investments, quality investments, and staying with the program."

"Can you go over asset allocation?" Betty asked. "I know it's in the Notes, but it would help if you explained it."

"Okay," Ted said, walking to the blackboard and drawing three large boxes, labeling them *equities, fixed income,* and *cash equivalents.* "Equities," he said turning back to the class, "could be common stocks or real estate or anything you own that can appreciate in value. Fixed income investments," he said, tapping the middle box, "are generally corporate or government bonds that pay interest on money you loan the corporation or government, with a pledge on their part to repay the loan at a given future date. Cash equivalents are checking or savings accounts, certificates of deposit, money market accounts and Treasury bills.

"Asset allocation means the percentage of your investment assets that you allocate to each of these three categories. The more you allocate to equities, the more risk you take, but also the greater potential return you have over the long term. The more you allocate to fixed income and cash equivalents, the more safety you have, but at a lesser expected return over the long haul. Nevertheless, with fixed income, you can expect some appreciation or depreciation in value as interest rates change; you can realize a gain or loss if you sell them before their maturity date. Cash equivalents, on the other hand, provide safety of principal with little or no fluctuation in value, but they usually provide the least long-term return on your money.

"Now," Ted said as he returned to the blackboard and wrote in some numbers, "if you're age 30 with a 30-or 35-year time horizon to retirement, you might be very aggressive and allocate 80 or even 90 percent of your investment assets to equities. If you're age 60, that might be 40, 50, 60, or 70 percent to equities, depending on your tolerance for risk, your job situation, planned retirement date, health, and other factors. That's asset allocation. In large measure, it will determine your total investment return. You need to design an asset allocation strategy that fits your particular situation."

"So the older you get, the more you go into fixed income and cash," Betty said.

"Typically," Ted answered, "because you have less time to recover from a loss on the equity side. But you still want some equities," he added, "even at age 70 or so. You still want a hedge against inflation."

"Thank you s-o-o-o much," Betty said. "I have a better picture."

"So, if at all possible," Ted said, erasing the numbers on the blackboard, "invest a steady amount on a regular basis. It's called 'dollar cost averaging.'

Check Table B in your Notes. Good things happen to consistent investors. Just be aware, though, that the market is not as steady a progression as Table B would imply. Table B is a compound interest table, it's not the market. There will be fits and starts and slumps and jumps in the market. There will be volatility; that's reality, that's life. But that's where asset allocation will help you. That's where 'dollar cost averaging' will help, too. Just stay the course and let time do its work."

"Ride that bull," Frank said.

"Now," Ted said, nodding his agreement as he dusted imaginary chalk from his hands and sat behind the desk, "I want to give you some quick hits related to your Reading Notes.

"First, we talked about hiring an investment advisor. You want to find one that you're comfortable with, one with unquestioned personal integrity, one with experience, and one who will respond to you, personally. By that I mean more than just a person who will give good service, return phone calls, and so on; I mean one who will represent your interests in a second marriage. You don't want one whose judgment might be clouded by the fact that he or she is handling a larger portfolio for your husband or wife."

"But what if my husband's broker has been successful and I don't have a broker? Wouldn't he want to do a good job for me too?" Cris asked.

"He probably would," Ted answered. "But just remember that you don't want to surrender responsibility. This is your program. It should fit your needs, and you need to stay in control. That's all I'm saying. Just be sure that he or she respects you, listens to you, and has *your* personal interest at heart."

"I have a different kind of problem," Anne said. "My first husband had life insurance and left it in a trust for me at the bank. But I'm not a big, big account at the bank. They gave me an 800 number to call. I get a different person every time I call; they look me up in the computer. Then, to make matters worse, my first husband's best friend is the designated trust advisor, but he's too busy to pay attention to my account, although he wouldn't admit that. Anyway, he convinced me to hire an outside advisor to advise the bank about my investments. But my account is small potatoes to the outside advisor, too, and I think the friend is just trying to cover his own you-know-what because he's not doing anything. In the meantime, I'm paying fees to the bank and to the outside advisor, and I'm not happy with either one."

"Are you paying fees to the friend?" Ted asked.

"No, but he has made passes at me more than once!" Anne said.

Betty laughed out loud. Cris was shocked; Frank smirked; the others showed no reaction, but Ted felt flushed. "It's a jungle out there," he said. "And you don't know what the arrangement might be between the friend and the outside advisor. They could be doing other business with each other, and referring your account to the outside advisor might be part of a tradeoff."

"I'd change trustees," Cris said.

"It's not that easy," Anne responded. "The trust agreement ties my hands. Besides, if I force a change, the bank will charge a 1 percent fee just to transfer the assets to a new trustee. And I would have to sell some of their in-house mutual funds and pay taxes on that. It's a mess. I feel like I've been hung out to dry."

"You need to have a talk with the friend," Ted said. "If he's not adding anything, he should resign. Same with the outside advisor. Maybe if you get rid of those two you would get more for your money at the bank. If not, change trustees. That 1 percent can be negotiated. Get an attorney."

"Can't your husband help you out?" Cris asked.

"I want to keep him out of it," Anne said, shaking her head. "It's not his concern."

"Maybe she doesn't trust him," Frank piped up. "She's afraid if he knew what she had, he would change their deal."

"It's none of your business," Anne said, glaring back at Frank. "I'm sorry I brought it up. Let's move on." She slapped her notes on the desk, glared again at Frank, and then looked at Ted as if to say, "DO SOMETHING!" Ted gave a knowing nod and pointed to Frank's raised hand.

"Sorry if I offended you," Frank said, with an emphasis on *offended*. "Ernie has the same issue, except in his case it's the house. He pays the mortgage and everything, but, as he says, it's his wife's house; it's her investment."

"It's not the same issue, Frank," Ted responded, "but it's an issue just the same. In his case, he does live in the house, so he's getting something of value."

"Not to mention a marriage," Betty added.

"What he's not getting," Ted continued, "is his part of the appreciation in value of the house."

"That's what I mean," Frank said. "To me, it's a matter of fairness. And in her case," he said, nodding in Anne's direction, "maybe her husband feels the same way. Maybe he's paying more of their expenses than he should."

Anne just shook her head.

"All right," Ted said, "let it go. Fairness is an issue, and it should be dealt with as part of developing a financial plan. It's up to the couple involved to decide what's fair. For tonight, we're talking about investments, so let's stay on course. We have several more matters to cover." Ted could see that Anne had been stung by Frank's remarks, and who wouldn't be?

"Thank you for sharing with us, Anne," Ted said, shifting his gaze to Frank. "We can learn from each other's experience, so let's be considerate and stay open to that." Anne nodded her appreciation for the comment; Frank avoided Ted's look. Ernie knew he'd been used—the price of his openness—but still, he thought, it's good to know that others see his situation the same way he does. He hadn't yet talked with Jennie.

"Speaking of fees," Ted went on, "I just want to make two points. First, there is nothing wrong with having to pay a fee or a commission. Just make sure that it's fair and that you understand how it's charged. You want to make sure that it's a *competitive* charge and you're getting *value in exchange*. The fee or commission might be charged by a financial advisor, a broker, a trust department, a mutual fund, or an insurance company. It might be up-front, rear-end, sideways, or other ways; just know what it is and how it's computed.

"The second thing is, you can save on fees and commissions if you do it yourself. For example, you can do your own research and trade online, or you can do your own research and invest in no-load stock and bond mutual funds. But if that's not really your thing, if you don't really get into it, you would be better off paying a fee to a professional. A professional may also have access to other investments not available to you as a retail investor. But the key is to know yourself, know what you do best, and know what you have time for. If it's not your thing, hire a professional.

"Let me give you an example of one case gone bad over fees. A woman had $300,000 worth of CDs at the bank. She thought she should be doing more with the money, but didn't know what. She didn't know how to invest, but she didn't want to pay anyone a fee either. The bank quoted her an annual fee of $3,000 to invest and manage her funds. That seemed like a lot of money. She was then befriended by a female investment advisor who said that she, the advisor, could handle it without charging a fee. The investment advisor met the woman at the bank each time a CD matured; the woman had six of them. The investment advisor sold the woman a $50,000 tax-deferred annuity, which was not appropriate due to the woman's age and tax bracket, and then got her involved with a bad apple investment guy to handle the rest of it. He churned her account and lost half of her money in the market. In retrospect, the $3,000 fee at the bank would have been a bargain."

"What about the broker who stole all that money from some of Cleveland's biggest names? Millions!" Cris said.

"At least $125,000,000," Ted said. "There's an embezzlement going on somewhere every minute; you have to be vigilant."

"That guy was slick, though," Frank added. "Did it over 15 years working for two different firms."

"Just find someone who's honest and who knows what he's doing," Dan said.

"That's right," Ted agreed. "All you can do is pick reputable people with reputable firms, and keep a close eye on it. Review your statements monthly, have meetings, ask questions, periodically verify your holdings. What else can you do?"

"Insured CDs," Betty said.

"Nah," Ted laughed, "you know better than that."

"Okay, but what did you mean when you said he churned her account?" Betty asked.

"That means the stockbroker did excessive trading in her account, just buying and selling securities to generate commissions for himself."

Betty nodded her understanding.

"In addition to people who befriend you just because you have money, who else might you avoid when it comes to handling your investments?"

"Your husband," Betty answered.

"Oh, and why might that be?" Ted asked.

"Because it could lead to marital problems, arguments," Betty said.

"It could lead to marital problems if he doesn't," Cris added.

"Obviously that is an area where all kinds of facts, circumstances, and personalities come into play, not to mention knowledge of investments," Ted said. "But when it's all said and done, I think in a second or subsequent marriage you should share your ideas, but keep your investments separate. They should be in separate accounts under separate control, but with open communication and sharing of information. After all, you *are* married.

"In a first marriage," Ted went on, moving to his right, looking at Cris as he spoke, "it's more of a team approach, all for one, one for all. In the end, if anything is left it goes to the kids. But this is the second time around; you've both been jolted by the termination of your first marriages; you've both been hurt financially, are older, feel more vulnerable, are concerned about the expenses of old age, and have different children to consider. It's a different ballgame."

"I think you should be able to work those things out," Cris said. "After all, you love this person you've married. You're partners. You've pledged to care for each other. I think it should still be all for one and one for all, and, in the end, if anything is left, it should go to all of your children."

"That's a nice model," Ted said to Cris, his eyes as wide open as an innocent child's. "I wish it could always be so. Unfortunately, things can change over the years. Sometimes a surviving spouse will change his or her will and leave it all to his or her own children. We'll talk about that in a few weeks. For now, though, we'll stay with the investment side of it. It would be ideal," Ted continued, "if we could all follow Cris's model. But I don't think it's realistic for most people. That being the case, I think separate investment accounts with separate control is the best way to go."

"But," Frank asked, "what if one is willing to take risks and grow his net worth, while the other just sits in certificates of deposit and loses out to inflation?"

"What if he loses his butt in the stock market?" Betty snapped back, but with a twinkle. "Then those CDs might look pretty good."

"There's no simple answer," Ted said. "I do like Cris's model; it's ideal, but it's not for everyone. Some have a different model, and with good reason. They know their own situation. For them, separate investment control is the answer."

"It seems like all their money might be needed to take care of both of them anyway," Cris said.

"Maybe, maybe not," Ted replied. "And don't forget that their children might have different needs and ideas."

"The kids should stay out of it," Ernie said under his breath.

"I agree with what Bob said last week about communication. I think good communication is the key," Dan said, looking at Ted, then Cris.

"But some want to keep their finances to themselves," Frank said, nodding toward a preoccupied Anne.

"There's no pat answer," Ted concluded. "Each couple needs to work it out."

"They need to trip the light fantastic and forget about it," Betty muttered.

Ted responded with a smile, welcoming the lighter note.

"Here are a few more things you should be aware of," he said.

"First, for most of you, it would be a very bad idea to trade on margin, to borrow money to invest. It's a way to magnify your gains, but it's also a way to magnify your losses. It seems like every down market brings out a few crybabies who want to sue their brokers, claiming they didn't understand the risks involved. When the market is up, they're geniuses. When the market is down, it's the broker's fault. Don't let that be you. Remember, there are birds of prey out there, and you're just learning to fly.

"Next, you need to know that chasing after last year's winners is usually not good strategy. Look at what happened to some stocks in the year 2000, for example. Yahoo! was down 86 percent; Lucent was down 81 percent; Amazon was down almost 80 percent. Cisco was down I don't know how much. And look what has happened since. Those were all hot stocks. Some investors rode them up, rode them down, and then got off. That's real volatility. Some bought at the top, rode them down, and then got off. That's a real loss. For most of you, buying and holding good quality securities or mutual funds, with periodic review, is your best strategy. A little venture into other waters for some excitement and a shot at higher returns might be okay, but just make sure you can stand some losses.

"Finally on this point, know that there is risk in the market, and even though you have good asset allocation, be prepared for some volatility; be prepared to assume market risk. There will be ups and downs, but that's how you can realize growth in your net worth. And know that the market is an efficient place; news travels fast. The professionals are going to know more than you do and know it before you do; therefore, don't try to outguess them; don't try to time the market by moving in and out of it. Your goal should be long-term; get the best return you can, given the amount of risk you're willing to take. That will represent an efficient portfolio for you.

"And," Ted continued, "along those lines, you could do some outside reading, or take a course, or check our web site references and learn more about what might be most efficient for you. Learn about mutual funds and the difference between active management and passive management, or index funds. Arm yourself with enough information to help you communicate effectively with your advisor and to make sound, reasoned decisions in designing your own efficient portfolio."

"What's the difference between active management and passive management?" Anne asked.

"It's the difference between telling your husband to mow the lawn and waiting for him to get around to it," Betty chirped.

"It refers to mutual funds," Ted answered with a twinkle to Betty. "Active management is where a fund manager buys and sells securities in an attempt to beat a given index, the Standard & Poor's 500 Composite Index, for example. Passive management is where the fund just mirrors the index, buys securities that are in the index, and doesn't try to beat it. Actually, there are many different kinds of index funds, not just the S & P 500. You can get large cap, mid cap, small cap, growth funds, value funds, international funds, bond funds, the whole range. It's not a bad way to go if you take a balanced approach; in fact, some think it's the smart way to go. It's certainly less stressful than active management.

"You can also buy individual stocks called ETFs, Exchange-Traded Funds, on the American Stock Exchange that reflect a given index, such as the S & P 500. That particular one is called a SPYDR. Another, called the QQQs, tracks the NASDAQ 100-index. Those are the two biggest ones. There are others that track the broad market, technology, mid-caps, small caps, and international."

"What's the advantage of using ETFs?" Dan asked.

"The advantages are lower expenses than a mutual fund, lower capital gains distributions, and the ability to trade them any time of day through a stock bro-ker. If you're interested, you can get information at WWW.AMEX.COM, or through Morningstar, or through your broker."

"Why wouldn't everyone do that?" Cris asked.

"Well, not everyone wants to have a broker. Also, ETFs haven't been around as long as mutual funds; public awareness isn't as great. In addition, if you're a long-term investor, you don't need to trade any time of day, and if you're an IRA investor you don't care about capital gains distributions because your taxes are deferred. Also, ETFs might appeal more to a younger computer savvy generation than to an older crowd…but that's just a guess."

"Which is better," Anne asked, "active management or passive management with Exchange Traded Funds or index funds?"

"It depends," Ted answered, "but the S & P 500 has outperformed most actively managed funds, not every year, but over a period of years. And index funds, whether they're mutual funds or ETFs, have lower costs, too. Finally, if you have to pay taxes currently, they're good from a tax standpoint, because they don't sell securities as often as an actively managed fund; you don't have as much to report each year in capital gains.

"On the other hand," Ted continued, "they're not exactly all-weather funds either. Morningstar reported in its March 2002 *Fund Investor* bulletin that the large cap index funds did better in good markets than actively managed large cap funds, but that the opposite was true in down markets and mixed markets. The report also showed that actively managed small-cap funds, and mid-cap growth funds, did better in general than their index counterparts. So, if you use index funds for the large cap part of your portfolio, you should be all right, at least if you believe we'll have more bull markets than bear markets."

"So you like index funds?" Dan asked.

"I do, but they're pretty boring, so I have some of each: some actively managed funds and some index funds."

"So you don't know which is better," Frank said.

"I thrive on competition," Ted admitted with a smile.

"Now," he said, getting onto his feet and stretching open hands to the class, "I want to switch gears for a few minutes and give you a little quiz based on your Reading Notes for tonight. Let's see who's doing his duty and who's dozing," he said with a wink.

"First, based on your Notes and the 1925 to 2002 Ibottson study, what lessons can we learn about investing? Yes, you raised your hand first," Ted said, pointing to Ernie who had new glasses and was wearing a suit and tie.

"Well, if you want to beat inflation and taxes, you can't just be in cash accounts like the money markets and certificates of deposit," he said, pointing to the faint outline left on the blackboard. "You have to be in equities to get some growth; real estate or stocks mostly."

"Right, you have to take some risk, and for most of us, stocks or stock mutual funds are easy investments to make; they're liquid, and you can easily diversify your investment portfolio. Okay, what else?"

"Inflation is bound to happen, even if it's just a little from year to year. It adds up, and you need to allow for it."

"Correct," Ted agreed. "And how much would you allow? Say you were looking ahead 20 years…"

"About 3 percent to 4 percent a year," Ernie answered.

"I'd personally allow 4 percent," Ted said. "Some planners even use 5 percent to be conservative."

"What else?" Ted asked, pointing to Cris.

"Don't put all your eggs in one basket."

"Right, you want to diversify your investments," Ted agreed. "You want to spread the risk over a broad range of stocks, bonds, and cash equivalents to avoid large losses in any one investment, or even any sector of the economy."

"Unless of course you have a real winner and use stop orders to sell," Frank said. "Or you have employer stock, or your own company; then you just keep a good eye on your basket. That's what I want someday, my own company."

"If you're one of the lucky few," Ted nodded agreement, "you can win big with employer stock or your own company…but you can lose big too. Even those folks should diversify as best they can, pull some money out, and spread it around to other investments.

"And, incidentally, for those of you who don't know," Ted said with a note of approval, "the stop order to sell that Frank mentioned would put a floor under a security so that it would be sold if the price falls back to a given level. It's a technique to preserve your gain."

Anne noticed the look of satisfaction that crossed Frank's face. He just needs more attention, she thought.

"What else?" Ted nodded to Dan, who had raised his hand.

"You can't plan on past performance when you look ahead, especially for a short period like 5 to 10 years. Your particular period could be boom years in the market, like the 1990s, or it could be as rolling as the Black Hills, or as flat as the Mojave Desert."

"Or as deep as the ocean," Betty sang softly while tapping her foot to imaginary music. "I do Little Richard, too."

"Okay," Ted said (at least she was paying attention). "So what's the lesson here?" Betty's eyes deferred to Dan.

"You need a cash reserve," Dan said, "and short-term bonds to carry you through a few bad years. But given enough time, say over a 15-year period, the averages should work for you. At least you might plan on it, given that amount of time."

"And what would those averages be?" Ted asked.

"About 10 percent to 12 percent for stocks," Dan answered, "and about 5 percent or so for bonds and about 3 and a half percent or so for cash equivalents like CDs or Treasury Bills. Those are the long-term averages."

"That's right," Ted agreed, "but we may have a new reality going forward. Some experts are projecting a future return on common stocks of only 7 to 9 percent, down from those historic averages. That's really an important prediction because the future is where you and I will be living. So, given that prediction, I'd consider an 8 percent total return on stocks as I look ahead, rather than 10 to 12 percent.

"Now, what about income taxes?" Ted asked.

"Unless you have a tax-sheltered account, income taxes will reduce those returns," Dan answered.

"And inflation will reduce them further," Ted added. "So what's the bottom line?"

"You need equities," Cris spoke up, "but you need a good balance between short-term reserves and a balanced long-term program for growth."

"In other words," Ted added, "you need asset allocation, and you need diversification of investments...both fitted to your risk and return requirements. And also, in most cases, you need to add to your investment fund on a regular basis." There was a nodding of heads. "Good," Ted said, hoping those points had found a home.

"Now, one more thing I want to emphasize," he said, moving from behind the desk, "I mentioned it before, but what do we mean by *market risk?*"

"It's what happened after 9/11," Frank answered.

"Yes," Ted agreed, "but it was happening before then, too. The market started drifting down in March 2000. The Federal Reserve was lowering interest rates to head off a recession even before the terrorist attacks. The market was down, then went down further after September 11. But, despite three back-to-back years of a down market, it was up in 2003. History tells us that, given time, the market does come back. But history also tells us that's why you need a reserve to carry you through; cash equivalents and short-term bonds to cushion the effect of a setback in your equity portfolio."

"I'd like a big reserve," Betty said. "At least you won't lose your money."

"Well, we all have to find our comfort level with that," Ted said, "but believe me, long-term, you have to have equities, you have to take some risks."

"One point I want to make," Frank said, "is that not all stocks will come back, and also most mutual fund managers did poorly during the 2000-2002 period, worse than the market in many cases. What can you say about that?"

"Some of that was market risk, but, in addition, a lot of stocks were overpriced; some fund managers had loaded up on overpriced tech stocks, and you know what a hit technology took," Ted answered. "Asset allocation, diversification, and choosing quality investments—ones that are not over-priced—that's all you can try to do long-term."

"How do you know you're making the right choices?" Frank asked. "How do you know you're getting diversification and value?"

"It's tough," Ted said, "but that's where you have to do your homework or hire an investment advisor to help you...that's where an advisor can add value. For example, regarding diversification, an advisor can get you mutual funds and money managers who will stay the course they advertise, who will stick with their area of expertise, be it growth or value, and who won't advertise one investment style and then drift to another just because its hot at the moment."

"Tracking that wouldn't be easy," Frank said.

"You're right, it's not," Ted agreed, "but if you don't do it you can become overloaded in one sector, like tech. You can wind up with too much risk, or a bunch of funds chasing last year's returns.

"As to value, you need to use common sense and have self-discipline. Let me give you an example. Say a company expected to earn $10 per share this year: How much would you be willing to pay for a share of that stock? Ten times earnings…$100? 30 times earnings…$300? 50 times earnings…$500? Think about it! You're saying you'd be willing to wait 10 years, 30 years, even 50 years to earn back what you paid for the stock!"

"Why would anyone be willing to wait 50 years?" Cris asked.

"Even 75 years or more in some cases," Ted said.

"Because they don't think it will take that long," Dan said. "They think the company will increase its earnings, or they think they'll find an even greater fool willing to pay more for the stock than they did."

"That's right," Ted agreed. "And it may or may not work out that way. But know up-front what you're paying for a share of stock, or shares of a mutual fund. It's called the price/earnings ratio: divide the earnings per share by the price per share to learn how many years worth of earnings you're buying with that investment."

"That's where valuations can get out of whack," Dan added. "People get blinded by greed and are willing to pay high multiples in the hope that they'll make a big profit down the road. In some cases, the companies don't even have earnings. Then, when the bottom falls out, they wish they hadn't been so greedy."

"Yeah, but if you'd bought Dell Computer early on, you wouldn't be sitting here now," Frank said.

"I'd rather be lucky than smart," Betty said with a twinkle.

"Now, to move on," Ted nodded in agreement, "the final investment we need to cover tonight is one that Frank alluded to earlier, the small, closely-held business. For this segment, I'm going to read straight from Bob's notes so I don't screw it up. This is Bob's specialty." Ted, sounding a lot like Bob, began to read:

Let me tell you about the person who owns his own business. In the game of money, he's a genuine risk-taker. He may have started from scratch or he may have expanded an existing business. I say he, it could be she. Either way, at one time or another, an entrepreneur has had to put it all on the line. This is a person who gave up a job, a salary, and fringe benefits because he got excited about having something of his own. He knew his product and the market, and he saw an opportunity. He struggled to survive even if he was right on all counts. Many, if not most, fail.

If he survived, it was because he had a single-minded intensity. He made it because he wouldn't quit. The resulting business is now his baby. It may also be his biggest investment, maybe his only investment. I say investment…in reality it may just be a job, or it might even be a liability. In any event, it's time-consuming, and in terms of investments he may have all his eggs in one basket; everything he has may be tied up in his business, especially in the early years. For some that's a disaster, for others it's a wealth builder. Having your own business can be a cash machine…but it's high risk unless you know what you're doing. Even then, you need some resources behind you. A little luck doesn't hurt either. On the other hand, we're talking about a special breed, and many an entrepreneur has burned his bridges and made his own luck.

Ted waved his notes and said, "Those are Bob's comments, and he will discuss this again in the retirement planning and estate planning sessions. As a divorce attorney, I will just add that I've seen both sides of this. The start-up years can put a strain on a marriage; the hours are long, the bills can pile up, and some spouses don't like risk. For tonight, though, what do you think of the small business as an investment in a second or subsequent marriage?"

"It's different than other investments," Dan finally spoke up. "My wife didn't invest money in my business; she didn't even work in the business, but she still contributed to it."

"How so?" Ted asked.

"Well, just being supportive, raising our boys, being a homemaker, being a steady influence; she helped a lot. I wanted to succeed and do well for her and the kids, and she made that possible. I thought of it as our business, not just mine."

"I understand," Ted said, "and would it be the same in a second marriage? Say the only thing a guy came out of his divorce with was his business. Then, say he remarried."

"I think it should stay his business, his investment," Ernie said. "He paid heavily for it one way or another."

"Still," Cris said, "it's not like he has a passive investment, like a stock portfolio. How he feels in the morning when he goes to work really matters."

"That's true anyway," Frank added from the back. "Even if he counts eggs, it matters what his home life is like. Besides, in this case, the guy already had the business."

"Okay," Ted said, "we'll let that wrap it up. You can see where this could get pretty involved, especially when the second spouse, or a son or daughter from the first marriage, is active in the business."

Ted surveyed the group as he opened his leather attaché case to put his notes away, and then added: "The real question is, how should the value of the business be used to benefit the surviving spouse vis-à-vis the children from a prior marriage?

"We'll talk more about that when we get to Chapter Ten. For now, suffice it to say, it's a different kind of an investment; it's the largest single investment some people have, and it's a difficult investment to put a value on. Take a look at Appendix G of your Reading Notes. Even that might not give a true picture. Most of the business value might depend on the energy, knowledge, and personality of the owner himself.

"That's it for tonight, let's go home," Ted concluded.

"This is starting to get complicated. Are you going to pull all of this together for us?" Anne asked.

"That's Bob's job," Ted laughed, then relented when Anne feigned a pout. "Okay, in a nutshell, when it comes to investments, it's having a plan instead of being driven by fear or greed. It's asset allocation, then diversification with quality investments, and then it's patience. Attentive patience, I should say."

"Sounds easy," Anne whispered as she got up to leave.

"But it does get interesting when there's real estate or a closely-held business," Ted added.

"One more point," he said with raised voice to the group as they gathered themselves to leave. "As important as your own investments are to you, in a second or subsequent marriage...as you will see in Chapter Seven...your spouse's investment program is just as important. You could have the perfect portfolio, but if your spouse is off track on his or her asset allocation, has poor investment performance, you could have a ticking time bomb, or it could be a parasite that consumes you both in the years ahead."

"Oh no!" Anne winced.

"Wowie-ka-zowie!" Betty said. "I knew he might be a problem, but I didn't know the half of it! A parasite! You mean he could bite my assets?"

"Something to think about," Ted said. "But parasite might be too strong."

"You don't know the half of it," Betty said as she pushed up from her desk.

"Don't look at it that way," Cris said from the doorway. "If you did it my way, it wouldn't be a problem. You'd be in it together." She looked over her shoulder for Ted's response as she left.

"That's Bob's answer, too," Ted called after her.

"We need to talk more about this," Anne said as she turned to leave.

"Fine with me," Ted said.

Chapter Six

Insurance

It was 8:00 a.m. on a cloudy, misty Wednesday morning as Ted pulled up behind the Mercedes stopped at the light. He immediately recognized it as Cris's just washed, glistening, black C-320 with the vanity plate "LIST AGT." Cris, the Realtor, on her way to a sales meeting, he guessed. Too early for an open house. She was alone in a car that fit her like a little black dress; Ted couldn't help wishing he were with her. He watched as her hand tilted the rear view mirror and she fussed with her eye make-up, unaware that he was watching. She was still fumbling with something on the seat as she pulled through the light. How do they do it? Ted wondered as he turned right and headed to Starbucks for a little jolt on the way to the office. His thoughts lingered on Cris. She set off a spark within him. They had shared wine and conversation that one time at the bank reception; it was pleasurable to recall her smile when she had seen him. And he was aware of her attention in class. Those pure blue eyes, full of interest and curiosity, following him from one side of the room to the other. She was smart, and behind those tortoise-shell frames, actually a beautiful woman. But she was assertive. Maybe it was just a sales facade. There was assertive, and there was real estate assertive. He could live with assertive, but not real estate assertive.

Ted's thoughts moved back to the traffic and the deposition he had scheduled for 10:00 a.m. He was well prepared with his documents and stack of note cards, a question on each one. He would go slowly through the questions, and his prey, relieved to see the stack of cards dwindle down to the last one, would start to visibly relax. Then Ted would reach down and pull another stack of cards from his briefcase. It was a technique he used to tire, frustrate, and anger the deponent, wear him down, corner him, trap him. He was a trained and disciplined marksman, a cold, patient, and deadly hunter. This case, the case of the dumb-ass, asset-hiding husband, could be won in the deposition. Ted had the trace evidence in his briefcase. It would be a fun day.

Cris hadn't noticed Ted at the light. She was a faithful listener to Imus, but today her thoughts overrode his resonant voice and were caught up in an internal struggle: What to do with her life?...Men were so hard to meet (good ones, anyway)...Should she marry this man? They weren't formally engaged, but they talked more and more about marriage and family. There were a lot of things to consider, mostly whether this was really right for both of them.

They had met two years before when she was still a nurse on the oncology floor at St. Stephen's. His wife was in and out of the hospital at the time. He would have supper every night in the cafeteria; a lonely figure surrounded by tables, tiles, stainless steel, and meaningless chatter. She would use her break to go down and provide him with company and conversation. He was strong, but still a sad, little figure, a reminder of her father who had died when she was a girl.

Cris had attended his wife's funeral and then not seen him until he called a year later; he had found her through a friend at the hospital. She was out of nursing by then, a dream dimmed by paperwork, heavy caseloads, long hours, and motherhood. She needed more time for Casey, her son, and she needed to earn more money for their future.

They had met and caught up with each other over supper at a steakhouse he liked. The rapport was immediate—a rekindled friendship—and she was excited to tell him of her new career in real estate. Real estate: he was shocked and amused. But she had taken to it instinctively and was fortunate to have experienced early success. It was a different world, she told him, with its own stresses and competitive, impersonal demands. She had invested in clothes, weekly trips to the hairdresser, and her beloved C-320 in order to look the part of a successful real estate saleswoman. The bonus was she had flexible hours and more time with Casey. The only problem was her precarious financial life. She had to make sales regardless of market conditions or interest rates. She had to make sales. She was the breadwinner, and it was scary. He understood.

She also shared her past with him that night. She told him of being knocked over and flattened emotionally and financially when Chuck, her husband, had been convicted in a city contract scandal seven years earlier. Chuck, a morally weak man, always playing the victim, went to prison for bribery and assault on the company whistle-blower. He did his time in Grafton, the aptly named medium security correctional facility. Cris divorced him while he was there. Upon his release, he left the state, and she was glad; she didn't want him in Casey's life. Her friend understood that, too; his eyes were loving, uncritical. They ended the evening hand in hand.

That's how it had started with Dan. Now they were sorting through their feelings, their children's feelings, their finances, and their plans for the future. He was seventy. She was thirty-nine and had a 10-year-old. They had signed up for the

Money and Marriage Two course to get information, but were sitting apart; they didn't want to draw attention to their relationship.

Cris moved through the traffic to her office. She would work until 3:00 p.m.: first a sales meeting, then a group tour of new listings, then finalize and present an offer at 1:00 p.m. on the refurbished Bell Street colonial, then the telephone, the bank, the cleaners, and finally home for a few hours with Casey. The hours were flexible; she was glad that she had been able to stay home with Casey on Monday, Columbus Day, and work from there.

—— ◇ ——

That night, the class began with Betty's announcement that insurance was a bore. "I could paper my room with insurance policies and read a little each night before bed," she said to Ernie.

"I agree," he replied. "I'd rather clean the garage."

"Bob is missing in action again," Ted began. "He had to go back to St. Louis…when your biggest client calls, you go. But he told me he'd be here next week, and for the rest of the course. So you're stuck with me one more time." Anne smiled and loved him with her eyes. They had plans to meet for a drink after class.

"There are a few things I want you to be aware of to supplement your Notes," Ted began as he surveyed the group, "and then I want to discuss some issues that are of specific importance in a second or subsequent marriage.

"First, as a practical matter, you can't avoid risk, and you can't afford to insure all possible losses."

"The Indians didn't have insurance," Betty said, hoping to get Ted off and running about the old west again.

"Not as we know it," Ted laughed, "but I'm not prepared to discuss the ways of Native Americans tonight. I already gave you my pitch," he said with a smile. He was tired from his day, but still felt keyed-up, perhaps in anticipation of his plans with Anne.

"I'm already insurance poor," Frank announced to no one in particular.

What a cop-out, Ted thought. You're not too poor to be driving a Lincoln LS. "Well, Frank, what you want to do is review your Cash Management Statement and see what you can afford. Take a look at your Reading Notes and that 10 percent of income idea. Then cover your most important risks. That's all you can do. Life's a gamble; we self-insure most of it. Insurance is just a safety-net to catch the losses we can't handle."

"But what if 10 percent doesn't cover all you need? What if it takes 15 percent?" Frank asked.

"If it takes 15 percent to cover what you need, then I would spend the 15 percent," Ted said, "but I would sure try to increase my income so that my insurance cost would be closer to 10 percent. And incidentally, I'm using the 10 percent as a guide. You have to analyze your own situation. Obviously, if you're either wealthy or poor you will have a different standard."

"How do you prioritize what you need?" Frank asked.

"Well, I'd cover my hospital/surgical/major medical first," Ted answered, "then my property, casualty, liability insurance…auto and homeowners. Then, I'd cover disability income needs, then life insurance, then an umbrella policy. Later, I might substitute long-term care insurance for the disability and maybe life insurance. But, personally, I'd try to do all that within 10 percent of my income…I'd work at it."

"It seems like the life insurance is where you have the best chance to save money…I mean why not just buy term insurance?" Frank asked.

"Having a job with insurance benefits is the best way to save money," Ted answered. "The life insurance question is a tough one, though: you have to determine what you need, and then, assuming you're buying insurance for the death benefit instead of as a tax shelter or retirement fund, buy it with as few of your dollars as you can. As your Notes said, term could be the answer, but it isn't always the answer."

Dan, turning to Frank, said, "The answer depends on how soon you're going to die."

"That's right," Ted agreed. "Tell me that, and I'll tell you what kind to buy."

"Why not buy the variable universal life mentioned in the Notes?" Ernie said. "It seems like that's the best of all worlds."

"It might be the best," Ted answered, "…the cheapest in the long-run…but I wouldn't buy it if I were you."

"Why not?"

"I wouldn't buy it if I were in my mid-50s or so because I wouldn't want to assume the investment risk. If I'm buying life insurance for the death benefit, I want to know that the death benefit is secure. I'll do my risk taking some other way. If I buy variable life or variable universal life where I'm taking the investment risk…and if I'm 55 or so…I may not have enough years left if the market heads south, or if I make some bad choices…if I zig when I should have zagged with my investments…I'd worry about that. If I were in my 30s, it would be different; I'd have time to recover. Even there, though, I think you should be reasonably conservative investment-wise with your life insurance. You can take your market risks with your stocks, bonds, and mutual funds. Still, some people like a variable life product; it has its place."

"And what's that?" Frank asked.

"It's fine if you're in a high tax-bracket looking for more retirement tax-shelter…and can use the insurance. But when you're in your 50s, and you're a middle-of-the-roader, I think there's a better way—a more cost effective way—to invest for retirement, and I wouldn't gamble with my life insurance dollars, that's all."

"It might not be gambling if you do it right and balance your investment mix," Ernie said. "I've seen proposals with a mix of stocks and bonds that projected a 10 percent future return."

"That's your call. But it sounds to me like they pushed the wrong key on the computer. Be aware that any cash value product is going to have a hefty premium at your age, and if I were you, I'd be prepared for that. To assume a 10 percent return on your sub-accounts is to assume the market is going to pay a good part of that premium for you. I wouldn't count on a 10 percent investment return to carry the load for me. No way. Did you read the prospectus?"

Ernie ignored the question. "What should I be looking at then?" he asked.

Ted had made his point and didn't press it. "If you're buying it for the ultimate death benefit, whether the death benefit is for your wife, your children, or for estate taxes, I'd look at regular whole life, or universal life with a reasonable interest assumption, say 5 or 6 percent, or if I wanted a variable product, I'd look at a 6 percent assumption on the investment return, not 10 percent. That's being realistic. Remember, you're not going to get a 10 percent compound return over the years without having heavy reliance on equity returns, and that means volatility and risk. It means you're going to have to come out of pocket with more premium money if things don't work out."

"But over 15 years or so it should work out," Ernie said.

"It could; I just wouldn't want to risk it with my life insurance at your age, that's all."

"I can get a guaranteed death benefit rider to keep the policy in force if the investment account goes down," Ernie said.

"As I said, it's your call," Ted said. "Just remember what happens when something goes down for the third time. And incidentally, I'd price that rider, and I'd also understand how the insurance charges and surrender charges work vis-à-vis that investment return. The investment return you're looking at, whether it's positive or negative, is only applied after monthly deductions, including mortality and expense charges. You won't *net* 10 percent even if you make 10 percent. In other words, the insurance company first has to cover all its charges out of your fund. Understand how that works. And, in the case of universal life, make sure you understand the difference between the current non-guaranteed return, like 6 percent or so, and the guaranteed return, like 4 percent for example. And in the case of *all* performance based policies, like universal life, variable life, and variable universal life, make sure you understand the difference between current *non-guaranteed* mortality and expense charges and the *guaranteed* charges, which will always be higher. If the insurance company falls back to its guarantees, you could find that you either lose your cash value and coverage, or you have to put in more money to keep the policy going. That's why I say, Ernie. I would be careful if I were you.

"And," Ted said to the group, "here's the bottom line. Always keep in mind the purpose of the insurance: Is it for your spouse…your children…your retirement…or to pay debts and taxes? Is it a temporary need, or an ongoing one? How much do you need? How much premium can you afford? How much risk do you want to take? Answer those questions first and then decide on the policy you want.

"So," he continued, getting back to his outline for the night, and looking past Ernie, who was now doodling on a yellow pad, "you'll want to make sure the insurance company you choose is one that is big enough and strong enough to absorb lots of claims and losses, including investment losses. How can you evaluate that? How can you evaluate the financial strength of an insurance company?"

No answer. How do you make this stuff interesting?, he wondered, picking up his notes.

"There are no guarantees, but there are rating services that evaluate the financial strength of insurance companies. I've listed the web sites of *MOODY'S, FITCH, WEISS RATINGS, A.M. BEST, AND STANDARD & POORS*, all of which are in your Notes. They all have different symbols for relative financial strength, but if you choose an insurance company that makes it into the top four rating categories with at least three of those services, you should be fine. If it meets that test, you can concentrate on other things like price, contract provisions, service, and experience in the market. You can also get a wealth of information, including *Standard & Poor's* and *Fitch* ratings, at WWW.INSURE.COM. It's well worth a look. Lots of information there.

"Next, you want to choose an agent to buy from."

"They work on commission don't they?" Ernie asked, looking up from his doodling.

"Most do," Ted answered. "But a few sell no load or low load policies for a fee. Those products may or may not be better in a particular case. You have to compare the numbers."

"How do you pick an agent," Frank asked. "Or do they pick you?"

"Well, choose an agent carefully; one with knowledge and experience. Some have professional designations…CLU, ChFC, CFP. As Dan said last week, work with an honest person who knows what he's doing. Choose one who will sell you what you need, not what he wants. There are good professional agents out there; just be sure you're getting the most bang for your buck. There are important differences in companies and in policies, so you have to do your homework. Compare, analyze, ask questions. Don't buy bells and whistles and smoke and mirrors you don't understand. Life insurance can be complicated. Slow down the process until you thoroughly understand the policy and how it works. And don't be afraid to get outside help if it's a big decision. Get the opinion of a fee-based financial planner or an estate planning attorney."

"Can't you buy a policy on the Internet yourself?" Frank asked.

"You can, and exploring the Internet can be part of your homework. But you have to make sure you know what you're doing. I still like to have an agent, a live person, eyeball to eyeball," Ted answered. "One example would be getting term insurance quotes and shopping for price on the net. You might buy a policy with a low rate and then have the cost jump dramatically unless you can pass another physical at the end of the first term. In other words, it might be renewable at an affordable rate, but only if you're in good health at the time. That may not be apparent to you and may not be what you need. You could miss things like that without the help of an agent."

"O.K.," Dan said, leaning against the blackboard to ease his back, "say you're working with a good agent and only considering financially strong insurance companies. How do you compare different kinds of life policies?"

"That's a good question," Ted answered, "and your Notes go into it." He began to wonder if people were reading the Notes. Maybe they just wanted to hear everything.

"First, with the help of an advisor and your own research, you narrow down the companies you want to consider. Maybe it's two or three you have found to be in the top tier regarding financial strength and the type of product you want—that is, term insurance, whole life, variable life, etc. And be aware that the best carriers at whole life may not be the best at term insurance or variable life. Know what you need first, and then do your homework."

"But how?" Dan asked.

"If you're buying term insurance, you can compare premium cost and policy provisions regarding renewal and conversion rates," Ted answered. "If you're buying whole life, you have to ask yourself if you're doing it primarily for the ultimate death benefit...or as part of your retirement program. And as an aside, I would suggest to you that you buy life insurance for the death benefit; period. There are better ways to fund your retirement.

"Now, the insurance industry has developed apples to apples cost comparison standards that you can use to compare one company's policy to another company's policy of the same type. If you're buying the policy for the death benefit, you can compare the projected *net payment index*. That shows the interest-adjusted cost of the death benefit. If it's for the lifetime use of the cash value, such as at retirement, you can compare the projected *surrender cost index*. That shows the interest-adjusted cost of the insurance if you surrender the policy after a period of years, typically 10 or 20. Remember, these are only projections, but they do give you something to compare that considers the value of money invested over time. Make sure both indexes are shown as part of the sales proposal because you never know what you might do with the policy. Your best bet is a policy that compares favorably under both measures. Check your Notes on this. Also, make sure of two things, both of which are covered in your Notes: the first is that you're comparing the same type of policies; the second is to get *actual past results* as well as future projections. It's your money. You want reality, not an illusion that makes you smile like Alfred E. Newman."

"What…me worry?" Betty chirped.

"What about variable life and universal life?" Dan asked, easing back into his seat.

"There you have to look at contract guarantees and past performance. With variable life and variable universal life, you're taking responsibility for future policy values. Read the prospectus; get outside help if you need it. At least with universal life there's a minimum interest guarantee. But either way, you're shifting the investment risk from the insurance company to yourself. That's okay for some, but it's not for everyone. In fact, it could be a disaster for some people. And watch out even on the universal life. If you start with low initial premiums and assume a high interest rate, or assume low mortality and expense charges, you'll find yourself in a lot of pain later with escalating premiums if those assumptions aren't met." Ted noticed that Ernie was unfazed; maybe he already knew what he was doing.

"Sounds like I need my financial planner, my psychologist, and my fortune teller for that one," Betty muttered.

"Amen," Ernie answered, shifting in his seat.

"But where would you get performance information for the variable life?" Dan persisted.

"You can do a preliminary performance screen on the Internet at a particular insurance company's web site," Ted answered. "In addition, you can check the *Morningstar* ratings for that company's sub-accounts, such as its bond fund or aggressive common stock fund. You can also do that through INSURE.COM. But then I would get more information and performance data from the insurance company's agent. Compare several companies' performances. Selecting your sub-accounts is the critical thing with variable life. Remember asset allocation? That's what this is. It's like buying stock and bond mutual funds inside an insurance policy. If you select poorly, you will have poor performance. If you select well, you could have great performance. But try to achieve reasonable balance. You're in this for the long haul. It's really like a variable annuity with a big kicker if you die."

"Some kicker," Betty muttered.

"Well, that's right," Ted said as he returned to his notes. "Remember: It's a life insurance policy. You don't want to confuse it with anything else."

"O.K.," he said with a gesture meant to signal a change in the discussion. "Let's talk about some second marriage issues.

"I'm not going to talk about property casualty and liability insurance or hospitalization and major medical insurance. All of that is covered in your Notes, and it goes without saying that you have to have those coverages. However, I *am* going to raise some issues about disability income insurance, and about life insurance and long-term care insurance.

"As we saw in the session on financial planning, both a husband and a wife have a legal duty, not to mention a moral duty, to support each other. But the legal duty of support is only while you're living! You don't have a legal duty to support your spouse after you're dead. In other words, you don't have to have life insurance for your spouse. Buying life insurance for your spouse's benefit is voluntary; it's not required. Providing support for your spouse during his or her disability, or confinement in a nursing home, however, is *not* voluntary; it's required. And that, as long as you have the means, is true even if you yourself are disabled or confined." Ted paused to make sure that every pair of eyes in the room understood his point.

"Let me repeat that," he said. "As long as you have the means and are breathing, you have a legal duty to financially care for your spouse. That duty ends when you die. Even then, though, your estate may be liable to the state for Medicaid payments that the state made to a nursing home. In the end, the state may get your house.

"So, Frank, what does that mean to you?"

"Sue me, sue me, what-cha gonna do me? Can't get blood from a stone."

"That's fine," Ted answered, "as long as you don't have much. In fact, the answer to all of this might be to live at the poverty line and let the chips fall where they may."

"That's a depressing thought," Anne said.

"Or have enough assets so you don't have to worry," Betty added.

"Agreed," Ted nodded, wondering if Betty did have anything put away, "but most of us are in between; we're part of the great middle-class. If you're at the low end of that class, you might run out of money. If you're at the high end, you're still at risk; you might see your estate shrink to the size of a six-pack." Ted shook his head, smiling wanly at his own silliness. He had conducted a tough all-day deposition. It was like trying to catch a barracuda with his bare hands. Now he felt like having a beer.

"When figuring the financial risk of disability or incapacity," he continued, "start with figuring what kind of income you can count on from your own resources. And do the same thing for your spouse. I mean interest income, dividend income, Social Security, pensions, and so on. And then figure your expected, and often unexpected, expenses. Chances are your income will not cover your expenses. The point I want to make in a second or subsequent marriage is that your resources may be used up for your personal care, or for the care of your spouse. In other words, not only may you not leave your kids an estate, but you may run out of money supporting yourself, or supporting your spouse."

"So what?" Frank said. "That's life."

"You could always divorce him," Betty added.

"Well, that has happened," Ted responded. "But for now let's try to keep things together, and try to stay out of bankruptcy while we're at it. With that in mind, you can try to close the gap with disability income insurance. Try to protect your *earned income*," he said with emphasis.

"Who can afford it?" Ernie asked rhetorically.

"I figure I'm healthy as a horse in springtime," Frank said, tossing his pencil onto the desk.

"Shtick happens," Ted answered. "If your earned income is needed in order to make ends meet, then you need disability income insurance. If your spouse is the breadwinner, then you need to protect his or her income, too. Having said that, I won't beat a dead horse," he said, winking at Betty as he straightened his papers on the desk like a deck of cards. "Check your Reading Notes."

"Speaking of death, what about life insurance?" Ted asked. "We said that you don't have a legal duty to provide it, but should you provide it. Do you have a moral obligation?"

"I think you do," Cris said, "for your children, or for a spouse who needs it." She had spoken to Ted, then quickly looked across to Dan. Dan was staring at the wall behind Ted, but then turned and looked at Cris. She couldn't read his look; they needed to talk. She didn't even know if he had life insurance.

"Your Notes cover the question of financial need," Ted continued. "Assume you have a financial need and you want to buy life insurance. Maybe you feel a moral obligation or you love someone or you just like to buy insurance. The question now is: Who should control the policy?"

"What do you mean?" Cris asked.

"I mean, who should own it?" Ted answered. "Remember, a life insurance policy is a private contract, and the policyowner is the one who can name and change the beneficiary. Except for community property laws and the augmented estate rules we'll talk about in a few weeks, a life insurance policy is not subject to re-direction by the probate court. It gets paid to whoever is named the beneficiary, period."

"I think the guy who pays the premiums should control it," Ernie said.

"The guy?" Betty mocked, wide-eyed.

"Yes," Ernie said, "I have some life insurance for my kids. It's their estate. I'm putting everything else I have into my marriage, just paying the bills. But I want my kids to have something."

"I think that's nice," Anne said, conveying a note of genuine empathy. "It shows you love them."

"Maybe he just feels guilty," Frank breathed.

"Maybe I do," Ernie said, turning to Frank.

"Divorce is hard, hard, hard for everyone involved," Ted said, taking control of the conversation, "and there's nothing wrong with wanting to leave something to your kids."

"I've done that too," Dan said, "whether they need it or not." He knew this would soon be a talking point with Cris; may as well get it on the table.

"You said the policyowner could change the beneficiary," Cris said to Ted. "So if my intended already has life insurance, he could change the beneficiary if he wanted to."

"Right," Ted said, "and vice versa. Even if you were the named beneficiary, he could change it to someone else; for instance, he could name his kids, his mother, or his high school sweetheart."

"Wow," Cris said. "How can you protect against that?"

"You could become the owner of the policy on his life," Ted said. "That's one way."

"How?" Cris asked.

"He could assign the policy to you; he could transfer ownership as a gift. The insurance company has forms for that. He could also get a new policy if he's insurable; then you could be the owner from the start. In that case, you would apply for the policy and you would own it and control it."

"But would I have to pay for it?" Cris asked.

"Yep. As the policyowner, you have to pay the premiums to keep the policy in force. But maybe you could get him to pay the premiums as a gift."

"Like a little bauble," Betty muttered softly.

"And I could name myself or my son as the beneficiary?"

"Name yourself as beneficiary. Name your son as contingent beneficiary, or better yet, have a trust as contingent beneficiary for your son."

Cris looked across to Dan for affirmation, but he was staring straight ahead.

"And, speaking of trusts, you can have an irrevocable trust own the life policy, and that can have important tax and other benefits…but we won't get into all that tonight." Ted noticed Dan staring off into space and thought he had better move on.

"Our last topic is long-term care insurance. Let me just make this point and then see what you think. You know that long-term care is going to be expensive. If you're in a nursing home, you could burn through virtually all of your assets. Then what happens? You start to burn through your spouse's assets. Everything you and your spouse own has to go toward your long-term care until you get down to your house, your essentials, and in this state, $1,500 for you, the so-called institutionalized spouse, and about $90,000 for your spouse, the so-called community spouse. At that point, you can qualify for Medicaid.

"As bad as that is in a first marriage," Ted continued, "it's even worse in a second or subsequent marriage. Why? Because you're burning through someone else's assets. You're burning through the assets of another marriage, one before your time.

Your spouse, and the children of that marriage, are not going to be happy. And, of course, the reverse is also true. Your spouse could burn through your assets. So, the question is, should you have long-term care insurance? What do you think?"

"If you've been married a long time, the kids might not mind your using up the assets," Ernie said.

Frank raised his hand. "I saw a study in the paper where it said older people are healthier these days, living better because of diet, exercise, and new drugs. The number of people in nursing homes has actually gone down. Even your Reading Notes say you probably won't need long-term care, especially if you're a guy. So why spend the money for insurance?"

"Good point" Ted nodded, and then acknowledged Cris's raised hand.

"What if one spouse is in a nursing home and the other spouse is still working? Could they take her earnings?"

"Good question. And what you mean is your spouse may not qualify for Medicaid if your earnings are sufficient to pay his nursing home bills. Is that right? How old is your fiancée anyway?" Ted asked, joking. Cris's cheeks flushed, and she shook her head.

"He's a young guy," she lied. "It's just a question." She saw Dan glance her way and was glad to see his apparent amusement.

"There are formulas for determining income and support obligations," Ted said in answer to Cris's question, "and they vary by state. But yes, you may find that some of your earnings have to be used for your spouse's care. It's a complicated formula that's governed by the different states as well as the federal government. In this state, you could keep between $1,500 and $2,200 a month of income to cover all your expenses, your housing, everything."

"Can't you just gift your assets to your kids and go on Medicaid?" Ernie asked.

"You might consider that," Ted answered, "but you had better know how and when to do it. And incidentally, will you also get your wife to give her assets away?

"It's a problem," he finally said, answering his own question. "Yes, there are gifting ideas, and annuity ideas, and trust ideas, but you need to know what you're doing. See a specialist. Medicaid planning is beyond the scope of this course, but the short answer is this: If you want to rely on Medicaid, be prepared to impoverish yourself. And incidentally, about half the people in nursing homes are there on Medicaid.

"Yes," Ted said, acknowledging Cris's raised hand.

"In answer to Frank's comment about not needing long-term care insurance, I heard that half the women in this country now turning 50 will live to be 100. That's a scary thought."

"All the more casseroles for me," Frank said.

"You pig," Betty laughed.

"But that would wipe most people out," Cris said. "There wouldn't be anything left for the children."

"Well, if you're going to buy it, buy it for yourself, don't buy it for your kids' sake," Frank said. "Kids today are less involved in parents lives. They live away, and most don't need their parents help; they're making it on their own. I know I am; I didn't get any help from them."

"And most parents have already provided for their kids by educating them," Dan added.

"Not everyone would see it that way," Ted said. "Some kids educated themselves. But if you do take that approach and don't care about leaving anything for your kids, then spend your principal as well as your income. Spread all of it over your lifetime like an annuity, or even with an annuity."

"What *is* your take on long-term care insurance?" Frank asked. "Inquiring minds want to know."

"I think of it as a safety-net," Ted answered. "I think it can help preserve your personal dignity, as well as your assets and your spouse's assets. Of course, you have to be able to afford it. But I think it's a good thing in moderation…say 3 years for a guy of 60 or so, 3 to 5 years for a woman. I would look at it if my investment assets were between $400,000 and $1,400,000. But I would limit the benefits. Maybe $100 to $150 a day with the 5 percent compound inflation rider. Self-insure the rest. That's just my opinion. And I would shop carefully for the policy. Know your ADLs, your *activities of daily living*, and know the difference between *hands-on-assistance* and *stand-by assistance*. Get a policy that covers assisted living, and home health care, as well as nursing home care. Do your homework. Check the references in your Notes and compare policies."

"I like the idea of hands-on-assistance," Betty said, wrinkling her nose. "I've got all the stand-by assistance I need right now."

"You wouldn't if you knew what it meant," Frank said.

"But won't policies change in the future?" Dan asked.

"Probably, but we can't wait forever," Ted said.

Cris flushed with embarrassment. Dan didn't seem to notice the inference, unintended though it was.

"That's it for tonight," Ted said. "Bob will be back next week. Remember Bob? He's the guy running this course. Next week we talk about retirement."

A short time later, Ted and Anne arrived in separate cars at The Straw Grass Club, an out of the way country-western lounge darkened for boots and denim romance. Anne had kidded Ted about learning the Texas-Two-Step.

They took a small table inside the bar, away from the dance floor. Ted had traded his shirt, tie, and jacket for a work shirt and black baseball cap with a truck stop logo. Anne played the part with a denim skirt, white blouse, and red, white, and blue kerchief. A straw hat completed the country girl look. She confided to Ted that she relished the role. Together, they fit right in. The waitress came by a moment later and took their order: a 16-ounce Foster's draft for Ted and a vodka on-the-rocks for Anne. Citron Absolut.

Ted drew deeply from the head of beer, a trucker's reward for a long day on the road, or in this case, Ted mused, a deposition and the classroom. No matter, a long day is a long day. Anne sipped at the cold clear ice and enjoyed the sensation of the vodka as it touched her lips and slipped down her throat. They smiled their mutual approval. This could be their place; they felt happy and secure with each other.

The background music, replete with longing feelings and lost love, carried them along into their second drinks. Ted relaxed and drank more slowly. Anne mellowed nicely, he thought. She had a beautiful smile, beautiful hair, good figure, and damned if she didn't really like him.

"Ted," Anne said, leaning forward, "I know we can't, but I wish we could run away. I want to ride on a Harley with you and race across five states. I want to be free."

"Wow. Sounds good," Ted grinned, straightening up a little. "I had a Harley once."

"Bet you had long hair too."

"Yeah, for a while, after high school."

"What happened?"

"That's when I joined the army, decided I had to turn my life around before I killed myself."

Anne looked at him and saw the youth he must have been. She felt a power she hadn't felt in many years. "Ted, I love being with you. It's exciting…I feel alive. I think we've really got something together."

"Yeah, I agree, but you've also got a husband, Anne."

"I know, but you're different, Ted. We can make this work; I know we can. It can be like nothing we've ever had before." Their eyes met in a swim of desire.

They left The Straw Grass Club an hour later, hand in hand to the strains of Keith Whitley, warmed by the alcohol and the touch of each other.

When they reached her car, bathed in soft lamplight, Ted kissed her neck, her cheek, and sought her mouth, but then Anne stepped back a half-step, uncertain, and took his hands into her own. "Ted, I'd better go now."

"Oh," he said, holding her hands, disappointed, "well can't I at least have a hug?"

She drew him in, put her arms around him, and responded with her whole being. Neither noticed the white van with the darkened windows and rapid clicking lens just ten yards away.

Chapter Seven

Retirement Planning

Dan was one of several on the practice tee, a familiar face there; he came to the divot-riddled driving range every week (when weather permitted) to work on his irons and fairway woods. He gripped the five iron now; the three and five woods lay used on the ground next to his bag. Rhythm and balance, he thought, rhythm and balance. He hit the next dimpled devil 140 yards, fading it to the right. Adjusting his weight slightly, with a short pause at the top of his backswing, he flew the next shot straight at the 150-yard marker. Satisfied with the adjustment, he proceeded to use different clubs, with mixed success, trying for consistency of grip, weight distribution, and backswing while keeping his head steadily in place. "Rhythm and balance," he said aloud, wrenching his last long iron off to the left. This game is like life, he thought. It takes patience, for one thing. Too bad he had taken it up so late; should have started as a teen, if not earlier.

Dan had played golf sporadically but was now seriously trying to learn the game from a Tommy Armour book he'd had for almost 50 years. Who knew if Armour's theories still held? But golf was golf, and if it worked then, it should work now. He didn't have the time then; he had it now. He finished the bucket of balls with pitch shots, wedging them a bit to the right of his target, which was eighty yards out. I need to open my stance a bit to the left, he thought, without knowing for sure. Maybe it was something else. Maybe some lessons would help. But he feared that another set of theories would just confuse him. Besides, lessons cost money. He wanted a good game, but didn't want to spend a lot to get it; he would save that buck for now.

Leaving the range behind, Dan eased the clean but dated blue Le Sabre into traffic, put in a Beach Boys tape, and cruised across town past his old machine shop to Connor's Diner for an after-workout special. Cholesterol was a real concern, but ice cream was his weakness. He needed a daily fix. He would let the vanilla, chocolate, and strawberry duke it out with the Lipitor.

Banana splits were a favorite, and Dan sat nursing this one, thinking about Cris. She wanted security for herself, and Casey. He was a lot older but that was okay; you can't change your age, but age doesn't change what you have together. Their bond was real. They both enjoyed movies, music, history, politics, a good laugh, and just being together. She liked books and was a sometime churchgoer. He liked golf and football. They would be fine. And he could give her the security she wanted. Likewise, she could give him what he wanted: love, caring, company, a shared life. Cris being a trained nurse was a comforting bonus. Casey, that ragmuffin, was a second chance. These days, Dan had the time to spend with him that he hadn't had for his own two boys, now in their forties. Casey's teenage years might be a challenge, but he would teach him to play golf. They would be buddies. Dan felt he could handle things, at least for the next 10 years. Thinking again of football, he would see if Casey wanted to go to the high school game of the week this Friday night: Mayfield at Solon. Nothing like a crisp autumn evening and a big game under the lights. Dan pondered the future as he spooned the chocolate sauce in search of the elusive juice-laden ruby he had saved for last. Rewarded, he put the spoon down and, still thinking of Casey, absentmindedly arranged the salt, pepper, ketchup, and mustard into a straight line on the table. He was a good kid; things would work out.

Money was something else to think about, but Dan wasn't too worried. He had gotten a good dollar for the machine shop, invested it, and today had about $700,000. That and a paid-up $40,000 life insurance policy was it. It would last him, and there should be something left for Cris and his own two boys. He knew the boys were worried about his relationship with Cris, worried that he was being schmoozed out of his money. But they would get half. That was enough. Meanwhile, he and Cris could have a good life for a few years, maybe a lot of years, and she would get the other half. That should take care of Casey's education and give her a base, a safety-net. She would probably remarry later anyway. Meanwhile, she would have a better life with him than if she married some young buck with no future. (He'd already looked-off a couple of those when he and Cris were out together.) There was more to life than steamy, dreamy romance. Dan knew he couldn't give Cris everything, but he could help her, assuming good health, and assuming his money lasted. Life was a gamble, but they were adults and their caring was real. He had already given her his heart, impaired though it was. Without Cris and Casey, his life would be a flat-liner, a lonely march to the quiet camp of the stone soldiers. With Cris, it would be lived anew. She wasn't the aggressive saleswoman she projected; she was a positive life force, warm and sensitive, fun loving, an empathetic friend, a rainbow. He needed her, and he loved her; she would keep him young. With that thought, Dan drank the last of his water, paid the check, and headed back to his condo for a shower and a short nap before class. He had to take life in smaller bites now; he didn't have the same energy he'd had even 2 years before.

Bob had called Ted in advance to alert him to the change. They were being moved to a smaller room that was adjoined with the principal's office. It had a conference table, and Bob liked that; it would be a cozy setting. Ted was uneasy, but it wasn't within his power to change the school's decision. They didn't really need a whole classroom, but he had looked forward to relaxing in the back and letting Bob run things. Now he would have to stay actively involved at close range.

That night, the group arrived by ones and twos, having found their way with the help of signs and arrows. They sat and chatted for a few minutes about the new room (everyone liked it) and Bob's trip to St. Louis (only Betty, Anne, and Ernie had been there). Yes, he liked the city; the Marriott was fine; no, he didn't eat ribs, tour the brewery, or go up in the arch. Betty had done that once, but she almost got stuck in the egg; helping hands had pulled her free. Never again, she said, but the view from the top was breathtaking.

Bob sat at the head of the table, with Dan on his right, then Ernie and Betty, with Anne on his left, then Frank and Cris. Ted sat at the other end with Betty on his left and Cris on his right. Ted noted the small initials carved at his end of the nine-foot heavy oak table, just below the top and out of plain view, a permanent impression once made by some detainee of the school principal. I wish you well, "CUB," Ted thought, may you be free and in a better place.

"Well," Bob began, "hope everyone is comfortable. This brings us closer together and will help us share with each other over the next few weeks. Let's start with what you got out of your Reading Notes on Retirement Planning. And incidentally, the Retirement Notes, and the Notes for the rest of the course, along with Chapters One and Four, are ones that I prepared, so you can blame me. Ted prepared Two, Three, Five, and Six, and I want to thank him for that."

Heads turned and Ted acknowledged the credit, ignoring a secret wink from Anne.

"Anyone have a comment?" Bob asked.

Looking up from his Notes, Frank said, "How can anyone figure all this out? It's one assumption built on another. A supposition based on a presumption, whatever that means. It's about as clear as mud to me."

"After reading that, I'm afraid to let Hank retire," Anne added. "We may need his income."

"I think it's like having babies," Betty analogized. "If you wait till you can afford 'em, you'll never have 'em."

"What do you think?" Bob asked a doodling but attentive Ernie.

"I'm just plugging away," Ernie answered with an easy smile. "I'm going with the flow. It should all work out if I can solve the housing thing."

"Well, there are lots of things to consider," Bob said, "and housing is one of them. Home equity is good, but you can live without it. Housing is part of a larger picture, and housing needs can be met if there's enough income. If there isn't enough income, you can't afford to retire even if you have home equity. But that's a generalization. We'll have some ideas about that later.

"For now, let's look at the larger picture and a different approach that I know Ted, for one, thinks is reasonable. *And* it's easy to understand. With this approach—I'll call it Ted's approach—you first determine the age when you will fully retire in the sense that you no longer work. You truly and finally retire. That's the age when your earned income, salary, wages, commissions, fees, etc., stop completely. You don't even work part-time. Your financial independence will then depend on your Social Security, your retirement accounts, your personal savings and investments, and your long-term care insurance, if you have any.

"Then subtract your stop-work age from age 90. The difference represents your payout period. For example, if you plan to completely stop earning income at age 65, you have a payout period of 25 years to age 90. You may, of course, not live to age 90, or you could live a bit longer. Realistically, if you plan to age 90, you have covered most bets. You've outlived most actuaries who calculated your life expectancy in the first place. If you're a woman under age 55, you might use age 95 instead of 90.

"Now, this approach is based on two suppositions, as Frank would say. The first is that you will not use any tax-sheltered retirement account money, or personal saving or investment account principal—notice I said *principal*—for living expenses, until your earned income stops completely. It's assumed that until then your earned income from full-or part-time work, plus Social Security, plus the *income* from your personal savings and investments will cover all of your living expenses. If that income doesn't cover your expenses, you can't afford to retire yet. Cut back your expenses, keep working, keep saving, and don't spend principal before you retire.

"The second given is that you will spend-down your principal, your retirement account money, and your personal saving and investment accounts, over the payout period, 25 years in this case, from age 65 to 90. You will live on Social Security, your income, *and* your principal. If you die before 90, the money you leave behind represents a minimum estate for your family. If you live beyond 90, your family or the government can take care of you; you've paid your dues. That's Ted's approach. Straightforward. What do you think?"

"So," Betty chuckled, turning to Ted, "at 90 you suddenly become a family man!"

"Or a fatalist," Frank added.

"That's because 90 is a long way off for him," Dan said.

Bob nodded his agreement, then acknowledged a signal from Ted.

"As Bob said, I think it's a reasonable approach. I don't worry about living past 90. In fact, if I had 3 years of long-term care insurance, I'd cut-it-back to age 87. But I don't disagree with the approach to longevity outlined in Bob's Notes. That makes sense too. I just like 90 because it's simple and it's a generous number for men—and even generous for most women. The main thing I like about the approach, though, is the idea of a clean cut-off age and a set pay-out period: age 65 with a 25-year payout in Bob's example; when earned income stops, you spend every dollar you've got by the time you hit 90."

"What then?" Frank asked.

"Just smile and pretend you like everybody," Ted said. "You'll be fine."

"I can't believe that! I think you're kidding us," Anne said.

"Only a little," Ted laughed. "My point is you don't know what the future holds. Take your best shot and forget about it. Enjoy life."

"Okay," Bob continued, "whether we use 90 or some other age, the idea of longevity is well covered in your Reading Notes and is one important element to be considered. Now, what are some others? Cris?"

"Inflation...investment earnings...future health care costs...changes in government policy..."

"Right, and we generally have no control over those, except of course we can influence our investment earnings through asset allocation and investment choices. But even at that, we can't control the S & P 500 or the NASDAQ.

"What are some of the factors we *can* control? Yes...Ernie?"

"Our budget for living expenses."

"That's the main one," Bob agreed.

"Why not just buy an annuity?" Dan asked. "Then you know you can't outlive the income. At least that solves the longevity problem; you can live to be 110 and still get a check every month."

"True," Bob said, looking up from his notes, "but the question is how much would it buy in 20 or 30 years in terms of goods and services? If you have a fixed annuity, say $1,000 a month, that you bought 20 years ago, you know it doesn't buy today what it did 20 years ago, and it won't buy as much 20 years from now. That's inflation. You'll lose out to inflation with a fixed annuity. And if it's a variable annuity, it might keep up with inflation, but it might not. It depends on the markets and your investment choices; you could even lose money. So an annuity is worth considering, but it's not without risk."

"What about this?..." Frank interjected. "What if you just withdraw a certain percentage each year from the total of all your investments? Say 6 or 7 percent. That way there would be an inflation hedge. Your investments would grow each year with inflation, and your withdrawals could grow with the inflation! Or what if you used half your assets for a fixed annuity and the other half for a withdrawal plan like that? That way you would have some money you couldn't outlive and some money that grows with inflation. What about that?"

"Sounds good," Cris said.

"Well, that general approach has its supporters," Bob said, "but it's not without its problems. For instance, you said your investments would grow each year with inflation. Maybe not. Those are two different things. You can have inflation without growth of your investments. And studies have shown that a withdrawal rate of 6 percent or 7 percent could spell disaster. Something around 3 and a half to 5 percent is a safer level, a more realistic long-term withdrawal rate."

"Cripes, I can earn 3 and a half to 5 percent without even trying," Frank said. "That's nothing; I wouldn't even touch my principal at that rate."

"Well, the studies disagree if you consider market volatility and cost-of-living increases," Bob said, leafing through his notes for a citation. "You have to look at this over a long period, 20 to 30 years through all kinds of markets, good and bad. And remember, since World War II, inflation has averaged about 4.15 percent a year. Here's what I'm looking for," Bob said, pulling the papers from his briefcase. "It's an article by William P. Bengen, CFP, published in the May 2001, *Journal of Financial Planning*. Bengen has studied this question and has published articles over the years; with this article he makes some adjustments to his earlier work; he refines his study based on Stein's book, cited in your Reading Notes. Bengen shows the probability of a given investment portfolio lasting 30 years at different rates of withdrawal. It's recommended reading if you're thinking of taking a percentage-withdrawal approach."

"What do you mean by percentage-withdrawal?" Betty asked.

"Well," Bob said, "one approach is to withdraw a fixed dollar amount based on a percentage of your portfolio as it exists when you retire, and then withdraw that same dollar amount each year. For example, if your investment portfolio at retirement is $500,000 and you withdraw 5 percent, you would withdraw $25,000 the first year, and $25,000 every year after that. It's like a fixed annuity without a longevity guarantee; in other words, you will suffer loss of purchasing power over time, and theoretically, you could run out of money because your principal could suffer market loss.

"Another approach is to withdraw a given percentage, such as 5 percent, of the investment portfolio as it exists at the beginning of each year. In this case, you withdraw $25,000 the first year, and if your portfolio goes up to $550,000 after one year, you withdraw $27,500 the second year, or if it goes down to $450,000, you withdraw $22,500 the second year. This approach is okay as long as you don't set your percentage too high. You should never run out of money, but you might wind up living on very little…at least in theory. If your investment principal went down to $300,000, for example, your 5 percent draw would be down to $15,000.

"Another approach, the approach essentially taken by Bengen, but with his own refinements, is to take a given percentage of your investment portfolio at retirement—say 5 percent, or $25,000 in our example—and increase the withdrawal amount by the rate of inflation each year. For example, if inflation increases by 4 percent the first year, you will withdraw $26,000 the second year: $25,000 plus 4 percent of $25,000. If inflation increases 3 percent the second year, you will withdraw $26,780 the third year—$26,000 plus 3 percent—and so on. The potential problem, the danger with this approach, is the same as the $25,000 fixed dollar withdrawal: you could run out of money if the markets go sour. In other words, your investments could shrink even though inflation keeps going up."

"That could happen anyway, couldn't it? I mean, if the market goes bad?" Cris asked.

"True," Bob said. "But it's an approach that can be used, as can the approaches taken by Stein and Hebeler in your Notes. Hebeler, in fact, describes the risks and costs of what he calls 'reverse dollar cost averaging,' and that's the negative effect a withdrawal plan has on a retiree's principal in a volatile or down market. Withdrawals of principal can hurt you in a down market, especially if it happens early in retirement. Also on that subject, take notice of the Monte Carlo web sites listed in your Notes."

"Can you summarize the recommendations of those writers you mentioned in the Notes?" Dan asked.

"Sure. Hebeler, in *Your Winning Retirement Plan*, thoroughly analyzes all the factors involved—investment return, longevity, inflation, and so on—and has tables and worksheets to calculate income and expenses. He then develops what he calls his *autopilot method*, which involves adjusting and fine tuning your retirement plan to keep you on course so you don't run out of money. He believes in doing a completely new analysis each year instead of just using an inflated value for expenses. It's a good concept, the work of an engineer, a very conservative approach. I think of it as the *science* of retirement planning.

"Stein, in *The Prosperous Retirement*, takes a broad look at the whole subject and breaks down the retirement years into phases he calls the *active retirement phase*, the *passive retirement phase*, and the *final retirement phase*. He discusses the idea of making the most of your good years, while at the same time you work with a well conceived plan that you monitor and adjust as you go along. He takes a positive, confident approach based on good planning. I think of it as the *art* of retirement planning.

"Bengen, in his articles in the *Journal of Financial Planning*, shows the probability of a retirement fund lasting for 30 years given different market cycles that we've had in the past, and assuming an asset allocation of 63 to 65 percent in tax-deferred equity investments and the balance in intermediate-term government bonds. Then he shows initial withdrawal rates ranging from 4.15 percent to 6.5

percent, increased each year by an inflation factor. For instance, one example shows the fund having an 85 percent chance of lasting 30 years if the initial withdrawal is 4.75 percent, but only a 43 percent chance if the withdrawal rate is 6.5 percent. His charts also incorporate Stein's Prosperous Retirement concept with its three phases of retirement. All in all, it's a thought-provoking study.

"These are all good resources for you to read: Hebeler, Stein, and Bengen. But in this course, we want to concentrate on the basic *survival approach* outlined in your Notes. That approach, together with an annual checkup with your financial planner, is your foundation in a second or subsequent marriage. Once you have the basic survival budget, and related comfort and transition budget concepts in hand, you can get more sophisticated."

"Do people really do that survival budget stuff?" Frank asked, rendering his opinion with the question.

"It's critical," Bob answered without looking up. "Intelligent people do it instinctively.

"Now," he continued, ignoring Frank's smirk, "what are some of the things people have trouble with when trying to plan for retirement?"

"They procrastinate," Frank said, using a four-syllable word.

"Right, manyana, manyana; I'll get to it tomorrow," Bob agreed, amused but glad to see a positive response. "And what else?"

"They don't set goals and write them down; they don't make a commitment," Ernie said.

"What kind of goals?"

"They don't project living expenses and set monthly income goals."

"Very, very necessary," Bob nodded. "Anything else?" he asked.

"I think people are intimidated by all of this," Ernie added. "I mean income, expenses, budgets, investments, taxes, inflation...how can you figure all that?"

"I agree," Bob said, "especially as you look ahead...it's hard to know what your situation will be...but you have to try. There are things you can do to help yourself, and those are the flip-side of what has just been said.

"First, set specific goals: your date of retirement, what kind of retirement you want, how you will use your time, where you will live, and, most important to our discussion, what your monthly living expenses are likely to be during that first year of retirement. Say, for the sake of discussion, you plan to retire at age 65 and your monthly expenses will be $4,000.

"Then, determine how much income you will have from Social Security, your pension, your 401(k), your IRA, and your present savings and investments. You have to project those to their future values at retirement. Say, for discussion, you project your monthly income to be $3,000.

"Third, determine how much money, as a single sum, you will need at age 65 to fund the difference between the $4,000 of expenses and the $3,000 of income, or $1,000 a month in this example. Project it all the way through your life expectancy, say to age 90 to be conservative. For that calculation, assuming a given inflation rate and a given investment return, you will need a financial calculator or the help of a financial planner.

"Fourth, determine how much you must save each month, starting now, in order to have that amount at retirement. Again, you will need to do calculations using assumptions about investment return and inflation."

"What's a financial calculator?" Betty asked.

Bob reached down and pulled one from his briefcase. "I use a Hewlett-Packard HP 12-C," he said, passing it down to Betty. "There are others available."

"Wow, that's small," Betty said, "I expected something the size of a toaster oven. Is it hard to use?"

"It's not that hard," Bob said, taking back the calculator and returning it to his briefcase. "If you can use an adding machine, you can use a financial calculator."

"The skill would be knowing the inputs," Dan said.

"That's right," Bob agreed. "That's where you may need help.

"Now," Bob said, glancing at his notes, "some of your income, such as dividends or a pension with cost-of-living adjustments, can be considered inflation protected, and some, such as a fixed pension or fixed annuity, as not. That distinction needs to be considered and accounted for when you calculate how much of a gap you need to close. In other words, there will be loss of purchasing power when income doesn't increase with the cost-of-living. You will need to fund an additional amount to cover that loss; see the example of Joe's fixed pension in your Reading Notes. Finally, be aware that yearly Social Security increases may not keep pace with inflation either, and that also represents a loss of purchasing power that you may want to fund."

"What do you mean?" Betty asked.

"Well, if Social Security says that the cost-of-living increased 3 percent last year according to its calculations, when other measures show that it increased 3 and a half percent, your Social Security increase this year will not fully cover the increase in inflation. That adds up over time to a loss of purchasing power."

"Can they do that?" Betty asked.

"It's something to keep an eye on," Ted answered.

"Man, this gets complicated," Frank said with an edge. "There may come a time when you just wear down on the job, call it quits, and go with what you've got. If you run out, the kids can pitch in."

"Kids have their own lives," Ernie said without looking up, still doodling. "I'd rather live in a box."

"I think there comes a time when you're entitled to retire. You've put in your time, you've earned it," Frank said.

"Yes, but what kind of life will you have?" Dan asked.

"I look at it like a military campaign," Ted said, leaning forward in his seat. "You can either just wander down the trail chattering away, sniffing the flowers, and hoping you'll make it, or you can have a strategy and go in prepared to win."

"It seems to me," Ernie said, looking over at Bob, "that people merely adjust their expenses to whatever their income is. They just cut back."

"There's a lot of truth to that," Bob agreed. "People merely adjust…but that's what we're trying to avoid here. We're trying to give you, as Ted said, a strategy to win, a way to live the way you want to live."

"My folks didn't live long enough to matter," Frank said. "They only had Social Security, the house, and a little savings…they never lived high anyway…and they just died before they ran out."

"That's sad," Anne said to Frank. "I hope all of us can do better."

"Well, it starts with planning," Bob said, folding his hands on the desk, "and that requires an understanding of all the things we've talked about, especially budgeting, investments, and tax planning, as well as a healthy respect for inflation and financial emergencies. But it really starts with commitment, with the right attitude," he said, glancing from Frank to Ernie, "and with the discipline to save today for a future you can't see but you know is coming.

"Now, I want to return to the idea that is central to this course. It's the idea of the survival budget in your Notes," Bob said, glancing at Frank. "You can't afford to retire until you can cover your individual survival budgets. And you may not want to retire until you can cover all three budgets outlined for you as a couple: your survival budget, your transition budget, and your comfort budget."

"If you're a survivor, you'll survive," Frank said without looking up.

"Prob-ab-ly true," Bob agreed, not wanting to get off track, "but hopefully you will plan to survive as a couple."

"That's something that really struck me," Anne said, "the idea that *together* you could live fairly decently, but separately you might struggle to even survive."

"It's the woman who has to struggle," Cris added.

"At least she can cook," Frank said.

"The truth is," Ted interjected, "the people who are in the best position to retire and live comfortably are the ones who stayed married, stayed with one job, and saved their money."

"Amen," Bob agreed, grateful for his own situation. "Staying with one job may be arguable in this day and age, but few would argue with the idea of one marriage."

"I could argue it," Betty muttered.

"Well, anyway, the critical idea I want to get across," Bob continued, "is this: don't contribute more to your mutual expenses than an amount equal to your individual survival budget minus your individual personal expenses, unless you're certain you can cover your survival budget the rest of the way. If you can do more, that's fine, but your survival budget may be the most you can put toward mutual expenses. By limiting your contribution that way, you're not spending money you may need to live on your own. And, to make the point again, the combination of both of you contributing an amount equal to your individual survival budgets means that together you can live better than either of you can live alone. In the example in your Notes, Wendy and Joe together, in the first example, dealing with after-tax investment accounts, can plan on something approaching their comfort budget to age 75, then their transition budget to 85, and so on."

"It's the 'so on' that worries me," Anne said.

"Don't worry, be happy," Betty said, mimicking the tune.

Ted, listening carefully to Bob's presentation, shifted slightly in his seat and accidentally bumped Cris's foot. "Sorry," he whispered, withdrawing, as Bob answered a question at the other end. "It's okay," Cris whispered back with a flip of her hair and a glance at Ted. Ted was sure he caught a flush of embarrassment and something in Cris's look that said she really didn't mind. He waited a minute as Bob continued and then, with growing anticipation, slid his foot slowly, silently, until he made contact with Cris again. She didn't move. Ted breathed soft relief; the risk taken had found reward. A small dare had paid off. His every nerve was now tuned into his contact with Cris. He felt the excitement of a schoolboy: Cris liked him. Behind those tortoise shell frames and navy dress, he saw her beauty anew. She looked at him quickly again, but without expression. Her eyes were as blue as heaven. Ted knew something had changed; he had something going with Cris; he knew he had a chance. Suddenly he loved this room, and he loved the conference table. The seed of hope, buried, began to bloom. His mind raced in new directions. Meanwhile, Bob was emphasizing the difference between before-tax and after-tax investment accounts.

"You'll notice in your Notes that if we assume Wendy and Joe's investment accounts are after-tax, that is, monies that have been accumulated out of personal savings, out of take-home pay so to speak, or money received as a gift or an inheritance, that Wendy and Joe can afford to retire and meet most of their goals. But, on the other hand, if their investment accounts are tax-deferred such as IRAs, annuities, or employer 401(k) accounts, and the accumulated earnings have not yet been taxed, they have a real problem. They clearly cannot afford to retire. Why? Because untaxed principal and accumulated earnings are going to be taxed at 20 percent, or 30 percent, or whatever their effective tax rate will be during retirement. Probably about 30 percent in their case. It's *critical, critical, critical* that you understand that distinction and the effect it has on your spend-able income during retirement.

"Now, granted, you can pay the tax in installments over a period of years. You can stretch out receipt of the money for your lifetime with an annuity, and you can defer receipt of your IRA to age 70 and a half—and then stretch it out over 27.4 years—but, the problem is, you may need the money sooner than that in order to pay your bills!"

"Where did you get 27.4 years?" Ernie asked.

"It's from the minimum distribution table in Appendix F. You take your IRA balance as of the previous December 31 and divide it by the number shown in that table for your age. You divide by 27.4 at age 70…26.5 at 71…25.6 at 72…and so on. You can take out more if you want to, but that's the minimum you must take out."

"It's confusing," Anne said, "especially when you mix in taxes, inflation, investment projections, and my accounts with my husband's accounts; it's a lot to absorb."

"The key," Bob said, turning to Anne and then scanning the table, "is to calculate your individual survival budgets and what it takes to fund them. That's the key. Yes, you have to make some guesses, but if you use conservative assumptions you should be all right. I know it's not an exact science, but there's help available. That's what a financial planner is for. You can also check the web sites and the books referred to in your Notes."

"Maybe we'll all inherit a bunch of money," Anne laughed. "That would solve the problem."

"I wouldn't count on it," Bob said. "It was projected that 10.4 trillion dollars would move from one generation to the next by the year 2040, but that was before the 2000-2002 bear market. That took 8 trillion off the table."

"It'll come back," Ted volunteered.

"Wow," Frank said, "that sure wasn't my case. I didn't inherit much of anything."

"I'm in the same boat," Ted said, "but it will save some baby boomers." He moved his sleeping foot and tapped it silently. Cris did not follow his move and gave no hint that there had been any contact between them.

"Okay," Bob continued as he shuffled the top sheet of his notes to the bottom and glanced up from a new page. "Does everyone have a good grasp on the survival budget concept and the individual versus couples budgets? In a nutshell, we're saying that with good planning you can achieve a better life doing it together, but neither of you should spend more than your individual survival budget allows. That's the key.

"And," he continued, looking from face to face around the table, "study the fundamentals involved. Revisit your Chapter Five Reading Notes. Investment return, risk, and asset allocation are concepts you need to understand. And be knowledgeable about longevity, taxes, and inflation. Use conservative assumptions.

Also be aware of increasing health care costs and possible shifts in government policy that will affect your Social Security and Medicare. Health care costs are rising faster than the general cost of living, and you could be hit with increasing health insurance premiums, as well as higher deductibles and co-payment levels. Finally, who really knows about the future of government programs? I expect them to be there…but I expect they will change, too."

"Not much you can do about that," Ernie said.

"So live within your means now and save," Ted added, still tapping his foot.

"As I said, people can only spend what they have," Ernie repeated.

"True enough," Bob said, "but that's the reason you need to plan."

"How do you know how much to save every month?" Cris asked, focusing her attention on Bob.

"It's hard to project your standard of living or your income needs 25 to 30 years from now," Bob said. "Just try to save at least 10 percent of your gross income, if not more, and invest it in a well diversified program for the long-term…with an emphasis on equities. When you get to be 50 or so, you'll have a good idea of your future earning potential and standard of living. You can fine-tune your projections and your investment program then; you can work with web site programs and a financial planner to monitor things on an annual basis."

"What do you mean *fine-tune your investments?*" Betty asked.

"Well, the experts would have you look at three distinct periods," Bob answered, wondering what Betty did have to invest, knowing she drove a Cadillac, but having seen her in an old beater, too. "The three periods are the long-term accumulation period such as I was suggesting to Cris, then a re-balancing period, and then a retirement income period. The gist of the idea is to tone down your aggressive investments around age 50 to 60 as you go into your re-balancing period, and then ease into a retirement income portfolio by the time you retire. At that time, when you retire, you want to reduce your risk and emphasize more income, but at the same time, keep enough in equities to hedge the inflation monster. That's why you can't just assume you'll earn 8 or 9 percent compound investment returns over your retirement years. You need to tone down your exposure to risk, and that means some fixed income investments with lower returns."

"But," Ted began, "in lieu of some fixed income investments, you could mix in a few conservative stocks or conservative stock mutual funds. The dividends they pay could be as much as the interest you'd earn on bonds or certificates of deposit, and the maximum tax rate on the dividends is only 15 percent! You'd have better appreciation potential too."

"Good points," Bob added, "but I wouldn't go overboard with that. You still need the stability that fixed income provides."

"I'm going to invest as if I'll live to be 100," Frank said.

"That's fine if you can stand the volatility." Bob grinned, "It should be a wild ride. Just have a reserve for those rainy days."

"But what about taxes? Won't you have to pay taxes as you do your re-balancing?" Cris asked, feeling the snuggle from Ted's foot again, and returning it this time with a little nudge of her own. As she spoke, Dan was gazing at her with pride: her youth, the blush in her cheeks, the smile playing at her lips. He had never seen her look more radiant.

"That's true if you're talking about non-tax-deferred investments, like personally owned stocks or mutual funds. But that's the beauty of your tax deferred accounts like IRAs or 401(k)s or tax deferred annuities, because you can make sales and purchases and re-balance your portfolio without having to pay current income taxes. You can change them to your heart's content.

"We could spend more time on this," Bob continued, "but I want to touch on two other subjects: use of your home equity, and then semi-retirement from a closely-held business."

Bob noticed people start to fidget (Ted included) and knew he had better keep it moving.

"Let's say you own your home and have plenty of equity. For example, maybe you paid $100,000 for it some years ago and it's now worth $200,000 and there's little or no mortgage. So you have $200,000 of equity. But you also have a $200,000 asset that is producing no income and, in fact, is costing you money for taxes, maintenance, and insurance, maybe even major repairs. Assuming you need more to live on, how can you get money out of the house?"

"Well, you could sell it, invest the money, and then rent or buy something smaller," Ernie answered.

"That's right," Bob nodded, "but for this example, assume you want to stay in the house." Bob found himself surveying a table of blank faces; a couple, especially Dan's, showed signs that it was getting late.

"Well, Ernie was partly right. You could sell the house, invest the money, and rent something, but in this case you rent your own house back from the buyer. It's called a sale-leaseback. It would typically work best with your own adult child or children as the buyer. They would get rental income and some tax deductions, and you would get income from your new investments, plus you would stay in your own home. Pretty nifty, huh?"

"Not bad," Ernie answered, making some notes. "But your investment income would have to be more than your rent, wouldn't it?"

"Right," Bob agreed, "and you would have to consider the tax effect of all that, but it's an option you can look at.

"A variation on that," Bob continued, "is a reverse mortgage. With a reverse mortgage, you contract with a specialized lender and you borrow against the house…except in this case you don't have to repay the mortgage loan. It stays as a lien against the house, and it gets bigger each year because you don't pay the interest; the interest is added to the loan balance. The loan gets paid when you sell the house and move, or when you die. And part of the deal is that insurance is used to pay off the excess loan if the loan balance exceeds the value of the house when it gets sold.

"Another approach is a reverse annuity mortgage. Here you divide the value of the house into two theoretical parts, one representing the present value of renting the property for the rest of your life and the other representing the so-called remainder interest, the value of the property after deducting the value of your rental interest. The two values are technically called a life estate and a remainder interest.

"Let's say, for example, that your house is valued at $200,000, and the present value of your life estate, a value gotten from an IRS life expectancy table, is $80,000. That means the remainder interest is valued at $120,000: $200,000 less $80,000. Under a reverse annuity mortgage, or RAM, as it's called, you live in the house rent-free for your lifetime, and meanwhile you get paid the value of the remainder interest you sold, the $120,000, plus interest, in installments over a period of years. Upon your death, or the death of you and your spouse if you structured it as a joint and survivor annuity, the purchaser of the remainder interest gets the house. That could be one of your children, or it could be an outside lender."

"So the buyer gets a $200,000 house for $120,000?" Frank asked.

"Right. It could even be worth $300,000 by the time he gets it," Bob answered, "but remember, he won't get it until you're gone. It could be years from now; you could live to be 100; it's yours rent-free as long as you live."

"Wow, you would really have to figure that out," Frank said. "You could die a week later. It could be a windfall for the buyer."

"It could," Bob agreed, "but it's a tool that can be used, especially in a family situation. In fact, it could be used in the 'Wendy and Joe' case in your Notes to get their income up to their comfort budget."

"Which is better, the sale-leaseback, the reverse mortgage, or the RAM?" Ernie asked.

"That would have to be figured out for a given situation," Bob replied. "No easy answer."

"Wouldn't they all raise tax and estate planning issues, though?" Dan asked.

"Absolutely," Bob nodded, "the tax issues need to be understood; but in most cases they won't cause a problem. As you can guess, though, this isn't a do-it-yourself project. You need to work the numbers with your CPA. As to estate planning, it all depends on who owns the house, who the buyer is, when it's sold, what's paid for it, and what's done with the money you get."

"Complicated," Ernie said with a note of tired resignation.

"It's a broad family decision," Bob agreed, "and it does have some potentially sharp estate planning edges in a second or subsequent marriage. But it's an option that can be used to raise your income. And you can stay in your own home. If those two things are important to you, that is, raising your income and staying in your own home, you can work the rest of it out."

"We have just one more thing to cover tonight," Bob said, checking his watch—a Rolex, Anne noted.

"If you have your own business, or professional practice, you're in a good position to ease into retirement. It's not always a slam-dunk, though. You still have to be productive, you still have business expenses, and you still have customers, clients, or patients to serve. You also have to keep current in your field. But all told, you're in a good position."

"I agree with Bob on that," Ted added from the other end, still nuzzled up to Cris, "but understand you won't be able to move to your dream location. You'll be stuck where you are until you let go completely and sell."

"If you're *able* to sell," Bob said, gathering that Ted knew the client he was thinking of.

"All too true," Ted agreed. "Sometimes your business is just a job without a boss, and when you stop, the business stops too."

"Even so," Bob continued, "you might be able to work part-time, have a source of income, and, within limits, have some perks like a car, and insurance coverage, and a retirement plan. And, if you're fortunate, you have an asset that you can sell someday."

"Or maybe you just let your kids run the business and hope they don't run it into the ground," Ted added, with an emphasis under the table that brought a smile to Cris's lips.

Dan was watching Cris with growing pleasure; life was good. He had Cris, he had a paid-for Buick that ran like a Bulova watch, he had money in the bank, and he had as much golf as he wanted. He even had the Golf Channel on a 32-inch flat-screen Sony. Casey was a bonus. Dan was able to catch Cris's eye and, tired though he was, smile his pleasure. Cris straightened a little in her chair and warmly returned his smile.

"That's a good point about the kids running the business," Ernie said, "but assuming they can run the business, doesn't that raise estate planning issues?"

"It does," Bob agreed, "and we'll touch on those during our Estate Planning session; it's time to wrap it up for tonight and let the cleaning crew in. Sorry to cut it off, but I see them outside the door. We'll start down the estate planning road next week when we talk about wills and trusts."

"Can't wait for that one," Betty said as she pushed off with both hands and lifted out of her seat, glancing sidelong at Ted, then Cris.

———— ◇ ————

Several days passed and Anne became more and more anxious. She had not heard from Ted since they had waved good-bye after class. He didn't want her calling the office, but she knew something was wrong. She grew more anxious and frustrated when his secretary said he was in a meeting or in court or in a deposition or on the telephone or out of the office. E-mail was no help; he either didn't check it or was ignoring it. She couldn't reach him at his apartment either; only his resonant "Hi, this is Ted, leave a message."

What's wrong? she wondered. Didn't Ted want an emotionally romantic relationship? Was he just using her? He would be sorry if he was. Anne continued to ponder this as she sat looking into the vanity mirror. She would need an eye tuck in a few years. She examined her face and neck, just beginning to show signs of age. But she still looked good. Maybe she would try Botox treatments. She stroked her throat with Lancôme Rénergie. Hank was a good provider; he enjoyed buying her clothes (not that she couldn't do so herself); she had the best hairdresser in town, and she still had her youthful figure. Her legs were outstanding, and she knew it. Dammit…if that shithead army brat was dumping her, he would be sorry. He couldn't just kick her to the curb. Didn't he care? Why didn't he call?

Anne wiped away a tear. "All I want is to be loved," she groaned. Inside, she felt empty and fearful. Her hand trembled as she laid the hair dryer down and lifted a vodka-tonic to her lips. She felt sorry for herself and didn't want to. Her marriage was a failure. Hank was on the road so much, and he wasn't there for her even when he was home. Making money, tennis, and his butterfly collection…that's all he cared about; she was just a trophy wife to be shown off at the club. That was it, dammit! Anne removed the picture of Tim from a vanity drawer. She missed his smile and warmth…missed him…the hurt never went away…they'd had such good years together. With a flash of feeling, she missed their daughter. She'd call Terry tonight, maybe run down over the weekend.

"I have to pull myself together," she said, getting up and moving about the room, "I have to take control; I deserve a lot better than this, a lot better." Ralphie, her small five-year-old beagle, also began to move about. Anne put her things away and admired the trim figure before her in the full-length mirror. She then put on a bright cocktail dress for lunch at the club. A sapphire pin and Gucci bag completed the outfit. She moved through the kitchen and tossed Ralphie a biscuit before activating the garage door. She looked forward to the acceleration of her Beemer convertible. It always responded to her touch. And Joseph, the valet at the club, was always glad to see her.

Chapter Eight

Intestate Succession, Wills, Trusts

The sounds of George Duke faded from Betty's mind as she pressed the eject button on the dash and, with practiced precision, swung the year-old, silver-gray Cadillac into Ace's underground parking garage and parked it next to the dark blue 8-year-old rusting stick-shift that she loathed driving. The rust bucket was her other car, the one she used every day, the one Baker knew about. The Caddy was her real car now, the one she and Ace, her accountant, knew about.

Betty's other secret was: she was rich, rich beyond anyone's dreams—at least anyone she knew. Only Betty and Ace knew she was rich: $40,000,000 RICH!!! Betty didn't want her husband Baker to know she was rich until she had everything figured out down to the last dollar (if then). Maybe he would never know. Her trust in Baker had been corroded over the years; Baker could not be trusted when it came to money.

It was twelve months since Betty had won the Ohio Lottery Mega Millions Jackpot. She had looked at the ticket, and looked at the ticket, and looked at it again, and didn't know what to do. She memorized the numbers: 04, 15, 17, 19, 38, 46. She had then put the ticket in her bra and taken the rapid transit downtown to see her younger sister, Mandy. Mandy worked at John Q's, the renowned steak house on Public Square. Mandy had been to college and she would know what to do. But Betty changed her mind on the way; she didn't want Mandy involved; Mandy might talk. When Betty got downtown, she walked around for an hour until she had an idea: she would get an accountant. He would know what to do, and he wouldn't talk.

Within twenty minutes, Betty was sitting in front of Ace Charles, a tax specialist with a small office on the second floor of the old Rockefeller Building. Betty had gotten his name from a splashy ad in the Yellow Pages that had a map complete with arrow showing his office close to the rapid transit. She liked him immediately. He laughed that, despite his initials, he didn't charge much.

Ace worked wonders in no time. First, they went downstairs and opened a safe-deposit box at the bank. The ticket went into the box with a note stating that it was Betty's ticket. Next, when they were back in Ace's office, he outlined a clever plan to assure Betty of anonymity. Ace would set up a limited liability company with only two Members: Ace, for a small share, say 3 or 4 percent, and a trust that Ace would set up. They would name it after the building and call it "The Rock Trust" for short. It would be Betty's trust, and Ace and Betty would be co-trustees. He could get this done in a few days—a week at most, he said—and there would be no fee. He liked her; she was a very genuine person, and she obviously had a good heart. It sounded good to Betty; she liked Ace's ideas, and she liked his emphasis on the importance of solid planning.

The plan was to contribute the ticket to the trust and then have the trust contribute the ticket to the limited liability company (the LLC, as Ace called it), and the LLC, as ticketholder, would claim the prize. Ace would do the paperwork for all of this. The money, after taxes, would be brought as a lump sum into the LLC. Ace would be the front man for that, which is why he needed to be a Member for a small share, say 5 percent, which would include expenses, he said. The LLC would then distribute the money out to its Members: 95 percent to The Rock Trust and 5 percent to Ace for his time, expenses, and expertise. Ace would handle everything. They would invest the trust together as co-trustees until Betty decided what she wanted to do. The important thing, as Ace said again and again, was privacy. This set-up would assure her privacy. Of course it was important not to start splashing money around, and she would have to start filing a separate income tax return from Baker. Betty said the only thing she wanted right off was some jewelry for her daughter to have someday, and a new Cadillac. She wanted a car with class…a silver-gray Cadillac would do nicely, thank you. Ace said he would arrange it, and Betty agreed she would only drive it now and then until they got all this figured out. The figuring out part would take awhile because Betty wanted to consider her children, her grandchildren, her church, Baker, and some kind of fund—a good-size fund—to help troubled teenagers. Ace liked the fund idea and said he could arrange a fund like that.

With all of these thoughts swirling in her mind, Betty chugged the old stick-shift out of the BP Tower parking garage (Ace had moved his office across Public Square to an upper floor of the BP Tower several months before) and headed home to Baker. Baker didn't like her being out every Wednesday night, but she said she needed to take a course if she was going to be a legal secretary.

———— ◇ ————

Bob started week eight's class with a question: "How many of you have a will?" Three hands went up: Anne's, Ernie's, and Dan's. "What about the rest of you?"

"Haven't gotten around to it," Frank answered. "Don't figure I'm gonna die soon."

Cris said: "I plan to do it when I do the prenup and get married, but I wanted to take this course first."

"I'll get to it soon," Betty said.

"On the other hand, you should know that not having a will can be a deliberate second marriage strategy," Bob said, looking around the table. "You forego the chance to name your executor, but beyond that, it may suit you just fine. Your estate is administered under the supervision of the Probate Court, the administrator posts a bond to assure faithful performance of his duties, and arguably everyone gets a fair share of your property."

"And you might not have much to probate anyway," Ted said.

"Right," Bob agreed. "Most of your assets might pass outside of probate. They might be in a trust or life insurance or an IRA or whatever. Those would be paid directly to your beneficiary."

"But everyone says you should have a will," Anne offered.

"And I agree with that," Bob said. "Especially if you have minor children, and besides that, it picks up any loose ends, it's neater."

"I do want to be neat," Betty said. "No use leaving a mess."

"Your Notes give you the gist of intestate succession, and we won't spend time on it here unless you have questions," Bob added. "I would rather spend our time on wills and trusts…an area where you can shape the course of events and not just let the chips fall where they may.

"One thing I will point out about the intestate succession laws, though," Bob continued, "is their emphasis on protecting the surviving spouse. The spouse gets the homestead allowance, exempt property, and family allowance provisions, in addition to a specific monetary share in some states, and then a percentage of the net estate, such as one-third or one-half. The effect in smaller estates, unlike the one in your Notes, is that the surviving spouse will usually take the entire estate. That makes sense in a traditional first marriage situation. That's the model. The law provides protection for the traditional family as the basic unit of society. Times have changed, though, and today, with second marriages and children from a first, you might want a different model. If so, you will have to take specific steps to provide more for your children. Your will or a trust can help you do that, as well as non-probate transfers like life insurance and P.O.D. accounts."

"What's the difference between a will and a trust?" Betty asked.

"At least $1,000," Frank said.

"Easy now, you're getting on my turf," Bob laughed. "Actually, a trust does cost more than a will, but a living trust—one where you re-title your assets into your name as trustee—will save your family more in costs and attorney fees when you die than what you spend to set it up."

"And," Ted interjected, "apart from that, a will is public and involves government supervision—the Probate Court—whereas a living trust affords privacy in most states…It's a contract between you, the donor, and a trustee; someone you trust to carry out your wishes. People don't know what you have or who you're leaving it to."

"On that note, though," Bob added, "remember, a will and the probate process provide more protection than a trust. Unfortunately, sometimes a person we trust doesn't deserve that trust. Having said that, I believe that most trusts work very well.

"Now," Bob went on, "let's make sure we understand the second marriage issues inherent in different types of wills and trusts.

"For openers, what's the danger in having simple mutual wills where husband and wife each leave everything to each other?"

"The survivor can make a new will," Ernie said.

"Right," Bob agreed, "but so what?"

"She might leave everything to her own kids," Ernie said.

"And where does that leave your kids?"

"Out in the cold."

"They're out in the cold unless they can prevail in a will contest (which we'll discuss next week) or unless they can produce a contract whereby the couple agreed not to change their wills."

Ernie said, "I thought it was interesting in the Notes that a contract not to revoke a will would have to be proved in a court other than the Probate Court."

"That's right," Bob agreed. "It could be done in a Court of Common Pleas in this state. Then, if you get a judgment, you enforce it in the Probate Court against the estate, or the receiver of the property if the property has already been distributed from the estate. The executor of the estate, or the recipient of the property, holds the property as a constructive trustee for the beneficiary of the contract. But that's a hard way to go. Still, if you're going to have mutual wills, you have to have a written contract not to revoke those wills."

"What if you totally trust your partner?" Cris asked.

"That's your call," Bob answered.

"Blood is blood," Ted interjected.

"Now," Bob said, signaling a change, "my comment regarding the use of a joint will—one instrument signed by both husband and wife as being his will and her will—is this: *Don't do it!* There are just too many problems identifying the property to be covered. Is it the property each of you own when you sign the will, or the property owned when the first spouse dies, or the property owned when the second one dies? But, despite that warning, if you *do* use a joint will, have a separate written contract that spells it all out."

"People might think that a joint will shows love and unity," Anne said. "I can see people doing that. It might be cheaper, too."

"Penny wise pound foolish," Ted added from the other end. At that, he could feel a chill from Anne all the way down the table. He had avoided her all week, not wanting to deal with any hurt. He would have to face that tonight, though; they were meeting for a drink after class. With one thought leaping to another, Ted recalled his week with Cris, who was now so close that if he moved his hand an inch he would touch her.

Ted had called Cris the previous Thursday morning and they had talked, but neither mentioned playing footsie the night before. He asked her to have lunch but she declined. He then asked about lunch for Friday, and again she declined, but she said she jogged every weekday morning at 6:00 a.m., and if he wanted to join her he could. Ted was enthused and got directions. She said she jogged for 40 minutes and then was back home to fix her son's breakfast and see him off to school. "Sounds great," Ted said.

That night, Ted went to the mall and bought a Casio runner's watch and a pair of Nikes. He hadn't jogged since his army days, but it wouldn't be a big deal. He was still in good shape, he thought, recalling early morning P.T. with the troops. And back then it was in combat boots, not Nikes.

The next morning, he arrived at 6:00 on the dot to be greeted by a ferocious bark from Cris's unseen dog, Tony. Tony turned out to be a gentle black lab, a loving pal for Casey, Cris's ten-year-old fifth-grader. They then jogged a 40-minute course through Cris's neighborhood; except for the streetlights it was dark, being the last week of daylight savings time. The darkness only added to the mystery of this special time with Cris.

Ted felt a tuck in his side after the first five minutes but managed to tough it out and stay with Cris's 8-minute-mile pace, managing some conversation as they went. Upon their return, he admired her Halloween decorations, said how much he had enjoyed the run, and then got into his Blazer to rest and recoup. They agreed that it had been fun and they would do it again on Monday.

They did do it again Monday, and again Tuesday, and today, Wednesday, except today she asked him in for juice and coffee while she fixed some scrambled eggs for Casey—and Ted too if he wanted. He did, and he met Casey for the first time. They liked each other immediately. Casey already knew that Ted had been a soldier, and he was full of questions. Cris enjoyed it too. Ted could feel the rapport and sensed what it might be like to be a family. He could visualize their life together, the two of them with Casey, and Tony, a warm friend at his feet.

Enamored by the thought, Ted returned to the moment and eased his right foot over against Cris. He felt the pressure returned. They would jog again tomorrow morning and he would talk with her. With that decision made, he returned to his notes and the agenda for the night.

"Next," Bob was saying, "in a second or subsequent marriage, when might you use a will that contains a testamentary trust, a so-called trust will?"

"What is that again?" Dan asked.

"It's a trust that arises from your will after you die. It begins when the Probate Court appoints a trustee; usually the person that you, the testator, have named as trustee under your will. The testamentary trust receives the residue of your probate estate, and maybe life insurance or other non-probate assets made payable to the trustee after your death. So…when might you want to use a testamentary trust under your will?"

Silence followed. No one volunteered a guess. Finally, Ernie met Bob's eyes, raised his eyebrows, and shrugged…He didn't know.

"In a second or subsequent marriage," Bob said, looking to Ernie, "you might consider a testamentary trust when your overall estate—probate and non-probate—is less than the lifetime estate tax exemption amount and when you want the continuing Probate Court supervision provided by most jurisdictions. Perhaps you want to provide income to your spouse, and then, in case of your spouse's death, have the principal held in trust until your children are older. For instance, you might want to keep the money in trust until a child is age 25, or maybe you want a child to get half at age 25 and the rest at age 30. Right now, if you have a minor child and just a simple will, the child could inherit your assets at age 18, and you may not want that; that could mean Corvette City."

"You may want a testamentary trust for that reason even in a first marriage," Ernie said.

"True," Bob agreed. "In fact, you would probably have mutual wills that leave everything to each other and then to a testamentary trust in the event of a common disaster. But in a second or subsequent marriage, having the Probate Court involved may also lessen confrontational issues that could arise between a surviving spouse and children from a prior marriage. The court is impartial, and it will require accountings of the trustee to assure that your assets are properly handled and that your wishes are being met.

"In contrast to that, a pour-over will distributes your estate to the trustee of a living trust, a so-called *inter vivos trust* you establish during your lifetime. You use a pour-over will in conjunction with a living trust when you have a larger overall estate and you want to avoid probate. You transfer your assets into the name of the trust during your lifetime and those assets avoid probate; they're already in the trust when you die. The pour-over will is there to pick-up any assets you didn't get transferred during your lifetime; it pours them from your estate into your trust."

"Can you go over that again?" Cris asked. "How do you transfer assets?"

"You change the title to your assets from your own name into the name of the trustee after you sign the Trust Agreement or Declaration of Trust. For instance, if you act as your own trustee, you would change the title to your bank accounts, mutual fund accounts, brokerage account, et cetera, into your name as trustee, 'Cris Smith, Trustee.' That puts the account into the trust and avoids probate of those assets."

"And you still control them?" Cris asked.

"Yes, assuming it's a Revocable Living Trust, one you can amend or revoke. You can do whatever you want with your trust assets: sell them, take them out of trust, give them away, or whatever. You also have better control of them for estate planning purposes."

"What do you mean?" Betty asked.

"You can better control who gets what, how much, and when," Bob answered, "and that gets to the heart of this class."

"It gets to the heart of the whole course as far as I'm concerned," Ted added. "Face it, the probate laws of wills and intestate succession favor a surviving spouse. In this state, though, you can leave all of your living trust assets to your children if you want to, and cut your surviving spouse out completely! Not nice maybe, but it can be done."

"Yes, and let me give you a recent Ohio case on that," Bob said. "It's the *Dumas* case cited in your Table of Cases. I was going to cover that in a minute anyway.

"In *Dumas,* Mr. Dumas set up a Revocable Living Trust and put $450,000 into it two years before he died. Upon his death, the trust left the assets to his children from his first marriage; it didn't leave anything to Mrs. Dumas, his surviving spouse from his second marriage. Mrs. Dumas took it to court and claimed that the assets were transferred to the trust by Mr. Dumas with the intent to defeat her rights as a surviving spouse. She sought a court order to compel the trustee to give her all the property she was entitled to as a surviving spouse.

"The court rejected her arguments and upheld the trust. It stated that a valid living trust bars the settlor's surviving spouse from claiming a share of the trust assets under the Statute of Descent and Distribution even though the settlor is the trustee, gets all income from the trust, can withdraw assets from the trust, and reserves the right to amend or revoke it anytime."

"What's the Statute of Descent and Distribution?" Anne asked.

"It's her share under the intestate succession laws…It's what she would get if he died without a will," Bob answered.

"Wow, she got screwed," Frank said.

"Maybe, maybe not," Ted interjected. "She also had a trust of her own."

Bob, nodding at the comments, continued: "The *Dumas* case was a 5 to 2 decision. The majority based its decision on an Ohio statute which specifically states that a trust of this type is not a testamentary trust and therefore is not subject to the law of wills.

"It also based the decision on its prior decision in the *Smythe* case decided over 30 years earlier. The *Smythe* case set the standard in Ohio stating that such a trust, established for the benefit of the donor during his life, with the remainder to go to others upon his death, is a valid trust as soon as property is titled to it and transferred to the trustee, and that it is not testamentary in nature and therefore, again, not subject to the Statute of Wills. That precedent was affirmed by the majority in *Dumas*."

"What about the other side? What was the minority opinion?" Dan asked.

Bob paused over his notes and then said, "The minority said that by rigidly applying the rule of *Smythe,* the court was allowing one spouse to disinherit the other. The minority said that the state legislature, by allowing a surviving spouse to elect against a will that did not sufficiently provide for her, had clearly intended to protect the interest of a surviving spouse, but with *Smythe,* now affirmed by *Dumas,* the court was giving a deceased spouse an untrammeled right to use a trust to sacrifice the interest of a surviving spouse.

"In support of its argument," Bob continued, "the minority cited the *Sullivan* case, a Massachusetts case that rejected that state's own version of the *Smythe* rule. *Sullivan* stated that the estate of a decedent shall include the value of assets held in an *inter vivos* trust, a revocable living trust created by a deceased spouse. In other words, the trust assets in Massachusetts would be subject to a surviving spouse's elective share the same as if there were no trust. That court reasoned that if a spouse would be entitled to a share of the other's assets upon a divorce, why should she be denied that right upon his death?"

"Makes sense to me," Cris said.

Betty leaned toward Cris and said, "But shouldn't you be able to leave your property the way you want to? Wouldn't you want that for your son?"

"I guess," Cris said, looking toward Dan, "but you have to be fair."

"That's the crux of the matter," Bob said. "That's what the courts are struggling with. On the one hand, they want to protect the surviving spouse. On the other hand, they want to protect your individual freedom to transfer property.

"Incidentally," he continued, "whereas Illinois is another state that agrees with the Ohio position, New York is another state that agrees with the Massachusetts position. In the *Reynolds* case, Mrs. Reynolds set up and funded a trust for her children upon her death—leaving her husband out of it—but she retained a right to change the distribution…She retained a power-of-appointment to change the beneficiaries. The New York court ruled that retention of a power to change the beneficiaries made the Reynolds trust testamentary, and, as such, it violated her surviving husband's right to a share of her trust assets."

"So how do you know what the law is?" Frank asked. "What if you want to start fresh and take a job in another state?"

"See someone like Bob when you move," Ted said.

"Or even before you move," Bob added.

"It seems like it's something you could get around though," Ernie said. "I mean, with beneficiary designations, T.O.D. accounts, joint and survivor accounts, and so on. With that you can avoid probate altogether, and get money to your kids if you want to."

"You're right, except in some states you have community property laws, and in others you have Uniform Probate Code augmented estate rules, and in New York, North Carolina, and Pennsylvania, for example, you have statutes that catch those kinds of transfers. But we'll look at all that next week. For now, I want you to see the split of state court decisions related to Revocable Living Trusts and know that the *inter vivos*, or living trust, is still a viable option in this state—and some others—to leave your assets to your children."

"What about the federal courts?" Ernie asked.

"It's not a federal issue," Ted answered. "They don't have jurisdiction."

"Okay," Bob said. "Against the background of the Revocable Living Trust, and realizing that the surviving spouse may be able to claim part of the trust assets in some states, like New York, Massachusetts, or next door in Pennsylvania, for example, let's look at a few common types of trusts and how they can be used in a second or subsequent marriage."

"When you talk about these trusts, you mean the part that's left in trust after a surviving spouse claims what's hers under state law," Ernie said.

"That's right," Bob agreed.

"First, the Marital Trust and the Credit Shelter Trust are two sides of the same coin. They spring from a Testamentary Trust or a Revocable Living Trust, and they're used to minimize estate taxes. After the testator or donor dies and the bills are paid, and any share due the surviving spouse is set aside, the trustee divides the trust into two parts: the Credit Shelter Trust and the Marital Trust. The Credit Shelter Trust may be (but doesn't have to be) funded up to the level of the lifetime exemption amount in effect when the donor dies, which, as your Notes show, is $1,500,000 in 2004 and 2005, $2,000,000 from 2006 to 2008, and $3,500,000 in 2009. The Credit Shelter Trust could be funded with less if you want the surviving spouse to have control of more of the assets. The Marital Trust is then funded with any amount not allocated to the Credit Shelter Trust.

"The Credit Shelter Trust typically provides that all income is to be paid to the surviving spouse, but principal is to be paid only if the trustee is given authority and it's needed for the spouse's health, education, support, or maintenance. Then upon the death of the surviving spouse, the Credit Shelter Trust principal is paid to the donor's children...all at once, or in stages, such as at ages 25, 30, and 35."

"Can't the surviving spouse get at that principal herself?" Betty asked.

"I can tell you she can't," Anne answered.

"That's true," Bob said. "The tradeoff to loss of access by the surviving spouse is a saving in estate taxes. In a second or subsequent marriage, though, the surviving spouse may not care about the taxes...They aren't due until after she's gone."

"And just so I understand, if you live in Massachusetts or New York or some other state that doesn't let you cut your wife out, the amount you can leave in trust might be less than the amount you can leave in trust here? Is that right?" Frank asked.

"That's right," Bob agreed.

"That would also be true if they live in a community property state, and might be true if they live in a Uniform Probate Code state," Ted added. "Adjustments may have to be made; in the end, the trust can only consist of assets the settlor owns free and clear of spousal claims."

"Or with assets put into the trust with the consent of the other spouse," Bob added.

"But isn't the purpose of a Credit Shelter Trust to save estate taxes?" Ernie asked. "Isn't that the whole idea?"

"It's a big part of the idea, I agree," Bob said. "But, subject to protective statutes and court decisions for the benefit of the surviving spouse—things we'll talk about next week—it can be used effectively in a second or subsequent marriage to block a surviving spouse's access to those assets."

Betty looked over to Anne, but Anne broke eye contact, not wanting to discuss her own situation further.

"But if she needs money to live, can't she get it?" Cris asked.

"Yes," Bob said. "In an ordinary case, the trustee has a duty to pay principal from the trust if she needs it for her health, maintenance, support, and education... In other words, the trustee can help her maintain her standard of living if she doesn't have other resources to pay her bills."

"And who is the trustee?" Cris asked.

"Whoever the donor has designated," Bob answered. "It could be a trust company, a bank, or an individual such as one of the donor's children."

"Uh oh," Cris said, "I see a problem there."

"Maybe," Bob said. "But the trustee has duties and responsibilities to the beneficiary. The trustee will be held to a high standard; he must act only in the interest of the beneficiary, and not in his own interest."

"But the child himself might be a beneficiary," Cris said, "and what if you didn't get along?"

"I agree," Bob said. "In a second or subsequent marriage, it's better to use an independent trustee and avoid any conflict of interest.

"Now, in larger cases," Bob continued, "the testamentary or living trust assets can exceed the lifetime exemption amount used to fund the Credit Shelter Trust. The excess assets will then be used to fund the Marital Trust, and that's where a major decision needs to be made when designing the trust. Who knows what that decision is?"

"The decision is whether or not to let the surviving spouse have control over the Marital Trust assets," Anne said.

"Spoken like one who's been there," Bob smiled.

"Yes, and I can tell you it would be better to have that money yourself than to leave it at the bank."

"Many spouses would agree," Bob said, "but there *is* another side. Investment expertise and asset management can be an issue. Also, even in a first marriage, there may be concerns about remarriage, and in our case, we already have a second or subsequent marriage. Either way, whether it's a first marriage or a second or subsequent marriage—especially a second or subsequent marriage—the donor can be legitimately concerned about his children's inheritance. Remember, this is his money; money he worked for and accumulated."

"Or her money," Betty whispered.

"Don't forget the contribution of the spouse," Anne added. "And anyway, that money can be protected by a prenuptial agreement if she remarries…Isn't that right?"

"Yes it can, but, in a second or subsequent marriage with children from a prior marriage, the surviving spouse can still cut out the donor's children if she's able to withdraw money from the Marital Trust. She can make a new will and leave that money to her children, and then, if she wants to go down the aisle again, she can protect her own children with a prenup. That doesn't protect the donor's children. That's the problem with a so-called Power-of-Appointment Marital Trust."

"You guys must not trust the women in your lives," Cris said.

"I'd trust my mother," Frank said.

"Well, anyway, you see the issue," Bob said. "That's why the QTIP Marital Trust is popular for larger estates in a first marriage, but even more so in a second or subsequent marriage. With the usual QTIP, the donor provides for his surviving spouse, but the surviving spouse can't withdraw the money, and can't decide who gets it when she dies…It goes to his children along with the balance in the Credit Shelter Trust."

"So his kids get everything," Cris said.

"That's the way it works," Bob said.

"That's Ohio," Ernie said.

"Right…that's Ohio, but for the assets left in trust after the estate is closed, it's the other states as well. Remember we're only talking about the assets the settlor owns free and clear of spousal claims. The real difference is that, in Ohio, that might be all the couple's assets, but in California, for example, it might only be half the couple's assets due to community property law. In other separate property states, it might be something in between."

"What if you live in a community property state and all the property is in your name, and what if you leave it all in trust for your wife's benefit while she's living, but then it goes to your kids?" Frank asked. "What would happen then?"

"That's a good question, and we cover it in two weeks when we get to estate planning. The short answer is that it might have been done with your wife's approval, but maybe it wasn't," Bob answered. "Either way, absent a prenuptial or post-nuptial agreement, upon your death she has a choice: let it ride as is, or elect out and take her half of the community property."

"Wow," Betty said. "You need a Philadelphia lawyer."

"It wouldn't hurt," Bob agreed, "but I don't actually know of anyone who sets up housekeeping in one state or another based on all of this."

"No kidding," Frank said. "Gimme a break!"

"Why can't we all just be friends?" Betty said, winking at Cris.

Bob nodded silently, turned a page in his notes, and continued: "The next item is what I think of as a mom and pop trust, and that's the Joint Trust. A lot of estate planning attorneys don't like Joint Trusts for the same reason they don't like Joint Wills. But I like them under the right circumstances. The ideal candidate for a Joint Trust is an older couple in a first marriage. Say they already have 40 years of marriage behind them, they're retired, they have their house, life insurance, and other assets of $300,000 to $1,000,000, they're conservative investors, and they own almost everything in joint and survivor form. Their plan is that when one dies, the other owns it all and there's no probate. Problem is, when the second one dies it all goes through probate. With a Joint Trust, all the couple's assets are in the trust and there's no probate for either estate. Now, it's fair to say there may be state estate taxes that could have been saved in a few states with a Credit Shelter Trust, but here we're talking about a couple who wants to keep it simple, wants control. In effect, they want a joint and survivor account that avoids all probate."

"What about that in a second marriage?" Ernie asked.

"You have to be careful in a second or subsequent marriage, but it can still work," Bob answered. "I would look for the same profile…long-standing harmonious marriage, retirement age, $300,000 to $1,000,000 in assets, joint and survivorship approach to homeownership and investments."

"But what about the kids? What happens when a spouse dies?" Cris asked.

"Make the trust irrevocable upon the death or incapacity of one," Bob answered. "In other words, lock in the plan for distribution of assets at that time."

"And the surviving spouse could continue to live in the marital home?" Ernie asked.

"That's the usual case," Bob answered.

"And who would be trustee at that point?" Ernie asked.

"It could be the surviving spouse or you could use an independent trustee or, in the right situation, you could use one or more of the children."

"But, you're saying that the surviving spouse could be the trustee, and could still live in the house," Ernie confirmed.

Bob nodded his agreement.

"That sounds pretty good," Ernie said. "But I can see that there might be a problem if someone else were the trustee…especially one of the stepchildren."

"It all depends on how the trust agreement is drafted and on the relationship you have with those kids," Ted chimed in.

"Okay," Bob said, "let's move on. I want to spend a few minutes on other types of trusts that might fit a particular situation.

"First, the Irrevocable Life Insurance Trust, or ILIT, is normally used in larger estates to provide liquidity for estate taxes. The trust is established with an independent trustee to own life insurance on the life of the donor, or to own a policy on the joint-life of the donor and his spouse; a so-called second to die policy. If it's done right, the insurance proceeds are received income and estate tax free by the trust."

"You said donor," Betty said. "Is that the same as settlor?"

"Yes, donor, grantor, settlor, trustor; they all refer to the one who sets up the trust."

"The sugar-daddy," Dan said.

"Or sugar-mommy," Betty mumbled.

"In a second or subsequent marriage, a donor-parent can use an ILIT to leverage gifts to his or her children and create a significant estate for them free of the probate process, and free of the surviving spouse's claims for an elective share. This will work in states like Ohio, in Uniform Probate Code states if the trust is in effect for at least two years before you die, and also in states like Massachusetts and New York because the trust is irrevocable."

"What about community property states?" Frank asked.

"It will work there too if you can show that the premiums came from your separate property. But, as with all questions like that, you have to sit down with an estate planning attorney in that state. Community property laws vary from one community property state to another, just as the Uniform Probate Code as enacted varies from one UPC state to another, and just as judge-made case law like *Smythe, Sullivan,* or *Reynolds* can vary from state to state."

Ted leaned forward and said, "Like we talked about at the beginning, we're giving you an overview and raising issues for you to consider. You have to follow up with someone on the ground, so to speak. We've got 50 states and all of them put their own spin on this."

"How do you find a no spin zone?" Frank asked.

"You can't, this is hardball," Ted answered with a wink.

"It can be hardball," Bob agreed, "but there's still room to be fair."

"The Medicaid Trust, Generation Skipping Transfer Trust, Asset Protection Trust, and Dynasty Trust are mentioned in your Notes, and we cover the Asset Protection Trust again in the estate planning session, but those are specialized types of trusts that generally go beyond what we're trying to give you in this course. People concerned about GST Trusts, APTs, and Dynasty Trusts already have high-powered law firms doing their work.

"The Retained Interest Trust, as your Notes indicate, has charitable applications for estate tax purposes, but you don't want to use it to shelter assets in a second or subsequent marriage because you don't need to in a state like Ohio where a living trust works just fine, or in a community property state where you don't have to shelter your own assets…And it won't work in a Uniform Probate Code augmented estate state, or a state like New York or Pennsylvania. But we'll talk about all that next week."

"Well, what is it anyway?" Frank asked.

"I'll give you an example," Bob answered. "With a regular Retained Interest Trust, you give assets to your children, but retain the income stream produced by those assets. Let's say you give $200,000 of assets irrevocably in trust to your adult child from a prior marriage, but you continue to receive the $10,000-a-year income it produces. That's a Retained Interest Trust. The income could be fixed at 5 percent or more of the initial asset value, or it could vary…It could be 5 percent or more of the year-to-year market value. Upon your death, the income stops and the trust distributes the assets to your child. It's an irrevocable gift of the remainder interest to your child. A variation on that is a Qualified Personal Residence Trust, which is a Retained Interest Trust used for estate planning purposes. With a QPRT, you can give your house to your children while you continue to live in it."

"That works in this state?" Ernie asked.

"The QPRT works for estate tax planning purposes, but that's not our focus here. As for a regular Retained Interest Trust," Bob continued, "it's not designed to shield assets from a spouse's elective share of your estate, but you can see how it might be styled as a Medicaid Trust to remove the asset from the reach of the state. Needless to say, though, special rules apply and careful planning with an expert is needed before you do something like that."

"Sounds creepy to me," Anne said.

"What about that Total Return Trust?" Ernie asked.

"That's a fairly new approach," Bob answered. "It's a trust investment concept along the lines of what we talked about in Chapter Five: setting goals and then figuring your risk tolerance and your required rate of return. It looks to the future and considers inflation and the effect that lost purchasing power will have on the next generation of beneficiaries."

"So it invests more in equities," Ernie said.

"Yes, if that's what it takes to meet the goals of the trust," Bob said.

"And that's where the rubber meets the road in second or subsequent marriage trusts," Ted added. "The surviving spouse wants as much income as possible, *now*, but if you invest to maximize current income, the kids may get a pittance down the road in terms of original purchasing power. And that's true whether it's a Credit Shelter Trust or a QTIP Marital Trust. When the kids finally get it, it may look like the same trust the trustee started with; the dollar amount of principal may even be the same, but it's been gutted by inflation."

"Well at least the spouse has something to cheer about," Frank said, nodding toward a preoccupied Anne.

"It's a tough problem for the trustee," Bob said. "And I agree with Ted: it's a tougher problem in a second or subsequent marriage than it is in a first marriage. The conflict of meeting the needs of the income beneficiary, the spouse, versus meeting the needs of the donor's children with a future interest, is a very real conflict of interest for the trustee."

Cris looked to Bob but then glanced at Dan as she said, "Hopefully the donor works that out when he sets up the trust."

"Balance," Dan said with a tired grin, "it's all about rhythm and balance."

"What about my husband?" Betty asked. "Does he have any interest in this? Say I had a trust and just wanted the money invested for my kids someday."

"There could be a conflict issue for the trustee in that one too," Bob said. "Your husband could argue that he's a third party beneficiary of your trust. In all fairness, the trustee has a duty to ascertain your income needs—the income you need in order to carry your fair share of the expenses as a partner with a mutual obligation of support—and if the trustee invests for future growth instead of investing to meet the income you need to carry your fair share of the expenses, then it could be argued that the trustee is breaching a duty to your husband. This goes right back to Chapter Four."

"That's a reach," Frank said.

"It might seem like a reach," Ted said, leaning back in his chair, "but I'd take that case given the right facts. The trustee has a duty to generate adequate income to the surviving spouse, along with principal if needed for maintenance and support, and if the new spouse in this second or subsequent marriage is getting a hose job paying the bills, I'd take the case! A trustee has nice deep pockets. It is a bank, isn't it Betty?"

"I don't have any trust!" Betty laughed. "I was just curious."

"On that note, let's call it a night," Bob said. "This week we've looked at what you can do with wills and trusts; next week we'll see how the surviving spouse can protect herself...or himself."

"The Empire Strikes Back," Betty said.

"Yeah, there's got to be a catch to all this somewhere," Frank added.

—— ◇ ——

Shortly after class ended, Ted and Anne arrived by separate cars at The Straw Grass Club. It looked different to Anne. Drab. Ted had finally called yesterday, but Anne knew this was a kiss-off meeting; why else had he avoided her all week? They went in together and took the same table, except this time neither was dressed for boots and denim romance. Anne ordered a Citron Absolut; Ted a Dewars on the rocks.

"Ted, what's wrong?" she began. "You've been avoiding me all week. That really hurts."

"I'm sorry, Anne, that's the last thing I want. You're a terrific woman, a beautiful woman, and I'm flattered that you like me, but you've got a husband, and I just can't do this anymore."

"Is it something I've done, Ted? Something I've said? Something I should change? You've *got* to tell me."

"It's nothing like that, and I don't want you to change a thing. You're fine just the way you are, believe me."

"Well what is it then?"

"I just can't do this to your husband. I'm no saint, but I'm not going to be a home-wrecker. I just can't do it; I know what it feels like from the other side."

"What do you mean?"

"I mean my wife was seeing someone while I was in the army, and when I learned about it from a buddy I couldn't do anything. I was out on bivouac and couldn't get away. It was agony...believe me, it was misery...and I'll never forget it."

"Where were you?"

"Fort Knox."

"Where was she?"

"Who knows? She was supposed to be home."

"Oh, Ted, I'm sorry. I didn't know; this is all news to me. I only know what I feel, and I feel that I want to be with you."

Ted downed the rest of his scotch and signaled for another. "Oh God, Anne, I wish I didn't have to hurt you."

"We were doing so well, Ted." Anne paused to take a sip of her drink. A memory of her mother flashed to the surface: She had never met her mother's expectations, she had never been good enough.

"Ted, you aren't wrecking my home. Hank won't know...and I don't think he'd care if he did know. But he won't. I think you still care for me, Ted."

"Of course I care, Anne, but we have to stop. I'm sorry."

Anne began to cry softly and didn't want him to see it. "I have to go, Ted," she said, and started to get up. She had hardly touched her drink.

"I'm sorry, Anne," Ted mumbled without looking at her.

He left a $20 bill on the table and walked Anne to her car, put her in with more apologies and assurances, and gave her a kiss on the cheek. He watched her crawl across the parking lot and then saw what a BMW 330 Ci can do from a standing start.

Tasting the salt on his lips, Ted turned toward his Blazer and kicked a small stone. "Shit," he said, "shit, shit, shit."

Nearby, an unseen figure punched a 213 area code and telephone number into his cell phone. "Something has happened here. It might be over," the figure said.

"Keep an eye on it. I'll be back in two weeks."

Chapter Nine

Probate, Spousal Elections, Will Contest, Trust Contest

It was 4:00 p.m. on Wednesday, and Bob sat in his office looking out the window at the nearby lake. It always brought memories of Liz and their early boating journeys with friends up to the Erie islands. Those were fun days. He looked at the family pictures on his credenza before the window: candid shots of Liz and the girls at Christmas, at Easter, and on vacation in Florida. There were also school pictures of the girls and a picture of Liz and him on their wedding day. In the middle was a candid of the two of them with his parents, now gone. Family meant everything to Bob. But now he needed to talk with someone. He had tried to catch Ted for lunch, but he was out. Via an exchange of voicemails, they had agreed to meet at the athletic club for a beer that night after class.

Bob was used to solving his own problems, but now he needed help. He continued to ruminate on his life, how he'd wanted to be a Jesuit, how he'd studied and prepared, both academically and spiritually. Then how, in the middle of his seminary life, with help from his spiritual advisor, and with test results in hand, it was understood and agreed, with tearful acceptance by his mother, that the priestly life was not his calling. It was then that he enrolled at John Carroll and began dating, really for the first time. It was *then* that he met Liz, and he never looked back...or to either side. Together they had plunged straight ahead into marriage, and shortly thereafter, family. Twenty-three years, he mused. They had been good years, but now things were changing, and he had a dilemma.

By whatever providence was at work, he found himself torn by thoughts and feelings he could not block out. His marriage was based on love and respect, but it was a dull everyday thing; the beat went on and everything got done, but it was a steady sameness without the intimacy and spark he and Liz had once known. They had grown over the years, sometimes together, sometimes separately, but more separately as of late. Liz was involved with the girls' lives and with her bridge group and club work. He was too involved with his practice, he admitted. For years now, he'd been one-dimensional. Was he hiding from his life, from his marriage? Was this career of his a shield? The one truth he knew for sure was that he felt like an outsider at home, the lone male in a female club, the lone dissenter in three-to-one decisions. He had become his father, and Liz her mother, and together they were living a new-old drama without direction. Like his father, he was not without power, but its exercise only isolated him further. Like her mother, she busied herself with all things, except for him. Now, as if a bolt from nowhere, the door was open to an intimacy and excitement he'd not experienced even in his earliest days with Liz. The thought of three days in New York with Anne filled his mind and every nerve.

It had been a sudden crossing of hearts with Anne; she had called just two weeks before to schedule lunch. He was open that day, and they met for two and a half hours, talking at first about the course, then the office. She asked about Ted and what he was doing…but then the conversation turned to themselves and their lives. They talked from their hearts; she opened up about her personal sadness and her unhappy marriage; he found himself opening up to her like he'd not done to anyone in years. She was a beautiful woman, a good listener, more understanding than anyone he'd ever known. She charmed him with Opium perfume and dark eyes, full of interest. He felt they struck a profound cord that day, forging an emotional tie that seemed like a lifeline to a palm island. It was on that day that he began to see a world beyond Liz. He began to see freedom.

Bob had met or talked with Anne every day since. He was immersed, he knew, and was aware that the palm island might only be a mirage; he could only try to stand outside himself for some dim perspective. Maybe Ted could help. He knew that Ted would be shocked: this would hit Ted like a hammer; he'd say to break it off; that it was wrong; that it was something he'd regret; that Liz didn't deserve this; to think of his family. Still, the pull of Anne was an undertow, and he was swimming alone; Ted could only call to him. With that thought, he looked at the reservation lying on the credenza. He was scheduled to be in New York in early December for a three-day estate planning seminar at the Grand Hyatt. Anne said she'd been planning a shopping trip to New York to buy clothes and things. She said they could meet; she could even stay at the Hyatt and they could have dinner at a little ethnic restaurant or bistro on the Upper East Side, then have a drink at Le Cirque. He had waffled his answer in a way that left it up in the air. Now he needed help.

Bob turned back to his desk, confused about what to do next, then shoved the Smith-Winter file aside; it was time to prepare for the evening. Despite the internal conflict, he looked forward to seeing Anne and feeling her presence at his side; his growing desire smothered his pangs of guilt.

——— ◇ ———

After a few minutes of meaningless chit-chat, Bob breathed the hint of perfume on his left, made brief eye contact with Ted, and with a nod began: "Our first topic for tonight is one that's taken a lot of flak over the years, and that's probate."

"Be still my heart," Betty said.

"Your Notes cover the basics, but I want to make a point before we look at specific issues. The point I want to make is one in defense of probate…Actually I have four points: *first*, that smaller estates are granted relief from administration, so, in effect, there is no probate in the usual sense—no inventory or accounting—and that saves time and expense; *second*, there is an effort to speed up the process…it's really on a fast track in this state, the court wants most estates closed in six to thirteen months; *third*, the probate process clears up creditor and title issues pretty quickly, which may take longer if the assets are in a trust; and *fourth*, with the court's oversight, the process assures proper administration and distribution of the decedent's property. That oversight is lacking where a living trust is used to avoid probate."

"Is that a problem?" Frank asked.

"It's led to increased trust litigation in our Probate Court," Bob said.

"The fox is in the hen house," Betty whispered.

"It's happened," Bob said. "A trustee isn't on a leash with the court like an executor is."

"It seems like probate gets knocked for its cost and delays," Ernie said.

"And lack of privacy," Ted added.

"Well, the delay issue is being tightened up," Bob said, "but there are times when it just takes longer. A prime example would be where there's a federal estate tax payable and there are valuation issues, such as the valuation of a closely-held business.

"The cost issue is one that sometimes gets blown out of proportion…especially if someone is trying to sell you more life insurance. Court costs are usually nominal, a few hundred dollars at most. The heavier costs involve attorney fees and the executor's fee, and it's true, those can be heavier if there's a full administration in the Probate Court. A living trust, funded before death, does avoid probate in most cases and it will save costs."

"So what are the fees?" Dan asked.

"Executor fees are generally a percentage of the gross estate for estate tax purposes, and may range from 2 to 5 percent, depending on the size and type of assets, how they're owned, and what state you live in. For attorney fees, a number of factors can be considered, including the size of the estate, the complexity of the matters involved, the experience of the law firm, and the time expended. The bottom line is that attorney fees must be reasonable and necessary under the circumstances, and they must benefit the estate."

"And they're tax deductible," Ted added.

"All right," Bob went on, "to probate a will is to prove its validity as the last will of the decedent. It's usually a straightforward process, but one with built-in safeguards. The basic safeguard we use in Ohio is an examination of the will by the Probate Court and proof that notice of probate was given to all interested persons within two weeks of the will's submission to probate. Anyone interested in the will can then examine it at the Probate Court, and legal action to construe the will, or to contest the will, can be initiated on a timely basis. A will contest in Ohio needs to be initiated within three months of notice of probate being given to all interested parties.

"But we'll talk about will contests later; for now I want to talk about two issues that might crop up in a second or subsequent marriage where the relationship isn't the best between the surviving spouse and the children from the decedent's prior marriage.

"First, let's look at a situation where there's an effort to remove the fiduciary who's handling the estate. The *Henne* case cited in your Table of Cases involved squabbling siblings, but the issues presented could easily happen in a second or subsequent marriage where the decedent's children object to the way the surviving spouse is handling the estate. The court in *Henne* stated that the Probate Court has discretion to remove a fiduciary who is not 'suitable.' It said a suitable person is one who is reasonably disinterested in the estate, and one who can fulfill the obligations of a fiduciary. It went on to say that, although there is deference to the person named as executor in the will, the court may consider other factors, including the nature and extent of the hostility and distrust among the parties, the degree of their conflicting interests, and the underlying and aggregate complexities of the conflict."

"In other words, if it gets into a cat-fight," Anne said.

"That wouldn't be a good thing," Dan said without looking down the table.

"Hopefully we're all above that sort of thing," Cris said as Ted nudged her foot, still not aware of her relationship with Dan. (Ted was still jogging every morning with Cris, and their friendship had grown into an easy, flirtatious thing for Cris, but much more than that for Ted. Ted had fallen in love.)

"Another type problem can arise," Bob continued, "if there's an allegation that assets are being concealed and not shown as part of the Inventory, the listing of property subject to probate. That problem can arise in any estate, and it can also arise with a trust."

"Same thing with embezzlement," Ted said, straightening in his chair.

Bob nodded in agreement and continued: "If it happens in an estate in Ohio, the Probate Court, once it's notified of an allegation, will initiate a quasi-criminal hearing to determine what's going on. If assets have been embezzled or concealed, there will be a judgment for the value of the assets, plus a 10 percent penalty will be assessed against the wrongdoer. If the allegation is against the trustee of a living trust, however, a civil lawsuit will have to be filed to get a money judgment. The Probate Court doesn't have the authority to initiate a hearing in a living trust case like it does for a probate matter."

"Score one for probate," Frank said.

"Right," Bob agreed. "If something goes wrong in probate, you can be glad that the Probate Court is directly involved."

"What if the executor or trustee is bonded?" Ernie asked.

"Good question," Bob said. "If he is, and if he absconds with funds, the bonding company will make the estate or trust whole, and will then go after the wrongdoer."

"Most wills and trusts dispense with bond, though," Ted added. "People trust members of their own families."

"True enough," Bob said, "and it usually works just fine." Looking around the table, he continued: "Okay, those are two issues I want you to be aware of: removal of an executor in a bad case, and what can be done if assets aren't shown as part of the estate. Now let's move on. The next subject is our main one for the night: it has to do with the spousal election, the election by a surviving spouse to take against the will of a deceased spouse."

"Does that happen often?" Ernie asked.

"Not often in a first marriage; it's more likely in a second or subsequent marriage where the decedent wants to leave property to children from a prior marriage."

"The big picture is this," Ted interjected: "The law wants to protect a surviving spouse from disinheritance, but that idea can clash with the idea that you can freely dispose of your property as you see fit...to your children, for example, from a first marriage."

"Let me give you some background on this," Bob said. "First, picture a business partnership. Say you and a friend start a consulting business, 50-50: you're going to share profits and losses equally.

"Of course you both have your own separate property apart from your interest in the consulting business. Your separate property might consist of your house, your car, your bank account, et cetera. Maybe you inherit property while you're working the business, or maybe your Uncle Ozzie gives you some money as a gift. That's all your separate property. It has nothing to do with your partner or the consulting business.

"Then, say the partnership breaks up: most partnerships do, you know. So you and your partner split your partnership property 50-50. Your partner has no claim against your house, your car, your bank account, your inheritance, or the gift from your Uncle Ozzie. It would be ridiculous if he did...That's your separate property, right? Is everyone in agreement on that? Seems fair, doesn't it?"

There was general agreement around the table, except for Frank who said, "But a marriage isn't a consulting business."

"No," Bob agreed, "but it can be viewed as a partnership. A partnership view lets a couple balance their joint income and marital property the same way they balance their roles as breadwinner, homemaker, and caretaker; it doesn't matter who brings home the bigger paycheck, or who changes the baby. That's the modern view. Everything is muddled up and shared…ideally 50-50. And that's how community property law works. And that's what I'm trying to describe. In a community property state, each party to the marriage has his and her own separate property to do with as he or she wishes, but they each own half their marital property 50-50, like partners, except they each actually own 50 percent of the property itself instead of 50 percent of a legal entity called a partnership. Incidentally, community property law covers nine states, ten if you count Alaska, and that covers over a quarter of our population."

"Does it matter whose name the community property is in?" Ernie asked. "For instance, could it all be in her name?"

"It doesn't matter; it could be in his name, her name, their names jointly, or in one trust or another. If it was earned during the marriage it's community property, and it's owned 50-50. Whose name is on the title doesn't change that unless the couple agrees to transmute community property into the separate property of one or the other."

"And vice versa. They can transmute separate property into community property," Ted said.

"By 'transmute' you mean 'change'," Ernie said.

"Yes, by conduct or agreement," Bob nodded.

"You'd need a bookkeeper," Betty whispered to Cris.

"Not really," Bob smiled. "Those folks are familiar with their own community property laws."

"Learned it at daddy's knee I'll bet," Anne added.

"More like momma's knee," Frank said. "But what about the income realized from separate property? Is that separate property or community property?"

"Good question," Bob said. "The answer, unfortunately, isn't uniform. The pure partnership idea would keep income from separate property separate, but Texas, Idaho, and Louisiana treat income from separate property as community property. The others treat it as separate property. Importantly, they all treat appreciation in value of separate property as separate, but that's become a bone of contention because of the great increase in value of some assets. Nevertheless, for our purposes, just keep the basic community property model in mind with income and appreciation in value treated the same as the property that generated the income or appreciation. We want to compare that concept with the 1990

Uniform Probate Code accrual concept...the elective share percentage of the augmented estate."

"Are you going to explain that?" Anne asked.

"The outline is in your Notes," Bob said, smiling at Anne, not wanting to get bogged down in details, but not wanting to slight her either. (A second glance assured him she was not offended.) "The elective share of an augmented estate is a practical way for separate property states without a community property history to approximate a community property result. The theory is that the longer a couple is married, the more of their property is marital as opposed to separate. After fifteen years, it's all deemed to be marital. As background, incidentally, Professor Lawrence W. Waggoner of the University of Michigan Law School was central in developing the concept and is a strong advocate of its simplicity and fairness. And what I want to do here is simply give you the rationale for the concept, the reasoning behind the details, and contrast that with the forced share system used in other separate property states, like Ohio, and then compare those two to the community property system."

"Let me give you the augmented estate concept in a nutshell," Ted said, wanting to convey a caring note to Anne.

"The gist of it is this: When the first one of the couple dies, you add up all the property each of them owned, controlled, or with some exceptions gave away, and you get a combined total amount. Then the surviving spouse gets a percentage of the total amount depending on how long they were married. After 5 years, 30 percent of a couple's property is deemed to be marital so the survivor is entitled to half of that, or 15 percent of the total. After 10 years, 60 percent is deemed marital so the survivor gets 30 percent of the total. After 15 years, it's 100 percent marital so the survivor gets 50 percent. In each case, the survivor is entitled to a minimum of $50,000. Then you offset against the surviving spouse's share what the surviving spouse already owns, controls or gave away, and what he or she got from the deceased spouse...either at death or earlier by gift. At that point, if the surviving spouse is short, the deceased spouse's estate or other beneficiaries have to kick in to make up the difference. The survivor could get more than those amounts if the survivor owned most of the property to begin with. The bottom line is this: You aren't able to disinherit your spouse by use of living trusts or retained interest trusts or joint and survivor accounts or beneficiary designations on IRAs and life insurance. Your spouse gets a percentage of the total property owned or controlled by the two of you, and the percentage depends on how long you were married."

Anne acknowledged the explanation coolly, then returned her attention to Bob.

Before Bob could continue, Ernie asked, "Did you include separate property in that calculation?"

"Yes," Ted answered. "The separate property of both spouses is included, and that means the survivor could get property that the decedent owned before the marriage, or property the deceased spouse inherited or received as a gift during the marriage. It's not likely in a short-term situation, but it could happen in a longer-term marriage when it's a 50-50 split. And you can see how that differs from Bob's community property partnership model."

"But," Anne asked Bob, "if the surviving spouse had enough separate property of her own, she wouldn't get any property from her husband, is that right?"

"That's right, and as Ted said, that's likely to be the case in a short-term marriage."

"But, in a longer-term marriage, if she had more separate property than her husband, would she have to give some of her property to his children to make it even?"

"No," Bob answered. "She keeps the excess."

"So it's not really 50-50," Ernie said.

"In that example it's not," Bob agreed.

"So his kids get screwed," Frank said.

"I don't think so," Anne said. "They just don't get any of her property, that's all."

"You both have a point," Bob said, "but—bottom line—it can favor the surviving spouse in some cases."

"So," Frank said, "if you're the one with more property, you better outlive your spouse or otherwise some of your property could go to her kids."

"Who cares?" Dan said, glancing toward Cris.

"I do," Betty mumbled.

"Now," Bob said, turning a new page, "let's move on. I want you to see another model, the model based on who has title to the property when the first one dies. This is the model used in the other separate property states—the ones that didn't adopt the UPC augmented estate concept, and that's most of the states, including this one. This model, with its English origin, grew out of the concept of dower and curtesy and was later reformed into the broader forced share statutes, which provide one-third to one-half of the net probate estate to a surviving spouse."

"By 'forced share', do you mean the surviving spouse can force the executor to give her part of her husband's estate if he didn't leave her much?" Cris asked.

"That's right," Bob confirmed. "Typically one-third to one half…That's what you'd get by electing against the will."

"But the bad guys found a way to beat the system," Frank said.

Bob half nodded, half shook his head side to side, acknowledging the comment but neither agreeing nor disagreeing.

"The object of the statutes in forced share separate property states is to protect the surviving spouse, but to do it within a traditional legal framework based on title to property, on ownership."

"It's the woman who needs the protection," Cris said.

"Usually," Bob agreed. "And, as Frank implies, there are ways around the statute in a number of states by use of trusts, survivorship accounts, beneficiary designations, and so on. It's still easy in some states, including this one, to bypass the surviving spouse's elective share."

Cris looked down the table to Dan who winked his reassurance.

"So," Bob continued, "before the UPC came along with the augmented estate idea, you had the community property states and the traditional separate property states. The two systems operated, and still operate, like two countries within one, with each country having sovereign states within it making their own rules and giving their own interpretations to the laws of their states, be it the community property states or the separate property states."

"And, to confound it further," Ted added, "people move freely from one state to another…more now than ever before. They move within the community property states, and they move within the separate property states, and they move from the community property states to the separate property states and vice versa."

"It sounds like a mess," Betty said, thinking that, despite the lure of Vegas, she wasn't making a move until she had all the answers.

"Not really," Ted said, "you just have to be aware that there are differences."

"Fortunately, I've lived here all my life and don't plan to move," Anne said, hitching her chair a half-inch to the right.

"Now," Bob said, smiling, flattered by the small attention just paid him, "go back and add the 1990 Uniform Probate Code to that picture. The UPC is designed to avoid disinheritance, while at the same time it's an attempt to bridge the gap and mold forced share spousal election statutes into a kind of partnership, a 50-50 result for longer term marriages. It's an attempt to approximate community property results in separate property states."

"But," Ernie interjected, "you said that in community property states you keep your separate property separate, while in augmented estate states your separate property is thrown into the mix."

"True," Bob said, "and as we've said, that can cause distortions in some cases. But overall, an accrued elective share of an augmented estate is a workable approximation of how a couple's total assets would be divided under a partnership approach to marriage. It's a simple calculation based on the length of the marriage."

"The key words are *simple* and *approximate*," Ted added.

"How many states have adopted the UPC?" Ernie asked.

"We've listed twenty in your Notes," Bob said, "but the Uniform Probate Code is a vast body of law and the augmented estate concept we're talking about is only part of it."

"And not all states adopted that part," Ted said.

"That's right," Bob said, "and each adopting state is free to put its own spin on the Code, which, of course, some have. Just look at Florida and Michigan in your Notes and Appendix I, and compare them to the model 1990 UPC."

"The thing is," Ted said, "each of the states already had probate statutes in place before the Uniform Probate Code was drafted, and then in some cases, they grafted parts of the UPC, but not all of it, onto their existing system."

"So," Bob said, agreeing with Ted as he turned another page of notes, "there you have the big picture in three primary colors: the community property states, the traditional separate property forced share states, and the UPC augmented estate states which try to achieve a community property like result while keeping a separate ownership of property framework."

"Do I need to know all this?" Anne asked.

"Not if you don't plan to move," Frank said.

"But once you know it you might want to move," Ernie added.

"That's a point," Ted said. "If you plan to move, get the lay of the land. All states but one have spousal election laws."

"Which one doesn't?" Frank asked.

"Georgia," Bob answered.

"Been meaning to visit my cousin in Atlanta," Betty mused.

"Well, there's one more color we need to add to the picture," Bob said. "And that's the color added by the courts and legislatures in several of the traditional forced share separate property states that didn't adopt the UPC but have adopted part of the augmented estate idea. New York and Pennsylvania would be examples. Those states add living trusts, retained interest trusts, and survivorship accounts to the property which is subject to the surviving spouse's election. Ohio and Illinois, on the other hand, and Michigan, a UPC state, are examples of separate property states that have refused to do that."

"So what does all that mean?" Frank asked.

Ted leaned forward and said to Frank, "It means the community property states are the poster boys and California girls that some states want to be. Problem is they can't be; they were born different."

"Well here's what I think the answer is," Bob said, putting aside his notes with a glance to Dan, making sure Dan still had room at the table.

"The issue consists of two related parts: it's a matter of freedom, and it's a matter of protecting the surviving spouse against disinheritance. What's fair might be arguable, but if you use the community property states as the standard for fairness, they seem to handle the issues of freedom and spousal protection naturally. They operate like the partnership model I gave you earlier. Contrast that with many separate property forced share states where the protection part can be circumvented by the use of trusts and so on. The surviving spouse can be disinherited. The accrued elective share of an augmented estate is an attempt in separate property states to build a bridge toward partnership."

"Problem is," Ted said, "the partnership idea doesn't always work. In long-term second marriages, the separate property of the two spouses gets blended into the 50-50 formula, and if the one with a lot of separate property dies first, that one's separate property is treated as marital property; it's shared with the other spouse."

"At the expense of the dearly departed's kids," Frank added.

"They may have intended that anyway," Cris said. "After all, they were married for some time."

"Agreed," Bob said. "And remember: along those lines, one spouse can always make provision for the other that is over and above the legal minimum. One can voluntarily leave separate property to the other."

"But also remember," Ted said, "that the couple can make a written agreement under the UPC, as they can in community property states, to waive their rights to marital property, or to change the classification of property from separate to marital or marital to separate...They can make their own deal."

"Why don't the separate property states just become community property states?" Anne asked.

"Why don't cardinals become bluebirds?" Frank mumbled.

"It's not gonna happen," Ted said.

"Personally, I think the accrued elective share of an augmented estate concept is a good one," Bob said. "It provides protection where it's needed, it's shown to be workable, and it approximates community property results in most cases."

"An alternative that I like," Ted said, "is the deferred-community property elective share system advocated by Akron University's Associate Professor of Law, Alan Newman. Professor Newman advocates that the separate property states keep separate property separate, but split the marital property 50-50, and that would be all property acquired during the marriage except gifts and inheritances. The system would operate like a partnership, like community property law, and it could be done in separate property states at the time of the first death."

"We could all be California girls," Betty laughed.

Bob smiled: "Yes, you could, but as a California girl you would have to track what was separate property and what was marital property, and you would need to keep tabs on that throughout your marriage and not co-mingle the two."

"That shouldn't be hard in a second marriage," Anne said. "You both bring your separate property to the marriage, and you just keep it that way."

"That's how it works," Ted agreed. "Upon the first to die, you split the marital property 50-50, and separate property stays separate. The result would be similar to what happens when a marriage ends in divorce. In a divorce there is an effort to grant each party his and her separate property, and to allocate the marital property equitably, if not equally."

"Divorce isn't always fair," Cris said.

"I agree," Ted said. "But that's the general pattern across the country in divorce cases: there's an attempt to keep separate property separate and to split marital property. And arguably, the results should be the same whether the marriage ends in a death or divorce."

"Alimony and child support can be factors in a divorce though," Ernie said.

"True enough," Ted said. "But the community property states manage to straighten those kinks out while still treating the division of property like a partnership...whether it's a death or divorce."

"Here's the problem as I see it," Bob said. "Ernie...let me use you as an example, okay? Okay. You said your wife owns the house; she brought it to the marriage as her separate property. Meanwhile, though, over the years, you paid the mortgage, the taxes, the insurance, the upkeep, and you made improvements. And through the years the house has continued to appreciate in value. So, is the house still your wife's separate property, or is it now marital property? In a divorce, Ernie, you could testify as to all that you did. But you couldn't if you were dead. And for that matter, your wife couldn't if she died first. In either case, what kind of records would there be? And would the split be equitable? You can see where it could get messy. A judge's discretion and legal presumptions would get involved. In the end, would you really have a better partnership result? And face it, the probate court would rather not get into all that. It wants ease of administration."

"You're saying that even in a second or subsequent marriage people would co-mingle property?" Dan said.

"Sure. In many cases. Just like Ernie. And I'm saying that I think the accrued elective share of an augmented estate would be easier to administer in separate property states, and it's a reasonable approximation of the partnership model. I also think it's a reasonable compromise of your freedom to transfer property. Finally, it assures protection for a surviving spouse, and as you know, I favor that."

"I can live with it," Ted said, "but I do think people would keep records and separate accounts if it meant that more of their property could go to their kids."

"It would still be a muddle for most people," Bob said. "On the plus side, though, I think that would be a good thing for the marriage. Let people muddle their property as long as you can approximate a fair settlement when you need to, and as long as it's not too much trouble."

"So where does that leave us?" Frank asked.

"Hopefully it leaves you with a better understanding of what's involved," Bob answered. "As a practical matter, you need to get specific legal advice from your estate planning attorney when you plan your estate. Know the elective share rules in your state. If you move to another state, you need to understand the elective share rules in that state, too. And know that things can change…Ohio, for instance, might adopt the UPC augmented estate idea someday."

"If it does, it will put its own spin on it," Ted added.

"A lot to think about," Betty said.

"A lot might be at stake for your kids," Ted said.

"You can still be a supportive spouse and achieve a fair result for your children no matter where you live," Bob added "It just takes planning."

"Of course we want to be fair, but there is a lot to think about," Anne said.

Betty nodded her agreement.

"Not everyone has a lot at stake," Frank said. "It probably works out all right for most people the way it is."

"You still need to know what you're doing," Ted said. "In most cases, the protections for a surviving spouse trump the protections for the children, at least adult children, and in a second or subsequent marriage, you may want to do something about that."

"All right, let's get into our final topic for the night," Bob announced, tucking one file into his briefcase and retrieving another. "Let's look at will and trust contests."

"Yeah, let's have some action here," Frank said, rubbing his hands.

Ted gave a wink to his partner as Bob continued: "First, let's look at trust contests where the surviving spouse wants to include the trust in the pool of assets subject to an elective share. These cases fall into one of two categories: either it's claimed that the trust was set up to defraud the surviving spouse from receiving an elective share, or else it's claimed that the settlor retained such power and control over the trust that the trust is no more than the settlor's alter ego. In other words, it's not really a trust at all; the trust is illusory."

Bob picked up his handwritten notes and Anne noticed how neat and legible they were compared to Ted's, which she knew consisted of scribbles. Bob read to the class: "To paraphrase Black's Law Dictionary: The elements of fraud include an intent to deceive another into relinquishing a legal right, or something of value, by misrepresenting—by allegation or concealment—a material fact, with reliance by the other on the misrepresentation, with damage suffered as a result.

"If a trust contest is to be filed on the basis of fraud, the facts of the case should reflect those three basic elements: misrepresentation, reliance, and damages.

"The *Dunnewind v. Cook* case from Indiana is an example of an alleged fraud case. In *Dunnewind,* the wife, after learning she was terminally ill, set up a living trust and transferred her assets to the trust. She then died within a few months. Given those facts, the court found the transfer to be fraudulent; the court said she intended to deprive her husband of his elective share of her estate."

"She was probably just trying to protect her children," Anne said.

"A guy's gotta live too," Frank mumbled.

Bob acknowledged both comments with a single nod, and continued to read from his notes: "An example of an illusory trust claim is the *Newman* case, a landmark case from New York.

"*Newman* involved the typical transfer of assets to a revocable living trust. Instead of basing its decision on fraud, however, the court found that the trust was illusory in that the settlor had retained the power to revoke it, and had retained other controls. The court said a trust should be judged by its substance rather than its form. It said the transfer of assets to the trust in this case was only a mask covering the settlor's effective retention of his property.

"And, as your Notes indicate," Bob continued, "New York has backed that up with a statute bringing revocable living trust assets into the spousal election pool."

"It would be easier to plan an estate if every state had a statute regarding living trusts and other non-probate transfers," Ted said. "But they don't. In the states without a statute, the issue of including revocable living trust assets in the spousal election pool is decided on a case-by-case basis and legal precedent."

"That's why we need you lawyers," Frank said with a grin.

"Gotta check it all out," Betty sighed.

"I agree," Bob said. "Check it out with an estate planning attorney in whatever state you're in."

"I'm in a state of blissful confusion," Betty sighed again, rolling her eyes to Cris.

"Me too," Cris said, nudging Ted with her foot.

"Now," Bob continued, "apart from fraud or illusory trust cases, the most common complaint in a will or trust contest is that the person lacked legal capacity, or the person was subject to the undue influence of another. Allegations of forgery, of course, or defective execution, mistake, lack of intent, or revocation of the will or trust might also be the basis for a suit, but those are less common than the two that Ted's going to review for you."

Bob looked to Ted, and Ted, who had been studying his notes, shifted his chair, put down his notes, and spoke to the group, eyeing each person in turn around the table, starting with Anne:

"The *Niemes* case is an old one, but it's the seminal case in Ohio regarding lack of testamentary capacity. In *Niemes*, a jury trial was had in the Probate Court to decide whether John Niemes had the mental capacity to make a valid will. The trial court decided he did not have legal capacity. The Appellate Court, however, ruled that the Probate Court had erred in allowing certain laypersons to testify regarding the mental capacity of Mr. Niemes. The case went to the Ohio Supreme Court, which used the case to set out the four-part test for legal capacity outlined in your Chapter Eight Notes. The Supreme Court then went on to say that laypersons could testify…not as to legal capacity, which was a question for the jury to decide…but as to their opinions of the person's mental state: Was the person of sound or unsound mind? Was the person capable of understanding important business matters? Such testimony, the Court said, is competent as reflecting on the testator's power of thought and comprehension and the general strength of his mental faculties."

"So anyone might testify about a person's mental state; they don't require an expert medical opinion," Ernie said.

"Right," Ted nodded. "They allow a wide range of testimony to shed light on the person's state of mind, with all its strengths or weakness, and its powers or limitations. Of course, expert medical opinion might be introduced too. And from it all—along with instructions from the judge—the jury will decide the question of legal capacity."

"Interesting," Anne mused.

"Legal capacity can be determined more easily, I think, than undue influence," Ted said. "And undue influence is the other common complaint in a will contest.

"The *West v. Henry* case is good authority on that issue in Ohio. *West* sets out the elements necessary to sustain undue influence. You also have those elements in your Chapter Eight Notes. The *West* case makes clear that the mere existence of undue influence isn't enough, and unless the undue influence is exerted at the time of execution of the will, or is done so near in time to the execution of the will that it's part of the *res gestae*…as we say…the will won't be set aside on account of undue influence. *West* involved a mother who felt pressure from a son who was close at hand. He wanted her to leave him the bulk of her estate, and she made out a will to do just that. Then, while visiting her daughter in North Carolina, she told her daughter that she'd signed something prepared by her lawyer back home that she shouldn't have. When her daughter asked her why, she said tearfully: 'Either do it or not have anything to live on.'"

"Sounds like undue influence to me," Frank said.

"But the Court deemed that statement, and other evidence, to be too remote in time from the signing of the will to prove undue influence," Ted said.

"So," Ernie asked, "do you have to have your arm twisted while you sign your will?"

"That would help," Ted answered.

"But the case of *In re Estate of Smith* is also instructive," Ted continued. "In *Smith*, the trial in the Probate Court found that Mrs. Smith was not legally capable of making a will because she was under restraint and subject to undue influence. She was in a nursing home, in a wheelchair, and died within two weeks. The Court of Appeals reversed that decision, finding that being in poor health does not establish that a testator is 'susceptible' to the influence of others. In the *Smith* case, Mrs. Smith had manually inserted her son's name into a typed will that had previously been prepared for *her* signature. She then initialed her change. The Court of Appeals found this to be strong evidence that Mrs. Smith was not in a weakened or susceptible mental state. It was evidence that this is what she wanted; it was her will."

"Strong lady," Frank said.

"Right," Ted agreed.

"It seems like strength of personality makes a big difference," Anne said. "Look at the difference between Mrs. West and Mrs. Smith. People have different resistance levels."

"I agree," Ted said. "It can get complicated. Your notes spell out some things you can do to protect yourself, though. And those things are important because the court won't find undue influence in this state unless the undue influence is exerted at or near the time of the signing of the will."

"Whatever happened to old-fashioned trust?" Cris asked of no one in particular.

"Well," Bob said, "that's where the problem is most acute: People trust those who have a confidential relationship with them…and that includes caregivers, close friends, attorneys, accountants, and financial advisors, as well as children and spouses. If you're interested, see the *Krischbaum* case in your Table of Cases. That case involved a lawyer. Here, though, our concern is with the spouse and children."

"If undue influence were found to exist, would that cancel the whole will or trust agreement?" Ernie asked.

"It would invalidate the wrongful bequest," Bob answered. "The rest would be okay."

"What about that no-contest clause mentioned in the Notes?" Frank asked. "You say that some states enforce it and some don't. What's the story on that?"

"Ohio will enforce the 'no-contest' if the contestant loses," Bob said. "Of course, if the contestant wins, the will is normally set aside and the no-contest clause is set aside with it. Some other states say they won't enforce the no contest clause against a losing contestant if the contestant acted in good faith, and if there was probable cause for bringing the action. There are cases from Colorado to New York to that effect, with Texas, Florida, Wisconsin, and Pennsylvania in between. The majority of the states take that approach. Fewer states take the tough approach we take here in Ohio, but those states do include California, Massachusetts, Michigan, and Missouri."

"Tough love," Dan said.

"Tough something," Frank mumbled.

"But if you're going to use a no-contest clause," Ted added, "it's worth considering some kind of bequest to the person you want to cut out. Otherwise, he has nothing to lose by contesting the will. For instance, a gift of one-fourth of what that person would have expected to receive might be enough to discourage a will contest. If he contests the will and loses, he gets nothing, or at least he gets nothing in this state. So rather than risk getting nothing, and having to pay attorney fees, he might take what's provided in the will."

"Another way to discourage will contests," Bob added, "is to make serial wills… make the same will every six months right up to the time you die. If they successfully contest the last will—say for incapacity or undue influence—it will, if it's done right, resurrect the immediately preceding will as being your 'last will.' In other words, a successful will contest would only give new life to a previous will which has the very same provisions. The contestant may have to go back several years and prove incapacity or undue influence with a new will contest every time."

"That would discourage just about anyone," Anne said.

"Well, it should be easy to defend one of those wills, that's for sure," Frank said.

"That's the idea," Bob agreed. "Now let's go home," he said with a smile to Anne. "We're running a little late."

"Remember," Ted said, "it's estate planning next week, and then two weeks from tonight it's our last class, and we want to hear what you plan to do with these issues in your own lives. Do you want to favor your spouse? If so, how? Or, if you want to favor your children, how are you going to do it?"

"You can have a happy medium," Bob said as he got up from the table. "You can have a close family and provide financial security for your spouse and children at the same time." At that moment, a little dart of fear struck him: only Liz would have noticed. In an instant, he realized the fullness of his risk, but then was drawn to dark eyes, warm with interest.

Trouping outside into the chill of the early November night air, the small group said their good-byes. Bob buttoned his London Fog and gave Ted a wave. Ted signaled a thumbs-up as he headed for his car, and then to the East Side Athletic Club to see what was up with Bob. Bob lingered for a moment to talk to Anne before going to his car.

Chapter Ten

Estate Planning

Ted awoke at 2:00 a.m., sad and confused: Was it a dream, an illusion, or did it happen? Did he finish their 40-minute jog that morning, have breakfast, joke around with Casey, go upstairs to see his Cleveland Browns poster, notice the pastel blue, yellow, and cream colors of Cris's room in passing, and then see the boy off to school? Did he two minutes later start to leave the kitchen, and on impulse, take Cris's hand, draw her to him, and kiss her lips so tenderly that, upon parting, the slightest tissue of her lip clung to his, not wanting to leave, while all the while her blue eyes, usually bright with intelligence, now softened with unspoken feelings, never moved from him? Did she then, without a word, with his hand in hers, lead him to the front door...and following his look toward the stairs, ask him to sit down for a minute? Did she then, as she talked with his hand in hers, say that she could not see him again...that she planned to marry another? Did he not then speak without stop for twenty minutes? Did he not say how much he wanted to be with her always, how he looked forward to seeing her each morning, how every Wednesday night he wanted to go home with her after class, how much he wanted to do things with Casey, how much he needed her in his life, how much he loved her? Did she then stand, look at him with loving eyes, crying, tissue in hand, hug him, say how sorry she was, and then, with soft pleading, repeat that she could not see him? Had he not said once more how much he loved her...to no avail? Had he then left angry, sad, frustrated, and defeated?

Ted was awake now, but groggy...had it all been a dream, an illusion, or did it happen? Was it over with Cris? If it was, how could it be over just like that...just when it was getting started? Ted was angry and confused with alcohol-laden thoughts of love and loss. He managed to sleep more, but the night was fitful, and the morning was worse—with heavy head and heavier heart. Had it all been a bad dream? Who was this other guy, anyway? Why wouldn't she tell him? Ted groped for the aspirin and headed for the shower. It was Wednesday morning and he had a pre-trial hearing in Judge Grant's chambers at 8:15 a.m. He would see Cris that evening...Maybe they could talk after class. As he entered the bathroom, he shouted, *"The team that won't be beat can't be beat."* He then stood naked in the shower, turned the cold water faucet to full blast, and let out a primal scream.

With coats and jackets laid across chairs in the corner of the room, everyone settled in around the conference table. Cris gave Ted only a polite smile when he eased his foot over. She didn't return the pressure, but she didn't break the connection either. Dan, looking at Cris, thought she had seemed distant before class, distracted. She said she'd had a bad day. They needed to talk. Maybe he could relieve some of the pressure. At that moment, he heard the stir of papers as Bob got ready to start the class.

Bob was less aware of Dan on his right than he was of Anne on his left. He drew in the light scent of her perfume, a new one he did not know (it was *Boucheron Eau de Parfum,* her husband Hank's favorite). Bob hoped he could see Anne alone for a few minutes that evening; he wanted to talk to her. "This will be our last meeting in this room," he began. "Next week we'll be back in the old classroom to wrap up the course. We'll discuss what each of you plan to do with all of this, or at least what you plan to do with something you got out of the course. Any questions about that?"

"Should we bring our significant others?" Frank asked, amusing himself with the thought.

"It's up to you," Bob answered. "Your spouses are welcome so long as we can have an open and honest exchange with each other."

"That'll be the day," Betty mumbled.

"Okay," Bob continued, "let's get to it; we have important ideas to get across tonight. The first one is this: there are a lot of people out there who say they do estate planning, but who shouldn't be doing *your* estate planning. There are people with a product or service to sell and even some lawyers who shouldn't be doing estate planning." Bob then looked to Ted for his reaction.

"I agree," Ted said, nodding a head still nursed with aspirin. "In fact, with all the Internal Revenue Service rules, combined with the ethical issues and the various states laws, I wouldn't touch it...especially in a second or subsequent marriage."

"That's the point I want to make," Bob said. "Estate planning in a second or subsequent marriage is complex. In addition to organizing and analyzing data, and preparation of documents and doing periodic reviews, you have federal income, estate, and gift tax issues, and you have state laws concerned with spousal protection. Given all of that, you need expert legal analysis and drafting skills.

Now, having said that, I have to say that the one who calls you with a product or service to sell may be the catalyst who gets you moving…and that's good. Without a catalyst, some people wouldn't do anything."

"But I thought the idea was to have an estate planning team," Ernie said.

"It is," Bob agreed, "but the team concept assumes that each person on the team plays his or her proper role. It assumes, for example, that a financial planner might get the process going and lay out an overall game plan. Then, if you don't have competent people you're already working with, the planner might bring in an insurance agent with specific insurance products and a stockbroker or investment advisor with specific investment products and an estate planning attorney to go through all the steps outlined in this week's Reading Notes. And it also assumes that people communicate with each other and work together; good ideas can come from any member of the team. But what it doesn't assume is that someone from the financial world or a divorce lawyer—sorry Ted—does your estate planning!"

"No offense, believe me," Ted muttered.

"That's where you, the client, have to stay in control," Bob continued. "You have to be the captain of the team and control the whole process. It's your money."

"But a lot of estate planning seems to involve insurance and annuities and investments," Ernie said.

"Yes, and that requires an expertise all by itself," Bob said. "And I agree that it's the life insurance agent who will deliver a $50,000 check or a $500,000 check to your widow, not your attorney. But you need to make the distinction between insurance and investment products that might be used to build an estate, or that need to be coordinated with an estate plan, and the estate plan itself."

"It sounds like it could be a turf war," Dan said.

"But it shouldn't be," Bob replied.

"Here, let me give you an example. I had a doctor come to me with a real estate corporation he'd had on the side for years. It was loaded with cash and common stock investments as well as real estate. Apart from the tax issues it presented, I was working on a plan for corporate succession that would meet his goal of security for his wife, but with an ultimate transfer of control to his son. Meanwhile, he met a stockbroker at a party and switched all of his investment accounts over to the new broker. The broker wanted to look good and do all the doctor's work, so he gathered information to do estate planning. Then, as part of his so-called estate plan, he switched the real estate corporation's investment account to the doctor's living trust. He did it to avoid probate, he said. The problem is that the transfer was treated as a dividend: it created a horrendous tax problem. The broker didn't understand the distinction between the doctor owning the shares of the corporation and the corporation owning the investment account. To him it was just another one of the doctor's investment accounts. That's what I mean by people playing their proper roles."

"Seems like the doctor was naive too," Ernie said.

"He was getting cocktail party advice for nothing," Ted said. "Very costly."

Bob nodded his agreement, then continued: "Professional insurance and investment people know their products and know how to use them to build or protect an estate. But the attorney is the one who knows state law and is the one who has studied property law, business organization, corporations, future interests, wills, trusts, estate planning, domestic relations, and the federal income, estate, and gift tax laws, and it's the attorney who knows how it all goes together in drafting documents and administering estates. Put the responsibility for your estate plan where it belongs. Enough said."

"And," Ted added, "beware of people who are just marketing estate planning documents."

"Right," Bob agreed. "There are boiler-plate living trust mills out there where one size fits all. Use a law firm for your estate planning, not a marketing firm.

"Okay," Bob continued, "all of that is *very* important, but so is this: Once you've been motivated to do estate planning, and once you've contacted an attorney, you need to discuss the ethical issues. Is the attorney going to represent you as an individual, or you and your spouse as a couple? As a person in a second or subsequent marriage, you need to understand all that that implies, and you need to have your understanding with the attorney reduced to writing in the form of an engagement letter. I'll leave it at that; you can review those issues in your Reading Notes."

Bob sifted through his class notes and then said, "In a nutshell, here's what you want to do once you've engaged an attorney: *first*, present all of your financial, investment, insurance, business, and family facts to the attorney; *second*, articulate the goals you have for your spouse, your children, and any charities; *third*, have a discussion about how your goals can be accomplished…and that involves a discussion of financial management, investment management, tax management, and personnel management as outlined in your Reading Notes; and *fourth*, emphasize that you want to minimize estate expenses. It's as simple as that."

"It doesn't look simple when you read the Notes," Dan said.

"And in many cases it's not," Bob agreed with a nod and a grimace.

"If you don't have a lot," Frank said, "it can't be that complicated."

"It might not be," Bob agreed. "It all depends on how your property and your goals match up. But if you don't have much in the way of assets, then that itself is an estate planning problem. You need to concentrate on building an estate; you need to figure out a way to cover your needs."

"I'm working on it," Frank said.

"All right," Bob continued, "here's the other side of the coin. Here's the challenge you give to your estate planning attorney: he or she needs to take all of your separate property and marital property that might be transferred with a will or trust, together with all of your property that might be transferred with a deed, together with all of your P.O.D. and T.O.D. accounts, insurance company products, and retirement accounts that might be transferred with a beneficiary designation, together with all of your close-corporation, partnership, and limited liability company interests that might be transferred with buy-sell agreements—*in other words, all of your property that might be transferred by law or contract or probate*—and he or she needs to coordinate all of those property components and transfer methods with the types of assets and timing needed to pay estate taxes and expenses, and then meet your goals for education funding, your goals for disposition of business assets, your goals for transfer of tangible personal property items, and your overall goals for your spouse, your children from a prior marriage, and for your favorite charity. He or she needs to understand it, chart it out, and then draft the documents and instruments that will accomplish it all. That's estate planning: it's stitching and weaving all of those elements into a seamless cloak for conservation and distribution of your lifetime of accumulated assets—maybe your parents' lifetime too—and it's doing it against the financial, investment, and tax background discussed in your Reading Notes, and it's doing it with the personal variables you bring to the table."

"That's mind boggling," Anne said.

"Well I'm no doctor with a fancy corporation, so it's no big deal," Frank said. "A will, a power-of-attorney, a couple of beneficiary designations, a pull-the-plug directive, and I'm done."

"That's not a bad plan," Bob said, putting his notes down, "but you should consider a living trust, or at least a testamentary trust. You have young children, don't you?"

"Yeah, two boys under sixteen months."

"Well, you need to designate a guardian for your children, of course, in case of a common disaster that takes both you and your wife. And you should consider a trust so that, in case of a common disaster, your children won't get everything at age 18. With a trust, you can have it held until they're older. In the meantime, the trustee can use the money for their education, medical expenses, and so on, and they can get the balance in installments, or in a single sum, at age 25, 30, 35, whatever you decide. You can also have your life insurance and other benefits made payable to the trust."

"What happens if my wife survives me?"

"Your will can leave everything to your wife in that case, or it can leave part to your wife and part to the trust. And she can have a mirror image mutual will that contractually leaves everything to you if you survive her, otherwise to a trust, or part to you if you survive and part to the trust.

"And as you said," Bob continued, "you should have durable general powers of attorney that would enable either of you to handle the other's financial affairs if one of you becomes incapacitated. It can be a very comprehensive instrument, and it may save you from having to set up a guardianship. It's cheap insurance."

"What if we're both incapacitated?"

"You can have a back-up in your powers-of-attorney.

"Also, you mentioned advance healthcare directives," Bob said. "I think that's a good idea, even though you're young. You'll make your own healthcare decisions as long as you can speak for yourself, but when you can't, a living will or healthcare power-of-attorney can speak for you."

"Not everyone wants that," Cris said.

"I have them for myself," Dan said.

"It's a personal choice," Bob added, "but it's worth considering. Life support in a hopeless case can be emotionally draining as well as expensive."

"Something else you can do," Ted interjected, "is have a joint and survivor deed with your wife. You can even have a T.O.D. deed here in Ohio for transfer of real estate on death. It avoids probate."

Bob nodded his agreement, and said, "All of that adds up to a good estate plan for young couples who don't have much, and it wouldn't be expensive to do. If you can afford it, use a living trust instead of a testamentary trust and avoid probate altogether. If you have second or subsequent marriage issues, you would probably use a living trust anyway."

"Even if I didn't have much?" Frank asked.

"Well, maybe not if you didn't have much. But that's where term life insurance might be called for; a young couple can cover a lot of their needs with term insurance payable to a living trust. With a living trust, in this state at least, you can give your wife what you want her to have and give your children what you want them to have. Pretty simple. Check it out though if you move 60 miles from here to Pennsylvania, or 120 miles from here to New York, or to a Uniform Probate Code augmented estate state, all of which make living trust assets subject to a spouse's elective share. Even if you move a few hundred miles west of here to Indiana, or up to Michigan, the courts will decide the living trust issue on a case-by-case basis. So if you plan to move, you have to know the lay of the land in your new state. But a living trust is generally a good way to go, and with a living trust in Ohio, you still call the shots."

"I'm staying put," Anne said.

"I might stay too," Betty said. "Got family here for one thing."

"Stick around," Ted said, "the Indians are rebuilding."

"Okay, to go back to Frank's point," Bob continued, "...if you're in a second or subsequent marriage, and you don't have much, you might use wills with testamentary trust provisions like we talked about, or you might use simple mirror image wills with a separate contract not to change or revoke them unless you do it together, or you might use a joint trust with a separate contract not to change or revoke the joint trust unless you do it together, or you might use living trusts with pour-over wills. It all depends on your situation."

"But what about other things like life insurance policies and IRAs? Those are things you can change on your own," Ernie said.

"You can make irrevocable beneficiary designations on those," Bob answered, "but I wouldn't recommend it because you lose flexibility. Too many things can happen. Besides, you can use life insurance, IRAs, joint accounts, P.O.D. and T.O.D. accounts to shape what you want to do for your spouse or your children…subject, of course, to community property and augmented estate rules in some states."

"I'd like to say something more about the point Frank makes," Ted said from the other end, "because I think a lot of people are in the same boat that Frank is in."

Not likely, Frank thought, picturing Sally near the Pittsburgh airport, and Marcie a few miles from where he sat.

"A lot of these people are young to middle-age, and they may have children from this marriage as well as children from a prior marriage. They may have a house with a mortgage, a car or two, a bank account, some life insurance through work, a small IRA or two, maybe a 401(k). But they have liabilities, too…Maybe a chunk of credit card debt, or maybe alimony or child support obligations from a prior marriage. They have bills to pay and not a lot of cash. So simple wills or testamentary trusts with a separate contract not to revoke, or a simple joint trust with a contract not to revoke, together with joint accounts, a survivorship deed, and coordinated beneficiary designations on insurance and IRAs…can all be inexpensive ways to meet their needs."

"It seems like those people would leave everything to the other spouse anyway," Ernie said.

"Probably right," Bob agreed.

"All right," he continued, "the things we just talked about are basic for couples who don't have much, and they can easily be used by couples in a second or subsequent marriage. But for larger estates with estate tax exposure, the QTIP Trust/Credit Shelter Trust combination is a no-brainer if you want to preserve something for your children."

Nothing's a no-brainer when you've got Sally in William Penn land and Marcie here, Frank thought. Got to move one of them.

"With a QTIP/Credit Shelter Trust combination," Bob continued, "you can combine estate tax planning and asset protection planning in one package. It's a cost-effective tool to protect your children from a prior marriage, while at the same time you save estate taxes and provide for your surviving spouse."

"How much money should you have to do that?" Ernie asked.

"If your assets exceed the federal estate tax lifetime exemption, you should consider it, but if your assets are less than that, less than $1,500,000 in 2004 or 2005, or less than $2,000,000 in 2006, 2007, or 2008, for example, you don't need it…You can get by with a standard revocable living trust, which will, upon death, serve as a stand-alone Credit Shelter Trust.

"Remember," Bob continued, "with a Credit Shelter Trust, you can leave everything to your children outright, or you can keep assets in trust and have the income paid to your surviving spouse, or you can have the income sprinkled among your spouse, your children, and your grandchildren. If you wish, the principal can be used to help your spouse maintain his or her standard of living, with any principal remaining at your spouse's death then paid to your children. The QTIP Trust can do the same thing except the income *must* be paid to your surviving spouse. These trusts can also incorporate generation skipping provisions whereby income and principal can be used for your children during their lifetime, but with principal kept in trust for ultimate distribution to grandchildren. In short, with a QTIP/Credit Shelter Trust combination you can control and direct the timing and distribution of your assets."

"Subject to the spousal election laws in your state," Ted said.

"Right," Bob nodded. "You can only deal with what is yours…and as we've seen, what is yours to deal with depends on where you live. But I'll say this," Bob added, looking around the table, "the basics we talked about a few minutes ago with Frank, together with a revocable living trust that divides into a Credit Shelter Trust/QTIP Trust combination upon death, will cover 90 percent of the people in second or subsequent marriages. That's a guess, but it's not far off."

"But what about the other 10 percent?" Betty asked.

"Well, for those in the other 10 percent," Bob answered, "I'm going to ask you to review your Chapter Eight Reading Notes for different types of trusts, and your Chapter Ten Reading Notes for background on limited partnerships, corporations, and limited liability companies. Then talk with your estate planning attorney. Those are all tools that can be used to achieve particular goals in a second or subsequent marriage, but they all come under the heading of advanced estate planning. For example, life insurance—either in an irrevocable life insurance trust or a family limited partnership—can be an effective way to provide liquidity, business protection, and a guaranteed estate for your children from a prior marriage. And in addition, you can structure it so it's both estate tax-free and immune from spousal claims. But obviously, planning like that takes a particular expertise."

"In addition, if you have a family business," Ted said, "you must have a plan for business succession and control. That might mean a buy-sell agreement, or an irrevocable life insurance trust, or use of a family limited partnership or limited liability company in connection with a closely-held corporation, or it might mean a voting trust, an asset protection trust, a SCIN, or any combination thereof. A creative estate planning attorney like Bob can use those tools to design a business succession plan."

"What's a SCIN?" Dan asked.

"It's a self-canceling installment note," Bob answered. "Say a business owner sells his business to a son or daughter from a prior marriage and takes back an installment note. By the terms of the note it's canceled upon the seller's death. And when that happens…Poof! The child has the business…and the note isn't part of the estate."

"Is that what you *do?*" Anne asked Bob.

"I've looked at a few," he answered. Bob's tone caught Ted's ear and he saw a blush as Bob nodded and smiled. Ted began to wonder about Bob: he wondered if Bob was losing his grip on his personal life. They had met as planned the week before, but Bob was vague about what he wanted to talk about. Ted had the feeling he wanted to talk about his marriage…but then didn't. They talked about the course instead and, Ted now recalled, Bob wanted Ted's opinion of each person in the class, including Anne…who Bob had saved for last. Ted knew how appealing Anne could be, and he hoped his instincts were wrong. Bob and Liz were a natural together. Anne would be totally out of character for Bob; it would be a disaster.

"Just a couple more things before we get to the heart of tonight's class," Bob said as Ted studied the two of them at the other end of the table.

"The first one is this: If your spouse is not a U.S. citizen, and if your assets are likely to exceed the federal estate tax lifetime exemption, you'll want to have special trust provisions added to your QTIP Marital Trust in order to defer and minimize the federal estate tax. They're called *qualified domestic trust* provisions and they're designed to prevent a non-citizen surviving spouse from taking assets out of the country to escape our federal estate tax system."

"Not my situation," Betty laughed.

"Didn't think so," Bob said, "but here's one that could be: Say you have a trust to benefit your children, and say your children are married but you see signs of trouble. What can you do to protect your assets from your children's spouses?"

"Let your kids have the money," Dan said. "It's their life."

"Well, it is their life," Bob said, "but it's your money. And since it's your money you can have trust provisions that say principal will only be distributed to your children if they have prenuptial or postnuptial agreements in place that will protect the assets from spousal claims."

"Wow," Dan said. "I say let them have the money."

Ted saw Betty make a note to herself and recalled his conversation with Bob: There may be more to Betty than meets the eye.

"One more thing," Bob said, "remember to review all of your beneficiary designations periodically. Check for primary and secondary beneficiaries. Those assets might in fact represent most of your estate. Maybe you want them to go to your spouse, or maybe you want them to go to your children. And look at stretching your IRA payments out as long as possible…That can be part of your estate plan as well as your plan for income tax deferral.

"Finally," Bob said, "don't forget gift ideas. If you have a good size estate— something beyond your lifetime exemption amount, and something beyond what you feel you need to live on—you can make gifts to your spouse, your children, your grandchildren, or your favorite charity."

"On the other hand, if your estate is smaller than that, don't forget about long-term care insurance," Ted added. "That can be a basic strategy to protect your estate."

The sound of Ted's voice and his near presence were a comfort and, at the same time, a cause of angst for Cris. She had feelings for Ted that wouldn't go away (she thought about him every day), and she knew she would forever treasure that moment in the kitchen. She had stopped the relationship from going further because she didn't want to lose control; she was afraid to let emotions cut through the woven fabric of her life. She had made one mistake; she couldn't afford another. And Ted was an unknown quantity: his first marriage hadn't worked; he'd never been a father; he might be a workaholic; he looked right now as if he'd had too much to drink…In a word, he was a risk. She couldn't afford to risk Casey, or herself. Dan was a known quantity; he'd had a good marriage; he'd raised two boys; he was steady. Still, Cris's heart reached out for Ted: he stirred something lost within her. She wished she could again take his hand in hers…a hand now just inches away…a hand she felt would never be so close again.

"Okay," Bob was saying, "let's get to the heart of the matter. Let's talk about how to maximize benefits to a surviving spouse, and then about how to minimize benefits to a surviving spouse while you maximize benefits to your children. I will then talk about how you might achieve a balance between the two…and you know that that is my preference."

"And you know I say keep your assets separate, and take care of yourself and your kids first," Ted said.

"Support your spouse first," Bob chided, smiling at Ted, "then just be fair."

"All right, let's get to it," Bob said as Ted looked around for reactions to his and Bob's different views, which defined the course in a nutshell. There were none other than Ernie jotting a note to himself, and a muffled, inaudible sound from Betty, accompanied by heavy shifting in her seat.

"First," Bob continued, "it's easy to maximize benefits to your spouse…You just do it. You leave everything to your husband or wife by way of joint accounts or your will or trust, and by way of all your beneficiary designations on IRAs, P.O.D. accounts, life insurance policies, et cetera, or you just gift everything over to your spouse during your lifetime."

"Not recommended," Ted said.

"But why would you do any of that when you have children from a prior marriage?" Ernie asked.

"Well, maybe there's estrangement from those children, or maybe this is your second family. Perhaps you and your second spouse have a child or two, and your children from your prior marriage are already grown and doing well on their own," Bob answered.

Dan glanced at Cris, but then looked away.

"On the other hand," Bob continued, "your Reading Notes mention that while you may want to give your spouse the benefit of your accumulated estate, you may not want to give him or her control of the assets. I won't go into all of that here, it's in you're Reading Notes, but suffice it to say that if that's your goal, you will want to consider the QTIP Trust/Credit Shelter Trust combination as a basic tool. In most cases, you won't need more than that."

"And those trusts come into being when you die," Ernie confirmed.

"Right," Bob agreed. "They're trusts that come into being at death from your Revocable Living Trust or Testamentary Trust."

"Couldn't your kids contest it if you left everything to your second wife and nothing to them?" Frank asked.

"They could," Ted answered, "but they would have to show lack of legal capacity or undue influence or fraud, et cetera. It's not an easy case to make."

"Review your Chapter Nine Reading Notes on that," Bob added. "In addition, make sure you mention those children by name in your will and trust. You don't want them to claim that you forgot them."

"Fat chance," Dan said.

"Leave them a dollar each," Ted said.

"Okay," Bob continued, "let's switch gears: Say you want to leave everything to your children from a prior marriage. Say your spouse already has sufficient assets, or say your marriage is broken—it's dead as a doornail—but you don't want to get a divorce. Remember, in a divorce, marital property will be divided as the court deems equitable, and there may also be support issues, but that's not what happens when you die. So, say you want to leave all your assets to your children from a prior marriage. How do you do that?"

"Probably can't," Dan said.

"Why?" Bob asked, shifting his chair back a few inches and turning to Dan.

"You can do it pretty well here in Ohio," Dan answered, "but not in a lot of places. For instance, you couldn't do it in a community property state like California or Texas."

"Not so," Bob said. "You can give them your separate property and your half of the community property…and that's all you own in those states. You just can't give them your spouse's half of the community property, or your spouse's separate property."

"Unless your spouse consents," Ted added.

"That's right," Bob agreed. "If your spouse consents, you can put everything into your name and leave it all to your children from a prior marriage."

"But that's not going to happen," Ted said, "at least not in the usual case."

"I agree," Bob said, "but you could consider the idea of negotiating more income for your spouse in exchange for his or her assets ultimately going to your children. See your Reading Notes on that."

Without looking at anyone in particular, Dan said, "I can see some people doing that…Say one person didn't have much separate property and the other one did. Income from the wealthier one's separate property might mean more than having half the community property."

"It might," Bob nodded, "but most people still like to have their own property."

Everyone at the table agreed.

"Now, in Ohio and Illinois," Ted said, "and other separate property forced share states like them, you can go further: If you can manage to get everything into your own name, you can leave it to your children and disinherit your spouse if you want to."

"Does that ever happen?" Cris asked.

"Not often," Bob answered. "We're looking at the extreme case here. The point to be made, though, is that it can be done…You just have to live in a state that allows it and then title all of the assets into your name. With that you can leave it to your children with T.O.D. deeds, joint and survivor accounts, living trust accounts, beneficiary designations on life insurance, IRAs, and so on."

"The survivor would still get priority claims, though, wouldn't she?" Cris asked. "I mean homestead, family allowance, and all that?"

"Only if there were assets in the probate estate," Bob answered.

"You would have to be mean-spirited not to even provide that," Cris said.

"Well," Bob answered, "both Dan and you have mentioned prenuptial agreements, and that's where you want to deal with all of these issues." Cris's eyes dropped to the table at the mention of her name with Dan's. Dan again noticed that she didn't seem to be herself. Maybe all of this was starting to get to her. He wanted to reassure her that none of it would be an issue when they did their prenup.

"That T.O.D. deed would need the other spouse's signature though, wouldn't it?" Ernie asked.

"Yes, to release dower," Bob agreed.

"So," Bob said, hitching his chair closer to the table, "that's community property and certain forced share states, but what if you live in a 1990 Uniform Probate Code augmented estate state? What then? How do you leave everything to your children and disinherit your spouse?"

"Have a post-nuptial agreement if it's allowed," Ernie said.

"Okay, but assume your spouse won't agree to it," Bob said.

"Then make gifts to your children," Ernie said.

"If it makes sense, you can do that," Bob agreed. "Gift your assets away at least two years before you die, or with annual exclusion gifts until your assets are equal to or less than your spouse's assets. Then, apart from priority claims, your spouse will have no election rights beyond a possible minimum $50,000 elective share."

"And if that isn't enough," Ted said, "if you can't achieve your goals through a spousal agreement, or gifts—and under gifts I include the irrevocable life insurance ideas mentioned in your Reading Notes—you can either establish domicile in a more favorable state or go into the asset protection arena."

"How many people do that asset protection stuff?" Frank asked.

"Not many," Bob answered, "but you might if there's enough money involved."

Betty turned to Ted with wide eyes: "Do you have to live on one of those little islands offshore?"

"No, but you might like to visit your money now and then," Ted said.

"Probably change planes four times and end up in a two-seater," Frank snickered.

"I picture a yacht or a private jet," Betty smiled.

"Okay," Bob concluded with a grin, "you get the point…It takes money, and if you've got it, you can make it happen."

"But for the rest of us, we'll have to give assets to our kids during our lifetime with no strings attached—perish the thought—or else we'll have to live in a state like Ohio or Illinois," Ted said.

"I'd like to perish that thought," Betty muttered. "Cold in winter."

"That's right," Bob said, "and the same is true—even more so—if you live in a state like New York or Pennsylvania…states that are not only cold in winter, but ones that include living trust and other assets in the surviving spouse's elective share, but then don't allow an offset for the surviving spouse's own assets."

Betty turned to Ted, again wide-eyed, and sang softly, "New York, New York!" and then, in a loud whisper: "*Broadway! Forty-Second Street!*"

"I like it there too," Ted laughed. "I'm not trying to disinherit anyone."

With the mention of New York, Bob glanced at Anne who was enjoying Betty's theatrics. He planned to let Anne down easy after class; his whole fantasy had come back to one reality: he loved Liz, she was home. He needed to reach into the core of his character and do the right thing. He wasn't going to ruin their lives. Funny, he thought, how the truth had hit him twice at unexpected moments during the previous Saturday: First in the morning, when he saw Liz ironing a blouse, unawares in jeans, a flannel shirt, and floppy slippers, and then later that evening at a party, when he saw her laughing with a friend. Bob realized in those moments just how much he loved her, how lucky he was. He had decided to talk with Liz after class and ask her to go to New York with him in December; they could rekindle their romance there in a dozen ways. He was relieved with his decision, but still uneasy. He needed to talk with Anne; he hoped she would be understanding, and quiet.

"Okay," Bob said, "you can review your Reading Notes on asset protection. And, as an aside, realize that asset protection in estate planning isn't just used to protect assets from spousal claims; sometimes it's your spouse who needs the protection…sometimes it's her own kids who want the money. But, to get back to the point here, if you want to leave everything to your children from a prior marriage, the most important thing to do is sit down with your estate planning attorney and lay it all out. Then you can see how asset protection fits into the picture.

"Now, let's move on and get into the world where most people live. Let's look at how to balance all of this between a surviving spouse and children of this marriage, if there are any, and your children from a prior marriage.

"For discussion purposes, let's look again at the *Gross* case that we talked about in week three…the class on prenuptial agreements. You'll recall that Mr. Gross had assets of about $550,000 when he got married in 1968, and assets of about $8,000,000 with a net worth of about $6,000,000 when he got divorced 14 years later in 1982."

"Whoa," Frank said, mimicking Betty's initial reaction to those numbers.

"Most people don't have that kind of wealth and never will," Ernie said.

"I know," Bob said, "but let's pretend. Let's pretend we're Mr. Gross and we didn't get a divorce. Assume we've been married for 15 years and we're doing estate planning. Let's say we want to achieve a fair balance between our spouse and our two imaginary children from a prior marriage.

"To shape the discussion," Bob went on, "let's keep our analysis within the framework set out in your Reading Notes. There we have three models showing how you might split assets between your spouse and your children: the California community property model, the 1990 UPC accrued percentage of an augmented estate model, and the intestate succession model which assumes you arrange all of your assets and benefits, including non-probate assets and benefits, to be distributed in accordance with the Statute of Descent and Distribution in your state. We'll use Ohio as an example for that. Also, for our discussion, let's assume Mrs.

Gross has no assets. Finally, let's ignore priority claims: With a $6,000,000 estate, we have enough to work with.

"Okay, who wants to take the California model?"

"I will," Anne said.

"Go," Bob smiled, impressed that Anne would jump right in.

"It's simple," Anne said. "Mr. Gross had $550,000 of separate property when he married and he has $6,000,000 now. The difference is $5,450,000, and that's marital property; half would be hers." Anne stopped to make calculations on her notepad and then said, "She would get $2,725,000 and his children would get the other $2,725,000 plus his $550,000 of separate property, or $3,275,000."

"Agreed," Bob smiled. "And what do you think of that?"

"Well, I think his children did very well considering they weren't involved," Anne said.

"You say that because the growth of assets took place while he was married, right?"

"Yes," Anne said.

"Fair enough," Bob said. "How about the 1990 UPC augmented estate model? Who wants that one?"

"I'll do it," Ernie said. "The augmented estate total is $6,000,000, and they were married for 15 years, right?"

"Right," Bob agreed.

"Okay," Ernie said, turning to his Chapter Nine Reading Notes to get the elective share percentage based upon the length of the marriage. "With a 15-year marriage, the surviving spouse's share is 50 percent of the augmented estate. That's $3,000,000 for the surviving spouse and $3,000,000 for the children."

"Based on these facts, you can see how she'd be better off if they lived in an augmented estate state like Minnesota," Bob said.

"Talk about cold," Betty mumbled.

"All right, now let's look at a Statute of Descent and Distribution model using Ohio as the example. Who wants it?"

"I'll do it," Dan said. "Ignoring the priority claims," he began, "and assuming Mr. Gross had at least two children, the split would be one-third to his surviving spouse and two-thirds to his children. So the $6,000,000 would be split $2,000,000 to Mrs. Gross and $4,000,000 to his kids."

"Correct," Bob said. "So to summarize, the surviving spouse would get $2,725,000 in California, $3,000,000 in a state like Minnesota, but only $2,000,000 in a state like Ohio. Now let's say they were only married for 5 years instead of 15 years…Does that change the result?"

"It wouldn't change the result in California or Ohio," Ernie answered, "because those rules aren't affected by the length of the marriage. She'd still get $2,725,000 in California and $2,000,000 in Ohio."

"Right," Bob agreed, "but what about a 1990 UPC augmented estate state like Minnesota?"

Ernie turned to his Chapter Nine Reading Notes before saying, "The elective share percentage for 5 years is only 15 percent. So 15 percent of $6,000,000 is $900,000. The wife would get $900,000 and the kids would get $5,100,000."

"Fair?" Bob asked.

"They weren't married long," Dan said.

"True enough," Bob said, "and that's a factor you can consider as you look at the issue of fairness. So, in those simple examples you could say that out of a $6,000,000 estate, a surviving spouse might get anywhere from $900,000 to $3,000,000 depending on how long they were married. You could argue that any number in between represents a fair share for the surviving spouse."

"I like that $3,000,000 number," Anne said.

Bob smiled without engaging Anne, shuffled his notes, and said, "One last example and then we'll finish up. Let's say we have a retired couple and he had assets of $500,000 when they married and she had $300,000. Let's say they live on their income from Social Security and the income from those assets. Assume they invested in certificates of deposit and the asset values have not changed. They both have two children from prior marriages. What are the splits?"

"Let me take this one," Frank said. "Under California community property law, they each have separate property and there's no marital property because nothing changed since they got married. So, subject to priority claims, he could leave his $500,000 to his kids if he wanted to, and she could leave her $300,000 to her kids."

"Very good," Bob said. "And would that be fair?"

"Maybe not," Cris said. "What if she had a health problem, or a child who needed help?"

"I agree. There are other factors to be considered," Bob said, "and that's where your personal analysis comes in. Now, what about the 1990 UPC…What if they lived in Minnesota, for instance? How much is the augmented estate?"

"It's $800,000," Cris said. "His $500,000 plus her $300,000."

"And what would she get from his estate?" Bob asked.

"If they were married for 15 years or more she would get 50 percent of $800,000, or $400,000," Cris answered. "But then you have to offset the $300,000 she already has so she would only get $100,000 from him."

"And if they were only married 5 years?" Bob asked.

Cris thought for a moment and said, "She'd get 15 percent of $800,000, which is $120,000, but since she has $300,000 of her own, I don't think she'd get anything from him."

"That's right," Bob agreed.

"What about Ohio?" Dan asked. "Would she be entitled to a third of his $500,000?"

"Yes," Bob said. "She'd get about $167,000."

Bob looked around the table and said, "You get the idea. She would get nothing from him under California community property law; she would get anywhere from nothing to $100,000, depending on the length of the marriage, under the 1990 UPC; and she would get about $167,000 under Ohio law."

"And remember, you can change the game when you move from one state to another," Ted said. "Remember that, absent an agreement, community property travels with you, and separate property can become community property."

"No wonder some ballplayers don't move when they get traded to another team," Frank said.

Betty just rolled her eyes.

"Here's the whole point of this," Bob said. "The three models we discussed give you boundaries you can use in determining what might be considered fair regardless of where you live. You can look to those models when you're looking for a balance between what's fair for a surviving spouse and what's fair for your children from a prior marriage. That's all we're doing here."

"What would you do?" Anne asked.

"Ah-ha," Bob sighed. "This is hypothetical of course, but I know I would do more for my wife than her elective share in Ohio, which is one-third of my probate estate. I'd look at the three models we just talked about, and then I'd work out something I thought was fair. I would first analyze my wife's needs and then my children's needs. I would consider any special needs, such as if I had a handicapped child. The main thing is, I would make sure my wife had enough to live on, make sure that she could meet her survival budget during retirement, and then some. That would be my floor."

"You'd do that even if your wife worked, or had assets of her own?" Frank asked. "Whatever happened to women's lib?"

"Yeah, women's lib aside, she deserves something just for being married to me," Bob laughed. Both Anne and Ted thought it an odd laugh for Bob, but Anne understood it better than Ted. She knew the awkwardness of the moment, and she also knew she couldn't see Bob after class, except to give him the note in her purse.

"Okay, to wrap this up," Bob said, "the goal in this segment is to achieve a fair balance between your spouse and your children. You have the three legal models to serve as a template, but you have to decide what's fair in your case. You have to decide what you want to do."

"What you want today could change tomorrow," Frank said.

"And it might," Bob agreed. "All you can do is set things up the way you want them today, and review your situation as you go along."

"Analyze it from year to year," Ted said.

"Analyze this," Betty said with a thrust of her left hand, "then analyze that," she said with a thrust of her right. "I've got my husband over here and my kids over there...and they should all be in psychoanalysis if you ask me," she grumped, then laughed. "What's a person to do?"

"Analyze their financial needs and their ability to handle money," Ted said. "Look at health issues, education needs, and retirement income needs. Do your financial planning homework as it relates to both your husband and your children."

"And despite what I said a minute ago, that includes what they have of their own in the way of assets and resources," Bob added, "including health insurance coverage. As Ted said, understand their needs."

"Financial management—if it's needed—is the most important thing," Ted said. "And that's your control over the use of your money...who gets it, how they get it, and when they get it. After that, consider the investment management, tax management, and personnel management issues we talked about. Put it all together based on what you have, what they need, and what you want to do for them."

"And how you want to be remembered," Dan added with a glance at Ted that caught Cris too.

"Right," Ted nodded. "That's the bottom line. How do you want to be remembered?"

"I want to be remembered for living it to the hilt," Frank said.

"Right!" Bob smiled. With that, he gave Ted a wink, closed his notebook, and said, "That's it! Next week it's your show; we'll hear what you want to do about all of this. We've covered a lot of ground over the last ten weeks; you've been a good class."

"Wouldn't have missed a word," Betty said.

"Well," Bob said, "you know my take on this: Protect your spouse first, you're *married* to each other; then think about your children. Work it out with your spouse...communicate with each other...listen to each other...take care of each other."

"I've been the devil's advocate," Ted said. "Most second or subsequent marriages don't last. You need to be a survivor, and your children will always be your children."

"Okay," Bob said, "either way, you know the issues, and you know how to get help. So on that note, Ted and I want to thank you for your attention, and if we can be of help in the future, please give us a call."

"Definitely," Anne said.

"See you for our final class next Wednesday at seven o'clock in the old classroom," Bob closed.

Ted had planned to see Cris before she left, but he was cornered by Ernie who wanted to discuss the format for next week. Cris was out the door and gone before he broke free.

Anne stopped for a moment outside and slipped Bob a note as she told him she had to head straight home; her daughter Terry had come in early for her school break. Bob shrugged, said he understood, turned up his collar against the chill of mid-November, and headed for his car. His salt-splattered Chrysler sat alone and cold against the building. He turned the ignition, switched on the overhead light, and read the note:

Dearest, sweetest, Bob…please destroy this note as soon as you read it. I know you will, I trust you.

Bob, I have decided it would be wrong to keep seeing you. You are a good, decent man and I want you to work on your marriage. Your wife sounds like a wonderful person, the right person for you. I'm going to work on my marriage, too. Hank and I had a long telephone conversation last night and we're going to make some changes in our life and make our marriage a priority. I would like you to meet Hank, so I am bringing him to class next week. I hope this will be okay. I think you will like him. As for us, I would still like to be friends. Let's stay in touch.

Affectionately,

Anne

Chapter Eleven

Class Presentations

From his window, he saw that the moon was full, a mottled sphere of gold sitting heavy on the trees, soon to ascend silver-white to its cold throne on high. Frank was fascinated by the moon and mystified by its effect on oceans and people. He knew it affected Marcie; it made her a little crazy. Well, he thought, she would see the moon from Vegas tonight. Marcie had cleaned out the apartment and left him only an angry goodbye. Frank pushed the play button and listened to her voice one more time:

> *"You louse, Frank! My sister saw you with a woman and two kids at a mall in Boardman last night. You were pushing a stroller! You're married, you bastard! I thought something funny was going on. I'm getting the fastest divorce you ever saw…then I'm headed for California to be with Matt. You remember Matt, don't you?! Get lost, you little creep!"*

Frank, though stunned by the rush of words and the emptiness around him, shrugged: If you live on the edge, you're going to take a fall. This, though, was a big fall, and his second one today: he'd lost his job that morning. There's got to be a silver lining here somewhere, Frank thought as he stood stoop-shouldered and watched the moon climb an invisible ladder into the night. Keep on truckin', he said to himself. Keep on truckin', you'll survive. With that thought, he turned from the window, crossed the empty room, and closed the door behind him. Frank headed for class, but would be glad when it was over. He needed to think about getting a job: he had a family to support and would need a paycheck before the moon turned full again.

———— ◇ ————

Hank sat in the back with Anne smiling beside him. He'd met each person in turn, and thanks to Anne, he knew something about all of them. He needed no primer for Ted and Bob who stood up front next to the teacher's desk, talking together. Hank had come a long way in the past week…not just from L.A. to Cleveland, but from the emotions of a jealous husband to those of a humbled man who, with pictures and tapes in hand, had made a life-changing decision. He had chosen forgiveness over anger and revenge; he had chosen love with all its joys, sorrows, and unknown depths of mutual dependence over the quiet safety of a solitary life without color, a life he knew had no more future than a worn dollar bill. He now craved a richer life for the years he had left. Before leaving L.A., Hank had destroyed the evidence he had of her indiscretions, burned it, and placed a telephone call to a lonely woman who needed his love, a love he had struggled to give, but now wanted to give without measure. He too needed forgiveness…He had been a distant husband; he needed to warm up, he thought, and he would have to learn to trust. He would have to change. Hank pondered that thought all the way back from the coast. Despite years in the same groove, he now wanted to take a new course, and he would start with what he saw as the essence of love. Anne was who she was, and he would embrace that: any lines she had crossed would be erased from his mind, and he would work to fill the void in her heart. The resonant sound of Bob's voice over the quiet chatter of Anne and Betty brought him back to the moment.

"Who wants to be first?" Bob asked, smiling as he moved out from behind the desk and surveyed the group, tonight expanded by two. He saw that Ernie had brought his wife, and he had already met Hank, who was now sitting in back across the aisle from Anne. Everyone had taken their usual seats, except Anne was now in back and Ted had moved up front and taken her old seat in front of Dan.

"I'll go first," Ernie said.

"Good," Bob said as Ernie got up and started to move to the front. "If you can," Bob said to the whole class, "tell us about your ideas for financial planning, estate planning, and retirement planning in your marriage."

"Okay," Ernie said as he faced the class.

Bob sat down.

"Financial planning. Jennie and I…and that's Jennie there, I wanted her to be part of this tonight…Jennie and I needed to talk about all of this…We had avoided the whole subject for so long; well, we just talked it through and it wasn't anywhere near as bad as we thought. Right, Jen?"

Jennie smiled her agreement.

"Jennie's biggest asset is her house. She doesn't want to lose the house—that's her anchor—and she wants to leave it to her daughters, Beth and Amy. And that's fine with me…but I've put a lot into the house, and I was worried about a place to live if anything happened to Jennie. So here's what we've worked out: Jennie knows I've paid the mortgage, taxes, insurance, and all the running expenses, so in exchange for that, she's going to give me a life estate in the house."

"Explain to us what you mean by that," Bob said.

"Well, if anything happens to Jennie, I can stay in the house as long as I live. I just have to keep it up and pay the taxes and insurance."

"And what if you didn't want to live there anymore, or couldn't live there?" Ted asked.

"Jennie's going to put the house into a trust, and I'll be able to direct the trustee to sell it and either buy something else for me, or invest the money and pay me the income. I could then use the income to pay rent on another place. The principal would stay in the trust, though. Then when I die, whatever is in the trust, either the house or the sale proceeds from the house, goes to Beth and Amy."

"Who's the trustee?" Bob asked.

"Jennie will be trustee while she's living, then her brother, followed by Beth and Amy."

"Sounds like a good solution," Ted said.

"I agree," Bob said. "The children will eventually get the house, or its value, but in the meantime, you have a place to live, or income to help pay your rent."

"You understand," Ted said, "that the children will lose the income they would have gotten if they had inherited the house right away and sold it. On the other hand, if their mother had had to pay the mortgage and taxes and insurance and upkeep over the years, they would have inherited that much less anyway."

"We do understand that," Ernie said, "and we're okay with it."

"But the children will get all the appreciation that takes place until the house is sold," Bob added, then asked, "Anything else?"

"Our two biggest hurdles are college costs for the girls and our retirement. Beth will start college next year, and Amy two years after that, so Jennie is going to go back to work for 5 or 6 years to help out. We figure that if the girls go to state schools and work summers we can make it. They may have to get student loans, but that wouldn't be the end of the world.

"Retirement planning is a bigger challenge because I've only got about 10 more years. But I've interviewed for a job with another company, and they made me an offer for more money. I start next week. It's a growing company, and they've got good benefits including a 401(k) plan and a company stock purchase plan. I'm going to max everything I can into those plans."

"That's great," Bob said. "Put away as much as you can and try to do something on the outside for diversification…maybe a ROTH IRA for example."

"Right," Ernie said.

"How about estate planning?" Bob asked.

"Well, if anything happens to me, Jennie will have her house, some savings of her own, Social Security, and my group life insurance and retirement plans from work. The group life will cover her until I retire, and then, hopefully, the retirement plans will be enough."

"What about your own kids?" Ted asked.

"I have some life insurance for them," Ernie answered. "I have to keep it up until I die, but I want them to have something. I've got four kids, and they could all use some help."

"And," Bob said, "if Jennie should predecease you, you'll have a place to live, and you'll have your Social Security and your retirement plans."

"Right," Ernie said.

"Anything else?" Bob asked.

"Nope."

"Okay," Bob said, "we thank you for that. Good job. It looks to me like retirement planning is your key issue."

Ernie nodded his agreement.

"Betty, you look like you want to go next," Bob said as Ernie moved back to his seat next to Jennie.

"That's fine with me," Betty said. Betty had given this a lot of thought and had decided two things: She would tell a half-truth to be credible, and she would keep it short and simple. Betty's fear was that Baker would want a divorce if he learned about the money. The 38 million after-tax had grown to 40 million. It wasn't inherited money, and it wasn't a gift, so it must be marital property that would be split upon divorce. Baker would walk for 20 million. She couldn't let that happen.

Betty moved to the front of the room, turned to face the class, and said: "Financial planning isn't a big problem with Baker and me. We just don't do it, never have. I keep the checkbook and handle the money, but to be honest, I don't keep close tabs on it. We live simply, except once a month we take a trip to gamble." At that, she paused to enjoy the looks she got, especially from Anne. "We take bus trips to Windsor, Ontario, or Niagara, but sometimes we hit Atlantic City. We get to Vegas once or twice a year because of the hotel and the swimming pool, and because Baker likes the Black Jack there. A little gambling's our only entertainment. That and TV."

"I hope you're not gambling with your retirement money," Bob said.

"No…I'm in CDs," Betty quipped, evoking a laugh, but then she got serious. "Retirement is part of my problem," she said. "I came into a little money last year and I want to make sure it lasts, and I also want to leave something for my kids. I don't want Baker to get it because he might gamble it. I need some kind of asset protection."

There was silence following this marital candor. Then, to test the advice Ace Charles had given her, she said, "I'm thinking of putting it into a trust or one of those limited liability companies. What do you think?"

"Can't say for sure," Bob answered, not knowing if Betty was pulling their legs, "but you should sit down with an estate planning attorney, and probably a financial planner, and work through your options."

"Okay," Betty said and started for her seat.

"Anything else?" Bob asked.

"Nope," she said as she sat down, "that's it. It's not a lot of money, but I don't want to lose it."

"You could lock some of it up with an annuity," Ted said. "That would guarantee a retirement income."

"I didn't like the sound of those annuities," Betty replied, satisfied that she had pulled this off but knowing she'd gotten nothing in return.

"And we shouldn't get too specific here anyway," Bob added. "Sounds like you need planning…financial planning, estate planning, and retirement planning. Before we move on, what's the one thing you can say you got from this course?"

Betty just shook her head: "Investments, I guess. I learned a lot about that, about asset allocation and stuff." She didn't say anything else, and Bob let it go. Betty was smug now: she knew what she was going to do.

"Who's next?" Bob asked, not thrilled with Betty's performance.

"I'll go," Dan said, getting up and moving past Ted, and then past Bob at the teacher's desk to the white erasable blackboard on which he drew three large boxes, one above the other two. He put a dollar sign in the top box, a stick figure with a skirt in the lower left-hand box, and two plain stick figures in the lower right-hand box. His plan would be a revelation to Cris because they had agreed to unveil their own unvarnished ideas for each other, and then reconcile them later. Turning to the class, Dan said, "Here's my situation…My fiancée" (tapping the lower left-hand box) "is younger than I am, and I'm thinking that a joint and survivor annuity would be a good thing for her. She's a lot younger than I am, so I'm thinking of a variable annuity with a 50-50 asset allocation, equities, and fixed income. That way we would both have an income for life, and there would be a good hedge for her against future inflation.

"For my two boys," Dan said, tapping the lower right-hand box, "I'm thinking of putting this into a living trust for them to get when I die. Meanwhile, my wife and I would have the income from the trust for as long as I live. What do you think of that?" Cris avoided Dan's glance and looked out the window.

"You've got the whole thing wrapped in two neat packages," Bob said. "Pretty interesting."

"Thanks," Dan said. "I want to keep it simple and make it so people don't quarrel about it."

"How about a prenup?" Ted asked.

"We're talking about it," Dan said with a quick look toward the windows. "My boys want me to do a prenup, and so does my fiancée, but they're not in total agreement as to what it should say, so I'm thinking about doing this. It seems fair to me."

"I recall from our first session," Bob said, "that you were concerned about how you would own things. Any further thoughts on that?"

"I'd like to keep it simple," Dan said. "I think we should each own what we have now, and then contribute our incomes to a joint account and pay the bills from there."

"Would your incomes be about the same?" Ted asked.

"She works," Dan said. He was now sorry that he had gotten into this discussion. Holding the teacher's pointer stick he'd gotten from the chalk tray, he shifted it from hand to hand and said, "Her income isn't as much as mine, although it might be someday. I have Social Security, and I have investment income," he said, tapping the top box.

"What about life insurance?" Ted asked.

"I have a little insurance."

"Long-term care insurance?" Ted asked.

"No, I don't plan on needing that. I don't picture myself in a nursing home." Dan turned aside and returned the pointer stick to the chalk tray.

"Well," Bob said, seeing that Dan was finished, and noting his decision about not going to a nursing home, "we thank you. The only suggestion I would make, Dan, is to sit down with a financial planner and chart your retirement income, and then come to a meeting of the minds with your fiancée."

"Makes sense," Dan said as he headed back to his seat.

Cris looked around the room, and when no one else volunteered, she stood, stepped to the front, took another look at Dan's blackboard plan, and turned to face the group.

"My biggest concern is for my 10-year-old son, Casey. I want him to have a good education, and that costs money. Then, of course, I'm also concerned about having enough to live on when I retire. I plan to be successful in my real estate career, but if that doesn't work I can always go back to nursing. That's my back-up.

"As I said before, I'm engaged to be engaged," Cris went on, speaking without looking at Ted in the front to her left, or Dan just two seats behind, "and my fiancée and I have talked about a prenuptial agreement, but I didn't want to do anything until I'd gone through this course. Now I think it's a must."

"What do you want from a prenup?" Bob asked.

"Well, I realize I have to take care of myself, and I realize my son is my responsibility, but I would like to have some help for his education, and I would also like some financial security for myself. After all, if we're married we'll be a family."

"Does your fiancée have children of his own?" Ted asked, seeing an opportunity to pry into an area she had once refused to discuss.

"Yes," Cris said, trying to hide the edge in her voice, "but I don't want to get into that; I just want to say that this course has shown me that I need a prenup."

"Is your fiancée insurable?" Ted asked.

Betty was enjoying this little show. She had picked up on these two while sitting at the end of the conference table in the other room, and she had a good idea who else was involved: With her very own eyes, she had seen Cris with Dan at the movies the week before, and she had been shocked, shocked, shocked. She now noticed that Dan, poor unaware Dan, was listening to Cris with a cocked ear.

"I don't know," Cris answered. "I suppose so." Dan opened his mouth to speak, but Cris shot him a look that said: Don't move! Don't speak!

Bob noticed that Cris, to his surprise, seemed nervous speaking before a group. He stood up and said, "Thank you, Cris. It looks like you have some things to negotiate yet for that prenup, but you still have time. And I agree with you: your career is your bedrock. Get yourself covered by a retirement plan, and try to save something for college every month."

"One final question though," Bob said. "Is there anything you learned from this course that stands out?"

"I don't care for annuities," Cris answered as she returned to her seat.

"Okay," Bob laughed, "you're not alone…but they do have their place. Look at Dan for instance."

"How about you, Frank, do you want to be next?"

"Sure, why not?" Frank got up and strode from back near the door, up the aisle past Dan and Ted, to the front where he faced the group. "I lost my job today," he said. A blend of groans was heard from Betty, Ernie, and Anne.

"So the first thing is, I've got to get a job; I have a family to support."

"Two baby boys," Anne whispered to Hank.

"But the good news is my wife and I are getting back together after a trial separation. That's the good news.

"Tonight I was going to talk about my financial plan and my estate plan, so I'll still do that. As soon as I'm working again, I'm going to see a financial planner. I need help with the whole idea, especially saving for college…how much to save every month and what to do with it. That's what I need to know."

"Your oldest is about 2 years old?" Bob asked.

"Not quite," Frank answered. "I've got 16 years or so to put something away. And that's the big question: How much?"

"A good financial planner will be able to help with that," Bob said. "The planner can do projections of future college costs, and can then convert them into monthly savings goals. You can also check the web sites we gave you in your Chapter Four Reading Notes."

"And you can look at Section 529 plans for investment," Ted added.

"Thanks, but my home is across the Pennsylvania line," Frank said. "I was only here temporarily."

"They have a Section 529 plan there," Ted responded, "but you can look at other state plans as well…You're not restricted to Pennsylvania."

"That's interesting that you live in Pennsylvania," Bob noted. "That means you're subject to their broader spousal election laws."

"It doesn't matter," Frank answered. "My estate plan is simple: I'm leaving everything to Sally. I have a form Will now, but as soon as I'm working I'm going to see an attorney about that testamentary trust idea, and I'm going to get some life insurance."

"You might also look at getting life insurance on your wife," Ted added. "With two little ones you'd have a tough time if something happened to her."

"I agree with that," Bob said. "And what about retirement planning? Any ideas there?"

"Haven't given that much thought," Frank said in a lowered voice. "Too much else happening right now."

"I understand," Bob said. "But work with your financial planner. Even small amounts set aside on a regular basis can make a big difference down the road.

"Anything else?" Bob asked, thinking Frank looked like a wet dog left standing in the rain.

"Nope, that's it!"

"Good luck on the job hunt," Ted added as Frank passed by.

"Your turn," Bob said, smiling, and extending an open hand toward Anne in the back. He had avoided calling on Anne until it was unavoidable. He was grateful for the way things had worked out, but now he wanted to avoid any further contact if he could…Her idea about staying in touch was ludicrous.

"Thank you," Anne said as she rose from her seat and smiled at Hank before starting to the front. She was dressy, as usual, with a delicate gold chain at her neck and a new diamond and gold bracelet from Rodeo Drive on one wrist to balance her ladies' Rolex on the other. The scent of Opium perfume moved up the aisle with her and cast a familiar net toward the recent objects of her affection. Both men shifted in their seats as they inhaled separate memories: Ted of the Copper Grill, Bob of lunch at John Q's.

"I'm happy to say," Anne began, looking from one side of the room to the other, but engaging no one except Hank, "that Hank and I have worked all this out.

"In terms of financial planning, Hank pays our mutual expenses, and we each pay our own personal expenses, except Hank buys me clothes and jewelry some-times…He just brought this back from California," Anne said, showing-off her new bracelet. "My daughter, Terry, will get this and other things when I'm gone.

"Terry will also get the trust my first husband set up for me at the bank; I'm getting the income from it, of course. In addition to that, because Hank doesn't have family, he also made a trust for me. It's set to go to charities when I die, but I think Hank's going to change that." Crinkling her nose, Alice said, "I think he might leave half of that to Terry.

"We're just now talking about retirement," she continued. "Hank is going to retire as soon as he can hire someone to take over his business. He wants to sell his distributorship and retire so we can spend more time together." At this point, Anne turned to Frank, who was sitting in the back by the door, and said, "Frank, I'm sorry to hear you lost your job, but I remember you saying that someday you would like to have your own company. Maybe you and Hank should talk. I know you're in sales." She then turned to Hank and said, "What do you think, hon?"

Hank, looking like a man who had just slipped on ice, turned to Frank and said, "Sure…call me tomorrow…we'll talk."

"Great," Frank said, hiking himself up in his seat. "That would be great."

"It would be wonderful," Anne smiled. "Hank wants to spend more time at home and be completely retired within a year. In the meantime, I'm going to travel with him when he goes out of town. That's our retirement plan: We're going to spend more time together.

"Oh," Anne concluded, "the one thing I wanted to be sure to mention is that I got a lot out of this course: I now understand the different kinds of trusts and I learned more about investments. I feel more in control of how things are done at the bank."

With that, Anne looked to Bob, raised both hands, and said: "That's it, really."

"Okay," Bob said, amused at how different Anne acted with Hank there, "it sounds like you've got it all together. And good luck on selling your business," he said with a raised voice to Hank. "There are ways to do that so it's a win-win sit-uation for both parties."

"Maybe you can be of help there," Hank said.

Bob nodded, "Glad to be of help." Cripes, he thought, what am I doing?

"Well," Bob then said, moving from behind the desk and aware that Hank was still evaluating him, "you all did very well. There's a lot to this, but I feel you have a good grasp of the issues, and you know where to get help. If there are questions in the future, check your Reading Note references, and feel free to call Ted or me. On that note, Ted and I want to thank you and wish you the very best. You've been a good class."

"What about you guys?" Ernie asked. "What are you doing about all this?"

"Well," Bob said, surprised but willing to respond without giving details: "As you might expect, I have a living trust that becomes a marital trust/credit shelter trust combination upon death for the benefit of my wife and two daughters. I have my life insurance payable to that.

"The big push," he continued, scanning the group and then coming back to Ernie, "is to save for college…but we're halfway there, and the girls know they'll have to help out. After college is out of the way, I'll concentrate on retirement. We have a buy-out plan at the firm for when a partner retires, but if the firm were ever to break up, I'd be out of luck…Not that I see that happening. Nevertheless, I need to save and invest more on my own. So," (with his hands open to the class) "I'm no different than you.

"And you, Ted?" Bob gestured with a smile as he backed toward the teacher's desk and sat on the edge. He knew Ted had a simple will that left his property to some cousins and a couple of charities.

Only half-listening while Bob spoke, Ted had used the rest of his mind to figure out what he might say. Unsure, he rose from his seat, looked across at Cris, and continued to look at her as he strode to the center of the room. Her eyes never left his until he stopped to face the class.

"There's a woman I'm asking to marry me," Ted said, staring at the back wall, and then, as his eyes dropped to meet those of the group in front of him, he continued, "and I'm going to tell you my plans for her."

"Oh, Ted!" Anne exclaimed. "Who is she?" Ted ignored the question and thought the look of shock on her husband's face was somehow fitting.

"When we get married," Ted began, "we're going to make all of our plans together. And she doesn't know it yet, but I want to adopt her young son as my own. We'll be a family, and I'll be his Dad…We'll do things together. And I'll see that he has money to go to college if he wants to.

"In addition, she and I will buy our own home," Ted said as he began to pace back and forth, noting the look on Bob's face, "and we'll take care of each other. I hope we can travel too, and someday get a cottage at a lake.

"Financially," he went on as he stopped in the middle again, "we can plan it out together…I'll get enough life insurance so she doesn't have to worry, and we can invest our savings for the future. We'll take care of each other and grow old like two peas in a pod. I love her…I want to spend the rest of my life with her.

"That's my plan," Ted said with a quick glance at Cris, then Bob, before he started for his seat amid a rush of questions and follow-up chatter. Ted ignored it all as he sat down and stole a look at Cris. She met his eyes until Bob eased off the desk and said, "When did this happen? You son of a gun, you never told me!"

Awkward and vulnerable, Ted grinned but did not answer. His words had come unscripted from a shaky place within. Now he wished he could disappear before their eyes.

"Wow," Bob said to the class with a wave to cut-short the buzz, "what better way to end the course than with a wedding announcement!"

The class gave Bob and Ted a round of applause with smiles from all and several thumbs up to Ted. The group chattered among themselves as they looked at Ted and gathered their coats and class notes, and headed out the door, down the hall, and through the outside door to the parking lot. Bob held Ted back and they stood at the top of the outside steps with Ted hedging questions until he saw something that stopped him in mid sentence: He saw Cris get into Dan's old Buick and watched them cross the parking lot and head down Jefferson Street. "I'll be damned," he said. "Did you see that? Did you see Cris leave with Dan?"

"Anything's possible," Bob said, "Do you think Dan's the guy she's going to marry?"

"Not if I can help it," Ted said, starting down the steps.

"Where are you going?" Bob called.

"I've got a load in the washer at the Duds and Diapers," Ted called back, "then I don't know where I'm going," he lied.

"Take it easy," Bob called, perplexed by the whole thing. He moved down the steps and walked toward his own car, wondering about Ted, but looking forward to getting home. Liz would have dinner waiting: two petite filet mignons with au gratin potatoes, caesar salads, and a bottle of good California cabernet sauvignon. Life is made up of moments; they come and they go. This would be a special moment with Liz. They were celebrating the end of the course and, for Bob, a new beginning with his precious friend.

As the Buick made the turn onto Chagrin Boulevard, Dan put an arm around Cris and patted her shoulder. "I'm glad that's over," he said.

"Me too," Cris replied, looking straight ahead. Just then, her cell phone went off in her purse. Retrieving it with alarm (she always kept it on so Casey could reach her), she said, "Hello?"

"Cris! What is going on? Is Dan the other guy? My God, I can't believe this!"

"I'm sorry, Mr. Henderson, I don't have the file, I'll have to handle that in the morning."

"I'm coming over to the house!" Ted said in a voice that hurt Cris's ear.

"No, Mr. Henderson, don't do that," Cris said in a rising voice, "We can talk in the morning." She then terminated the call and turned off the power.

"Who was that?" Dan asked. "I couldn't hear what he said, but whoever it was sounded like a madman!"

"It was just Mr. Henderson from the office," Cris said. "He gets mad if he thinks he missed a sale."

"We've got to talk about that," Dan said, "I think you're working too hard."

———— ◇ ————

Ted sat alone, looking out the front window of the empty laundromat. He had picked up a Geppetto's pepperoni pizza on the way over...his favorite comfort food. He had just finished his first slice and was taking a sip of diet Pepsi when headlights came through the window, full in his face, and then cut out. He sat up straight and blinked as a figure came through the door.

"Hi, Teddy, I thought this was the place. I heard you yell to Bob."

"Betty, what are you doing here?"

"I want to talk to you, Teddy, but first I have to ask you a question: If that woman doesn't marry you, what are you going to do?"

"I'll run with the bulls in Pamplona."

Betty laughed. "And if you survive that, what are you going to do?"

"I don't know."

"Teddy, I know you're mixed up now, but I've got an offer you can't refuse. This is going to make you a happy boy."

"What offer?"

"Sit down because this is going to surprise you. Teddy, I'm a millionaire forty times over! Can you believe that?"

"No," Ted said. (Is she nuts or what?)

"Can I have a piece of that pizza?" Betty asked. "It looks so-o-o good."

"Sure," Ted said, sliding the warm box across.

"Here's the deal," Betty said, "and I don't need an answer tonight; I've got to get home to Baker, and you and I can talk in the next day or two. Teddy, I can't prove this to you right now, but I won the lottery last year...I have 40 million dollars."

"You have 40 million dollars?"

"Yes...and I want you to handle it. I want you to figure out all that investment stuff and all that asset protection stuff. I don't want Baker to get it, or even to know about it. I know you won't tell him."

"Wow," Ted said. "*Wowie-ka-zowie.* Betty, I can't believe it...I'm sorry."

"I'll prove it to you tomorrow; I'll take you to meet Ace, my accountant."

"You don't mean Ace Charles!"

"Yes, I do indeed."

"You *do* need help Betty."

"We can talk about Ace if you want, but Teddy, I want you to handle everything for me. You can use Bob if you need to, but you're my man."

"If this is true, I'd have to use Bob," Ted replied, now giving full attention to the matter.

"We can work out the details," Betty said, "but I'm offering you a base salary of $150,000 plus half a percent of the assets invested."

"You've got 40 million invested…after tax?"

"Yep…and Ace tells me it's all in safe stuff."

Ted did the math: $150,000 plus $200,000. "I'd need a long-term contract," he said.

"I'll give you a 10-year guarantee on the base, rolling forward each year for another 10 years."

"That's a $1,500,000 guarantee," Ted said.

"Unless you quit," Betty said, "then there's no guarantee."

"Make it 5 years if I quit," Ted said. "I'd be giving up a career."

"Teddy, you're washing your clothes in a laundromat…I'm offering you a future, and I'll cover your travel expenses to boot. You ever been to Vegas? No? You'll like it, believe me!"

"I don't know, Betty. Even if this is all true, I want to marry a woman here…I said that tonight…and I'm supposed to make full partner next year."

"Teddy, we can work all that out; I know who you want to marry, and your firm can do my legal work. But, I want you, Teddy: We can be a team; you'll be like a son to me; we can do a lot of good together. I'm offering you a whole new world, Teddy. What do you think?"

"I think I'm interested," Ted said, taking a sip of Pepsi as he eyed the smiling woman before him in a pea coat, jeans, and tennis shoes. "I think I'm interested."

"Good," Betty said, "that's all I needed for tonight." She took Ted's hand as she bent over and kissed his forehead. "I'll call you tomorrow, honey."

"Thanks," Ted said as he stood and waved at the smiling woman going out the door and getting into a beat-up old car. This is nuts, he thought, shaking his head as he punched in the phone number to check his voicemail.

"Ted, I love you," the voice said, "and I want to marry you. Please call me tonight. Call me as soon as you get this."

Ted jumped up and down, yelling like a high school kid, but there was no one there to share his joy. He'd have to stop at Johnny Malloy's on the way home. First, though, he checked the time on the dryer and punched in Cris's number.

Postscript

The lives of Anne, Betty, Bob, Cris, Dan, Ernie, Frank, and Ted continue to swirl ahead. In the meantime, Bob and Ted are preparing to teach the Money and Marriage Two course to a new group, and you can be in the class if you wish.

If you would like to have your money and marriage experience reflected anonymously in *Money and Marriage Two—The Sequel*, you can get Bob and Ted's e-mail address at: WWW.MONEYANDMARRIAGETWO.COM. Click on "Contact Us." Please share enough information for Bob and Ted to help others with similar financial, estate, or retirement planning problems. If your story is used, it will be woven in with the experiences of others.

Money and Marriage Two—The Sequel will use a case study classroom approach. Old friends will flit in and out of the story. In addition to Bob and Ted, if you want to give Anne, Betty, Cris, Dan, Ernie, or Frank some advice, they can be reached through the same web site. Just click on "Contact Us." (If you wish, you can spice up their lives by contacting Baker, Casey, Hank, Jennie, Liz, Marcie, Sally, or Terry the same way.)

See you soon at Hunter-Wilson High!

J.F.

Chapter One—Reading Notes

Financial, Estate, and Retirement Planning

Financial Planning

Knowing what you want to achieve with money…and knowing where you stand at the moment: that is where financial planning begins. Your wants could include a vacation home, a college education for your children, a secure retirement, or anything else that requires a sum of money now or in the future. You need to convert wants into goals and then take an inventory of your assets. There is usually a gap between what you want and what you have. A financial plan is your written blueprint for closing that gap, for getting what you want.

Financial planning can include planning for current cash management (monthly income and expenses), insurance planning, estate planning, tax planning, and investment planning, as well as retirement planning and planning for specific shorter-term goals such as a new car, a special vacation, or a cabin at the lake. A comprehensive financial plan is a long-range plan that includes all of the above planning areas. It provides an all-weather track to your future.

A short-term specific financial plan can address any given subject, such as insurance planning, tax planning, or investment planning. It will concentrate on a current issue of importance to you. You might feel the need for a specific financial plan from time to time as problems arise, and if you do, you can consult with a specialist in that area, such as a tax or insurance specialist, to help you resolve the matter. But such specific financial plans are akin to crisis management; a better approach is to incorporate your specific financial plans into a comprehensive financial plan. In that way, all problems are analyzed within a balanced framework, and you are able to choose the most cost effective way to achieve your overall goals.

Financial planning in a second or subsequent marriage will ideally be a joint effort with common goals, but there can be different goals—stated or unstated—and different plans to achieve them. For example, a husband might put his planning emphasis on having a comfortable retirement with money for travel and on providing security for his wife upon his death. A wife might put her emphasis on having a nice home for the couple to enjoy, on helping her children along the way, and leaving an estate for them upon her death. Their separate goals might be reconciled as part of an overall comprehensive financial plan, but they could also remain disconnected and cause disagreements and secret manipulation of assets and income.

A number of financial planning issues will need to be reconciled in a second or subsequent marriage. Housing is one. Who will own the house? Who will pay the mortgage, insurance, taxes, utilities, repairs, and maintenance? How will major repairs and improvements be handled? How will appreciation in value be shared? Will it be shared?

Financial management is another issue. How will everyday living expenses be managed? Will your income—salaries, interest, dividends, Social Security, pensions, etc.—be co-mingled or kept separate? Whose money will be spent for everyday living expenses, and whose money will be saved and invested? Will savings and investments be jointly owned or separately owned? Who will control the checkbook? Who will make investment decisions?

These and other financial planning issues will be discussed in this course.

Estate Planning

Estate planning is a component of financial planning; it can provide important benefits for you, your spouse, and your children during your lifetime, and for your spouse and children—along with grandchildren and others, or charities if you so choose—after your death.

As part of a comprehensive financial plan, estate planning includes your plans to build and maintain an estate as well as your plan for its disposition. Building an estate can include building a business, investing in real estate or securities, and purchasing life insurance. Maintaining an estate includes investment planning, insurance planning, tax planning, gifting planning, and even retirement planning.

During your lifetime, you and your family will benefit from a broad approach to estate planning, and you, in a narrow sense, can take comfort in knowing that provisions have been made for your care in the event of your incapacity. In addition, you can have advance healthcare directives to avoid heroic or extraordinary efforts where the end is only prolonged.

Upon death, your plan can make use of specific estate planning tools such as wills, trusts, beneficiary designations on retirement accounts, and beneficiary designations on life insurance policies, as well as the use of deeds and joint accounts and transfer on death arrangements. There will be peace of mind in knowing you have a will and possibly a trust in place to assure an orderly and tax efficient disposition of your property. At death, your will, trust, life insurance, IRAs, etc., can provide for the distribution of your property to your loved ones and favorite charities at a time you desire. (With planning, you can control the use of your property for many years after your death, if you so choose.) You can also plan to minimize the publicity, expense, and delays of probate. In addition, your family will benefit from an estate plan arranged to save estate and gift taxes.

1-3

Estate planning in a second or subsequent marriage can be open and cooperative, or it can be a secretive thing where neither spouse fully discloses his or her plan to the other. Even in cases where it is open and cooperative during the lifetime of both spouses, it is sometimes changed by the surviving spouse after the death of the first spouse. A couple may have had a plan to leave everything to the surviving spouse, with the understanding that the surviving spouse would leave everything equally among all of their children. After the death of the first spouse, however, the surviving spouse may change the plan, make a new will, and leave everything to his or her own children. Old agreements and understandings can give way to repressed feelings and current pressures.

This course will discuss estate planning techniques in a second or subsequent marriage that will allow you to provide for a surviving spouse and yet protect your children from your prior marriage. You will be shown ways to have a cooperative plan with built-in safeguards. Nevertheless, you will also be shown planning techniques that will enable you to maximize benefits to your spouse, if you choose, or to minimize benefits to your spouse and maximize benefits to your children. Legal protections for a surviving spouse will be discussed at length.

Retirement Planning

Retirement planning is also a component of comprehensive financial planning; it starts with the following questions: When will you retire? Where will you retire? Why will you retire? How will you retire?

"When" you retire may be dictated by matters largely beyond your control. Your health or a job loss, for example, could force an early retirement, or market losses could cause a delay. Conversely, if your health is good and you have control over your job status, or if you already have sufficient assets, you can control when you retire.

Your answer to the "where" question will be influenced by your family relationships, the cost of living, health concerns, and your retirement lifestyle. Your happiness may depend upon where you retire. You may choose to move for family or for climate, or you may choose to stay where you are.

For some, the answer to the "why" question is as important as any other. Why retire at age 55, 60, 62, or 65? Or why retire at all? The answer may depend upon whether you will have meaningful activity in your life after you retire. "Meaningful activity," as used here, means that what you do with your time makes a difference in other people's lives, makes a contribution to the world, or is personally fulfilling. For some people, work is their most meaningful activity. If you are in this group, if you enjoy your work, you may choose to ease into retirement over a period of time or not retire at all. For others, there is no shortage of meaningful activities they want to pursue after retirement. They cannot wait to retire.

The "how" question, the financial one, is central to this course…Can you afford to retire? For example, how much will you need to spend each month after you retire? Do you base it on your current spending pattern? What about inflation? What about ups and downs in the market? How long does your money need to last?

In subsequent chapters, we will concentrate on the financial analysis you need to make in order to determine cost-of-living needs during retirement and the likelihood that your resources will be sufficient to meet those needs. Factors such as monthly expenses, income taxes, inflation, investment return, and longevity need to be carefully considered.

Retirement planning in a second or subsequent marriage will have the same challenges as retirement planning in a first marriage, as well as challenges of its own. If both of you have ample income and assets, retirement planning should be a smooth process even with separate estate planning goals. If you have limited income and assets and separate estate planning goals, you may have conflict and loss in the future. Still, if you have limited income and assets, a workable plan might be possible if you work together. This course will show you how to develop a workable plan…a survival approach to retirement planning which will serve you well both as an individual and as a couple. The object is to survive individually, and then as a couple, and then to live together as comfortably as you can, consistent with individual estate planning goals.

Chapter Two—Reading Notes

Property Ownership and Transfer

The word *property* embraces everything which you may own. The term includes your right to present or future possession and the right to use and enjoy the thing you possess. In general, it also includes the exclusive right of disposition: you can sell it, gift it, or leave it as an estate for others. Private ownership of property and freedom to transfer are fundamental rights in the U.S.A.

Nevertheless, as subsequent chapters will show, marriage carries with it legal curbs that limit your property rights. The law, derived from England, Spain, and France, is built upon a single marriage model: preservation of the marriage with mutual support and protection is in society's best interest. No one argues with that good intent, yet times have changed. You are in a second or subsequent marriage, perhaps with children. You have a new reality. A basic understanding of property law sources, terms, and concepts is needed, therefore, if you are to achieve your personal financial, estate, and retirement planning goals.

As background, property is classified as either *real* or *personal*.

Real Property

Real property is generally land and whatever is built upon or attached to land. A farm is real property. Your house is real property. The tacked down carpeting in your house is real property. Real estate and real property mean the same thing.

Real property, whether sold by contract or made the subject of a gift, is transferred by a written statement, a deed, signed by the property owner (or his or her authorized agent, e.g., under a power-of-attorney). Although the requirements can differ from state to state, a deed is usually signed in the presence of two witnesses with a Notary Public attesting the owner's or authorized agent's signature. If the owner is an individual owner and is married, it is recommended that his or her spouse (or authorized agent) also sign the deed to relinquish homestead or community property or his or her other legal rights in the property, known as dower for a woman, curtesy for a man. Delivery of the deed to the transferee and acceptance by the transferee completes the change of ownership. To evidence the change of ownership as a matter of public record, the deed must be recorded with the County Recorder where the real property is located.

2-2

Deeds

There are different kinds of deeds in use—with different warranties given by the transferor, and different estates created in the transferee:

- *General Warranty Deed*...the owner warrants that he or she owns the property and has the right to transfer it, that it is free from all liens and encumbrances, that no one will otherwise claim an interest in the property, and that the owner will defend the title for the transferee against the claims of all persons. The warrants extend not only to the transferee, but to the transferee's heirs, assigns, and successors, forever, against all persons. In order to supplement the owner's performance, the usual real estate contract will provide that the owner furnish the transferee with a title policy from an insurance company. When you give a general warranty deed, you (and more importantly, the title insurance company if a title policy is gotten) stand behind it forever.

- *Quit-Claim Deed*...provides no personal warranty or assurance of title; it transfers whatever interest or title the transferor may have in the property at the time. When you give a quit-claim deed you do not stand behind it. The protection of a title policy then becomes even more important to the transferee. A quit-claim deed might be used without a title policy in a family gift situation, or if you transfer ownership of real property to your own trust.

- *Limited (or Special) Warranty Deed*...essentially a warranty deed with a limited time frame, e.g., limited to the period of your ownership. It is not widely used, but is becoming popular in certain commercial and high-end residential transactions.

- *Fiduciary Deed*...A deed transferring an interest in real estate from an estate, trust, guardianship, or other fiduciary relationship. It essentially warrants that the fiduciary has the proper authority to transfer the property and is acting lawfully. It does not, however, warrant the title conveyed.

- *Joint and Survivor Deed*...could be in warranty form or quit-claim form. Either form provides for a present ownership interest in two or more persons (joint tenants) and a transfer of interest to the surviving joint tenant(s) upon the death of one. In this form, the property is not subject to probate administration upon a joint owner's death. You may own your home or other real property in joint and survivor form with your spouse, with a child, or with another person.

2-3

- *Tenants by the Entirety (or Estate by the Entirety) Deed*...a form of joint and survivor deed restricted in use to a husband and wife. It provides protection for the marital home against creditors of one of the spouses. Not all states recognize this form of deed.

- *Transfer on Death (T.O.D.) Deed*...could be in warranty form or quit-claim form. The T.O.D. deed names one or more beneficiaries who will become the owner(s) of the real property interest upon the death of the present owner. Like a joint and survivor deed and a tenants by the entirety deed, the property is not subject to probate administration upon the present owner's death. Unlike the joint and survivor deed and the tenants by the entirety deed, the named beneficiary has no ownership interest in the real property until the owner dies; the owner can change the beneficiary from one to another with a new T.O.D. deed. Again, if you are married, your spouse should also sign the deed. The T.O.D. deed is relatively new and recognized in only a few states.

- *Tenancy in Common Deed*...the most common form of co-ownership. Unlike the various forms of survivorship deeds above, the tenancy in common deed creates an estate of inheritance in each co-owner, i.e., upon the death of a co-owner, his or her interest vests in his or her heirs rather than in a surviving co-owner.

- *Mortgage Deed*...a deed given by the owner (and spouse) to a mortgage lender (typically a bank or savings and loan) that grants the lender a lien interest in the real property to secure payment of a loan obligation; the lender may seek foreclosure of the owner's title upon default under the loan agreement.

- *Deed of Trust*...a form of mortgage deed used in some states whereby a trustee holds legal title to the property until the loan obligation is satisfied.

Personal Property

Personal property is generally all property other than real property. It is classified as either *tangible* or *intangible*.

Tangible Personal Property

Tangible personal property has physical form and substance; the property itself may be seen and touched. Your furniture is tangible personal property, as is your automobile and your watch. Tangible personal property is transferred by a lawful change of physical possession. Where a title is required, such as to an automobile or a boat, the title must be signed by the owner and notarized, and the new owner must obtain a new title. Where a title is not required, mere transfer of possession with intent to transfer ownership, and acceptance by the transferee, is sufficient. Even where a title is not required, a writing such as a bill of sale in a commercial transaction, or an affidavit of gift for tax purposes, might still be used. Nevertheless, a writing is not always used: You can give your valuables to your children, for example, by mere transfer.

Intangible Personal Property

Intangible personal property is typically evidenced by a piece of paper representative of ownership, such as a stock certificate or stock option, a bond, mutual fund account, insurance policy, certificate of deposit, bank check, promissory note, or a patent, trademark, copyright, or goodwill. It includes intellectual and Internet property rights. Intangible personal property is transferred by a writing, an assignment, or a letter of authorization signed by the owner and given to the new owner. For an exchange of stock, the written instrument of transfer is typically given to the new owner through a third party, or transfer agent, who records the transfer. An example would be for you, as the owner, to sign the back of a stock certificate to effect its transfer or sale. Your stockbroker would then surrender the negotiable stock certificate to the transfer agent (usually a bank) and a new certificate would be issued to the buyer or the buyer's broker/dealer. (All of this may be done through accounting or "book entries" without the use of physical certificates.) A second example would be for you to transfer your interest in a limited partnership to your child by a written assignment evidencing the transfer. The transfer would only be effective if the limited partnership agreement allowed the transfer of a partnership interest. A third example would be for you, as an individual, to transfer mutual fund shares to yourself as trustee of your living trust. An assignment of ownership form would be provided by the mutual fund.

Your largest intangible personal property asset could be your retirement account, your IRA, or your employer-provided 401(k) account. The account will be held by a custodian or trustee for your individual benefit, and by law, it cannot be sold or transferred to another. Even your choice of beneficiary—clearly a second or subsequent marriage issue—may be governed by law. If the account is in an employer plan governed by the Employee Retirement Income Security Act (ERISA), your spouse must be the designated beneficiary upon your death unless you elect otherwise, and your spouse consents to the election. Community property laws, and the laws of certain other states, can also affect IRA accounts.

2-5

Property Ownership

The *ownership* of property may be *legal*, i.e., you (or you and others) have *title* to the property, or it may be *beneficial*, i.e., you (or you and others) are entitled to the benefits of ownership; you are the *equitable* owner(s). A trustee, for example, has *legal* title to trust property. Legal title may be held by more than one person, e.g., there may be two or three trustees. The beneficiary of the trust has *beneficial* or *equitable* ownership of the trust property and is entitled to its use and enjoyment as provided for in the trust agreement. There may be more than one beneficiary. As an example, you could live in your own home, but title to the property might be held by your 30-year-old twin daughters, as co-trustees, for your benefit. The trustees have legal title; you are the beneficial owner and may be said to have equitable title.

Sole Ownership vs. Joint Ownership

When legal title and equitable title are held together, there is outright ownership…whether by one person or by more than one person. If you alone have legal title and equitable title, you are the sole owner. If you share both legal title and equitable title with one or more other persons, you are a joint owner. Both real property and personal property can be owned individually or jointly with one or more other persons.

Forms of Joint Ownership

Joint ownership includes:
- Tenants in common;
- Joint tenants with right of survivorship (JTWROS);
- Tenants by the entirety;
- Tenants in partnership;
- Community property.

Tenants in Common

Tenants in common have equal or unequal undivided separate interests in the property (e.g., one-half each, or one-third each, or one-fourth to three-fourths, etc.) but share the common possession, use, and enjoyment of the property. If you and your cousin own Brownacre, a 200-acre parcel of rich farmland with known underground oil reserves, as tenants-in-common, you both can possess and use the whole property and enjoy the income proportionately. If you sell your interest to a stranger, your cousin and the stranger will then be tenants-in-common. If you die, your interest will become part of your estate. Your cousin has no right of survivorship. As a tenancy-in-common your cousin's separate interest will not be affected by the sale of your interest or by your death.

If you are married when your interest is sold, your spouse should sign the deed along with you in order to release dower, if any, and pass clear title. If you die instead, your spouse's interest in Brownacre will depend upon the state where Brownacre is located (e.g., Florida, Ohio, South Dakota, California, etc.), and whether or not you have a will, or whether the legal title to your interest is held in a trust. This will be developed further in Chapters Eight and Nine.

JTWROS

Joint tenants with right of survivorship in real property have equal (or in some states, it may be unequal) interests, acquired by the same conveyance, at the same time, with each having a right to the possession and use of the whole property. Generally speaking, upon the death of one, the whole property is owned by the other(s) who survive(s). Assume you and your sister own Greenacre, a 50-acre parcel of land ripe for development, as joint tenants with right of survivorship. If you die, your sister will own Greenacre outright. If you want to sell Greenacre, your sister will have to join you in the sale. If your sister is married, you will want to have her spouse sign the deed too. If you want to sell Greenacre and your sister does not, you can break the joint tenancy with right of survivorship—in some states—by conveying your interest to a third party, which will then create a tenancy in common. There are other states, like Ohio, however, where conveying less than the entire property will not break the joint tenancy with right of survivorship, but will merely substitute a new joint tenant.

JTWROS bank accounts are governed by state law, and during the lifetime of the joint tenants, the balance in the account is presumed to be owned proportionate to each joint tenant's contribution to the account. In states adopting the Uniform Probate Code (UPC) approach, the account is presumed to be owned equally if the joint tenants are married. Upon death (absent fraud or undue influence), account ownership passes to the survivor(s) by law. That result is conclusive in some states, but in other states following the UPC approach it is only a strong presumption. The presumption can be rebutted by clear and convincing evidence of a different intent. For example, the account may have been intended only for the convenience of a child who lives near an elderly parent.

2-7

Because property owned in JTWROS form is generally intended to pass upon death to the survivor(s), it is a popular form of ownership for husbands and wives to own bank accounts or a personal residence; it is fast and convenient; it avoids probate. But, at the same time, by avoiding probate the property is not part of the decedent's estate, not governed by a will, not subject—in many states—to the ordinary protections for a surviving spouse. For example, subject to state law, a bank account owned JTWROS by a parent and a child would, upon the parent's death, be owned outright by the child. It could, subject to state law, bypass probate and the surviving spouse.

Tenants by the Entirety

Tenants by the entirety is like JTWROS except:

A. The joint tenants must be husband and wife;

B. Neither spouse can cause a creditor to have any claim against the property without the consent of the other spouse; and

C. One spouse acting alone cannot break the joint tenancy and create a tenancy-in-common (although dissolution of the marriage will).

Tenants in Partnership

Tenants in partnership have an interest in specific property they own as partners, e.g., you and your neighbor can own an apartment building as partners. The property is possessed and used for partnership purposes and is subject to the claims of partnership creditors. There is no right to possess the property for your or your neighbor's personal use, and no claim may be made against the apartment building by your or your neighbor's personal creditors. The partnership itself, as a legal entity, is a form of intangible personal property owned by you and your neighbor as individual partners. Your ownership interest in the partnership is an interest in the profits and surplus of the partnership, not the assets of the partnership. Your *interest* in the partnership is subject to your personal creditors; your personal creditors might get a lien against your interest in the partnership, but not against partnership assets, not against the apartment building.

If you die, your partnership interest becomes part of your estate. What then happens to the partnership itself depends upon the partnership agreement, if there is one, or upon state law. The partnership interest may have to be sold by agreement to your partner, or provision may have been made for transfer of the interest to another person who will become your neighbor's new partner, or absent an agreement, the partnership may have to be dissolved. In any event, your surviving spouse has no right to become your neighbor's partner, unless the partnership agreement so provides.

A *limited partnership* can be an effective asset protection and estate planning tool, as can its younger half-brother, the *limited liability company*. Both can be used in a second or subsequent marriage and they will be discussed in Chapter Ten (Estate Planning).

Community Property

Community property is recognized in ten states: Alaska (if the couple so elects), Arizona, California, Idaho, Louisiana, Nevada, New Mexico, Texas, Washington, and Wisconsin. The term sometimes used in Alaska and Wisconsin is "marital property."

Generally, all wages and property acquired by either spouse in a community property state during marriage is community property, which means equal ownership and management by the spouses. Property received by gift or inheritance during marriage is an exception. Property acquired by gift or inheritance, along with a spouse's separate property acquired before marriage, remains that spouse's separate property. In some states, personal injury awards are also considered separate property. Nevertheless, depending upon the couple's conduct and intent, separate property can be transmuted and become community property. Each community property state has its own specific application of these general rules; no two community property states are quite alike.

Community property laws travel with the community property and are applicable to that property when a couple acquires it while living in a community property state and then moves to a separate property state, one of the other forty states. The couple can overcome community property law with a property ownership agreement between them that transmutes or reclassifies property from community status to separate property of one or the other. Nevertheless, it is an estate planning and tax issue, and couples in second or subsequent marriages need to be aware of the effect that moving from a community property state to a separate property state, or vice versa, can have on their estate plans. Professional help from an estate planning attorney is recommended, not only for those issues, but also to discuss the laws that control investment appreciation and earnings, and specific assets such as life insurance and retirement accounts, and their status (including spousal rights as beneficiary) under a particular state's community property laws. Professional help is also recommended when taking title to community property assets, and when a couple is planning to minimize estate and gift taxes. **2-9**

Sources of Property Law

Our laws come from elected and appointed state and federal judges through court decisions, and from federal and state statutes adopted by elected legislative bodies. Both federal and state statutes and case law play a role, but apart from federal tax and retirement plan laws, state laws control property ownership and transfer issues, and the laws of the states can vary one from another.

In years past, in an effort that will continue into the future, legal scholars and experts in various fields of law have encouraged state court judges and state legislatures to adopt laws which, to the experts and scholars, represent the best solutions to certain legal problems, solutions which will lead to predictable results across state lines. Individual scholars and experts express their views through law review articles and other publications, and as a body they speak through Restatements of the Law and through proposed Uniform Laws.

Restatements of the Law

Restatements are the work of The American Law Institute, a national body of prominent judges, lawyers, and teachers formed in 1923 in a general effort to codify legal principles and influence the common law, i.e., judge-made case law. The Restatement of most interest here is: *Restatement (Third) of Property: Wills and Other Donative Transfers*, Lawrence W. Waggoner, Reporter, Copyright 2003 by The American Law Institute. Portions of sections 8.1, 8.3, 9.1, 9.2, and 9.4 are reproduced or cited with permission. All rights reserved.

Uniform Laws

The National Conference of Commissioners on Uniform Laws was formed in 1892 upon the recommendation of the American Bar Association to draft laws where uniformity among the states would be "desirable and practicable." Lawyers with expertise in specific subjects are chosen by the states to draft laws for adoption. The final text as approved by the full Conference is then submitted to the fifty state legislatures for consideration, and, it is hoped, adoption.

To date, over two hundred Uniform Laws have been approved by the full Conference and proposed to the states, but only a few have been widely adopted. **2-10** The Uniform Laws as adopted are seldom uniform, however, because each state legislature is free to mold its own version of the law, and also because the Commissioners themselves sometimes propose later versions of the Uniform Law which are adopted as an update by some states but not by others. The *1969 Uniform Probate Code* and the *1990 Uniform Probate Code* are examples.

Following is a list of the Uniform Laws of most interest here. They are from a work by John H. Langbein and Lawrence W. Waggoner: *Uniform Trust and Estate Statutes, 2002-2003 Edition*, Copyright 2002 Foundation Press. Portions are reproduced or cited with permission. All rights reserved.

- *Uniform Disposition of Community Property Rights at Death Act (1971).* Adopted by fourteen states: Alaska, Arkansas, Colorado, Connecticut, Florida, Hawaii, Kentucky, Michigan, Montana, New York, North Carolina, Oregon, Virginia, and Wyoming. The list of adopting states is from: *Family Property Law: Cases and Materials on Wills, Trusts, and Future Interests (Third Edition)* p. 589, by Lawrence W. Waggoner et. al., © 2002 Foundation Press.
- *Uniform Marital Property Act (1983).* Adopted by Wisconsin.
- *Uniform Probate Code (1969).* Four states have adopted an elective share statute for a surviving spouse based upon the 1969 UPC: Maine, Nebraska, New Jersey, and Virginia. The list of adopting states is from: *Restatement (Third) of Property: Wills and Other Donative Transfers*, § 9.1, Reporters Note 3, Page 213.
- *Uniform Probate Code (1990).* Nine states have adopted an elective share for a surviving spouse based upon the 1990 UPC (modified by some states for formula or to exclude life insurance): Colorado (modified), Hawaii, Kansas, Minnesota, Montana (modified), North Dakota (modified), South Dakota, Utah (modified), West Virginia (modified). *See id.,* § 9.2, Reporter's Note 1, Page 225.
- *Uniform Premarital Agreement Act (1983).* Twenty-five states and the District of Columbia have adopted their own version of the Act: Arizona, Arkansas, California, Connecticut, Delaware, Hawaii, Idaho, Illinois, Indiana, Iowa, Kansas, Maine, Montana, Nebraska, Nevada, New Jersey, New Mexico, North Carolina, North Dakota, Oregon, Rhode Island, South Dakota, Texas, Utah, Virginia. Source: Legal Information Institute: *Uniform Matrimonial and Family Law Locator* (WWW.LAW.CORNELL.EDU/UNIFORM).

Uniform Laws and Restatements of the law influence and persuade our courts and legislatures because they are the product of our country's best legal scholars. Yet, due to political and other factors, they (especially the Uniform Laws) are not always adopted. Just as a state's Supreme Court may be liberal or conservative, so also its state legislature may be liberal or conservative, and further, its individual legislators may be subject to political pressures from various interest groups. Nevertheless, legislators are also attuned to public opinion, and they can be moved by their constituents. You, from your home, can be a lobby of one. If, after completing *Money and Marriage Two*, you would like to see the law changed in your state, you can help to do so: Write your state senator and state representative. Your voice will be heard. You, collectively, are the ultimate source of law.

Summary

As you can see, with its admixture of law and politics, property ownership and transfer is a complex maze which crosses federal and state legal boundaries. Yet property law is the framework you must use to achieve your financial, estate, and retirement planning goals. The basic terms and concepts outlined here will be our foundation for discussing the second or subsequent marriage issues which lie ahead.

Chapter Three—Reading Notes

Prenuptial Agreements

A prenuptial agreement, also known as a premarital agreement, or an antenuptial agreement, is a written contract you make before marriage to determine the rights you and your intended spouse each have to your own property, and to the property of the other, during marriage, upon the death of either, or upon your separation, annulment, dissolution of marriage, or divorce.

If properly executed and otherwise done in accordance with state law, a prenuptial agreement will be enforceable upon the death of either you or your spouse. The agreement generally provides for full disclosure of assets, obligations, and income, and a clear statement of rights being waived by the surviving spouse upon the death of the other. The courts generally will not enforce an agreement found to be unconscionable, one so unfair that it shocks the conscience, but even an unconscionable agreement might be enforced in some states if there is full and fair disclosure of each other's financial position before the agreement is signed.

Enforcement of the agreement upon separation, annulment, dissolution of marriage, or divorce is more problematic. Historically, the courts did not condone agreements that might be seen as promoting divorce, i.e., agreements where one could profit from a divorce. The courts supported the institution of marriage as a matter of public policy, and prenuptial agreements were not favored. The modern view is that prenuptial agreements, properly executed and otherwise done in accordance with state law, are generally enforceable as to property rights and the division of property upon separation, annulment, dissolution of marriage, or divorce.

Nevertheless, provisions in the agreement that relate to alimony or spousal support are generally only enforceable if they are found to be fair at the time the marriage ends. The court reserves the power to change support provisions previously agreed to by the parties. A change in circumstances since it was signed could make an agreement unconscionable at the time of enforcement. In the same way, the court will determine what constitutes adequate child support at the time the marriage ends. The parents cannot determine that by contract in advance.

In addition to assurance that the agreement was not entered into with a profit motive encouraging divorce, the court will want assurance that there was full disclosure of assets, obligations, and income, and that there was no fraud, coercion, duress, or overreaching by a more dominant, more sophisticated, or more clever party at the time the agreement was signed.

Because a contested prenuptial agreement will be carefully scrutinized by the court, the party defending the agreement will want to show that there was full and fair written disclosure of the type, value, and extent of all assets, obligations, and income, that both parties were represented by independent legal counsel, that there was adequate consideration for the agreement (promises made, or benefits conferred or denied), that the agreement was fair, and that it was voluntarily signed before the wedding (preferably at least a month before the wedding) without duress or coercion.

Twenty-five states and the District of Columbia have adopted the *Uniform Premarital Agreement Act (1983)* in an effort to achieve consistency. Among other things, the Act provides that a premarital agreement is not enforceable if the complaining party proves that the agreement was not signed voluntarily, or that the agreement was unconscionable when signed and, before signing, the complaining party: (1) was not given a fair and reasonable disclosure of the property or financial obligations of the other party; (2) did not voluntarily and expressly waive, in writing, any right to disclosure of the property or financial obligations of the other party beyond the disclosure provided; and (3) did not have, or reasonably could not have had, an adequate knowledge of the property or financial obligations of the other party. (See generally: *Uniform Trust and Estate Statutes, supra*; Page 701.)

In *Restatement (Third) of Property: Wills and Other Donative Transfers, supra*, § 9.4, it provides that, to be enforceable upon death against the surviving spouse, the enforcing party, i.e., the defender of the agreement, must show that the surviving spouse's consent was informed and was not obtained by undue influence or duress. A presumption of informed consent free of undue influence or duress arises if it is shown that, before the agreement was signed, the surviving spouse knew, at least approximately, the decedent's assets, asset values, income, and liabilities; or, the surviving spouse was provided—in timely fashion—with an accurate written statement of the decedent's significant assets and asset values, income, and liabilities.

In addition to such knowledge or written disclosure, the *Restatement* provides that the surviving spouse must be represented by independent legal counsel; or, if not, he or she must be advised in timely fashion to obtain independent legal counsel, and, in the event of financial need, he or she must receive an offer to pay the costs of said counsel. Finally, the agreement must state in ordinary laymen's terms the legal rights of the surviving spouse that were altered by the agreement, and the nature of the alterations.

Issues For Your Consideration

3-3

If you are contemplating a prenuptial agreement, you will want to consider the following:

A. What is your motivation for the agreement?
- To have your spouse assume your debts?
- To provide for a gift of property from your spouse?
- To keep control of your property during your marriage?
- To protect your home, investments, retirement accounts, and other property for your children in the event of your death?
- To protect your interest in a closely-held business?
- To bar your spouse from sharing a gift or inheritance that you expect to receive?
- To keep your property from your spouse should you separate or divorce?
- To provide for your support and housing if your spouse should die, or if you should separate or divorce?
- To provide for your children during the marriage, or after your or your spouse's death, or upon separation or divorce?
- To provide for certain estate and gift tax planning results?

B. Consider the value of the property you own: real estate, tangible personal property, intangible personal property (securities, bank accounts, business interests, retirement funds, etc.). Are you financially secure?

C. Consider the value of the property your intended spouse owns: real estate, tangible personal property, intangible personal property (securities, bank accounts, business interests, retirement funds, etc.). Is he or she financially secure?

D. Consider the source and amount of your income: salary, fees or commissions, investment income, business profits, Social Security, pensions, IRAs, etc. Is it adequate? Do you need additional support?

E. Consider the source and amount of your intended spouse's income: salary, fees or commissions, investment income, business profits, Social Security, pensions, IRAs, etc. Is it adequate? Does he or she need additional support?

F. Consider the inheritance either of you expect to receive from parents or others.

G. Consider your age, health, education, experience, and career status, and that of your intended spouse.

H. Consider the age, health, education, dependency, marital status, and career status of your children and your intended spouse's children.

I. Consider any claims you or your spouse will want to make against the property and income of the other:
   - during your marriage;
   - upon the death of the other;
   - upon separation or divorce.

J. Consider whether you or your children will be better off or worse off with a prenuptial agreement, or whether there will be no significant change in your financial condition:
   - during marriage;
   - upon death;
   - upon separation or divorce.

K. If there is to be a gift from one to the other in consideration of the marriage:
   - What is the value of the gift?
   - Will it be in the form of cash, securities, real estate, life insurance, an annuity policy, tangible personal property?
   - Will it occur before or after the wedding? Consider the gift tax effect if made before the wedding.

L. Should you or your spouse provide life insurance for the benefit of the other, or the other's children?

M. Should you or your spouse provide a trust fund for the benefit of the other, or the other's children?

N. Will any provision be made for the benefit of the less well-to-do spouse upon separation or divorce, or upon the death of the other?

O. Consider whether a surviving spouse's right to receive certain retirement plan death benefits will be retained or waived after the wedding. (A spouse, by law, must be the designated beneficiary of plan benefits covered by the Employee Retirement Income Security Act (ERISA) unless the covered employee elects another beneficiary, and the employee's spouse consents to the change during the marriage, i.e., *after the wedding*).

P. Consider whether you will reside in your former marital home, or your spouse's former marital home, or a home, condominium, or apartment that is new for both of you. Will one of you buy into or improve the other's home? How will you share the mortgage payments and the costs of insurance, taxes, repairs, maintenance, and improvements? How will you share appreciation in value? Upon the death of the homeowner, will the surviving spouse then own the home, or be able to stay there for a period of time? How long? For life? Until remarriage? What if the home is sold? What is to happen with the sale proceeds? Income from the proceeds? How will the deceased spouse's children be protected? A lien? Use of a trust?

Q. How will you share your mutual living expenses…food, clothing, medical care, travel, entertainment, etc.?

R. Who will provide support, maintenance, medical care, and education expenses for your minor children? Your spouse's minor children? How much will each of you contribute?

S. Will there be support, maintenance, medical care, or education expenses for the adult children or parents of either of you?

T. Do either of you have alimony, child support, or other financial commitments from a prior marriage? Are any retirement plan benefits vested in a former spouse under a Qualified Domestic Relations Order?

U. Do you or your intended spouse bring debt, bankruptcy, or credit rating problems to the marriage? Will one assume any debt of the other? Plan to exchange all financial information prior to signing the prenuptial agreement: credit reports (see Chapter Four Reading Notes for web sites), credit card statements, financial statements (assets, liabilities, and income), bank, investment, and retirement plan statements, etc.

V. Are there income tax issues with the Internal Revenue Service or a state or local government agency? Will you file joint or separate returns? Will there be a capital gains tax upon sale of a residence? If so, who will pay it? Will there be capital loss carry-overs from prior years? If so, who will benefit? How will income taxes be allocated? Exchange federal, state, and local income tax returns for the past 3 years (6 if warranted by the circumstances).

W. Finally, consider the marital rights to the property of the other that you will be waiving in a prenuptial agreement.

Rights Waived By Agreement

Each person contemplating a prenuptial agreement needs to know his or her legal rights in the absence of the agreement, i.e., what marital rights are being waived by the agreement?

Following is a list of marital rights you can anticipate waiving as part of a prenuptial agreement. Weigh them against the safeguards being provided by the agreement.

A. The right to dower or curtesy…the right to an interest in real estate owned by your spouse (or any statutory substitute for them);

B. The right to any share of your spouse's estate should he or she die without a will (otherwise you could be entitled to at least one-third or one-half of the estate, or possibly all of the estate);

C. The right, upon the death of your spouse, to exemptions provided by state law, and the right to remain in the residence, as well as a right to an allowance for support (possible benefits waived could include a right to your spouse's automobile(s), a right to temporary support, and a right to live in your spouse's house rent-free for a period of time, such as 1 year);

D. The right to elect against your spouse's will (without the agreement you could be entitled to at least one-third to one-half of the estate, possibly all of the estate);

E. The right to act as executor or administrator of your spouse's estate (the right to control property; the right to compensation);

F. The right to spousal support upon separation, dissolution of marriage, or divorce.

Summary

The safeguards and benefits to be provided by a prenuptial agreement can include preservation of your property for your children and provision for your support when the marriage ends by death or divorce. Weigh those safeguards and benefits against your legal rights in the absence of an agreement.

Before entering into or refusing to enter into a prenuptial agreement, you will want to consider the checklist above as well as the financial, estate, and retirement planning issues developed in subsequent chapters. A good agreement, one entered into after considering all the issues in a second or subsequent marriage, can benefit both you and your marriage.

Chapter Four—Reading Notes

4-1

Financial Planning

In its broadest sense, financial planning encompasses everything related to your future. It relates to where you live, how you live, how your children are educated, how you spend your leisure time, how much leisure time you have, where, when, and whether you travel, the medical care you receive, the amount you give to charity, the quality of your retirement, and the amount you leave to your children or others.

If you are young, planning for your higher education or job acquisition or career or business development may be where you start. At any point along the way, you may need to plan for debt reduction, purchase of a home, paying for a vacation, or purchase of a new car. The long-term concerns of most people relate to college funding for their children, retirement planning, and estate planning.

You will have other planning issues if you have already accumulated wealth. Wealth management will consist primarily of coordinating assets, information, and advisors to achieve effective investment planning, tax planning, and estate planning. Your investment planning will be concerned with asset allocation, diversification of investments within asset classes, growth, income, risk, safety, and overall achievement of your objectives. Tax planning will involve techniques to minimize or defer taxes, primarily the federal income tax. Estate planning will involve techniques to acquire and protect property to support your standard of living, and then to distribute that property to your beneficiaries with minimum taxes and expenses at death. Tax planning and estate planning will be ongoing family and intergenerational issues.

In a second or subsequent marriage, with each person coming from a different place, you will have to negotiate a number of matters related to money and its use. Your negotiations may be between equal partners or they may be one-sided. They may even be silent. Of necessity, you will negotiate or acquiesce to an everyday mutual financial plan for living expenses, but each of you may have a separate plan—by agreement or otherwise—related to other matters, such as estate planning. Your particular relationship, financial circumstances, attitudes, experience, and abilities will shape your financial plans. (It should be noted that the use of separate financial plans need not be adversarial. In fact, for many, it may be the most practical approach. Regardless of one's approach, the object is to meet your personal needs and goals while you achieve a workable and fair arrangement that will improve your marriage and family life.)

Questions To Ask Yourself

4-2

The following questions can serve as a guide for negotiating money matters in a second or subsequent marriage. The questions cast a broad net. The issues raised will highlight areas of easy agreement for a mutual financial plan and reveal other areas where further negotiation is needed. The end result may be a comprehensive financial plan for you as a couple, or it may be a combination of a mutual plan for some matters, and separate plans for others. In either event, your answers will clarify the issues and help shape your financial future. (Although the questions assume there is no prenuptial agreement, some questions are applicable even if there is a prenuptial agreement.)

A. What is important about money to me...to my spouse? Power...Control? Freedom...Independence? Security...Safety? Pride...Show? Love...Relationships?

B. Can we talk about money? Are decisions mutual?

C. Can I trust my spouse where money is concerned? Do I have reason to distrust him or her?

D. Am I willing to fully disclose my financial picture to my spouse? My income, spending, assets, liabilities, net worth...my expected gifts or inheritance? If not, what are the reasons?

E. Do we have the same tolerance for investment risk? Do we use the same investment advisor? Do we confer together or separately?

F. How do we share the expense of our mutual support and maintenance, i.e., food, clothing, shelter, transportation, insurance, utilities, medical and dental expense, education, personal care? What percentage does each of us pay? Is it fair? Should it be changed? Can it be changed?

G. How do we share the cost of travel, vacations, home entertainment, outside entertainment, and other life enrichments? Is it satisfactory? Should it be changed?

H. How do we share the cost of household repairs, maintenance, replacements, and improvements, e.g., a new kitchen or furnace, or lawn care, roof repair, etc.? Is it fair? Should it be changed?

I. What percentage of my salary, wages, fees, commissions, pension, or Social Security or other "earned income" do I contribute to our mutual support? What percentage does my spouse contribute? Is it fair? Should it be changed?

J. What percentage of my interest, dividends, annuity, capital gains, trust fund, or other "investment income" do I contribute to our mutual support? What percentage does my spouse contribute? Is it fair? Should it be changed?

K. Are my spouse and I able to control a desire for instant gratification? Do we buy things on credit that we cannot afford?

L. Who handles the mutual everyday expense money? Who signs the checks and does the banking? Is this satisfactory?

M. Does each of us have our own separate checking account? Our own separate funds for discretionary spending and investment?

N. How much does either of us provide for the support, maintenance, education, and medical expense of the other's children? Is this satisfactory?

O. Am I providing funds for my spouse's retirement and old age? Is my spouse providing funds for my retirement and old age? If not, what are the reasons? If so, how are we doing it?

P. Am I providing financial security for my spouse upon my death? Is my spouse providing financial security for me upon his or her death? If not, what are the reasons? If so, how are we doing it?

Q. Are we each planning to leave an estate for our own children upon our deaths? Should I provide an estate for my spouse's children? Should my spouse provide an estate for my children? Do either of us have charitable causes we wish to support?

R. Would my spouse continue our mutual estate plan after my death, or would he or she be likely to change it, e.g., make a new will? Would I?

S. Is our financial arrangement working? Do I feel that it is fair? Do I have enough freedom and latitude, or do I feel constrained?

T. Does our financial plan assure the long-term financial security of each of us as individuals, as well as the two of us as a couple?

Legal Duty of Support

As an underlying principle for all marriages, and as background for financial planning in a second or subsequent marriage, it should be noted that there are no hard and fast financial planning rules beyond the fundamental rule that each spouse has a duty to help support and maintain the other. The following state statutes, for example, reflect the broad application of the rule:

- California

  Husband and wife contract toward each other obligations of mutual respect, fidelity and support. (Ca. Code ξ 720)

- Illinois

  Every person who shall, without lawful excuse, neglect or refuse to provide for the support or maintenance of his or her spouse…shall be guilty of a Class A misdemeanor and shall be liable…in a civil action…(ILCS 750 15/1)

  4-4

- New York

  A married person is chargeable with the support of his or her spouse and, if possessed of sufficient means or able to earn such means, may be required to pay for his or her support a fair and reasonable sum, as the court may determine, having due regard to the circumstances of the respective parties. (N.Y.—McKinney's Family Court Act ξ 411)

- Ohio

  Each married person must support the person's self and spouse out of the person's property or by the person's labor. If a married person is unable to do so, the spouse of the married person must assist in the support so far as the spouse is able. (R.C. 3103(A))

- Texas

  Each spouse has the duty to support the other spouse. A spouse who fails to discharge the duty of support is liable to any person who provides necessaries to the spouse to whom support is owed. (TX Family Code ξ 2.501)

A legal encyclopedia—drawing on case law from across the country—has defined "maintenance and support" as follows:

> The terms "maintenance" and "support", it has been said, are not words of art, but have a relative meaning, according to the intention and surrounding circumstances of the parties, as well as the context in which they are used. Generally speaking, the words "support" and "maintenance" are used synonymously, to refer to food, clothing, and other conveniences, and shelter, including, in some cases, medicines, medical care, nursing care, funeral services, education, and reasonable personal care…" (Am Jur 2nd: 73, Support of Persons ξ 1)

The law, therefore, of practical necessity, establishes a flexible baseline that can be applied across the spectrum of human circumstances. But apart from the law, with its practical baseline, there is no model for mutual financial support, there is no set pattern of fairness which fits all couples. Each plan, to a large degree, will reflect the facts and circumstances, relationship, and force of personality of the parties involved. A given plan may be no more than an accord and satisfaction, an agreed compromise on major issues.

A worthy goal would be a financial plan agreed by both of you to represent a fair and equitable use of your resources, with assurance that the needs of each will be met during your lifetime, and with further assurance that the estate planning wishes of each will be honored, or enforced, in the future.

4-5

Develop a Financial Plan

Following is a brief guide you can use to develop a long-term mutual financial plan, or if needed, your own separate financial plan:

A. Set specific goals:

1. If you have debt, especially credit card debt, plan for its reduction, then elimination except for pre-retirement home mortgage debt. Set a date to be debt free. (Even if you are debt free, obtain your credit report. If there are errors or blemishes, write the agencies to correct the record and state your side of the story; work to clear and maintain your good reputation, a hidden asset.)

2. Build an emergency fund apart from your home equity and life insurance cash value...set a date when you will have at least 3 to 6 months worth of living expenses in a separate cash equivalent fund. (Longer-term goals might be 24 months by middle-age, 48 months by retirement.)

3. If homeownership is a goal, determine the amount of down payment needed and the date it is needed.

4. If you have children to educate, determine how much you will need for their education. When will it be needed? Estimate specific dollar amounts for each child. Consider the fact that college costs are rising faster than the general rate of inflation.

5. At what age will you retire? Where will you retire? How much monthly income, in today's dollars, will you need when you retire? Consider your current and projected standard of living. Consider long-term care needs.

6. Upon your death, how much of an estate do you wish to provide for your surviving spouse? How much for your children? How much for your spouse's children? How much for other family members or charity? Are beneficiary designations on life insurance policies, annuities, IRAs, 401(k)s, etc., consistent with your goals?

B. Summarize your current finances (see Appendix "A"...Personal Balance Sheet and Appendix "B"...Personal Cash Management Statement):

1. List all assets that you and your spouse own as joint tenants with right of survivorship.

2. List all your separate assets under **two** headings: (1) **pre-tax**, e.g., the taxable portion of U.S. savings bonds, tax-deferred annuities, individual retirement accounts or individual retirement annuities (IRAs—traditional, SEP, rollover), pension, profit-sharing, 401(k), and other "qualified" employer retirement plans; and (2) **after-tax**, e.g., all other personally owned assets: real estate; tangible personal property (approximate value of household goods and personal effects, jewelry, tools, computers, vehicles, etc.); and intangible personal property such as stocks, bonds, mutual funds, ROTH IRAs, business interests, life insurance policy values, and other assets, including cash equivalents (checking, savings, certificates of deposit, money market accounts, Treasury Bills), and the cost you paid into U.S. savings bonds, annuities, IRAs, etc.

3. List all your spouse's separate assets under the same two headings.

4. List all liabilities, credit card debt, notes, mortgages, loans, etc. under the same three categories: joint, your own separate obligations, your spouse's separate obligations.

5. List the source and amount of all current and near-term expected income and revenues, listed separately for you and for your spouse: salary, wages, fees, commissions, royalties, business profits, interest, dividends, trust income, Social Security, pension, proceeds from sale of assets, gifts, inheritance, etc.

6. List all current living expenses, and near-term expected purchase of assets. Examples include food, clothing, housing, auto payments, taxes, insurance, entertainment, new appliances, repairs, home improvements, etc. Use your last 2 years' actual expenditures from your checkbook and other sources as a guide, to be modified for expected future needs. Classify your payments under two headings: *fixed* (necessary) and *variable* (discretionary).

7. Calculate your net positive or negative cash flow by subtracting your expenses (6) from your income (5).

C. Analyze your financial information. Engage a financial planner, if needed, to help you do budget and cost-of-living projections, and to help you evaluate your goals and your prospects for achieving them:

1. Can your goals be reached given your current and expected assets, income, and expenses?

2. Can your income be increased or expenses reduced?

3. Can you save more? Are you willing to seek higher investment returns by assuming more risk? Can you get financial aid for education expenses? Are you willing to defer your retirement date?

4. Can you reduce taxes? Can you eliminate debt?

5. Are you adequately insured for large medical expenses? For disability? For personal liability? For long-term care? For death?

6. Do you need to change jobs (or get a job)? Does your spouse need to change jobs (or get a job)?

7. Do you need to modify your goals to ones you can reasonably expect to achieve?

D. Make a commitment to achieve your goals:

1. Reduce your goals and commitment to a written plan with specific priorities, dates, and amounts. Prepare a written Cash Management Statement along the lines of Appendix B, with revenues, expenses, and a savings margin tied to your goals. Allow some flexibility. Communicate your plan to your spouse and to your financial advisors.

E. Take action:

1. Reduce your expenditures, if needed;

2. Increase your savings, if needed;

3. Revise your investment strategy, if needed;

4. Revise your insurance program, if needed;

5. Revise your tax strategies, if needed;

6. Revise your estate plan, if needed;

7. Change jobs (or get a job), if needed.

F. Review your plan and your financial progress quarterly the first year, then semi-annually for the next 2 years, then at least annually. Anticipate changes; allow for flexibility; stay on course.

This is a brief overview of the process. Your particular analysis can be developed along the lines of a mutual plan where possible, or a separate plan where needed. For example, you may have a mutual goal for retirement, but separate goals for educating your or your spouse's children, or separate goals related to estate planning. You may also have separate plans for investments, for discretionary spending, or for making gifts to children or grandchildren. There may also be separate plans related to business assets, such as stock ownership in a closely-held corporation.

Get Professional Help

Professional help can add value to developing and implementing an overall financial plan. There are many variables, and key assumptions need to be made about risk, inflation, life expectancy, and investment return. Use of a Certified Financial Planner™ certificant (CFP®), Chartered Financial Consultant (ChFC), Personal Financial Specialist (CPA/PFS), or a member of the National Association of Personal Financial Advisors (NAPFA), is highly recommended in developing a comprehensive financial plan. Such a professional generalist will learn about you, see your whole picture, and then help you through the process one step at a time. You may start with a particular problem and then evolve your planning from there. There may also be a specific need for professional insurance, tax, investment, or estate analysis, and such a specialist can be brought in as needed. For example, a Certified Public Accountant (CPA) can be used for income tax matters, and an attorney should be used for estate planning.

An excerpt from a professional planning firm's questionnaire that will give you a sense of the financial planning process is attached as Appendix C. In addition, see The Certified Financial Planner Board of Standards, Inc. web site at WWW.CFP.NET to view the six-step financial planning process. Click on "Learn About Financial Planning."

A comprehensive financial plan will address issues in investments, insurance, income taxes, retirement planning, and estate planning, as well as cash-flow budgeting, and financial projections to fund education needs and retirement. It will also assist you in assessing your personal tolerance for risk. Subsequent chapters of this course will cover investments, insurance, retirement planning, and estate planning, including estate and gift taxes. The subject of income taxes is sprinkled lightly through the course. It is recommended, however, that you have a tax professional review all of your tax planning strategies.

Tax Planning

Following are items for you to discuss with your tax professional in the context of a second or subsequent marriage:

A. The rules relating to dependency, the so-called "kiddie tax," the capital gains tax, and the alternate minimum tax, if applicable.

B. Ideas regarding tax deferral:

1. Deferring the receipt of income; accelerating the payment of expenses;

2. Use of tax-deferred retirement savings vehicles, e.g., employer sponsored 401(k), Keogh, SEP, and SIMPLE Retirement Plans, ROTH IRAs, Deductible and Non-Deductible IRAs, and possible annuity or cash value life insurance plans for yourself and your spouse.

C. Tax credits which may be available to you:

1. Child tax credit;

2. Adoption tax credit;

3. Dependent Care Credit.

D. The availability of tax-favored education savings plans, tax credits, and deductions for education expenses:

1. Section 529 savings plans;

2. Coverdell IRAs (Education Saving Accounts/ESAs);

3. HOPE Scholarship Credits;

4. Lifetime Learning Credits;

5. Employer provided assistance;

6. Student loan interest deduction;

7. Deduction for higher education expenses.

E. The advantages and disadvantages of filing joint federal, state, and local income tax returns versus filing separate returns. Discuss how to share refunds or additional taxes owed.

F. The joint and several liability for income taxes you have when you file a joint return, i.e., you and your spouse are both liable for the tax, and it can be collected in full from either of you.

G. Applicability of the innocent spouse rules. Relief from tax liability is available to a spouse who can prove that she or he did not know, and had no reason to know, that the other spouse had underreported his or her income, or had claimed deductions for expenses that were not allowable. In filing a joint return, you will be liable for your spouse's underpayment of income taxes in the absence of innocent spouse relief.

Summary

Financial planning is an ongoing process, but just getting started is half the battle. Set your goals! Organize your data! Get professional help! Take action!

Following is a partial listing of web sites that may be of help to you:

FINANCIAL PLANNING WEB SITES

LOCATE PROFESSIONAL PLANNERS:

- WWW.CFP.NET — Certified Financial Planner™ consumer webpage with CFP® information and the six-step financial planning process.

- WWW.CPAPFS.ORG — American Institute of CPAs web site for Personal Financial Specialists. Find a CPA/PFS in your locale.

- WWW.FINACIALPRO.ORG — Society of Financial Service Professionals web site. Find a member Chartered Financial Consultant (ChFC) or Chartered Life Underwriter (CLU) in your locale.

- WWW.FPANET.ORG — Financial Planning Association web site. Click on "Public/Find A Planner" to find a member CFP® practitioner in your locale.

- WWW.NAPFA.ORG — National Association of Personal Financial Advisors home page. Find a fee-only financial planner in your locale.

OR…

- WWW.MONEYANDMARRIAGETWO.COM Provides links to all five sites.

COLLEGE FINANCE INFORMATION:

- WWW.COLLEGESAVINGS.COM — Section 529 Plans, Coverdell ESAs, IRAs for college, cost calculators, research resources.

- WWW.FASTWEB.COM — Free scholarship and college searches plus financial aid tools and more.

- WWW.FINAID.COM — Guide to scholarships and financial aid for college.

CHECK YOUR CREDIT RATING:

- WWW.CREDITREPORT.COM — For a fee, check your credit online. Information from the three major credit bureaus.

- WWW.FREECREDITREPORTSERVICE.COM Online credit reports from the three major bureaus and other debt-related information.

4-10

• WWW.MYFICO.COM	For a fee, check your credit as reported by the three major bureaus. Credit rating information.

MORTGAGE INFORMATION:

• WWW.BANKRATE.COM	Compare mortgage rates.
• WWW.HSH.COM	Consumer loan and home mortgage information.

INFORMATION FOR LOW INCOME AND DISABLED:

• WWW.DISABILITYRESOURCES.ORG	Information for each state on aid for the disabled.
• WWW.BENEFITSCHECKUP.COM	The National Council on Aging web site for people over age 55. Locate programs to help defray cost of living.

STEPFAMILY INFORMATION:

• WWW.STEPFAM.ORG	Educational information and resources for stepfamilies.

GENERAL FINANCIAL PLANNING WEB SITES:

• WWW.CNN.COM/MONEY	Broad-based CNN/Money Magazine site: personal finance, mutual funds, insurance, retirement, college costs, and more.
• WWW.FIDELITY.COM	Fidelity Investments home page.
• WWW.SMARTMONEY.COM	Personal finance, college, retirement, and other information.
• WWW.SOUNDMONEY.ORG	Minnesota public radio—personal finance.
• WWW.TROWEPRICE.COM	T. Rowe Price home page with calculators and more.
• WWW.VANGUARD.COM	Vanguard home page with calculators and more.
• WWW.YAHOO.COM	Yahoo! home page. Click on "Finance" for research and planning tools.

(Also check the mutual fund or brokerage firm site(s) of your choice.)

Chapter Five—Reading Notes

Investments

Investing money is not child's play, or a fool's game. 2000–2003 is proof of that. In 2003, interest rates dropped to the lowest level seen in 45 years. The stock market reflected the combined effects of job cuts, consumer uncertainty, war, terror, SARS, deflated prices, temporary tax cuts, and a world economy groping for traction. It is with this background in mind, as well as the run-up in the late 90s, that you must design and maintain an efficient and productive investment portfolio. If you are in a second or subsequent marriage, you will also want your spouse to have an efficient and productive investment portfolio because, whether your financial plans are mutual or separate, his or her investment results are going to affect your standard of living.

In that light, if you are an experienced investor, you can be of assistance to your spouse if he or she lacks experience. If you lack experience, you can learn investment basics, perhaps use a more experienced spouse as a sounding board, and then consult with a professional advisor. For many of us, use of a professional advisor will prove to be the most efficient way to gain long-term success.

By this time, you will have adopted a written financial plan, will have your goals, risk tolerance, and timetable before you, and will know how much you can invest on a continuing basis. The next step is to decide where to invest. It is a critical juncture, for many sirens call and conflicting advice is never far away. You can make your decisions alone, or you can hire an investment advisor to help you chart a course. The advisor you choose might be the same financial planner who helped develop your financial plan, but need not be. You might choose to implement your plan with a different advisor—a stockbroker or bank trust officer, for example—or other financial consultant.

Choosing an Investment Advisor

If you are going to hire an investment advisor, you will want to consider the following:

A. What is the person's background? What is the nature of his or her professional education, training, and experience?

B. What professional credentials does he or she have? For example, a person might be a financial planner, but is he or she a Certified Financial Planner™? A CFP® has adopted a code of professional ethics, has at least basic experience, and has completed a comprehensive course of study and testing. Nevertheless, this is not a litmus test for expertise in every subject. You must look more deeply into the person's investment background and experience; a professional designation does not assure you that the person has the depth of knowledge or experience you need. It is, however, a threshold, a door to be gone through, and a standard you can use to qualify prospective advisors.

C. Is the person part of a financially strong team or company having a depth of technical resources and a depth of management and research personnel, e.g., is the company a member firm of the New York Stock Exchange (NYSE), or the National Association of Securities Dealers (NASD)? How long has he or she been with the company? Is it his or her permanent career?

D. Has the person been recommended to you by someone you know to be an experienced and successful investor?

E. Are you comfortable with the person's integrity? Would you trust him or her with your money? Is he or she sincerely interested in helping you on a continuing basis?

F. How will the advisor be compensated? Fees? Commissions? A combination of fees and commissions? What is the formula? Is it competitive?

This is a screening process. It does not assure you of picking the right advisor, or of having a successful investment experience, but it greatly improves your chances. You will still need to monitor the relationship; if it does not work, you can change it.

Why not do it yourself? You can. It takes time, study, and discipline, but you can do it yourself. Many people do. You can chart your own course and captain your own ship. In fact, you should always be the person in control. Nevertheless, you will benefit a great deal if you have a good sounding board. You have to pay management fees or transaction costs in any event; why not have a professional on your side who can add value beyond his or her own marginal cost (especially if he or she can do a better job with your money than you can)? That, potentially, is your investment advisor. Interview at least three. Then, unless you are comfortable going it alone, hire one to share the driving, to be your co-pilot.

The balance of this chapter is intended to give you, the inexperienced investor in a second or subsequent marriage, the "101" basics you need in order to better communicate with your investment co-pilot.

Compound Interest

5-3

First, there is the concept of compound interest. One Thousand Dollars, today, has a present value of One Thousand Dollars. If you invest it, it can have a greater value in the future. How much greater depends upon how long you have it invested and the rate of return you realize.

Table A below shows the results of a single $1,000 invested for different periods of time at different rates of return. It shows that the longer the investment period, the greater the return. It also shows the effect of increasing the rate of return, e.g., in 30 years an 8 percent return is more than double a 5 percent return for the same period, and a 12 percent return is nearly triple an 8 percent return.

TABLE A

The Future Value of $1,000 invested at different rates of return.

PERIOD	5%	8%	12%
10 Years	$ 1629	$ 2159	$ 3106
20 Years	$ 2653	$ 4661	$ 9646
30 Years	$ 4322	$10,063	$29,960

Table B below shows the results of investing $1,000 per year at the beginning of each year for different periods of time and at different rates of return. It shows the benefits of continuous investing each year.

TABLE B

The Future Value of $1,000 per year invested at the beginning of each year.

PERIOD	5%	8%	12%
10 Years	$12,578	$ 14,487	$ 17,549
20 Years	$33,066	$ 45,762	$ 72,052
30 Years	$66,439	$113,283	$241,333

Although Tables A and B are based upon compound interest tables, you can easily get an idea of future values by applying the "Rule of 72," a calculation you can do in your head. The Rule of 72 is a simple but valuable tool to project the future value of an invested sum. Just divide the rate of investment return (e.g. 8 percent) into the number "72" and the answer tells you within a whisker how long it will take to double your money at that rate of return. For example, 72 ÷ 8 percent = 9 years. It will take 9 years to double the value of a sum invested at 8 percent. Or, 72 ÷ 12 percent = 6 years. Obviously, if money doubles every 6 years it will grow much faster than if it doubles every 9 years. That is compound interest. It is magic. With compound interest and the Rule of 72 as investment tools, you can be a master carpenter building your future.

Investment Risk

Next you will need to understand the concept of investment *risk*. You have heard the cliché "No pain, no gain." You have also heard "What goes up must come down." You have never heard "What goes down *must come up*." With investments, what goes down may not come back up. There is always that risk. Witness a company: Enron. Witness an industry: basic steel.

Current investment literature equates *risk* with *volatility*, meaning change in market value…the chance that an investment may go up or down in value from month to month (or day to day or year to year)…with higher risk investments having wider swings in value. One measure of that volatility, or risk, is "Standard Deviation," a measure of the fluctuation of returns around the arithmetic average return of an investment. History has shown that you can expect a security's total return (income plus or minus change in value) to fluctuate within one Standard Deviation of its arithmetic average return about 68 percent of the time, and within two Standard Deviations about 95 percent of the time. For example, if a security has a 10 percent average total return over a period of years with a Standard Deviation during the period of 18, the next year's return has a 68 percent chance of ranging between-8 percent and +28 percent, and a 95 percent chance of ranging between-26 percent and +46 percent.

U.S. Treasury Bills fluctuate little in value and therefore have a low Standard Deviation. Corporate bonds fluctuate more in value and therefore have a higher Standard Deviation. Common Stocks fluctuate even more, with small company stocks fluctuating more than large company stocks. They have the highest Standard Deviation, denoting the most risk. Your investment advisor can show you charts depicting the Standard Deviation for different securities, or portfolios of securities, or mutual funds. You can view their historic risk over different periods of time. The impression you may get is that things turn out all right if you keep the investment long enough ("Time heals all wounds"). That can be true. But risk can also be defined as the chance that the result you achieve will differ from the result you expect (which can be either good or bad). It can also be described as the chance that you will suffer a loss and not recover. You need to be able to discuss risk with your advisor. Some can accept more volatility, or risk, than others, but no one wants to suffer a loss. To paraphrase Warren Buffett and Yogi Berra: "You can win if you don't lose."

Risk and Return 5-5

Return is what you realize from an investment, what you get back in the form of income and change in value. You invest with an expected return in mind, one that you need in order to achieve your goals. There is risk that the return you actually realize may differ from the return you expect, or need. The greater the return you need, the greater the risk you have to take. If you only need a 4 percent return, you need take little or no risk to achieve it. You can expect to earn that over time with U.S. EE or I savings bonds, or insured certificates of deposit. If you need a 20 percent return, you will have to take significant risks. You will be a young robin flying in the shadow of hawks.

Know the return you need. A professionally prepared financial plan will show the return needed to meet your goals. Next, understand your personal tolerance for risk. Your financial plan should answer that question too. An evaluation of your risk tolerance will be made based upon a questionnaire completed by you, and it should be explained as part of your plan. The return you need to realize can then be matched to your risk tolerance to determine if your goals are realistic. You will not have a workable plan if you need to realize a 15 percent return but have a low tolerance for risk. You can have a workable plan if, for example, you need a 7 or 8 percent return and have a moderate tolerance for risk. If the return needed to realize your goals does not fit your risk tolerance, you either need to fit your risk tolerance to the return needed, or else revise your goals. This will be part of fine-tuning your financial plan. A workable plan requires a realistic balance between the desired return and your tolerance for risk. In finding that balance, look beyond descriptive labels such as "growth & income" or "moderate risk." Rather than accept such bland descriptions, ask whether the portfolio will pay for the risk you are taking. And, finally, consider your emotions. Examine the Standard Deviation for your particular portfolio: Can you stay the course through that range of volatility?

The concept of return needs to be further refined because of two outside realities: *taxes* and *inflation*.

Return After Income Tax

For our purposes, we will use an assumed "average tax rate" instead of a "marginal tax rate." Your average tax rate is generally found by dividing the combined federal, state, and local income taxes you pay by the adjusted gross income figure shown on your federal income tax return. Your marginal tax rate, on the other hand, is the rate of tax that would be applied to your next dollar of new, additional income. Use of your marginal rate (or a blend of your average and marginal rates) would be appropriate for receipt of assets that have not previously been taxed, e.g. IRA or 401(k) assets. Use of your average rate is appropriate for an existing "after-tax" investment portfolio.

5-6

If your average tax rate is 30 percent, and you earn 10 percent investment income, you will keep only 7 percent of the income after tax, your so-called after-tax income. But not all income needs to be taxed at your average rate: with planning you can lessen the taxes paid and improve your after-tax returns. First, note that until 2009, domestic and qualified foreign corporation dividends will be taxed at a maximum rate of 15 percent. Also, you may be able to invest in tax-deferred ways through your 401(k) plan at work or through Individual Retirement Accounts or tax-deferred annuities or U.S. EE or I savings bonds. With tax-deferred investments, you pay no tax currently; you keep all of your money working. Then consider tax-free municipal bonds, even variable life insurance if you are in the higher tax brackets.

You can also invest for capital gains instead of (or in addition to) ordinary interest and dividend income. The capital gains tax is a tax applied to the increase in value realized when you sell an asset. For example, if you pay $100 per share for a security and sell it for $150, you will have a capital gain of $50 per share subject to the capital gains tax, a tax that, if you own the security long enough, is levied at a rate lower than your marginal tax rate. Currently, the maximum capital gains tax rate is 15 percent for securities, and less for people in the lowest tax brackets. (Note: The 15 percent will become 20 percent in 2009 unless congress changes the law.) In order to qualify for capital gains tax treatment, you must own the asset for more than 12 months. Special rules apply to different types of assets.

Finally, you can plan to defer the receipt of income until you retire and are (perhaps) in a lower tax bracket. Deferred compensation, tax-deferred annuities, 401(k)s, U.S. savings bonds, and IRAs are examples of tax deferred investments. The combination of tax deferred growth and a lower tax rate in the future will enhance your total after-tax return.

Inflation

The other outside reality is inflation. It goes without saying that a gallon of gasoline costs more today than it did 10 years ago. The same can be said for food, clothing, shelter, medical care, and college costs. Looking ahead, it is safe to say that food, clothing, shelter, medical care, and college costs will all cost more 10 years from now than they do today. The inflation factor may not affect your standard of living today if you are working and realizing salary increases to keep pace. But your college funding, retirement funding, and standard of living during retirement will be seriously affected by inflation. You may have to save more now, or plan to work longer, in order to compensate. In addition, your investments will have to do even more work for you than anticipated; they not only have to realize the return required to meet your goals, but an additional return needed to offset inflation. Automatic annual Social Security increases will help that part of your income keep pace when you retire…assuming the continued viability of the system and assuming that built-in cost-of-living increases keep pace with inflation. But your investments will have to keep pace with the traffic as well. Therefore, for planning purposes, assume at least a 4 percent per year inflation factor. A 4½ percent factor is safer. Some planners, despite the recent low rates, even suggest 5 percent. Since World War II, inflation has averaged over 4 percent per year.

Your Real Return

As an example (to bring all of this together), assume that you need a return of 3 percent in today's dollars, after taxes and inflation and investment costs, in order to meet your future goals. That means you need a *real return* of 3 percent. If your combined federal, state, and local income tax rate (your *average* rate as opposed to your *marginal* rate) is projected to be 30 percent, and you assume a 4 percent rate of inflation, you will need a 10 percent *total realized return* on your investments after investment costs. *Total realized return* includes interest, dividends, and realized appreciation in value, or capital gains. A *total realized return* of 10 percent will net you *approximately* 3 percent in today's dollars after taxes and inflation (10 percent *total realized return*—30 percent in taxes = 7 percent *after-tax return*. 7 percent *after-tax return*—4 percent inflation = 3 percent *real return*).

Larger Returns Mean Greater Risk

Now, back to basics: *risk* and *return*. If you need a 10 percent *total realized return* you are going to have to take risks. You will not realize a 10 percent *total realized return* by investing in certificates of deposit or money market funds or savings bonds. The question then becomes, can you tolerate the risk you need to take in order to realize the larger equity return? If not, your goals need to be scaled back, or you need to save and invest more money. Over a period of years, using history as a guide, you probably can realize the larger return, but there is no guarantee. The picture in the rearview mirror may be rosy, but looking ahead, the scene is hazy. You could lose ground, suffer losses. Nevertheless, you still have to take calculated risks. If you take no risks you will lose ground to inflation, and probably taxes as well. A 5 percent no-risk savings account might lose 3 percent to inflation, leaving a 2 percent return before taxes. If the 5 percent is taxable, your real return will be negative. The so-called safe investment has its own assured risk...lost purchasing power because of taxes and inflation.

Types of Investment Assets

Cash

Despite historic low returns, there is a place for cash equivalent investments as part of an investment portfolio that includes stocks, bonds, and real estate. Your cash investments (checking, savings, money market accounts, certificates of deposit, Treasury Bills, and U.S. savings bonds) provide stability, an emergency fund, an anchor, liquidity, and peace of mind. They are a safe harbor in troubled times. They have a place in every investment portfolio. But you need more. You need equities.

Real Estate

Real estate equity in the form of homeownership will also provide stability, an anchor, and peace of mind. It is not liquid, but liquidity can be had through a sale or through borrowing on an equity line of credit. Your home investment provides potential for capital appreciation and is also afforded special tax advantages. Homeownership is a primary goal for most people, a foundation investment, so to speak. Beyond that, by using borrowed money (a mortgage) for leverage, your home can be viewed as an asset with extraordinary appreciation potential. Many bet on buying a large home with a large mortgage. Others disagree with that strategy. Not everyone lives in a growth market.

Other types of direct real estate ownership, such as open land or a rental property, may also be part of your investment program. Investment real estate can be a winner or it can be an ongoing headache. Location, location, location…if you have it, you have a winner. But you must consider all aspects of the investment, including management, tenants, taxes, repairs, maintenance, improvements, and insurance, as well as market cycles and lack of liquidity.

The Real Estate Investment Trust or fund (REIT) is an indirect form of real estate ownership. An equity REIT can give you a stake in office buildings, retail shopping malls, and income producing apartment buildings across a wide geographic area. A mortgage REIT invests in real estate mortgages rather than the properties themselves. On the upside, a REIT can be used to balance a portfolio of stocks or equity mutual funds; it can serve as a counter-weight to common stocks. On the downside, the investment is subject to real estate market cycles, and it carries a heavier expense load. But studies by the investment research firm Ibbotson Associates show that REITs hold their value well during a general market downturn; they produce steady income…and they are liquid. You could consider a 5 to 10 percent investment in selected REITs as part of a diversified portfolio.

Vacation real estate may be an investment, or it may be a mirage and only appear to be an investment. It could prove to be an expense. You have to be realistic in evaluating vacation property as an investment or as a lifestyle expense, or a bit of each.

Tangible Property

Collectibles and tangible property such as coins, stamps, antiques, cars, etc., might be thought of as having appreciation potential, but in most cases, they are better thought of as hobbies. Do not count on them for future income.

Business Interest

An interest in a closely-held business is the biggest investment—in some cases the only investment—some people have. It may be a cash machine. It may also be an all-consuming job and little more. It can be a dream realized and a wealth builder for some, but it can lead to bankruptcy for others. An investment of time (lots of it), money, and energy is needed. The return depends upon the ability of the owner, as well as outside factors.

Employer Securities

If you work for a public corporation with publicly traded stock, you may have stock option opportunities. They can be lucrative. They can also be a carrot never realized, or a carrot missing a large tax bite. Also, beware of having too many of your eggs in a stock option basket (or of having too much of your 401(k) account invested in employer stock).

Stocks and Bonds

The most likely investments for most people, after cash equivalents and home-ownership, are investments in publicly traded stocks and bonds. An investment in stocks and bonds might occur through direct ownership of stock in a corporation, or by direct ownership of bonds issued by a corporation, government, or government agency. (Indirect ownership of stocks and bonds through mutual funds is discussed below.)

Common stock means you have a residual ownership or equity interest in the corporation. As an owner, you are credited with your proportionate share of the profits of the business. Profits are realized from sales and revenues minus business expenses and taxes. Profits are the source of dividends paid to you, the shareholder. If the prospect for profits and future dividends is good, other investors may bid up the price of the stock. If that happens, you can realize appreciation in the value of your shares, i.e., capital gains.

Preferred stock has a preference when it comes to dividends, or liquidation of the corporation, but it does not have the appreciation potential of common stock.

Bonds do not give you an ownership, or equity, interest. Bonds represent a debt of the issuer, be it a corporation, a government, or a government agency. You are a creditor. You lend your money and are paid interest on your loan; you are investing for a fixed income. If you hold the bond until it matures, and if all goes as planned, the money is returned to you at the end of the loan period. Meanwhile, as interest rates change, the bond (other than a U.S. savings bond) will fluctuate in value; you will realize a capital gain or loss if you sell it before its maturity date. Long-term bonds fluctuate more in value and have greater risk-return potential than short-term bonds.

A History Lesson

According to a study by Ibbotson Associates, the compound average annual rate of return before taxes on various types of investments during the 1925-2002 period, including reinvested income, was: U.S. Treasury Bills (reflecting cash equivalent investments), 3.8 percent; government bonds, 5.5 percent; large company stocks, 10.2 percent; small company stocks, 12.1 percent. The rate of inflation during the same period was 3.1 percent.

The actual returns realized during that period were not as smooth and steady as compound interest. There was volatility from day to day, year to year. The 78-year 1925-2002 period included the Great Depression, World War II, the post-war boom, the Korean and Vietnam Wars, the Kennedy assassination, the Nixon resignation, recessions, inflation, the Gulf War, the 9/11 attack, Afghanistan, preparation for Iraq, and fourteen different presidential administrations. There were great changes in the U.S. economy and the world economy. Some old-line companies prospered, others disappeared. New companies were born like stars in the sky; some flourished, others died. Some investments had astronomical returns, others failed completely.

5-11

Against this background, four investment lessons stand out. *First*, based upon the Ibbotson study, if you need a total return on your investments of more than 5 percent, you need to have part of your portfolio invested in equities, and you need to be invested as an owner, not just as a creditor, such as a bond holder or a holder of certificates of deposit. You need to own common stocks, real estate, or a business of your own. The *second* lesson is that inflation is an historic reality, though it may seem to come and go from time to time. The 3.1 percent compound annual average from 1925 through 2002 cannot be ignored. The *third* lesson is that any single company, any single equity investment, could exceed its expectations or it could end in scrap. The *fourth* and final lesson is that the broad averages are likely to work themselves out over a period of years, but expect volatility along the way; they may not be met in any given period of 5, 10, or even 20 years. The Ibbotson study covered 78 years. Your timeframe is much shorter.

Asset Allocation and Diversification

Two specific strategies can help you to manage the risks presented by those four lessons. The first strategy is *asset allocation*; the second is *diversification* of investments.

Asset allocation means the apportionment of your investment portfolio in given percentages over cash equivalent investments, bonds, and equities…common stocks and real estate. For example, apart from the real estate investment in your home, you might have the following asset allocation strategy: cash equivalent accounts, 5 percent; bonds, 35 percent; equities, 60 percent. If you are in your 30s, your asset allocation might be: cash and bonds, 20 percent; equities, 80 percent. If you are in your 70s, it might be: cash and bonds, 70 percent; equities, 30 percent.

Your particular asset allocation strategy will be a reflection of your goals, the rate of return you need to meet your goals, your time horizon, and your tolerance for risk. If you need funds for a particular purpose in 3 years, you will want to keep those funds in cash equivalent accounts and short-term bonds for safety. If you do not need the funds for 15 years, you can invest in equities. If you need an 8 or 9 percent rate of return on your investments, you will have to invest a good portion in equities. Studies by Ibbotson have shown that your asset allocation formula is more important in determining your total return on investments than either individual security selection or trying to time the market, trying to "buy low and sell high." Your financial plan, with its syntheses of refined goals, required rate of return, time horizon, and risk tolerance, will shape the allocation strategy that is right for you.

5-12   *Diversification of investments* means you own a whole basketful of investments within your equity and fixed income allocations. The effect is to spread the risk of success or failure over a broad cross-section of securities and other investments. You achieve a leveling effect with balance and safety in numbers.

Equity Diversification

For your common stock investments, you can own shares in companies that represent growing sectors of the economy: growth stocks. Some might be growth industry leaders, large established corporations (large capitalization...large cap stocks). Some might be smaller, newer, faster growing companies (small capitalization...small cap stocks). Smaller companies are a greater investment risk, but represent greater return potential as well. Your asset allocation will determine what percentage of your portfolio is in growth stocks, and how it is split between large cap and small cap shares. You can then balance the growth portion of your portfolio with shares of older, established, basic industry leaders, or companies that are fundamentally sound but currently undervalued in the market, i.e., dividend paying value stocks. The value stocks will complement the growth stocks, and again, there can be an allocation between large cap industry leaders and small cap companies that represent a good opportunity but at a greater risk. Owning shares in foreign corporations can offer further diversification, with their own risk and return potentials.

Fixed Income Diversification

For your bond investments (the fixed income portion of your portfolio), you can own corporate or government bonds, foreign or domestic bonds. They can be short-term (e.g., 3 or fewer years to maturity), intermediate term (e.g., 5 to 10 years to maturity), or long-term (e.g., over 10 years to maturity). The corporate bonds can range from secured bonds issued by the largest, strongest corporations to low-rated so-called "junk bonds" which pay a higher rate of interest to compensate for the higher risk they represent. Government bonds can be U.S. Treasury bonds, U.S. savings bonds, bonds issued by agencies of the federal government, or municipal bonds issued by state and local governments. (Municipal bonds are not subject to federal income tax; if you are in a 33 percent tax bracket, a municipal bond paying 4 percent is the equivalent of a taxable bond paying 6 percent.)

You will also need to diversify your bond holdings because, despite the term "fixed income," bonds (other than U.S. savings bonds) are not without investment risk. Your bond portfolio can achieve diversification with a combination of corporate and government bonds (domestic and foreign) having different investment qualities, with different credit risks, different rates of interest, and different laddered maturity dates, e.g., bonds maturing 1, 2, 3, 4, 5, and more years in the future. (For a tax-deferred bond investment with built-in inflation protection, consider U.S. Series I savings bonds. They can be combined with regular certificates of deposit to build a laddered portfolio free of investment risk.)

Your required rate of return, your risk tolerance, and your time horizon should be used to shape your bond, or fixed income, portfolio.

Market Risk

Diversification, however achieved, spreads your investment risk by offsetting the results of one security, one fund, or one sector against the results of another. It balances risk and helps smooth the way. Nevertheless, diversification does not protect your investments from *market risk*. The market as a whole moves up and down from day to day, week to week, in reaction to, or in anticipation of, outside events, e.g., a change in interest rates by the Federal Reserve Bank, a change in the rate of unemployment or consumer confidence, inflation fears, recession, war, terrorism, oil price changes, etc. The moves are sometimes sudden. Your investment portfolio, no matter how well diversified, will ride up or down to one degree or another. Be prepared to ride with the market. With a nod to Lewis & Clark, just imagine you are on your own cross-continent expedition to your own Columbia…Pack enough cash equivalents and short-term bonds to carry you over the valleys—the recessions—that lie ahead. And keep your equities; stay on the path that will break the 10 percent tree line: Let historic market returns and the idea of compound interest be your barometer and compass.

Mutual Funds

You can achieve stock and bond diversification directly with your own portfolio of securities, or you can own shares indirectly through a mutual fund where professional managers select the securities and charge a management fee. Mutual funds can range from growth funds specializing in large-cap, mid-cap, or small-cap stocks, to value funds owning large-cap, mid-cap, or small-cap stocks, to bond funds of various types…corporate or government, long-term to short-term, foreign or domestic. Some funds specialize in international investments made in either mature or emerging economies, or in specific countries. There are also funds that specialize in a given sector of the economy, e.g., technology or health services. You will not avoid market risk, but you can diversify your portfolio with mutual funds.

There are thousands of mutual funds, more than there are stocks listed on the New York Stock Exchange. Your goal as a mutual fund investor is to find about six or eight that will give you the diversification you want…a blend of stock, bond, and cash equivalent funds suited to your needs. For example, you might choose two growth stock funds (one large-cap and one small or mid-cap), two value stock funds (one large-cap, one small or mid-cap), an international stock fund, a bond fund or two, a money market fund and, to add a little salt, a technology, REIT, healthcare, or other sector fund. The percentage of your total investment assets that you commit to each fund will be governed primarily by your required rate of return and your risk tolerance.

How, out of the thousands of funds available, do you find the funds that are right for you? You can either do your own research, or you can get professional help from a financial planner or stockbroker. For your own research, start with Morningstar. There you will find funds categorized by type, with historic total returns, risk ratings, and other information. *The Wall Street Journal,* your daily newspaper, and magazines such as *Money* and *Smart Money,* will also give you ideas. Your library and the Internet are additional sources. By doing your own research and investing, you can reduce your expenses. Look for "no load" funds which do not have a sales charge. The largest "fund families" offering no-load shares are Fidelity, T. Rowe Price, and Vanguard. Good quality smaller funds are also available. (If you are willing to pay for it, you can have the convenience of buying the funds of several fund families through a supermarket such as Charles Schwab, or the brokerage arm of a major fund family.)

If you use your financial planner or stockbroker to help you, he or she can suggest funds that fit your goals, required rate of return, time horizon, and risk tolerance. Your advisor can add value by providing research, recommendations, mutual funds, and other investments not available to you as a retail investor. Your advisor can also give you moral support and help you stay the course; you are less likely to hopscotch from fund to fund chasing last year's returns if you have a knowledgeable co-pilot to guide you.

Advisor Fees and Commissions

What is the cost of an investment advisor's service? It depends upon the type of investment program you have and the size of your investment. If you use "load" mutual funds, ones with a sales charge, the charge will vary depending upon the fund and the method of payment you select. You can choose to pay the commission charge up-front (typically up to 5.75 percent of the initial investment…"A" shares), or upon sale of the shares if sold within a given period of time (e.g., 5 years), with a charge that reduces from year to year over that period ("B" shares), or with a constant low-level annual charge, e.g., 1 percent, or no sales charge at all unless redeemed within the first year ("C" shares). Sales charges and other fees can be found in the fund prospectus, and with help from your advisor, you can choose the schedule that best suits your needs.

5-15

Your financial planner or stockbroker might suggest other avenues to asset allocation and diversification such as a managed account with a "wrap fee," e.g., .50 percent to 2.5 percent of the fund being managed, depending upon the size, with no separate commission or transaction charges. Diversification, as well as asset allocation, is then achieved by use of selected money management firms from around the country, or if your account is large enough, through establishing your own portfolio of securities in a brokerage account.

Summary

If your portfolio is well diversified with quality stocks, bonds, and short-term cash equivalents, perhaps along with a selected real estate component, and if your asset allocation is fitted to your particular time horizon, risk tolerance, and required rate of return, you have an efficient portfolio, an efficient investment plan. An efficient investment plan, especially in a second or subsequent marriage, is a must. Both you and your spouse must get the best return you can consistent with your tolerance for risk. You must not, however, take more risk than is necessary to achieve your goals; your investment return, and that of your spouse, may be critical to your survival. (See Chapter Seven.)

A Word about Annuities

Annuities can be a useful planning tool in a second or subsequent marriage because, like T.O.D. designations on regular investments of stocks, bonds, or mutual funds, you can name anyone the beneficiary to receive the annuity benefit upon your death...subject, of course, to community property laws and the augmented estate rules discussed in Chapter Nine. Also, unless your estate is the beneficiary, an annuity will not be subject to probate administration.

5-16

How Annuities Work

Annuities are a tax-favored insurance company product historically used to provide an income for a period of years, or for a person's lifetime. The concept of an annuity is for the insurance company to pay you a sum of money each month that is scientifically (actuarially) designed to exhaust an invested fund of its principal and income over a given period of years, or your (the annuitant's) life expectancy. If you live longer than your life expectancy, you continue to receive annuity payments for life, and thereby benefit financially at the expense of other annuity buyers in the actuarial pool. If you die sooner than your life expectancy, it benefits the other annuity buyers in the actuarial pool; funds are provided for the longevity of others. Reduced monthly payments can be elected, however, in exchange for a guarantee: you can have a refund of contribution feature in case you die soon after the annuity begins, or with another option, the payments can be guaranteed for a minimum period such as 10 or 20 years, or for the joint lifetime of two people. For example, a husband and wife can choose a joint and survivor annuity to provide a given monthly payment to both while they live, with an option to provide 100 percent or 50 percent of that amount to the surviving spouse for his or her remaining lifetime.

Provision of a lifetime income used to be the basic purpose of an annuity, but in recent decades annuities have been sold primarily as tax-deferred investments. Tax deferral means you do not pay tax on the income that accumulates within the annuity until you withdraw the money. As a result, the annuity is now seen more as an investment fund than as a stream of income during retirement.

Annuities are generally purchased through insurance agents or stockbrokers and can be purchased with a single premium or with periodic premiums paid over a period of time. There are "non-qualified" annuities, i.e., contracts owned personally, and "qualified" annuities owned through a retirement plan or IRA. There are "fixed annuities" and "variable annuities," meaning monthly annuity payments from the insurance company can be fixed in amount or variable.

Payments can begin immediately or be deferred to a future date (immediate annuities; deferred annuities).

Variable Annuities

The object of a variable annuity is to provide a hedge against inflation. A variable annuity provides an income that is tied to an index such as the S & P 500, and therefore it involves a risk that annuity payments will be decreased from time to time, although the hope is that they will be increased to reflect a rising stock market.

5-17

During both the accumulation and distribution period, a variable annuity will have a menu of internal stock and bond (mutual fund-like) sub-accounts for your investment. You can choose your own asset allocation. For an additional premium, some annuities allow sub-account equity investments, but still provide a guarantee of principal with a minimum rate of return. For a price, you can have your cake and eat it too.

The single premium deferred variable annuity has become a popular investment because of its tax-deferred internal mutual fund-like sub-accounts. For optimistic investors, the single premium immediate variable annuity is a popular retirement income vehicle because the life income feature is combined with a stock market index…a potential hedge against inflation.

Fixed Annuities

For conservative investors, or those who in recent years have lost money in the stock market, the single premium immediate fixed annuity may seem like a safe harbor. Some fixed annuities have a minimum interest guarantee during the accumulation period, with the potential for additional interest credits which are linked to an outside barometer such as the 5-year U.S. Treasury Rate, or the S & P 500 Index. Some fixed annuities have an automatic 3 percent increased payment each year once annuity payments begin.

The Downside of Annuities

Annuities are not without their drawbacks. Expenses will include commissions, mortality charges, administration and investment expenses, and they may also include a surrender charge during the first 5 to 10 years, depending upon the contract. In addition, withdrawals from a non-qualified annuity in excess of your cost are treated as ordinary income for income tax purposes, i.e., appreciation in value of the internal sub-accounts will be taxed when sale proceeds are withdrawn. Also, the first dollars withdrawn from a non-qualified annuity are considered income rather than recovery of cost, and if taken out before age 59½, are subject to an additional 10 percent penalty unless withdrawals are made in a series of substantially equal periodic payments generally based upon life expectancy. A similar mutual fund investment, outside of an annuity, will generally have lower expenses, no surrender charge, and, apart from year-to-year taxation of dividends and capital gain distributions at a current maximum of 15 percent, will qualify for capital gains treatment when sold—a maximum 15 percent until 2009.

Finally, for tax and estate planning purposes, a mutual fund will receive a "stepped-up" basis equal to its fair market value on the date of death, or if elected (and if it would result in a lower estate tax), on the alternate valuation date up to six months later. With a stepped-up basis, there may be little or no capital gains tax payable upon sale. With an annuity, however, there is no stepped-up basis: appreciation in value at the date of death is taxed as ordinary income when paid to the beneficiary.

Summary

An annuity, fixed or variable, may be seen by retirees who have limited assets as the best way to squeeze the toothpaste from the tube. Nevertheless, compare a tax-deferred annuity with comparable mutual funds. Read the prospectus for each product. Compare the expense aspect. Ask if there will be a market value adjustment upon surrender of the annuity contract. Compare the lifetime annuity idea with a mutual fund withdrawal plan. Also compare the deferred ordinary income tax treatment under the annuity with the current income tax treatment and deferred capital gains treatment of the mutual fund. (Your tax analysis should consider the type of investment account you will use—fixed income vs. equity— and your current and expected future tax bracket.) In summary, read the fine print and shop very carefully for an annuity: costs and benefits can vary widely. In addition, for a variable annuity, review the insurance company's past sub-account investment performance with a rating service such as Morningstar. Get outside help if needed.

INVESTMENT WEB SITES

REVIEW BROKER'S STATUS:

- WWW.ADVISERINFO.SEC.GOV   Check status of SEC and state registered advisors managing less than 25 million. Click on "Investment Adviser Search."

- WWW.NASD.COM   National Association of Security Dealers web site. Click on "Regulation," then "Investor Protection," then "About Your Investment Professional."

5-19

STOCK EXCHANGE WEB SITES:

- WWW.NYSE.COM   New York Stock Exchange web site. Get quotes and more.

- WWW.AMEX.COM   American Stock Exchange home page. (Click on "ETFs" for Exchange Traded Funds.)

CASH AND U.S. TREASURY INVESTMENTS:

- WWW.BANKRATE.COM   Compare bank yields for cash investments.
- WWW.IMONEYNET.COM   Check and compare money market fund yields.
- WWW.SAVINGSBONDS.GOV   Everything you need to know about U.S. EE/E, HH/H, and I Savings Bonds.

- WWW.TREASURYDIRECT.GOV   Information about a service that lets you buy Treasury Bills, Notes, and Bonds, and hold them electronically in accounts with the U.S. Treasury.

RESEARCH AND EVALUATION:

- WWW.FINANCIALENGINES.COM   Online fee-based investment advisory service.
- WWW.MFEA.COM   The Mutual Fund Education Alliance home page. Locate and evaluate mutual funds.
- WWW.MORNINGSTAR.COM   Locate and evaluate mutual funds.
- WWW.SMARTMONEY.COM/MAG   Morningstar ratings, stock and fund snapshots, REIT information, and more.
- WWW.VALUELINE.COM   Value Line research tools for investors.
- WWW.YAHOO.COM   Yahoo! home page. Click on "Finance" for funds, planning tools, and more.

MUTUAL FUND FAMILY WEBSTIES:

• WWW.FIDELITY.COM   Fidelity Investments home page with mutual
                            funds, tools, and more.

• WWW.TROWEPRICE.COM   T.Rowe Price home page with no-load mutual
                            funds, tools, and information.

• WWW.VANGUARD.COM   Vanguard home page with no-load mutual
                            funds, tools, and more.

     (Also check the mutual fund or stock brokerage site(s) of your choice.)

5-20

Chapter Six—Reading Notes

Insurance

To be alive is to be exposed to risk. To own anything is to risk its loss. Risk cannot be avoided. You can only try to manage it, control it, contain your loss. Risk management includes making sure you have adequate insurance protection. You will want to make sure that your spouse has adequate insurance protection, too; it is an important part of your own financial security.

Property, Casualty, Liability Insurance

This course will not cover property, casualty, and liability insurance except to restate what you already know:

A. If your house is destroyed by fire or storm, you have lost your home, your possessions and, in many cases, your largest investment.

B. If you injure or kill another person with your automobile, you may be sued and lose your house and all your other investments. Your future earnings may also be at risk.

The chance that either tragedy might happen is small, but the potential loss is great. Property, casualty, and liability insurance spreads the risk of loss over a large number of people. The result is an affordable premium cost for each insured person. For a small additional premium, you can purchase an umbrella policy that significantly raises your overall liability protection, e.g., $300,000 of liability coverage can be raised to $1,000,000 for about $0.50 a day in many parts of the country. (Check to be sure your umbrella policy, in addition to your basic policy, covers you from loss at the hands of an uninsured or underinsured motorist.)

Review your coverage with your property, casualty, and liability insurance agent. To be cost effective and avoid gaps in coverage, both you and your spouse should be covered under the same policy.

Health Insurance

Next, consider your hospital, surgical, and major medical insurance coverage. If you have not seen the cost of daily room rates and medical/surgical procedures lately, you will be shocked. Hospital, surgical, and major medical insurance is needed not only for obvious health reasons, but also to protect your savings and investments. A serious illness for either of you could be financially devastating for both.

If you are employed, your health insurance may be provided as a fringe benefit, or at least at a group rate if it is charged to you. Alternatively, you may be covered as a dependent on your spouse's plan.

6-2

If you are under age 65, and not covered under an employer sponsored plan, you will want to purchase an individual policy, typically a comprehensive major medical policy. An individual policy will typically cost more than coverage under a group policy, but use of higher deductibles and co-insurance can help lower your premium cost.

Cost may also be lowered through use of an HMO (Health Maintenance Organization) or PPO (Preferred Provider Organization). HMOs and PPOs are managed care plans designed to control costs. HMOs provide comprehensive healthcare services for a fixed membership fee. Your choice of hospitals and physicians is generally limited. PPOs provide comprehensive healthcare services for a reduced fee. Fees are discounted and paid as services are rendered. You have a greater choice in selecting your own physician under a PPO.

At age 65, if you are eligible for Social Security, you will be covered without cost by Medicare Part A. Medicare Part B may be elected; the monthly premium will be deducted from your Social Security. You can then secure (and it is recommended that you do secure) a separate so-called Medigap or Medifill policy to cover you for hospital/medical/surgical costs not paid by Medicare Part A or Part B. In selecting a Medigap policy, you will have a choice among several standardized plans. You can select an insurance company that offers the plan you want, at a premium cost that best suits you. Medigap supplemental insurance will be issued without regard to your health or insurability if you elect to take it when eligible at age 65. For more information, consult the current *Guide to Health Insurance for People with Medicare: Choosing a Medigap Policy* (CMS Pub. No. 02110) published by the U.S. Department of Health and Human Services, Center for Medicare & Medicaid Services, 7500 Security Boulevard, Baltimore, Maryland 21244-1850.

Disability Income Insurance

The next type of insurance coverage to consider is a policy to replace your lost earnings in the event of your disability resulting from accident or sickness.

Your employer may provide group short-term disability insurance as a fringe benefit. Upon disability, a portion of your salary or wages would typically be paid for 13 or 26 weeks, or in some plans, for up to 2 years. If your employer has a long-term disability income plan, it might provide benefits for a 5-year period, or even to age 65. Under a long-term plan, benefits of 50 to 65 percent of pay are typically payable after a 3 or 6 month waiting period.

If you are a professional person, such as an accountant or dentist or engineer, for example, group disability income coverage might be gotten through your professional association.

You may qualify for disability income payments under your state's Worker's Compensation laws if you are disabled because of a job related injury. Regardless of its cause, if your disability is severe enough, you may qualify for Social Security disability benefits. To qualify, your impairment must prevent you from doing any substantial work for pay, and it must be expected to last at least 12 months or to result in death in less than 12 months.

After considering the amount of employer or association group disability income coverage available to you, and setting aside the possibility of Worker's Compensation and Social Security benefits, you should consider an individual disability income insurance policy.

You will have the best protection if your individual policy is non-cancelable, guaranteed renewable, and covers your *own* occupation. You might consider a policy with a 90-day waiting period with benefits payable for at least 5 years, or to age 65 if affordable. You could elect to have a shorter waiting period than 90 days, but it is good risk management to self-insure small affordable losses and to purchase insurance for the larger, catastrophic losses (long-term disability). For example, good risk management would be to select a 90-day wait with a 5-year benefit period instead of a 30-day wait with a 2-year benefit period. Plan to self-insure the first 90 days from your personal emergency fund.

If you rely solely on your earned income (as opposed to investment income) to cover living expenses, the monthly benefit amount you purchase, together with any group disability insurance you have, should cover at least 60 percent of your earned income before taxes. Disability payments received from insurance purchased with your own after-tax dollars are received income-tax-free, and therefore the 60 percent benefit should, after allowing for tax on the employer provided benefit, replace most of your current after-tax earned income. You can take a different approach, however, if you have income producing investment assets and receive interest and dividends on a regular basis. Determine your monthly expenses that need to be covered, deduct the amount of your after-tax investment income, and insure the difference.

Finally, in addition to your own health insurance and disability income insurance needs, you will want to consider those of your spouse. Would your spouse's serious illness or loss of earned income cause financial hardship? Would your savings and investments be at risk? As previously stated, you and your spouse have a duty of mutual support. A loss to one could consume assets of the other.

6-4

Life Insurance

It cannot be denied: You can create an estate with the stroke of a pen, and life insurance proceeds are income tax-free. But between those simple bookends are volumes of philosophy, projections, rhetoric, and statistics about life insurance, a maze of information and misinformation, enough to boggle your mind. The answers to a few questions, however, can guide you through the maze: *Do you need it?; How much should you have?; What kind should you buy?; Which company should you buy from?; How should you buy it?; Who should own it?*

The last question is especially important in a second or subsequent marriage: The owner names the beneficiary.

As background, we know that a life insurance policy is a contract, a promise to pay a sum of money upon the death of the insured. The consideration given in exchange for that promise is the premium paid to the insurance company together with statements made in the application. The contract is a confidential one…typically between two parties, the insured policyowner and the insurance company. As such, life insurance gives the owner of the policy privacy and flexibility; it is ideal for estate planning in a second or subsequent marriage.

Needs and Wants

First, do you need life insurance? You personally do not need life insurance, and apart from perhaps using the cash surrender value, if any, in the future, you will not benefit from it. Nevertheless, you do benefit from peace of mind in knowing that you are meeting your responsibilities, from knowing that you are providing for those you love. In this light, you do need life insurance if you have financial obligations and there are not sufficient other assets to meet those obligations upon your death. Examples of financial obligations are debts owed to creditors, last expenses including funeral and medical bills, support of a spouse, education of children, and payment of estate taxes. Even if you do not need life insurance, you may want coverage for your spouse or your children.

Need vs. Affordability

Next, how much life insurance should you have? The question is really a two-part one: *How much do you need (or want), and how much can you afford?*

Calculate the Need

You might determine specific needs such as debts to be paid, support of children to age 18, college expenses, support of a surviving spouse to age 60 (when he or she becomes eligible for surviving spouse Social Security), or for life. Or you can determine your total needs. A calculation can be made to determine the *present value* of your total future commitments. From that amount you can deduct the amount of life insurance you currently have, plus the current value of your income producing assets. The difference is the amount of capital (or life insurance) needed to bridge the gap between what you need and what you have. For example, if the amount of all your future needs is determined to be $900,000, and if the present value of $900,000 discounted at 6 percent interest is calculated to be $500,000, and if you have existing life insurance and income producing assets of $300,000, you need $200,000 of additional life insurance. Present value is calculated by discounting a future dollar amount by a given interest rate to its value today. To turn this example around: If you died today, and if the present value of your income producing assets, together with the amount of insurance on your life, equaled $500,000, that amount, if invested at 6 percent, would be sufficient to meet your $900,000 of future commitments.

The present value approach to determining the amount of life insurance needed is a form of capital needs analysis, an approach developed many years ago by Thomas Wolfe of Aetna Life. You can do the computation with a financial calculator, or have a professional insurance agent or financial planner do it for you.

The answer to the question of how much life insurance is needed hinges on what is to be done with the capital: How are the life insurance proceeds to be used upon your death? If the life insurance principal is to be spent over time, along with the income it earns, the answer will be one amount. If the principal is to be kept intact as a future estate for your children, and only the income is to be used to meet your financial obligations, the answer will be a much larger amount. You may *want* the larger amount, but you only *need* the smaller amount. If you wish to hedge your bet and provide a cushion, some leeway for unforeseen future obligations, you might arbitrarily increase the smaller amount by a factor such as 15 percent.

If you are raising a family and want a *rough* idea of the amount of life insurance needed to replace your basic take-home pay, multiply your annual after-tax earnings by 5 (others would argue for a multiplier of 7 to 10). For example, if your after-tax earnings are $60,000 per year, the 5 times answer is $300,000. That could be considered the *minimum* present value of your future after-tax earnings; you might want to insure at least that minimum. Nevertheless, because formulas are no substitute for individual analysis, you will want to evaluate your own particular needs based upon a capital needs approach.

Determine What Is Affordable

6-6

That leads us to the second part of the question: How much life insurance can you afford?

Your financial plan and your Cash Management Statement will help you decide how much you can afford to spend for life insurance. For example, knowing that the purpose of all insurance is to protect you, your family, and your assets from the risk of large losses, you might reason that 10 percent of your income should be allocated to insure your earnings and assets against large losses of all types. You might (to use a sports analogy), allocate 10 percent to your defense (your insurance) and 10 percent to your offense (your savings and investments). The other 80 percent can then be allocated to your fixed and variable living expenses, including income taxes. That is one model. You will want to do your own analysis and allocation based upon your own particular facts and circumstances.

Using the 10 percent model, the following represents hypothetical allocations to cover various insurance needs, including life insurance. Say, for example, your gross income is $75,000. The 10 percent insurance allocation is then $7,500. It might be broken down as shown under either A or B below:

	A	B
Homeowners Insurance	$ 600.00	$ 600.00
Automobile Insurance	1500.00	1500.00
Hospitalization and Major Medical Insurance	4400.00	-0-
Disability Income Insurance	750.00	1400.00
Life Insurance	250.00	4000.00
Total	$7500.00	$7500.00

The unstated difference is that under "B" your employer is paying your hospitalization and major medical insurance as a fringe benefit. Chances are good that the same employer would provide you with some group disability income and group life insurance as well, although probably not all you need.

How much life insurance can you afford? Using these simple models, the answer is $250 per year under "A" or up to $4000 per year under "B." You can move the numbers around: the 10 percent formula is a winter coat, off the rack; it needs to be tailored. For example, under "A," you might choose to have higher deductibles under your homeowners, automobile, and hospitalization/major medical insurance in order to afford more disability income and life insurance protection. Also, just as a person without an employer contributing to the cost might spend more than 10 percent, a person with an employer contributing might spend less.

Kinds of Policies

6-7

Third, what kind of life insurance policy should you buy? If your life insurance budget is $250 per year, shop for term insurance. With term insurance you can buy the most coverage for a given premium outlay. If your budget is $4000 per year, you can consider a cash value type of policy. You can also consider a combination of the two: a basic cash value policy with a term insurance rider to enhance the death benefit for a period of time.

Term Insurance

Yearly renewable term (YRT) starts out at a low premium, and the rate increases each year as you grow older. This reflects the increased cost of buying a death benefit; mortality rates increase with age. Term insurance is purchased for a term of years, e.g., YRT, or 10 or 20 years, or to age 65 (in some cases longer, e.g., 30 years, or to age 95). It stops at the end of the term period, but is usually renewable for a limited term at a higher rate, and is typically convertible to a cash value policy prior to termination. Term policies other than YRT would typically have a level premium for the term. With some policies, the premium is guaranteed for a period of time, e.g., 10 years, and then the premium increases dramatically unless you re-qualify as a good risk. Be careful of such a policy; know what you are buying; if your health changes during the term period, you may want to convert to a cash value policy.

Term is often the ideal coverage for a young family in need of maximum protection on a limited budget. It is not ideal if you need insurance for your entire lifetime. Term insurance owners tend to discontinue their life insurance at older ages because the term premium increases with age. Many also drop the coverage because they no longer need it. Nevertheless, if life insurance is needed and your budget is tight, term insurance is the answer. In a second or subsequent marriage, you may choose to have term insurance for temporary coverage until your children are grown, or until other assets have been accumulated for a spouse's protection.

For example, a 10 or 20 year level term policy may meet your need to provide for a child's support or education, or it may give you time to rebuild your estate following a divorce.

Cash Value Whole Life

Cash value life insurance is designed to be carried for a longer period than term; it can be carried for your entire lifetime, and in fact (for tax reasons), can be carried for a period beyond your life expectancy, e.g., to age 115, should you live so long, before it matures for the face amount. The regular whole life policy has a level premium payable for life that is initially much higher than a term premium at the same age. The additional premium builds a fund, or cash value, within the policy. The cash value can be borrowed by the policyowner or it can be used to help pay the premiums. The cash value can also be viewed as an emergency fund. Upon the death of the insured, the beneficiary is paid the face amount of the policy, which includes the cash value. For example, a policy with a face amount (death benefit) of $100,000 might have a cash value after a number of years equal to $30,000. Upon the insured's death, depending upon use of policy dividends, if any (see below), $100,000 is paid to the beneficiary, not $130,000.

Critics of cash value life insurance would argue that the insurance element in this policy is only $70,000 because the $30,000 is really a return of your own money. They argue in favor of buying term insurance and putting the premium difference into other investments such as mutual funds. Upon retirement, you would have more money in your mutual fund, they argue, than in your cash value policy. Proponents of cash value life insurance would argue that most people would spend the premium difference rather than invest the difference, and therefore cash value life insurance constitutes a forced savings plan. Instead of having nothing, the policyowner would have the death benefit, or a guaranteed fund at retirement. They would also argue that most people drop their term insurance at older ages because of the increased premiums, and thereby have no life insurance when they die. The whole life policyowner might keep the policy, it is argued, because the premium will not have increased with age, and, in fact, the policy might be paid up with no additional premiums due. The policyowner would then have a guaranteed death benefit, or the cash value could be used for a lifetime purpose.

Cash value life insurance typically has a level premium payable for your "whole life," but it could have a gradually increasing premium, limited payment premium (e.g., 10 years, or to age 65), or even a single premium. Some policies also pay "dividends" which are really a return of excess premiums. Dividends are not taxable (unless they exceed the accumulated premiums paid) and can be paid in cash, accumulated with interest (which is taxable), used to reduce premiums,

6-8

or used to automatically buy paid-up life insurance or additional term insurance (e.g., $30,000 of additional term purchased with dividends would cover the cash value in the example above, and thereby provide a total death benefit of $130,000). You can be creative with dividends.

A whole life policy can be used in a second or subsequent marriage to provide an estate for children of a prior marriage, or it can be used to provide a lifetime income for your spouse. In a word, if you want to create an estate for your children that stands separate and apart from your present marriage, or if you want to assure your present spouse a minimum level of support, you can guarantee the result with a whole life policy. With this type of policy, you will have to pay the premiums for your whole life, or until the policy cash value and dividends can carry the premiums for you.

6-9

Partly in response to the term vs. cash value arguments, but also in response to changing financial and market conditions, the insurance industry developed new types of policies with elements of each.

Variable Life

Variable life is a form of whole life whereby the policyowner can have the cash value invested in equities or fixed income investments, i.e., in stock or bond mutual fund like sub-accounts with the insurance company. The premium is a whole life premium that will not increase with age. The death benefit is guaranteed to be not less than the initial face amount, but it could be greater. The cash value is not guaranteed; depending upon investment results, it will be more or less than a regular whole life policy. In effect, you are buying term insurance and investing the premium difference in mutual fund-like sub-accounts within the same policy. You, rather than the insurance company, bear the investment risk.

Variable life can be used in a second or subsequent marriage in lieu of a whole life policy if you want whole life-type coverage, but seek a better investment return for the cash value and are willing to accept risk in order to achieve it. If successful, you will increase the amount of death benefit payable to your spouse or children over that payable under a regular whole life policy, and the cash value will also be greater should you later not want the death benefit and decide to surrender the policy. If your investment results are poor, your cash value will lag, and that can jeopardize plans for an increased death benefit or future use of the cash value.

Universal Life

Universal life is a flexible premium policy whereby you pay—at your discretion—a premium that might be nearly as low as a yearly renewable term premium, or as high or even higher than a whole life premium, i.e., you can, within limits, make additional interest earning deposits. The policy is charged monthly with a deduction that includes mortality cost for the death benefit, an administrative fee for expenses, and other insurance company costs, e.g., taxes; it is credited monthly with interest. The mortality and expense charges in current use by the insurance company are not guaranteed rates. The guaranteed rates are typically higher. The interest credited to the accumulated cash value is a current rate declared periodically by the insurance company. The guaranteed interest rate is typically lower than that initially credited.

A universal life policy can have premiums payable for life, but it also affords premium payment flexibility. Premiums can be based upon a 10-pay life policy, for example, or premium payments can be kept at a minimum, whereby the policy will be like yearly renewable term and have the same drawback of escalating premium outlays in future years. Also, a decline in interest rates from those initially projected, or an increase in monthly deductions, will have an adverse effect; the cash value being built to cover future premium payments will not grow as anticipated, and therefore the cash value may not be sufficient to pay the premiums: You may have to put more money into the policy to keep it in force.

Universal life can be designed to have a level death benefit, or for an increased premium, an increasing death benefit to include recovery of the cash value or premiums paid. It can be used in a second or subsequent marriage in lieu of either whole life or term, but should be viewed as a term policy if premiums are going to be minimized.

Variable Universal Life

Variable universal life has elements of both universal life and variable life; it is like universal life with its flexible premium deposits, but it is like variable life with its internal mutual fund-like sub-accounts for investment of the cash value. Like variable life, you can select from a variety of sub-accounts, including stock and bond accounts, and you, rather than the insurance company, bear the investment risk. But unlike universal life, there is no minimum interest guarantee unless you select the insurance company "fixed account" for your investment.

The variable universal life death benefit, like variable life, is guaranteed to be not less than the initial face amount; it could be more depending upon investment results. Nevertheless, if investment results are poor, you may have to put more money into the policy to keep it in force. Like both variable life and universal life, variable universal life needs a healthy cash value in order to carry future mortality and expense charges.

Variable universal life can be used in a second or subsequent marriage in lieu of variable life if more premium payment flexibility is needed. Like variable life, if you surrender the policy the tax consequence will be the same as it is with a variable annuity: ordinary income could be realized. (See Chapter Five.)

Cost

There are other variations on the theme of premium, death benefit, and credits to cash value, including "current assumption," "low load," "no load," and non-commission fee based policies, but all are related to the types of policies discussed above. Regardless of policy type, life insurance is a financial commitment, a cost, and there are important decisions to be made. Do you want maximum coverage for the lowest initial outlay, or do you want whole life coverage with a level premium? If your choice is lifelong coverage, do you want guaranteed cash values, or do you want a policy based upon investment performance? Your answers will depend upon your need, your budget, your risk tolerance, and what you believe to be the most cost effective approach.

6-11

A primary goal should be cost effectiveness and, in that light, a life insurance policy is best viewed as a guaranteed death benefit. It may have future cash values which benefit the policyowner, but its reason for being is primarily to provide a death benefit. Based upon that, term insurance advocates will argue that term is the most cost effective way to buy a death benefit. That is clearly true if you die soon after buying the policy, and likely to be true if you die before age 65. Nevertheless, if you want to carry the policy for your whole life, and if you live according to your life expectancy, or longer, term insurance alone is not the answer: You will have to accumulate a separate investment fund (after-tax) to replace the expired term insurance. The alternative to term is a form of whole life…regular whole life, variable life, universal life, or variable universal life. Your particular needs in a second or subsequent marriage, and your budget, will dictate the type of policy you should have. Is the protection for your spouse or for your children? Is your need a temporary or a permanent one? Do you want guaranteed results, or are you willing to take risks that could increase (or decrease) the policy's value? The type of policy you choose will determine your cost.

Choose an Insurance Company

What insurance company should you buy from? There are several thousand life insurance companies. Your selection of a company, however, can be based upon just two criteria: first, the financial strength of the company; second, the cost of the type of policy you want to buy, yearly renewable term, regular whole life, variable life, etc.

Compare Financial Strength Ratings

The financial strength of an insurance company can be checked with rating services via the Internet. Rating service web sites are shown at the end of this chapter. They will give you a financial strength rating for each company you wish to consider. The financial strength of the insurance company will be relatively more important if you are buying term, whole life, or universal life than if you are buying variable life or variable universal life. With the latter two types of policy, your cash values are invested in sub-accounts apart from the general assets of the insurance company. Nevertheless, choose a company with high ratings from at least three rating services.

6-12

Compare Cost of Policies

Next, select a company that offers a cost effective policy of the type you want to buy. Not all companies are cost effective for each type of policy. Those companies that offer the most cost effective term policies are not necessarily offering the most cost effective whole life policies. Companies offering the most cost effective whole life policies are not usually offering the lowest cost term policies. Do insurance companies specialize in the types of policies they offer? It seems they do; they find their own niche in the market.

Term policies are "pure insurance," and premiums can be compared, "apples to apples," one company against another. Nevertheless, also compare the renewal rates and conversion aspects of the policy because you may want to renew the coverage or convert to a whole life policy in the future. If you are going to convert the policy, you have to look at it as a whole life policy.

Comparing whole life policies involves more than just comparing premiums or cash values. Get quotes from several companies. Request the projected "net payment index" and the projected "surrender cost index" for each policy. The net payment index is designed to measure the projected cost of the death benefit; it is designed to tell you, on a *present value* interest adjusted basis, the cost per $1,000 of the insurance. The surrender cost index is designed to measure the projected cost of the coverage if you surrender the policy after a period of years for its cash value; it is designed to tell you, on a *present value* interest adjusted basis, the cost per $1,000 of your protection. Past history and future index projections are your best methods of comparing whole life-type policies on an apples to apples basis.

Nevertheless, there are two cautions when you do your cash value policy comparison. The first is, if you are buying regular whole life, compare regular whole life to regular whole life. If you are buying universal life or variable life, compare universal life to universal life, and variable life to variable life. Do not compare a regular whole life policy to a universal life, variable life, or variable universal life policy. They are computed differently and the comparison (expected to favor the performance based policy) would be misleading. The second caution is to be wary of overly optimistic projections of future interest rates (universal life) or investment results (variable life). Ask for the past history of the "actual payment index" and the "actual surrender cost index." They will be available from each insurance company for its own products. In addition, you can find them in the library under *Best's Review (Life/Health Edition).*

Variable life policies use sub-accounts for investment of the cash value. You can select from a diversified common stock fund, a growth fund, a bond fund, etc. Comparison of one company's policy to another company's policy will involve a comparison of sub-account investment performance, as well as underlying charges for mortality costs and administrative expenses. You can check the company web sites for sub-account performance history. Look for actual year-to-year past sub-account performance; beware of misleading averages that smooth over the impact of down markets. You can also request information from the companies. Read their prospectuses.

6-13

Ownership and Beneficiary

How you might buy the policy and who might own the policy will be covered further in Chapter Ten (Estate Planning). For now, we can note that the insured person or another person who has a financial interest in the insured person—such as a spouse, a child, a trustee, a business partner, an employer, or a creditor—can own the policy. When the insured person owns the policy (as is most often the case), anyone can be named beneficiary (however, initially the beneficiary must have an insurable interest in the life of the insured, and as you will note in Chapter Nine, protection is afforded a surviving spouse in some states). When someone other than the insured person owns the policy, such as a spouse or a trust, that person or entity is typically the beneficiary.

Summary

Determining your need and comparing life insurance policies can be a complex undertaking. The essentials for you in a second or subsequent marriage, however, are: (1) selection of the amount and type of policy that meets your need (term, whole life, etc.); (2) selection of a financially strong insurance carrier; and (3) selection of a company with a cost effective policy of the type that you want to buy. Your financial planner or life insurance advisor (himself or herself carefully selected) can be of great help to you.

Long-Term Care Insurance

Everyone has heard of the increasing cost of long-term care in a nursing home. Costs vary by locale and are highest in the major metropolitan areas, but they are relatively high everywhere. Rates of $160 per day or higher are common. One year in a nursing home could cost $50,000, $70,000, $90,000, or more depending upon where you live and the particular facility you choose. Given that reality, you might consider long-term care insurance as a safety-net for old age.

The financial loss from a nursing home stay could be devastating. Not everyone will realize that loss, however, just as not everyone will suffer the loss of his or her home in a fire. The odds are favorable that you will not go into a nursing home at all, or if you do, that your stay will not be long-term. In *Guide to Choosing a Nursing Home*, the U.S. Department of Health and Human Services reported that 40 to 45 percent of 65-year-olds in 1990 would be admitted to a nursing home at least once during their lifetime. About half of those would stay fewer than 6 months. One in five would stay 1 year or more. One in ten would stay 3 years or more.

The government report is supported by a study done by Kemper & Murtaugh reported in *The New England Journal of Medicine (1991)*. The study said that of those turning age 65 in 1990, 43 percent are expected to be admitted to a nursing home at least once during their remaining lifetime. Of those, one in three would spend 3 months or more, one in four would spend 1 year or more, and only one in eleven would spend 5 years or more. Kemper & Murtaugh projected that two out of three in the study will never enter a nursing home at all or will spend 3 or fewer months there. Nevertheless, the study also projected that 13 percent of women will spend 5 years or more in a nursing home, as will 4 percent of men.

We cannot be certain of our individual or collective future(s). We know we have an aging population: about 80 percent of Americans will live past age 65. We also know that, with age, the likelihood of entering a nursing home increases. We know that women generally live longer than men and are more likely to need nursing home care. Based upon these facts, and the studies conducted, we could reason that, although long-term care of 3 years or more might be needed, intermediate-term care of 2 to 3 years is far more likely. Taking that a step further, we could reason that home care, short-term assisted living, or short-term nursing home care is even more likely.

You may not need long-term care...but if you do, it will be expensive. Should you hedge the risk with long-term care insurance? The questions again might be: *Do you need it?; Can you afford it?; How much should you have?; What kind should you buy?; Which company should you buy from?*

Need vs. Affordability

First, do you need the coverage, and can you afford it? You may need the coverage, but if your income is too low to pay the premiums for the rest of your life, you simply cannot afford it. In making this decision, you need to project your income and your expenses through your retirement years. Will your income be enough to cover all your basic needs and then some? (See Chapter Seven Reading Notes.) Conversely, if your assets can produce sufficient income to pay the nursing home cost, you do not need the insurance coverage even though you can afford it. For example, if you have $1,800,000 of investment assets (including proceeds from the sale of your house), you should safely realize $85,000 per year in total return (interest and dividend income, plus capital appreciation). Add Social Security to that, and you should have enough inflation-protected income to cover your nursing home costs. If you live in a less expensive market, $1,200,000 to $1,500,000 of income producing assets may be sufficient. If more is needed, you can nibble away at your principal.

6-15

If you are "in-between"—not well-to-do, but not poor—you may want to buy long-term care insurance. It may be needed and, if you choose to make it a priority, you can probably afford it. It is most affordable if you are still in your 50s or early to mid 60s. You can consider it at older ages, but it does get expensive. In deciding whether you should buy long-term care insurance, you will have to weigh the possible costs of nursing home care on the one hand against the certainty of an ongoing insurance premium on the other.

When you consider your need and whether you should buy long-term care insurance, you will want to consider this: Not only are your assets at risk with a nursing home stay, but those of your spouse are as well. As discussed below under Medicaid, both your assets and those of your spouse need to be "spent down" before you qualify for government assistance. This is consistent with state law requiring mutual support; if needed, each must contribute to the support of the other. In a second or subsequent marriage, long-term care insurance may be used to insure your *personal dignity*, as well as your (and your spouse's) *financial security*. In the glare of those headlights, you have to ask yourself if your spouse needs long-term care insurance as well. Do your assets need to be protected from the cost of his or her nursing home stay? You both need to evaluate your circumstances as you enter a different phase of your life together.

How Much Coverage Should You Have?

Next, how much long-term care insurance should you have? That depends on what you can afford. The studies show that although a stay of 5 years or more is possible, a stay of 3 years or fewer is more likely. Review a quote for 3 years as a start. For a daily benefit, consider $100 to $150 per day to get an idea of costs. A waiting period of 30 to 100 days can be considered. The longer the waiting period is, the lower the premium. That said, the longer the waiting period, the more you are self-insuring. How much do you want to self-insure? At a $160 to $200 per day nursing home cost, the 30-day wait is recommended if you can afford it.

What about inflation? Nursing home costs will surely be higher in the future, and the value of your assets may not keep pace. The answer: A 5 percent per year simple or compound interest inflation rider can be added to your policy. The compound interest rider is preferred, especially if you are under age 70. The inflation rider, to a large degree, is actually your reason for buying the insurance. You may be able to cover 3 years at $60,000 per year now, but can you cover $124,740 per year in 15 years? That is what today's $60,000 will amount to with 5 percent annual increases. The compound interest inflation rider will cover the higher cost, at least to the extent of 5 percent per year.

Affordability can be a problem. The problem is made easier if you are self-employed: Your long-term care premiums are, to a large extent, a tax-deductible business expense. That will help until you stop working. Also, using the 10 percent of income model for all your insurance needs, and anticipating a different phase of your life, you might substitute long-term care premiums for some or all of your disability income or life insurance premiums, ultimately your automobile insurance premiums. Finally, while planning your insurance budget, anticipate that the quoted premium may be increased in the future. Check the insurance company's history for premium increases.

Kinds of Policies

What kind of policy should you buy? The future trend of long-term care may be toward more home healthcare and assisted living care and less actual time in a full service nursing home. Look for a policy with comprehensive coverage for all three possibilities, home healthcare, assisted living, and nursing home care. Also, note that some policies may afford limited tax savings as an itemized deduction, but others may be more liberal in qualification for benefits. The tax qualified policy is now the standard, but you may want to consider the other type. *A Shopper's Guide to Long-Term Care Insurance* published by the National Association of Insurance Commissioners is "must reading." Your agent will furnish a copy with your proposal.

Choose an Insurance Company

Finally, which company should you buy from? There are reportedly about 130 insurance companies offering long-term care insurance. Concentrate your efforts on examining three or four companies that you find to be the strongest financially and the most committed to serve this market niche with competitive products. Compare them (there are important differences in premiums and coverage) then get a professional opinion from your financial planner. Make an informed decision.

Long-Term Care Insurance as a Rider

As a footnote to this subject, it should be mentioned that, for an extra premium, some insurance companies offer a long-term care insurance rider to a cash value life insurance policy or annuity. The basic idea is this: If you do not use the long-term care benefit, you still have the annuity or life insurance for yourself and your family. If you do use the long-term care benefit, the policy will pay a percentage of the annuity, or up to 5 percent of the face amount of the life policy each month (until the policy is exhausted), paid first from the cash value and then from the rider.

6-17

Should you cover your long-term care needs with a rider to an annuity or cash value life insurance policy? You will first want to do the basic analysis outlined above. Then ask yourself: *Do I need the annuity or the life insurance? Will I keep the life policy in force for my lifetime? Does the long-term care rider provide quality coverage? Is the price competitive?*

Short-Term Care Through Medicare
Long-Term Care Through Medicaid

Medicare and Medigap policies provide health insurance coverage, i.e., hospital/surgical/medical; they do not cover custodial nursing home care. Medicare and Medigap coverage for nursing home care is limited to a 100-day period, including an initial 20-day skilled acute care period following at least 3 days in the hospital, and thereafter only for skilled care needs during the balance of a period not to exceed 80 more days. Very little long-term care is classified as skilled; it is primarily intermediate (commonly called "custodial") care, and not covered by Medicare or a Medigap policy.

Medicaid is a joint federal and state program to provide long-term care for those who qualify. You do not qualify for benefits if your assets or income exceed certain minimum levels. Rules vary some from state to state. In Ohio, for example, the non-institutionalized spouse (the community spouse) can retain a house with furnishings, a car, and about $90,000 worth of other assets. The institutionalized spouse can have only $1,500 worth of assets. The balance of the couple's assets can be spent to purchase "exempt assets" or be used for the institutionalized spouse's nursing home care. Purchase of a house, or improvements made to a house, would be exempt asset purchases. There are others. Currently (in all states but New Jersey, Ohio, and Pennsylvania), the purchase of an annuity for the community spouse would also be an exempt asset purchase.

In some states, income is another restriction; in other states, it is not. Except for a small monthly allowance for the community spouse, or a family allowance for minor children, the income of the institutionalized spouse must be spent for his or her nursing home care. The total income of the community spouse can range up to a maximum of about $2,200 per month, depending upon various factors. The balance of the couple's income must be used for the institutionalized spouse's nursing home care. Exact income allowances vary from state to state and are subject to change from year to year.

6-18

As a married couple, you need to spend down your combined assets to the minimum before either of you qualify for Medicaid. Your remaining assets will be needed for the care of the community spouse. If the community spouse is later institutionalized, your house may have to be sold to cover costs. In any event, if the state Medicaid program has paid nursing home costs for either of you, the state can recover its costs from the survivor's estate.

In a second or subsequent marriage, the Medicaid rules are especially onerous; a child from a prior marriage may have his or her inheritance spent for the nursing home care of a stepparent. Consult a Medicaid specialist if you wish to learn about ways to protect your home and other assets for your children.

INSURANCE WEB SITES

GENERAL:

- WWW.INSURE.COM

A guide to auto, health, life, and home insurance, and annuities. Links to Standard and Poors and Fitch financial strength ratings. Click on "Insurance Company Guide," then "Financial Ratings."

GOVERNMENT:

- WWW.MEDICARE.GOV

Official U.S. Government site for people with Medicare.

CONSUMER HEALTH INSURANCE:

- WWW.HEALTHINSURANCEINFO.NET

State-by-state information from group plans to Medicaid.

NURSING HOME COSTS:

- WWW.LTCFEDS.COM

Check daily rates for cost of care. Click on "Planning Tools," then "Use The Tools."

FINANCIAL STRENGTH RATING SERVICES:

- WWW.AMBEST.COM

Ratings for over 1,400 companies; fee charged. Top 4 rating categories: A++, A+, A, A-.

- WWW.FITCHRATINGS.COM

(Can access via WWW.INSURE.COM) Ratings for over 220 American companies; fee charged. Top 4 rating categories: AAA, AA+, AA, AA-.

- WWW.MOODYS.COM

Ratings for about 700 companies; some free. Top 4 rating categories: Aaa, Aa1, Aa2, Aa3.

- WWW.STANDARDANDPOORS.COM

(Can access via WWW.INSURE.COM) Insurance and investment ratings; free service. Top 4 rating categories: AAA, AA+, AA, AA-.

- WWW.WEISSRATINGS.COM

Ratings for about 1,700 companies; small fee. Top 4 rating categories: A+, A, A-, B+.

VARIABLE LIFE SUB-ACCOUNT PERFORMANCE:

- WWW.MORNINGSTAR.COM

Investment rating service; fee charged.

- INDIVIDUAL INSURANCE COMPANY WEB SITES
  e.g., WWW.ABCLIFE.COM

6-19

Chapter Seven—Reading Notes

Retirement Planning

7-1

Start your planning with the questions *when, where, why, how, and who*. When will you retire? Why will you retire? Where will you retire? How ($) will you retire? Who will you spend your time with?

As a prelude, we can say that planning for some will be cut short by life events…health, disability, job loss. The poor hand dealt will have to be played "as is," or with help from family, friends, charity, or the government. Others will have inherited wealth or accumulated sufficient assets on their own. Their standard of living is assumed. But most people are in between, having to choose between spending for current consumption and saving for future consumption. In addition, taxes and inflation are constant impediments to savings and growth. They are systemic and impede progress in real terms. Add to this the setback that occurs when your first marriage ends in death or divorce. You may never catch up.

In a second or subsequent marriage, you will need a cooperative plan in order to maximize your injured potential. In some cases, however, a cooperative plan will not be had. Instead there will be separate agendas with each having separate assets, separate income, and separate investments; there is often a common checking account for mutual expenses. Knowingly or unknowingly, by agreement or otherwise, one may carry more than his or her share of the expenses. By agreement or otherwise, the other, perhaps moved by fear, may overtly or covertly harbor assets for his or her own long winter, or for the future…for his or her young to find when winter has passed. Depending upon the personalities involved, feelings of resentment—even bitterness—leading to a failed relationship, may result. For others, a cooperative plan will be achieved. The couple will live and nest as cardinals. In their own world, they will face the winter together; their young are seen as off and on their own.

But retirement planning is not all about planning for winter; it is also about planning for financial independence, freedom, discovery, and happiness. A whole world of ideas, places, and new adventures awaits. It is a once in a lifetime opportunity. The fullest realization of that opportunity, however, hinges upon those few critical questions raised in the first paragraph above.

When Will You Retire?

The question of when to retire is the first issue. You typically want to retire while you are young enough to enjoy life, while your health, energy, and interests are strong. Yet, you do not want to risk running out of money by retiring too soon. Suppose, for example, that you expect to live to age 85. If you retire at age 65, you want to know that your assets will carry you to age 85, and then, let us say, for 5 more years as a margin for error. That is 25 years. If you retire at age 55, the time period is 35 years. At age 70, it is only 20 years. If, for example, you need to realize $40,000 per year from your investments at retirement, and your return on investments is 6 percent, you will need $459,000 at age 70, $511,000 at age 65, or $580,000 at age 55. That is the sum needed in order to pay you $40,000 per year of amortized principal with 6 percent interest over the 20-, 25-, or 35-year period. As you can see, the earlier you retire, the more money you need. Viewed another way, the longer you delay retirement, the higher the standard of living you can enjoy with a given amount of assets: $580,000 at age 65 will provide a higher standard of living than it will at age 55. The question of when to retire, therefore, involves a balancing of health, energy, and interests on the one side, and your standard of living on the other. If you retire early, you may have to accept a lower standard of living, and we have not yet considered the effects of inflation.

Why Retire At All?

A related question is, why retire? Or at least, why retire at a conventional retirement age? You may enjoy your work, the challenge, the power, the status, the society, the perks, the income. As an alternative to complete retirement, you may elect semi-retirement; more time off but with a hold on your career and earned income. You may also keep working in order to maintain your standard of living, e.g., to continue driving a luxury car, or to continue taking expensive vacations, or to continue an active social life. Such lifestyle benefits may be more important, more satisfying, than retiring with fewer amenities. Finally, you may continue to work in order to maintain your health insurance, or pay off a home mortgage or other debt. In short, a deferred retirement, or semi-retirement, may give you added financial security, or enhance your overall quality of life.

Where Do You Want To Live?

Where to retire is also a critical question. It is related to the question of whom you will spend your time with. Family, friends, church, and clubs are lifestyle connections. For many, family trumps location; it is more important to be near children and grandchildren than to live in a retiree climate. Some couples are fortunate and able to mix two locations by spending a few weeks or months away from home during the worst months of the year. But you have only one domicile, and the selection of that home base will affect your quality of life and your cost of living for housing, utilities, medical care, insurance, and other items. It will also affect your access to work and recreation. Perhaps most important, it will affect your emotional well-being. You may want to golf year-round, but your spouse may not. Have you known someone who retired a thousand miles from home, only to move back?

Can You Afford To Retire?

The how question is directly related to the others and, standing alone, is the most challenging one, especially in a second or subsequent marriage. How can you afford to retire? Will you have enough money? How can you make it work? A number of important elements must be considered. Some will be known and some will be unknown.

Basic Assumptions

Every retirement plan will be built upon certain assumptions about the unknown elements. If the assumptions are conservative, your plan will absorb financial shocks as a building with the right design and foundation absorbs an earthquake. If the assumptions are too optimistic, they will batter your plan as heavy seas batter a beach house.

The assumptions that you need to consider as seriously as you would consider earthquake or hurricane planning are: (1) your longevity; (2) the future rate of inflation; (3) your return on investments; (4) your future healthcare costs (this assumes you have insurance); and (5) changes in government policy (tax law changes, Social Security changes, Medicare changes).

Those are the principal unknown elements that will affect your standard of living during retirement. The known elements are your present assets, resources, and income, and your present health, living expenses, and income tax rate.

Life Expectancy

First, you have to make an assumption as to how long you will live. You can consult actuarial tables, and you can consider how long your parents, grandparents, and other family members have lived. Consider their general health, lifestyle, and personal living habits. Consider your own general health, lifestyle, and personal living habits. From these considerations, you need to make an estimate of your own longevity. Then, to be conservative, many planners suggest you add 25 to 50 percent to your answer. For example, if you determine your life expectancy to be 20 years, add 5 to 10 more years. If 40 years is your estimate, add 10 to 20 more years. Remember, the actuarial tables of life expectancy show average life expectancy. That means one-half of the group will die before the expectancy age is reached, but one-half will live beyond it. Give yourself a margin for living beyond your life expectancy. That is being conservative.

7-4

Appendix D shows life expectancy tables used by the Internal Revenue Service. From this, you can derive a statistical life expectancy for yourself and for the joint life and last survivor expectancy of you and your spouse. For example, if you are age 65, the table shows your life expectancy to be 21 years. If your spouse is 3 years younger, your joint and last survivor expectancy is shown to be 27.7 years, meaning the survivor of you and your spouse is expected to live 27.7 years. For conservative planning purposes, add 25 percent to 50 percent: life expectancy at age 65 becomes 26.3 to 31.5 years instead of 21 years. The joint life expectancy of a 65-year-old with a spouse that is 3 years younger becomes 34.6 to 41.6 years instead of 27.7 years.

If your health is below average, you might use the IRS Table and still be conservative. If your health is average, you might add 25 percent to the table. If you are a preferred risk, e.g., a white female in good health, with good family history, you might add 50 percent to the table. Use your best judgment.

Inflation

Second, you are aware of inflation because you have lived it. Now, however, you must actually confront the reality of inflation. In the past, your increasing salary, wages, fees, and commissions hid that reality. Your income offset the effects of inflation and, in all probability, you increased your standard of living despite it. With retirement, your earned income will cease, but your cost-of-living will continue to grow because of inflation. As a result, some retirees must cut back the extras, the things they would like to enjoy, in order to afford the increasing cost of necessities. For some, one necessity is sacrificed in order to afford another: food for medicine, medicine for food.

Appendix E shows inflation as measured by the Consumer Price Index (CPI) for the years 1926 to 2003. The period covers many changes, including years of depression, wars, and recessions, and changes in oil prices, energy prices, farm prices, and interest rates. During this period, the economy moved (and is still transforming itself) from a manufacturing base to one based upon technology and service. But what of the future? It is difficult to predict the future rate of inflation. For planning purposes, 3½ percent might be considered realistic, based upon the past, but many planners recommend a 4 to 5 percent assumption. The higher rate reflects concern for future oil and energy prices and for products and services used more by seniors than by the general population, e.g., prescription drugs and medicines. For conservative planning purposes, a 4½ percent rate is suggested. The rate you select should be monitored from year to year with adjustments made as needed.

7-5

Investment Return

Third, you must also estimate the rate of return you will earn on your investments. "Return" in this sense means your total return: dividends and interest, plus or minus capital appreciation or loss. For example, if your equity investments earn 2 percent in dividends and appreciate 6 percent in value, the total return is 8 percent. If your fixed income investments earn 5 percent interest, with no change in value, the total return is 5 percent. Given those returns, a 50-50 portfolio of fixed income and equity investments would return 6.5 percent. If your asset allocation is 60 percent equities and 40 percent fixed income, your portfolio return will be 6.8 percent. If it is 40 percent equities, 60 percent fixed income, your portfolio return will be 6.2 percent.

An 8 percent portfolio return in the future is possible. It could be achieved with an investment blend weighted toward equities and with the equity return meeting its historic average of more than 10 percent per year compounded. Nevertheless, for planning purposes at retirement, an 8 percent return is aggressive, with added risk. A 6.5 percent portfolio return, equities and fixed income, is more conservative. Some would even recommend a 5 percent return.

Your own investment return, based upon your own particular portfolio, may dictate a different return to be assumed. Prior to retirement (and also during retirement) you can reevaluate your tolerance for risk, your actual realized returns, and your required rate of return. (See Notes to Chapter Five.) It is suggested that the total return you assume, like the rate of inflation you assume, be conservative, and that it be monitored from year to year with adjustments made as needed.

As you consider the investment return concepts in Chapter Five and the investment return concepts in this chapter, note that it is usual to assume a rate of return for your retirement years that is less than the rate of return you assume for your accumulation years. During your accumulation years, you can afford to take risks. The 30-year-old can take more risks than the 50-year-old, who can take more risks than the 70-year-old. The younger you are, the more time there is to recover from an investment mistake or a prolonged down market. For that reason, as you grow older, your portfolio will typically shift more toward fixed income investments in order to reduce the risk of capital loss and, at the same time, to produce more dividend and interest income. For example, over a period of time a given portfolio may go from 80 percent equities and 20 percent fixed income (e.g., at age 35), to 40 percent equities and 60 percent fixed income (e.g., at age 65 or 70). Put differently, the 8 percent total return you assume for your accumulation years can become the 6.2 percent or 6.5 percent or 5 percent you assume for your retirement years.

7-6

An old rule of thumb said that you should determine the equity component of your portfolio by deducting your age from the number 100. For example, a 65-year-old would have a portfolio with 35 percent equities. A 75-year-old would have 25 percent equities. There are modern variations of the formula that use the numbers 110 or 120 instead of 100. A better approach, however, is to analyze your own investment return needs in conjunction with your own tolerance for risk.

Regardless of your exact investment blend, an equity component is needed in order to offset future inflation. You need to share in the economy's growth; living expenses will surely be higher in the future. The tradeoff is risk: You will have to assume market risk. But what if you have to sell during a down market after you retire? If you do, you may realize a loss, and it will be a real loss, as opposed to a paper loss. That is the real risk: a sizeable loss, especially during your early retirement years, may be devastating. Part of your retirement planning, therefore, is to make sure your non-equity investments will carry your retirement budget through a prolonged down market without your having to sell equities. You want to have a cash equivalent and short-term bond reserve that will carry you for at least 3 years, if not 4 or 5, without having to sell any equity investments. A paper loss that is subsequently recovered with an upturn in the market is not a real loss. Your reserves need to see you through.

Healthcare Costs

Fourth, you can anticipate that healthcare costs will increase at a faster rate than the general cost of living. It is the law of supply and demand at work. More people will need healthcare, and there will be fewer people able and willing to supply it, thus an upward pressure on wages. Your budget for prescription drugs and medications can also be expected to increase with increased age and usage. A conservative estimate of the future rate of inflation (4 to 5 percent instead of 3 to 3½ percent) will help cushion future medical costs, but you might still add a special allowance for increased prescription drugs.

Income Taxes

Fifth, you must also consider the federal and state income tax you will have to pay on retirement income. (In addition, you may need to consider a local income tax, or an intangible tax on investment assets.) What rate do you pay now in combined federal, state, and local income and intangible taxes, 15 percent? 30 percent? 40 percent? For example, if your adjusted gross income is $75,000 and you pay $15,000 in federal, state, and local income taxes, your tax rate is 20 percent ($15,000/$75,000). (You can find your adjusted gross income at the bottom of Page 1 of your federal income tax return-Form 1040.) If you have tax-free income, or deductions for depreciation, you will have to add those amounts back to adjusted gross income and use a total revenue (cash-flow) figure in the calculation rather than adjusted gross income.

As an estimate for income taxes during your retirement years, apply your current tax rate (20 percent in this example) to your expected adjusted gross income. This is a conservative approach. It may overstate the amount you will pay in income taxes because you may be in a lower tax bracket after you retire. On the other hand, it will help absorb changes in government policy, e.g., changes in Medicare costs and reimbursements, or a decision to tax 100 percent of your Social Security instead of 50 percent or 85 percent. Also, it can help absorb what will amount to a hidden tax on Social Security if future cost-of-living increases in Social Security do not keep pace with inflation. Finally, the use of a conservative tax rate will help off-set possible changes in income tax rates, deductions, and exemptions.

Just as your assumptions about inflation and investment return can change, your assumed tax rate should be monitored and adjusted from year to year based upon your experience and a conservative look to the future.

In conjunction with use of a conservative tax rate assumption, you can also plan to minimize your taxable income during retirement. For example, you can adjust the rate at which you withdraw money from retirement plans; you can use tax-free investment vehicles; you can spend-down taxable investments before using tax-deferred investments; you can file a joint income tax return instead of filing separate returns. Your investment and tax advisors can assist you in planning to maximize income while you minimize taxes during retirement.

Summary of Unknown Elements

In summary, the first three unknown elements (longevity, the rate of future inflation, and your return on investments) represent the leading edge of the storm. Failure to prepare can result in irreparable damage. The other two unknown elements (future healthcare costs and changes in government policy) represent the backend of the storm; damage can still be heavy, though it's usually less severe.

Those are the unknown elements. They call for conservative estimates with necessary adjustments from year to year throughout retirement. (For a thorough presentation of retirement planning using conservative assumptions, see J.K. Lasser's *Your Winning Retirement Plan* by Henry K. Hebeler. For conservative investment return probabilities, see the "Monte Carlo" web sites at the end of this Chapter.)

7-8

The Known Elements

The known elements are closer at hand: your present assets, resources, income, health, and living expenses. You can take stock now and make adjustments that are within your reach. If you have years to go before retirement, you can make improvements across the board. Your options are limited if you are about to retire.

Estimate Living Expenses During Retirement

The emphasis here will be on living expenses, a known element you can control. Look to your Cash Management Statement…How much are you presently spending each month? How much will you need to spend each month after you retire? One of two approaches can be taken in answer to the second question: the *ratio* method or the *budget* method. (Using either method, estimate all expenses for your *first* year of retirement using *today's* dollars. We will account for future inflation later.)

The Ratio Method

The *ratio* method is easy to apply. You simply estimate how much your monthly expenses during retirement will be as a percentage of how much they are before retirement: 100 percent? Or possibly just 70 percent? Or something between 70 percent and 100 percent? The reasoning behind using a lower percentage is that you are no longer saving for retirement, and you will drop all employment related expenses such as F.I.C.A. taxes, work related lunches, clothes, transportation, etc., and most likely your income taxes will be lower. At the same time, you may increase certain expenses such as recreation and hobbies, dining out, travel, etc. Depending upon your lifestyle, your expenses may drop, or stay the same, or even increase for a few years. Arguably, the percentage could be 90 to 100 percent, but over time, as a middle of the road example, you might estimate your post-retirement living expenses to be 80 to 85 percent of your pre-retirement living expenses. That should enable you to maintain your present standard of living.

The Budget Method

The *budget* method calls for a detailed listing of all current expenses with side-by-side estimates of those same expenses during retirement, plus any new expenses. Some expenses may be reduced or eliminated, such as mortgage or debt payments, and work related expenses, but others may be increased, such as telephone and utilities, home repair and maintenance, and/or recreation and travel.

7-9   The budget method is recommended over the ratio method because the budget method forces a detailed analysis and discussion. As a couple, you can make policy decisions, agree on details, and divide areas of budget responsibility.

Major Purchases During Retirement

An important aspect of budgeting for retirement is to budget for major purchases. The approach taken here assumes that you pay for your major purchases as part of your everyday budget: if your car payment is $350 per month, the $350 is just part of your budget. Inflation factors incorporated into the planning process will account for higher car payments in the future. (As an interesting and worthwhile sidebar to budgeting technique, however, you might consider this: Henry K. Hebeler, in his book *Your Winning Retirement Plan*, recommends carving out a separate fund from your assets to cover the future purchase of major items, such as cars or special vacations. For example, if you plan to purchase two cars during retirement and the cost of one car today is $25,000, you would set aside $50,000 in a special "car replacement" fund, and plan your everyday expenses based upon income from your remaining assets. The theory of the separate fund is that the fund will grow in value and cover the anticipated higher future cost of the cars to be purchased. The separate fund idea—adaptable to the approach taken here—can be applied to any anticipated future purchase.)

Lifetime Budgeting

Your own retirement budget should break down into three separate budgets to take you from your retirement date through the rest of your life: (1) your *comfort budget*, which might be close to your pre-retirement budget; (2) your *survival budget*, which is just that: what you need in order to survive; and (3) your *transition budget*, which is the midpoint between the two, a gradual reduction from your comfort budget to your survival budget.

The Survival Budget

The first critical step to retirement planning in a second or subsequent marriage is to prepare a *survival budget* for yourself. A survival budget will show the minimum amount you need each month to live on your own. Inherent in the survival budget is personal dignity. Survival with dignity. The words "survival" and "dignity" will mean different things to different people; the words by themselves are ambiguous. As used here, however, they are concrete; they are to be used as you would apply them to yourself, with the understanding that a minimum standard of living with adequate food, clothing, shelter, and medical care is understood. It assumes you can pay your bills and live independently with dignity.

Therefore, what are the basic expenses for health, support, and maintenance that *you*, as an individual, will need in order to survive and live with dignity? You should prepare the budget based upon the cost of goods and services today, using today's dollars. This will be your survival budget before considering the effects of inflation. Next, have your spouse prepare a similar survival budget for him or herself. Then, with either professional assistance or the use of a financial calculator, you can project each budget, using conservative assumptions, to your retirement date and for the period from your retirement date through your life expectancy.

7-10

Next, prepare a survival budget on the same basis for the two of you to live simply, but with dignity, as a couple. You can then project that budget, using conservative assumptions, through your joint life expectancy. Needless to say, two cannot live as economically as one, but your couple's survival budget should be less than your combined individual survival budgets. For example, you might find that each of you separately needs about 65 percent of what you need as a couple, which means, separately, you would spend 130 percent of what you would spend as a couple. A second example would be if one needs only 50 percent, but the other needs 70 percent. That still adds up to 120 percent of what you would spend as a couple.

The Comfort Budget

Next prepare a *comfort budget* as a couple. What are the expenses you need in order to live comfortably as a couple? The word "comfort" is understandably nebulous and will mean different things to different people. Use it as it sensibly applies to you without increasing your present standard of living. Your comfort budget might typically be 80 to 100 percent of your pre-retirement budget.

The Transition Budget

Finally, as you work with your own particular details, formulate a plan whereby you use your comfort budget as a couple until you are about age 75, your survival budget as a couple after you reach age 85, with a transition budget (comfort to survival) for the years between 75 and 85. This approach allows for an active lifestyle transitioning to a more sedate lifestyle. The idea of planning a transition budget from active lifestyle spending to passive lifestyle spending makes sense so long as you do not overspend during the early years. (In his book, *The Prosperous Retirement*, Michael K. Stein postulates that retirees might expect to enjoy an active, healthy lifestyle until their mid-70s, with a transition to their mid-80s when a passive lifestyle is normally preferred, if not necessary. He shows how a couple can afford to spend more money in the early years of their retirement while they travel, pursue hobbies, and dine out more often. Conversely, Henry K. Hebeler, in *Your Winning Retirement Plan*, warns against spending too much during those years and thereby not having enough money later. You will have to weigh their arguments on your own scale.)

7-11

A Case Study

Against that background, let us look at a hypothetical couple in a second marriage. Wendy and Joe, both age 62, are now retiring and plan to live as they have, but do more traveling and play golf regularly until they are age 75. They then plan to reduce their outside activities but otherwise maintain their standard of living; two cars, dining out, etc. By age 85, they plan to just live with dignity in a safe and comfortable environment with needed services close at hand.

As a couple, Wendy and Joe have a pre-retirement income of about $109,000 per year, before tax. They feel they can live comfortably during retirement on $80,000, after taxes. They estimate they can survive with dignity as a couple on $60,000. Individually, each one needs $35,000 per year for a survival budget. (All budget figures are in today's dollars, which will be increased annually for inflation at 4½ percent.)

Wendy and Joe are planning a budget whereby they will live on $80,000 per year, adjusted for inflation, from their age, 62, to age 75 (their comfort budget), $70,000 from age 75 to 85 (their transition budget), and $60,000 after age 85 (their survival budget). Before they start spending the $80,000 to live comfortably, however, they need to make sure that they are not spending money needed by either of them to support an individual survival budget: $35,000 per year as adjusted for inflation. After they apply the survival budget test for each of them, they may have to scale back their comfort budget in order to assure each of them that he and she will have enough money to survive alone and live with dignity for the rest of his and her life.

The first goal of a second or subsequent marriage retirement plan, therefore, is to provide a built-in safety-net that assures each of you the ability to live out your years with dignity in the event of the other's death, or your divorce, or the incapacity of either of you. (The second goal, it is suggested, is to fashion the best lifestyle you can as a couple, consistent with your individual estate planning goals.)

Now, using the concepts outlined in this chapter, let us see what it will take for Wendy and Joe to retire at age 62.

Goals as a Couple

A. $80,000 Comfort Budget for 13 years (Ages 62 to 75);

B. $70,000 Transition Budget for 10 years (Ages 75 to 85);

C. $60,000 Survival Budget for 13 years (Ages 85 to 98...their joint-life expectancy from Appendix D...29.0 years from Age 62...plus 25 percent... 36.3 years total).

Individual Goals

D. $35,000 Survival Budget for Joe for 29.4 years...his individual life expectancy from Appendix D...23.5 years from Age 62...plus 25 percent for an average risk;

E. $35,000 Survival Budget for Wendy for 35.3 years...her individual life expectancy from Appendix D...23.5 years from Age 62...plus 50 percent for a preferred risk.

Retirement Assumptions

A. Longevity: life expectancy at age 62 from Appendix D, plus 25 percent for Joe, 50 percent for Wendy, and 25 percent using joint-life expectancy;

B. Inflation...4.5 percent annual compound rate;

C. Investment income...6.5 percent total return before-tax;

D. Income taxes...20 percent of adjusted gross income.

E. Healthcare costs...For simplicity of illustration, no extra inflationary adjustment is made.

It should be noted that by retiring at age 62, Wendy and Joe will receive only 80 percent of the Social Security they would receive at age 65. In addition, they will have to secure hospitalization and medical insurance from a private carrier for the next 3 years until they qualify for Medicare at age 65. (Memo: The example assumes full Social Security benefits at age 65. The age for full Social Security benefits is higher for those born after January 1, 1938. See: WWW.SOCIALSECURITY.GOV.)

7-12

Available Assets and Annual Income at Age 62

		Joe	Wendy	Total
Assets:				
Investment Assets	(A)	$450,000	$250,000	$700,000
Home Equity		100,000	100,000	200,000
Total Assets		$550,000	$350,000	$900,000
Income:				
Social Security at Age 62—estimated		$14,400	$7,200	$21,600
Pension - adjusted annually for cost of living			24,000	24,000
Pension - not adjusted for cost of living		18,000		18,000
Investment Income @ 6.5% (total return)		29,250	16,250	45,500
Total Income		$61,650	$47,450	$109,100

7-13

First Year After-Tax Retirement Income

		Joe	Wendy	Total
Social Security (Assuming 85% is Taxable):				
.15 x Social Security + .80 (Social Security x .85)		$11,952	$5,976	$17,928
Pension Income:				
.80 x Pension		$14,400	$19,200	$33,600
Basic Retirement Income	(B)	$26,352	$25,176	$51,528
Investment Income:				
.80 x Investment Income		23,400	13,000	36,400
Total After-Tax Income		$49,752	$38,176	$87,928

Smooth sailing or troubled waters? It appears that Wendy and Joe will have smooth sailing throughout their retirement. It looks as if they can meet all of their goals and even live on income alone without touching their principal. Individually, they both have after-tax income in excess of their $35,000 survival budgets. Together, their $87,928 after-tax income exceeds their couple's survival budget and their transition and comfort budgets, too. It looks as if they can actually live better than anticipated.

Unfortunately, Wendy and Joe have not considered the effects of inflation. What will happen in the future as their income, year by year, loses its purchasing power?

Effects of Inflation

		Individually Joe	Wendy	As a Couple
Survival Budgets	(C)	$35,000	$35,000	$60,000
Deduct Basic Retirement Income	(B)	(26,352)	(25,176)	(51,528)
Survival Budgets Exceed Basic Retirement Income	(C - B)	$8,648	$9,824	$8,472
Life Expectancy Assumed		29.4 yrs.	35.3 yrs.	36.3 yrs.
Present value of Survival Income Shortage for life expectancy...assuming after-tax investment return of 5.2% (.80 x 6.5%) and inflation of 4.5% [1]	(D)	$228,158	$307,030	$271,469
Present value of sum needed to maintain purchasing power of pension income [2]	(E)	160,136	-0-	160,136
Total present value of Survival Income Shortage (D + E)	(F)	$388,294	$307,030	$431,605
Investment assets exceed (fall short of) total present value of Survival Income Shortage (A-F)	(G)	$61,706	($57,030)	$268,395

7-14

Stated differently, using Joe as an example, we show a shortage of $8,648 per year between the $35,000 Joe needs to survive, and the amount provided by his Basic Retirement Income of $26,352 (Social Security and pension after-tax: $11,952 + $14,400). The question then becomes, how much money does Joe need today, invested at 5.2 percent (6.5 percent–20 percent tax), to pay himself $8,648 per year for 29.4 years, assuming the $8,648 is a moving target increasing at a compound rate of 4½ percent per year because of inflation? (Each year it will take more money to buy the goods and services that $8,648 will buy the first year...$8,648 becomes $9,037 the second year, $9,444 the third year, etc.) The answer is $228,158. That amount, $228,158, invested today at 6.5 percent before-tax (5.2 percent after-tax), will fill the gap...except for one problem. Although Social Security is assumed to increase each year with inflation, Joe's pension will not...it pays a flat $18,000 per year before-tax. Joe's pension will lose purchasing power over the years, and he needs to offset that loss with additional income. Therefore, how much money does Joe need today, invested at 5.2 percent after-tax, to provide the additional pension income he needs? The answer is $160,136. That amount, invested today at 5.2 percent after-tax, is needed to maintain the purchasing power of Joe's $18,000 annual pension. Joe's total Survival Income Shortage, therefore, is $388,294 ($228,158 + $160,136), meaning he needs $388,294 today, invested at 5.2 percent after-tax, in addition to his pension and Social Security, in order to pay himself $35,000 each year, adjusted for inflation, for 29.4 years. Visualize the $35,000 as a moving target increasing at a compound rate of 4½ percent per year ($35,000 becomes $36,575 the second year, $38,221 the third year, etc.). Joe's investment assets of $450,000 ("A" above) exceed the total present value of his Survival Income Shortage of $388,294 ("F" above), giving him a margin of $61,706 ("G" above). So far, Joe seems secure.

As a couple, Wendy and Joe have a projected margin of $268,395 (their combined investment assets of $700,000 exceed the $431,605 total present value of their Survival Income Shortage). As a couple, Wendy and Joe seem even more secure.

7-15 Wendy, however, has a projected shortage of $57,030. The $307,030 total present value of her Survival Income Shortage exceeds her $250,000 in investment assets. She could run out of money during her lifetime; her situation is critical and needs to be addressed before she commits to retirement at age 62. What can be done to close the gap for Wendy?

First, Joe can gift $57,030 to Wendy now. That will solve the problem for Wendy, but Joe will then have only a $4,676 survival margin ($61,706–$57,030). If that is a problem, Wendy can plan to liquidate her equity in the house at some point. As an alternative, Wendy can defer retirement for a few years: Deferred retirement will result in a higher Social Security benefit, give her assets more time to grow, and will shorten the payout period to her life expectancy. A contingency plan would be to have Joe name Wendy as a beneficiary under his will (if any) or life insurance (if any). The drawback is that Joe can change his beneficiary or drop his life insurance. Wendy needs to take a hard look at her options (apart from claims against Joe's estate) and plan now to cover the shortage in her survival budget. Otherwise, she risks impoverishment.

Viewed as a couple, however, the adage holds true: There is strength in numbers. The example shows that Joe and Wendy have a $268,395 cushion over and above the present value of their couple survival budget of $60,000 per year for 36.3 years, as adjusted annually for inflation. Together they are more secure; they can survive the winter better as a couple than either one can alone.

Next, we need to add a layer of income to their survival budget to represent their transition budget. They can afford the survival budget of $60,000 per year. Can they add another $10,000 for 23 years and afford their transition budget of $70,000 from age 62 to age 85? The present value of a sum equal to $10,000 per year for 23 years needs to be added to the present value of their Survival Income Shortage to take them from $60,000 to $70,000 for the 23-year period. The total of the two present values can then be added together and compared to their combined investment assets of $700,000.

The present value of $10,000 per year for 23 years, assuming an after-tax investment return of 5.2 percent (.80 x 6.5 percent) and inflation of 4.5 percent, is $213,924[3]. Add $213,924 to the total present value of their Survival Income Shortage as a couple, $431,605 ("F" above), for a total of $645,529. Compare that to their combined investment assets of $700,000 ("A" above). Can Wendy and Joe afford to use their transition budget from age 62 to 85? Yes. And they still have $54,471 left over ($700,000–$645,529). They have enough as a couple for their transition budget of $70,000 per year from age 62 to age 85, with a survival budget thereafter of $60,000 per year for 13 more years to age 98, their joint life expectancy plus 25 percent.

Now comes the comfort budget. Can Wendy and Joe afford to add another $10,000 layer of spending to their transition budget to take them to an $80,000 per year comfort budget, as adjusted for inflation each year, from age 62 to age 75, a 13-year period? The answer is probably "no," but it could be "maybe." The present value of $10,000 per year for 13 years is $124,934[4]. Wendy and Joe do have $54,471 left over from their transition budget, but that still leaves a shortage of $70,463 ($124,934–$54,471). They cannot fully realize their comfort budget unless they close that $70,463 gap.

7-16

Here is where home equity can come in. Wendy and Joe still have $200,000 equity in their house, and that can be considered an additional resource. They could sell the house, buy or rent less expensive housing, and invest the excess proceeds to generate more income. Nevertheless, they will still have housing expenses, be they in the form of rent or homeownership (taxes, insurance, and maintenance). The sale proceeds will have to cover those expenses as well as the $70,463 shortage. In short, they have a dilemma: Should they sell their house to support a higher standard of living, or should "comfort" for them mean staying in their present home, staying with their $70,000 transition budget, and having peace of mind with a $54,471 cushion? (The cushion could still be used for some extras, and their home may continue to appreciate in value: If so, the increased value could be tapped for additional spending.)

Adjustment for Tax-Deferred Investments

Now, an important concept and possible adjustment needs to be considered. The investment asset figures used—$450,000 for Joe and $250,000 for Wendy, and $700,000 for them as a couple—are shown as "after-tax," i.e., personally owned assets such as mutual funds or certificates of deposit…money saved and accumulated out of earnings after taxes have been paid on the earnings…or money received as a gift or an inheritance. That may not be true. The investments may instead represent annuities, or traditional or rollover IRA accounts or 401(k) accounts that have not yet been taxed. If that is the situation, we have to reduce the account values for income taxes yet to be paid, and our 20 percent assumption for combined federal and state income taxes is probably too low. Therefore, the combined federal and state income tax rate we will now use is 30 percent, as taxation of the untaxed principal is assumed to push Wendy and Joe into a higher effective tax bracket. In this example, if Wendy and Joe's investment assets are subject to tax, they will have to be reduced to $315,000 for Joe [$450,000–(30 percent of $450,000)] and $175,000 for Wendy [$250,000–(30 percent of $250,000)]. After deducting income taxes, Wendy and Joe both fall short of their individual survival budget needs, although as a couple they still have a margin of safety.

7-17

Taxation of Investment Asset Principal

		Individually		As a
		Joe	Wendy	Couple
Investment Assets before tax	(A)	$450,000	$250,000	$700,000
Income Tax @ 30%		(135,000)	(75,000)	(210,000)
Investment Assets after-tax	(H)	$315,000	$175,000	$490,000
Total present value of Survival Income Shortage	(F)	$388,294	$307,030	$431,605
Investment assets after-tax exceed (fall short of) total present value of Survival Income Shortage (H-F)	(I)	($73,294)	($132,030)	$58,395

In this example, Wendy and Joe would be wise to consider deferring retirement for a few years in exchange for more financial security. The combination of increased Social Security at age 65, plus additional investment growth during the deferral period, *and* the shortened payout period to their life expectancy, would enhance their individual security as well as their security as a couple. And that is the real issue for Wendy and Joe: Should they retire at age 62 while they are in good health and might most enjoy the time, or should they wait until they are more financially secure?

Wendy and Joe are only one hypothetical couple. The universe of possible factual situations is beyond the scope of this chapter. Needless to say, there will be couples who have more assets than Wendy and Joe and couples who have less. Couples will be older or younger, with similar issues and with issues that are unique to them. The purpose of this example is to illustrate the comfort budget, transition budget, and survival budget approach to retirement planning in a second or subsequent marriage.

For further refinement, it should be noted that if Wendy and Joe were age 45 instead of age 62, we would have done projections of their future retirement goals

17 years hence, with projected funding to meet those goals. For example, we could estimate a comfort budget of 85 percent of their current age 45 budget and then project that budget 17 years into the future at a 4½ percent assumed rate of inflation, plus as an added factor, 2 percent for expected salary increases in excess of inflation. Calculations can then be made to determine the amount they need to save each year from age 45 to age 62 to fund their retirement.

An additional refinement would be to consider the tax effect of funding their retirement with ROTH IRAs. The after-tax retirement income picture would be enhanced if the investment assets—(A) above—were ROTH IRA accounts where taxes had been paid before the money was contributed to the ROTH, and all withdrawals at retirement are tax-free. The ROTH enhancement over regular after-tax investments (e.g., personally owned mutual funds or certificates of deposit) is because the earnings on the regular after-tax investments are subject to tax. In our example, we reduced assumed investment earnings from 6.5 percent to 5.2 percent to account for taxes at a 20 percent rate. If the assets were ROTH IRA assets, the 6.5 percent investment return would be tax-free.

7-18

Summary

Other refinements can be made, and other approaches and theories can be tested against the comfort budget, transition budget, and survival budget approach. The two books mentioned, *The Prosperous Retirement* by Michael K. Stein and *Your Winning Retirement Plan* by Henry K. Hebeler, are recommended, as is *Comfort Zones* by Elwood N. Chapman, as revised by Marion E. Haynes, a holistic look at retirement planning. In addition, a number of web sites can be consulted, a few of which are listed below. Finally, with the use of available statistical tables and a financial calculator, you can do your own retirement estimates. Whichever method you choose, be aware that longevity, inflation, investment return, and tax assumptions are arguable; be watchful that the ones used are not overly optimistic. Remember the story of the three little pigs? One built his house out of sticks, one out of straw, but the third one, the smart one, built hers out of bricks.

Finally, regardless of the approach you take to project your retirement income and funding needs, it is recommended that you check your results with a qualified financial planner. A professional can give you one-on-one retirement planning expertise. In a second or subsequent marriage, especially, you need to evaluate your personal financial security—your personal survival with dignity—as well as your financial security as a couple.

RETIREMENT WEB SITES

GENERAL:

• WWW.AARP.ORG	Lots of information for retirees.
• WWW.ANALYZENOW.COM	Henry K. Hebeler's web site (author of J.K. Lasser's *Your Winning Retirement Plan*).
• WWW.BESTPLACES.NET	Information on over 3,000 cities with cost of living comparisons and more.
• WWW.CHOOSETOSAVE.ORG	Provides Internet planning tools and retirement calculators.
• WWW.ROTHIRA.COM	Dedicated to Roth IRAs.

7-19

MORTGAGE MANAGEMENT:

• WWW.MORTGAGE-CALC.COM	Calculates early mortgage payoff.
• WWW.REVERSE.ORG	Consumer information on reverse mortgages.
• WWW.REVERSEMORTGAGE.ORG	National Reverse Mortgage Lenders Association web site. State-by-state list of reverse mortgage lenders. Reverse mortgage calculator.

MONTE CARLO WEB SITES:

• WWW.EFFISOLS.COM	Portfolio software for sophisticated retirement projections.
• WWW.MONETECARLOSIMULATIONS.ORG	Monte Carlo information and education.

MUTUAL FUND FAMILY WEB SITES:

• WWW.FIDELITY.COM	Planning tools—retirement income calculator.
• WWW.TROWEPRICE.COM	Select "Tools." Retirement calculator shows probability of meeting income goals—check assumptions used.
• WWW.VANGUARD.COM	Personal investors/planning & advice/ planning tools—calculator shows how much you will need based upon your assumptions.

(Also check the mutual fund site(s) of your choice.)

FOOTNOTES... Present value calculations using couples budget model and Hewlett Packard HP12C Financial Calculator:

(1)

KEYSTROKES	DISPLAY
(g) [BEG]	8472
[CHS] [PMT]	-8472
1.052 [ENTER]	1.052
1.045 [÷]	1.0067
1 [-]	0.0067
100 [x] [i]	.6699
36.3 [N]	36.3000
0 [FV]	0 [FV]
[PV]	271,469

7-20

(2)

STEP ONE		STEP TWO	
KEYSTROKES	DISPLAY	KEYSTROKE	DISPLAY
(g) [BEG]	14,400	(g) [BEG]	14,400
[CHS] [PMT]	-14,400	[CHS] [PMT]	-14,400
1.052 [ENTER]	1.052	-	-
1.045 [÷]	1.0067	-	-
1 [-]	0.0067	-	-
100 [x] [i]	.6699	5.2 [i]	5.2000
29.4 [N]	29.4000	29.4 [N]	29.4000
0 [FV]	-0-	0 [FV]	-0-
[PV]	379,912	[PV]	219,776

Step One represents the present value (PV = $379,912) of Joe's $14,400 annual after-tax pension for 29.4 years at 5.2 percent after-tax interest and inflation at 4.5 percent compounded annually. Step Two represents the same present value (PV = $219,776), but with no inflation. The difference of $160,136 ($379,912–$219,776) measures the amount of inflation, the present value of the sum needed to offset lost purchasing power.

(3) | KEYSTROKES | DISPLAY |
| --- | --- |
| (g) [BEG] | 10,000 |
| [CHS] [PMT] | -10,000 |
| 1.052 [ENTER] | 1.052 |
| 1.045 [÷] | 1.0067 |
| 1 [-] | 0.0067 |
| 100 [x] [i] | .6699 |
| 23 [N] | 23.0000 |
| 0 [FV] | -0- |
| [PV] | 213,924 |

7-21

(4) | KEYSTROKES | DISPLAY |
| --- | --- |
| (g) [BEG] | 10,000 |
| [CHS] [PMT] | -10,000 |
| 1.052 [ENTER] | 1.052 |
| 1.045 [÷] | 1.0067 |
| 1 [-] | 0.0067 |
| 100 [x] [i] | .6699 |
| 13 [N] | 13.0000 |
| 0 [FV] | -0- |
| [PV] | 124,934 |

Chapter Eight—Reading Notes

Intestate Succession, Wills, Trusts

Intestate Succession

8-1

The intestate succession laws under the *1990 Uniform Probate Code* (UPC), and a cross-section of five non-UPC states, will be discussed in this chapter.

If you do not have a valid will when you die, your *probate estate* will pass to your *heirs* according to the *laws of intestate succession,* also known as the *Statute of Descent and Distribution.*

Probate Property

Your *probate estate* consists of property you own at death. It does not, however, include the following property: (1) property transferred at death to a named beneficiary (e.g., life insurance, annuity, 401(k), IRA, P.O.D. and T.O.D. accounts); (2) survivorship accounts owned with another (e.g., JTWROS, Tenants by the Entirety); (3) property held in trust; (4) property of another that you had a right to appoint by your will among a group of beneficiaries designated by the other; (5) community property owned by your spouse.

Heirs

Your *heirs,* as defined by the *Uniform Probate Code,* are those persons who would inherit your probate property according to the applicable state Statute of Descent and Distribution. Those persons could include your spouse, your descendants (e.g., children, grandchildren, great-grandchildren), your parents, or other relatives (siblings, grandparents, aunts, uncles, cousins, or more remote family). If you have no known heirs, your property will escheat to the state.

Deductions and Priority Claims of Surviving Spouse

Probate property can be distributed to your heirs only after deductions for taxes, debts, expenses, and estate obligations. Estate obligations include amounts set aside to satisfy priority claims of your spouse and minor children for *homestead*, *exempt property*, and the *family allowance.*

Homestead, or the homestead allowance, varies from state to state but generally provides for temporary living space for a spouse or minor children. It protects the primary residence for a period of time from claims of non-lienholders, or else it provides a monetary allowance for temporary housing. *Exempt property* which might be set aside for a surviving spouse or minor children includes household furnishings and, within dollar limits and depending upon the state, one or two automobiles and watercraft, the tools of one's trade, and other tangible personal property. The *family allowance* is a designated monetary sum for temporary support of a surviving spouse or minor children.

8-2

Personal Property vs. Real Property

The intestate succession laws that apply to *personal property* are generally those of your state of domicile, i.e., your legal home, your intended primary residence, your mailing address, the place where you vote, have your driver's license, and have other primary business, religious, or social connections. The laws that apply to *real estate* are those of the state where the real estate is located. For example, if an individual died intestate a resident of Chicago but had a condominium in Santa Barbara, the laws of Illinois would govern the disposition of all his property except his condominium. The condominium would descend to his heirs under California law.

Community Property

Since California is a community property state, one-half of the condominium—if he was married and if the condominium was not his separate property—would already have been owned by his wife, and only *his* one-half of the community property would be part of his probate estate and descend to his heirs. (Under California intestate succession law, his one-half of the condominium would descend entirely to his wife. Under Texas community property law—had his condominium been in Texas—his one-half would descend to his lineal descendants, e.g., his children, if living, otherwise grandchildren, etc. Under all community property intestate succession laws, all community property descends to the surviving spouse if the decedent has no descendants.)

Summary of Intestate Succession

To summarize the above points about intestate succession, we can say:

A. Personal property is distributed under authority of the court to heirs pursuant to the laws of the decedent's state of domicile;

B. Real estate descends, i.e., vests immediately (subject to control by the court to assure payment of debts, taxes, and claims) to heirs pursuant to the laws of the state where the real estate is located;

C. The decedent's probate estate consists of all property owned by the decedent other than that passing by law, contract, trust, or survivorship to another;

D. In community property states, probate property owned by the decedent consists of the decedent's separate probate property plus one-half his community property, which is subject to probate.

8-3

The Uniform Probate Code

The *1990 Uniform Probate Code* (a model code adopted with significant modifications by a number of states…see Chapter Two Reading Notes) can serve as backdrop to illustrate intestate succession for a hypothetical couple in a second marriage. Assume the decedent had two children, now adults, from a prior marriage. Further assume a probate estate of $500,000, $100,000 of which had been acquired by the decedent before marriage, and $400,000 of which, including a $200,000 residence, had been acquired after the marriage.

Under the UPC, $43,000 would be set aside out of the probate estate to satisfy priority claims of the surviving spouse. The surviving spouse can claim the following:

Homestead allowance (a flat amount)	$15,000
Exempt property (a flat amount)	10,000
Family allowance [1]	18,000
Total set-aside for surviving spouse as claims against the estate	$43,000

Assume for this example that funeral expenses, court costs, attorney fees, administrator fees, and other debts, claims, and expenses equal $37,000. The decedent's probate estate would then be distributed by the Personal Representative, i. e., estate administrator, as follows:

Debts and expenses	$37,000
Claims of surviving spouse for homestead, exempt property, and family allowance	43,000
Net estate distributable to:	
Surviving spouse - specific monetary share [2]	100,000
Surviving spouse - ½ remainder [3]	160,000
Total to surviving spouse	303,000
Adult children - ½ remainder	160,000
Total probate estate	$500,000

(1) The Personal Representative can pay a reasonable sum up to $1,500 per month for one year without court approval.

8-4

(2) The specific monetary share to the surviving spouse is $200,000 if a decedent has no descendants, but has a surviving parent. It is $150,000 if the decedent has descendants who are descendants of the surviving spouse, and descendants who are not descendants of the surviving spouse. It is $100,000 if the decedent is survived by one or more descendants who are not descendants of the surviving spouse.

(3) The remainder to the surviving spouse is ¾ instead of ½ if the decedent has no descendants, but has a surviving parent.

Under the UPC, the surviving spouse takes the entire estate if all the decedent's children are also children of the surviving spouse, or if the decedent has no children and no surviving parent.

The UPC has been adopted with various modifications (some significant…see Chapter Nine Notes) by sixteen states: Alaska, Arizona, Colorado, Florida, Hawaii, Idaho, Maine, Michigan, Minnesota, Montana, Nebraska, New Mexico, North Dakota, South Carolina, South Dakota, and Utah. A number of other states, including California, have adopted portions of the UPC.

Other Examples of Intestate Succession

Among the states that have not adopted the UPC are Illinois, New York, Ohio, and Texas. The intestate succession laws of those four states, together with California, as applied to our $500,000 (less $37,000) probate estate example, are shown in Appendix H. Appendix H is summarized as follows:

	Surviving Spouse			
	Priority Claims	Remaining Share	Total Share	Adult Children's Share
California:				
Probate Estate	$24,000	$79,666)	$303,666	$159,334
Surviving Spouse's		)		
Community Property		200,000)		
Illinois	18,000	222,500	240,500	222,500
New York	44,000	234,500	278,500	184,500
Ohio	67,000	145,333	212,333	250,667
Texas:				
Probate Estate	100,000	61,000)	361,000	102,000
Surviving Spouse's		)		
Community Property		200,000)		

8-5

The examples are based upon the above facts, and the assumptions contained in Appendix H, including the assumption of a 50-year-old surviving spouse and the author's valuation of a life estate for a Texas homestead owned as community property. Different facts will generate different results, e.g., there may only be one child from the decedent's prior marriage, or the decedent's children might be minors, or in addition to children from a prior marriage, one or more of the children might be children of the decedent's marriage to the surviving spouse, or the surviving spouse could be age 40…or age 80, or the homestead in Texas could have been the decedent's separate property. The facts in a given case, together with the laws of intestate succession for the decedent's state of domicile (and other states if there is "out-of-state" real estate), will determine the distribution of the decedent's probate property.

Other Aspects of Intestate Succession

Other aspects of dying intestate include the probate court's appointment of someone to administer the estate (spouse, child, other relative, creditor), and where necessary, the appointment of a guardian for the decedent's minor children. The court will also require that a bond (a special insurance policy) be provided to safeguard estate assets from misappropriation by the administrator.

In a second or subsequent marriage, dying intestate may only exacerbate an already difficult matter to be worked out between a surviving spouse and children from a prior marriage. But, turned around, to die intestate may be a deliberate strategy.

Wills

The benefits of having a valid will are apparent: The testator (the person making the will) can, subject to spousal protections discussed in Chapter Nine, provide for distribution of his or her probate estate as he or she wishes, can select who will administer the estate as the Personal Representative (executor, executrix), can provide for estate tax apportionment (who bears the economic burden of the tax), can dispense with the requirement of a bond, and can, subject to court approval, appoint a guardian for his or her minor children. (Note: The surviving spouse cannot generally be made to bear the economic burden of estate taxes...see Chapter Nine.)

8-6

The Will Must Be Valid

What constitutes a valid will? A will is valid if it is "admitted to probate" as being the last will of the decedent, and one that meets the requirements of the state's probate code. For example, not everyone can make a will. Ohio's probate code provides: "A person of the age of eighteen years, or over, sound mind and memory, and not under restraint may make a will" (RC 2107.02).

Having sufficient mind and memory, i.e., having testamentary capacity, will be found in Ohio where the testator: (1) understands the nature of the business in which he is engaged; (2) comprehends generally the nature and extent of his property; (3) knows the identity of those who have natural claims upon his bounty, and (4) is able to appreciate his relation to members of his family (*Niemes v. Niemes; Doyle v. Schoot*).

The law, as expressed in *Restatement (Third) of Property: Wills and Other Donative Transfers, supra* § 8.1, is premised upon implementing the testator's intent. The will, therefore, must be the *will of the testator*, and not that of another person, i.e., the testator must be free from restraint and the undue influence of another. In Ohio, if a will is challenged on the basis of undue influence, the challenger must prove the following: (1) susceptibility of the testator; (2) an opportunity for another to exert influence; (3) the fact that improper influence was exerted or attempted; and (4) a result showing the effect of improper influence. "The mere existence of undue influence or an opportunity to exercise it, although coupled with an interest or motive to do so, is not sufficient to invalidate a will, but such influence must be actually exerted on the mind of the testator with respect to the execution of the will in question, and, in order to invalidate the will, it must be shown that the undue influence resulted in the making of testamentary dispositions which the testator would not otherwise have made." (*West v. Henry.*)

In a second or subsequent marriage, the testator might be influenced by his spouse, or by an adult child, but the question is, was the influence "undue"? The claim of undue influence can be difficult to prove. An early Ohio case stated: "Actions to contest wills are inaugurated with a legal presumption in favor of the will and of the mental capacity of the testator and against undue influence." (*Beresford v. Stanley—1898.*) Nevertheless, a recent case stated that where a claim of undue influence is made against one having a confidential relationship with the decedent, the one charged must show by a preponderance of the evidence that he or she is innocent of the charge and that the decedent acted voluntarily and with full understanding of his actions. If the one charged is able to show such evidence, the one making the claim must then prove the charge of undue influence via clear and convincing evidence. (*Wallbrown v. Kent State Univ.*)

Further requirements for a valid will in Ohio are, generally, that it be in writing, be signed at the end by the testator or some other person in the testator's presence (and at his or her express direction), and that it be signed in the testator's presence by two or more competent witnesses who saw the testator sign, or heard him or her acknowledge, his or her signature (RC 2107.03).

8-7

Each state will have its own specific requirements for admitting a will to probate as being the valid last will of the decedent. It is recommended that your will be prepared by an estate planning attorney licensed to practice in your state of domicile, and that the attorney be one of the witnesses to your will. As a witness, your attorney will be able to testify to the circumstances surrounding its execution.

Per Stirpes vs. Per Capita Distribution

Before discussing types of wills, let us look at an issue common to all wills: the distinction between a *per stirpes* (by the roots) and a *per capita* (by the heads) distribution of property. If a testator has three children and leaves his or her estate equally to three living children, the children will share the estate one-third each whether the testator leaves it "per stirpes" or "per capita." But if one of the children is deceased, leaving children, there is a difference. A per stirpes distribution still leaves the estate in thirds (by the roots) with one-third shares to each of the two living children, and with the deceased child's children sharing equally their deceased parent's one-third. A per capita distribution leaves the estate equally to the testator's two living children (by the heads), with nothing left to the children of the deceased child. That is a basic example. More complex examples would get into questions of will construction, intent, and the laws of the various states…including anti-lapse statutes designed to protect "forgotten" descendants.

Common Patterns of Distribution

Next, regardless of the type of will used, the will can be seen as having a one-, two-, or three-step pattern of distribution. A one-step residual pattern would leave everything outright or in percentages to the designated beneficiary or beneficiaries, e.g., to a spouse, children, other persons, or to a trust or charity. A two-step pattern would bequeath the tangible personal property to selected persons, with all the rest and residue of the estate distributed outright to the residual beneficiary. A three-step pattern would bequeath the tangible personal property as above, then make specific devises (real estate) or bequests (other personal property, e.g., sums of money, shares of stocks, etc.) to specific persons, and then leave all the rest and residue outright to the residual beneficiary or beneficiaries.

8-8

The following example shows a general disposition of tangible personal property that can be used in lieu of gifting specific items to named individuals:

> I give all of my tangible personal property to my spouse and to my children to be divided among them as they may agree, or if they are unable to agree, as my executor shall decide.
>
> I request (but do not direct) that the division of tangible personal property among my spouse and my children take into consideration any list or memorandum left by me at the time of my death.

Types of Wills

Note, for our purposes, that wills can be classified as *simple wills* (and simple mutual wills), *joint wills, trust wills* (wills containing a testamentary trust), and *pour-over wills*. We will also discuss contracts related to wills.

Simple Will

A *simple will* is inexpensive and provides the protection of the probate process. The probate process finalizes creditor claims, clears title to assets, requires accountings by the Personal Representative, and provides evidence that property has been properly distributed to beneficiaries. A simple will can dispose of all probate property directly to the beneficiaries in one step, or it can make specific gifts to named persons (e.g., jewelry to daughter, stamp collection to son, $5,000 to Aunt Nellie, etc.) with "all the rest and residue" (the residuary estate) to a designated beneficiary or beneficiaries.

In a second or subsequent marriage a simple will can be used as a tool to leave all the probate estate to a spouse, or as an attempt to leave all the probate estate to the children...forcing the surviving spouse to elect against the will to obtain the minimum statutory share. A simple will might also be used in a second or subsequent marriage where neither spouse has children from a prior marriage, or where the probate estate is small.

Simple Mutual Wills

Trusting couples in a second or subsequent marriage will often have simple but separate mutual wills (reciprocal or mirror-image wills) which leave their property to each other, and then to their children—usually to all of their children equally. The fatal drawback to the use of simple mutual wills, however, is that absent contractual language (and preferably a separate written contract not to change the will), the surviving spouse can defeat the mutual plan and change his or her will after the other's death, leaving all the couple's property to the surviving spouse's own children.

A critical portion of a *simple mutual will* might read as follows:

Summary: All to spouse if surviving, otherwise equally to children of both.

I give, devise and bequeath all the rest, remainder and residue of my estate whether real, personal or mixed, of every kind, nature and description whatsoever, and wheresoever situated, which I may now own or hereafter acquire, or have the right to dispose of at the time of my death, by power of appointment or otherwise (herein referred to as **my "residuary estate")**, **to my spouse, (Name), if (he/she) shall survive me, but if (he/she) shall not survive me, per stirpes to my and my said spouse's lineal descendants** who shall survive me by thirty (30) days.

8-9

Joint Will

A *joint will* is a single instrument signed by both a husband and wife as being his and her will. It might have the same terms as separate mutual wills, but here the terms are merged into one instrument. The same will is submitted to probate upon the death of each spouse as being the will of that spouse. But what if the second spouse makes a new will after the death of the first? The question then becomes whether or not the couple intended the joint will to be a contract that neither would change. The question also arises as to whether the joint will covers property acquired by the couple after the joint will is signed, or property acquired by the surviving spouse after the death of the first spouse, or whether it covers all the surviving spouse's property? Presumptively, the joint will only applies to property owned by the spouses at the time of the first death, but the language used in the will may signal a different intent.

A critical portion of a joint will might read the same as a simple will, but with modification to reflect the property intended to be covered, the agreed ultimate disposition of the property, and the contractual intent of the parties. Nevertheless, a joint will is fraught with potential for litigation, and there are potential estate tax problems as well. Do not use a joint will unless your intent is clearly expressed in the will and in a separate written contract. There are better ways to assure children of their inheritance, e.g., through the use of separate mutual wills with a related written contract or with an irrevocable trust or with non-probate transfers, e.g., life insurance, JTWROS accounts, P.O.D. accounts, etc.

Trust Will

A *trust will* (a will containing a testamentary trust) leaves the residuary estate to a trustee of the testator's choice. Nevertheless, the trustee does not become trustee until formally appointed by the probate court after the will is admitted to probate; thereafter (in many states) the trustee remains subject to probate court supervision during the term of the trust. The trustee apportions and distributes assets received from the estate (as well as other assets, such as life insurance made payable to the trust) in accordance with the provisions of the trust. Use of a trust will provides the protection of the probate court during estate administration, but it lacks privacy, and it may have added court costs and the expense of a bond (unless waived), and added attorney fees if there are ongoing accountings to the probate court.

Subject to a surviving spouse's priority claims and right to elect against the will, a trust will might be used in a second or subsequent marriage to block or control a spouse's or child's access to property, or for estate tax planning purposes, or both. Such tax planning can be done with a Marital Trust or with a Credit Shelter Trust, either or both of which can arise from a trust will. (Both are discussed below.) The testator's control can be exercised through trust provisions related to apportionment of property and the timing of its distribution.

A critical portion of a trust will (hereinafter referred to as a *Testamentary Trust*) might read as follows:

Summary:

All to appointed trustee for benefit of surviving spouse and children.

I give, devise and bequeath all the rest, remainder and residue of my estate whether real, personal or mixed, of every kind, nature and description whatsoever, and wheresoever situated, which I may now own or hereafter acquire, or have the right to dispose of at the time of my death, by power of appointment or otherwise (herein referred to as **my "residuary estate"), to the Trustee hereinafter named, in trust, for the benefit of my spouse, (Name), if he/she shall survive me, and my lineal descendants who shall survive me, as provided for herein.**

Pour-Over Will

A *pour-over will* leaves the residuary estate to an already existing trust, an *inter vivos* or living trust known as a Revocable Living Trust. The living trust typically becomes irrevocable upon death, and then it provides for the apportionment and distribution of assets received from the probate estate, as well as other assets already held in the trust, or made payable to the trust, e.g., life insurance proceeds. Upon death, apportionment of living trust assets will typically be to a Marital Trust and a Credit Shelter Trust, as discussed below.

A critical portion of a *pour-over will* to a Revocable Living Trust might read as follows:

Summary:

All to trustee of living trust for benefit of surviving spouse and children.

All the rest and remainder of my property I give and devise to the acting trustee, as successor trustee, **in augmentation of the property held** by him, her, or it **under the terms of a certain Trust Agreement** known as The (Name) Trust **entered into previously** this date between me and myself as initial trustee, as the same may be hereafter amended in writing.

8-11

Contracts Related To Wills

Contracts related to wills include contracts to make a will (with a given pattern of distribution), contracts not to revoke a will, and contracts not to make a will, i.e., an agreement to die intestate.

Contracts are agreements between competent parties that involve an offer, acceptance, and consideration, i.e., something of value exchanged, e.g., the mutual promises of the parties. Couples in a second or subsequent marriage who intend to have a contract govern their wills must make their contractual intent clear to the drafting attorney: Do they intend with their mutual wills (or joint will) to bind each other not to revoke or change the will, or do the parties intend that the surviving spouse will be free to change his or her will and dispose of the survivor's property, or all the couple's property, as he or she chooses?

Contracts themselves are not wills, and therefore litigation to enforce the contract will not take place in the Probate Court. Allegations about breach of a joint will or a mutual will, or a contract not to revoke a will, must be filed in another court, e.g., a Court of Common Pleas, with the judgment then brought into the Probate Court. If the alleged breach of contract is found to be true, the injured party's remedy is either receipt of money damages from the decedent's estate, or through specific performance, i.e., receipt of the specific thing in question, e.g., the diamond tiara, or the parcel of real estate. The executor of the estate, or recipient of the property, would be deemed to hold such property in a constructive trust for the benefit of the injured party.

Trusts

The essence of a trust is to have one person hold legal title to property for the benefit of another. The one transferring property to a trust is called a donor, grantor, settlor, or trustor; the holder of the property is a trustee; and the person for whom property is held is the beneficiary. There may be two or more donors, trustees, or beneficiaries, but one person could also be all three. Finally, the trustee may be an individual, or may be a corporation such as a bank or trust company.

The Fiduciary Relationship

The relationship between trustee and beneficiary is based upon a trusting, confidential relationship called a fiduciary relationship. The trustee is a fiduciary, and the law holds a fiduciary to a high standard of behavior, i.e., the fiduciary must act in the best interests of the beneficiary. The fiduciary duties of the trustee will include: (1) a duty to adhere to the terms of the trust, i.e., carry out the lawful intent of the donor of the trust property, whether expressed or implied; (2) a duty to use caution and prudence in handling trust property, i.e., a duty to transact business for the trust with the care and skill one of ordinary intelligence would employ in conducting a like enterprise of his or her own with similar objectives (or with greater skill if the trustee possesses greater skill), including the duty to preserve, protect, and defend trust property, and to make it productive; (3) a duty to maintain the highest loyalty to the beneficiary, i.e., the trustee is prohibited from any kind of self-dealing with the trust and must avoid even the potential for a conflict of interest with the beneficiary; and, (4) a duty to treat all beneficiaries impartially, including those with a future interest as well as those with a present interest, and those whose present (or future) interest may conflict with others having a similar interest.

In a second or subsequent marriage, the trustee's duty to impartially consider the interests of future beneficiaries (e.g., children from a prior marriage), as well as the interest of the current income beneficiary (e.g., the donor's surviving spouse), is a ticklish one (see "Total Return Trust").

Trusts Created by Operation of Law

Although a trust may be imposed by law as a result of a given transaction (a "Resulting Trust"), or as a court imposed remedy to correct a wrong or to avoid unjust enrichment (a "Constructive Trust"), the usual trust is an express trust whereby one person, the donor of the property, intends to create a trust for his or her own benefit, or the benefit of another person, and titles property into the name of the trust.

8-12

Express Trusts

An express trust is a trust created by contract; it may be oral (not recommended) or written, revocable (can be amended or revoked by the donor) or irrevocable (cannot be amended or revoked). A revocable trust typically becomes irrevocable upon the death of the donor or upon the donor's loss of legal capacity, e.g., senility. At that point, the trust cannot be changed (absent provision in the trust to do so) because the donor is either deceased or does not have the requisite mental capability to handle his affairs (at least the trust cannot be changed without the consent of all beneficiaries and a court order…assuming that the purpose of the trust has been materially accomplished).

Trusts Created During Lifetime or Upon Death

A trust can be a living trust (in existence during the donor's lifetime), or testamentary (contained in a testator's will; the trust comes into existence after the testator's death). A living trust is a private contract that can be for the primary benefit of the donor during his or her lifetime, and, upon death, can be used to benefit the donor's family. During the donor's lifetime, another person (or a bank or trust company) can be trustee, but often the donor acts as trustee of the trust and plays all three roles: donor, trustee, beneficiary. Upon the donor's death or incapacity, a successor trustee replaces the donor as trustee. Upon the donor's death, the persons the donor then intended to benefit from the trust become the beneficiaries, and the successor trustee acts on behalf of the new beneficiaries. (A trust cannot fail for the lack of a designated successor trustee; society, through the law, and the Probate Court, will appoint a trustee to carry out the lawful intent of the donor.)

A Revocable Living Trust is simple in operation; it is the donor's alter ego: trust income is reported on the donor's personal income tax return. The primary benefit of a Revocable Living Trust is avoidance of probate upon the donor's death or incapacity (assuming all assets are placed in trust). A funded trust will ease estate administration, especially if there is out-of-state real estate that has been transferred by deed into the trust. A testamentary trust, on the other hand, is subject to the probate process. Nevertheless, either type of trust can provide for continuity of property management with a successor trustee, either one can be used to block or control a spouse's or child's access to property after the donor's death, and either one can be used for estate tax planning purposes.

Types of Trusts

There are different types of trusts and different names given to the same type of trust. In addition to the basic Testamentary Trust and Revocable Living Trust discussed above, we will touch on several other types of trusts and give their purpose and their application in a second or subsequent marriage. They are: (1) the *Marital Trust* with two variations (*Power-of-Appointment Marital Trust* and *QTIP Marital Trust*); (2) the *Credit Shelter Trust*; (3) the *Joint Trust*; (4) the *Total Return Trust*; (5) the *Irrevocable Life Insurance Trust*; (6) the *Retained Interest Trust*; (7) the *Medicaid Trust*; (8) the *Generation Skipping Transfer Trust*; (9) the *Asset Protection Trust*; and (10) the *Dynasty Trust*.

Basic Trusts used in Estate Planning

The *Marital Trust* (also called a Marital Deduction Trust, "A" Trust, or Spousal Trust) and the *Credit Shelter* Trust (also called a Bypass Trust, "B" Trust, or Family Trust) come into existence upon the donor's death as separate parts springing from either a Testamentary Trust or a Revocable Living Trust. Property left to a Marital Trust is deductible for federal estate tax purposes. Property left to a Credit Shelter Trust, within allowable limits, is exempt from the tax.

Marital Trust

The *Marital Trust* is established following the donor's death for the sole benefit of the surviving spouse. All of the income from the trust is paid to or for the benefit of the surviving spouse (unless it is an "accumulation trust"), and principal is payable to the surviving spouse at the discretion of the trustee, or as otherwise provided in the trust agreement.

Power-of-Appointment Marital Trust

If it is a *Power-of-Appointment Marital Trust,* the income is paid to the surviving spouse (although it could be accumulated and added to trust principal…a so-called "accumulation trust"), and the trust will generally give the surviving spouse either a right to withdraw principal from the trust during his or her lifetime, or a right to "appoint" the principal upon the surviving spouse's death to beneficiaries of his or her choice. A Power-of-Appointment Marital Trust is typically used in a first marriage, but it can be used in a second or subsequent marriage. The fatal drawback to a Power-of-Appointment Marital Trust in a second or subsequent marriage is that it allows the surviving spouse to withdraw all funds from the Marital Trust, or to designate beneficiaries to receive the Marital Trust principal upon his or her death, e.g., it could all be paid to the surviving spouse's own children…thereby disinheriting the donor's children.

A critical portion of a *Power-of-Appointment Marital Trust* in a second or subsequent marriage might read as follows:

Summary:	Commencing as of the date of my death, the trustee shall pay the income from Trust A, at least as often as quarterly, to or for the sole benefit of my spouse so long
All income to the surviving spouse, plus principal at the trustee's discretion.	as he/she shall live and, in addition thereto, such **amounts of principal as the trustee from time to time shall deem desirable** to provide for his/her comfort and welfare, taking into consideration his/her income from this and other sources known to the trustee.
Surviving spouse can withdraw principal.	**Further, the trustee shall pay to my spouse such amounts of principal from Trust A as he/she may from time to time request.**

Upon the death of my spouse, the principal remaining

8-15

Surviving spouse can direct that trust be paid to his or her children upon surviving spouse's death.

in Trust A, or any part thereof, and any unpaid or accrued income from Trust A at the time of my spouse's death (a) **shall be distributed as he/she may appoint, by specific reference hereto in his/her will,** to his/her estate, or in trust or otherwise; and (b) as or to the extent not effectively so appointed shall be paid to his/her estate in such amounts as his/her personal representative may request in writing to

Remaining unappointed principal to donor's children.

pay part or all of his/her debts, debts of his/her estate, administration expenses, and taxes (except generation-skipping transfer taxes), including interest and penalties, arising by reason of his/her death, without any duty on the trustee to verify such amounts or see to their application; and (c) **any property not so appointed or requested shall be added to and disposed of as a part of Trust B.**

QTIP Marital Trust

If the Marital Trust is a *QTIP Trust* (qualified terminable interest property trust), then all of the income *must* be paid to the surviving spouse. The principal can typically be used for the surviving spouse at the discretion of the trustee if needed for his or her benefit, but—contrary to the Power-of-Appointment Marital Trust—the surviving spouse has no right to withdraw principal during his or her lifetime (unless a limited right is granted), and there is no right to appoint the principal upon his or her death to his or her creditors or beneficiaries, or to his or her estate, i.e., there is no general power of appointment. Upon the surviving spouse's death, the principal is paid to beneficiaries who have been pre-selected by the donor, e.g., the donor's children. A QTIP Marital Trust can be used in a first marriage to protect the donor's assets for his or her children in the event that the surviving spouse should remarry, and it is frequently used in second or subsequent marriages to preserve the donor's property for ultimate distribution to his or her own children from a prior marriage.

A critical portion of a *QTIP Marital Trust* might read as follows:

Summary:

All income to the surviving spouse, plus principal at the trustee's discretion.

Commencing as of the date of my death, the trustee shall pay the income from Trust A, at least as often as quarterly, to or for the sole benefit of my spouse so long as he/she shall live and, in addition thereto, such amounts of principal as the trustee from time to time shall deem desirable to provide for his/her comfort and welfare, taking into consideration his/her income from this and other sources known to the trustee.

8-16

The only additional principal paid is that needed to cover the surviving spouse's additional estate taxes resulting from inclusion of the marital trust in the surviving spouse's "taxable estate" for estate tax purposes.

Remaining balance to donor's children.

Upon the death of my spouse, any income for the period between the last distribution date and the date of his/her death shall be distributed as he/she may appoint by specific reference hereto in his/her Will to his/her estate, or in trust, or otherwise; and, to the extent not effectively so appointed, shall be distributed to his/her estate. In addition, if all or any part of Trust A is taxable in his/her estate for federal or state death tax purposes, then the trustee shall pay to the executor of his/her estate (unless waived by such executor) so much of the principal of Trust A, if any, as such executor shall be entitled to recover from the trustee or trust distributees under applicable law or the terms of his/her will, not to exceed the amount by which total state and/or federal estate taxes actually payable, including any interest but not any penalty, exceed the taxes and interest which would have been payable if such Trust A property had not been included in his/her taxable estate. The trustee shall have no duty to see to the application of any funds paid over to his/her estate and the receipt of his/her executor shall be a complete acquittance to the trustee with respect thereto. The balance of Trust A shall be added to Trust B to be held, administered and distributed as a part thereof.

Credit Shelter Trust

The *Credit Shelter Trust* is a companion of the Marital Trust; it is established following the donor's death to receive assets in an amount up to the amount of property you can "pass on" without a federal estate tax. That amount, the lifetime exemption amount, is as follows under present law:

2004-2005	$1,500,000
2006-2008	$2,000,000
2009	$3,500,000
2010	Taxes Repealed

It is not clear what the law will be in 2011. The tax could be totally eliminated, or the lifetime exemption could revert to $1,000,000, or it could be set at a new level, e.g., $2,500,000, or some other amount.

8-17

The Credit Shelter Trust might be: (1) distributed outright following the donor's death to beneficiaries other than the surviving spouse, e.g., to the donor's children; or (2) held in trust for its beneficiaries, typically for the lifetime benefit of the surviving spouse, with the remainder paid to the donor's children upon the death of the surviving spouse. The income from the Credit Shelter Trust (depending upon the need for income and other considerations such as differing tax brackets of beneficiaries) can either be paid totally to the surviving spouse or "sprinkled," at the trustee's discretion, among a group of beneficiaries, e.g., the surviving spouse and the donor's children and grandchildren. If needed, principal can typically be paid to the surviving spouse for health, support, maintenance, or education. In addition, the surviving spouse is sometimes given a right to withdraw principal each year equal to the greater of 5 percent of the principal balance, or $5,000. The right of withdrawal might not be given in a second or subsequent marriage.

Flexibility can be added to the Credit Shelter Trust by giving the surviving spouse a limited power-of-appointment (exercisable during lifetime or by will at the surviving spouse's death) to appoint the principal remaining in the trust among a group of beneficiaries designated in the trust, typically among the donor's children, or perhaps the donor's children and grandchildren.

In addition to the lifetime exemption amount, the Credit Shelter Trust can be designated to receive the balance remaining in the Marital Trust upon the death of the surviving spouse, i.e., the entire amount if it is a QTIP Marital Trust, or the unwithdrawn or unappointed portion if it is a Power-of-Appointment Marital Trust.

A critical portion of a *Credit Shelter Trust* might read as follows:

Summary:	Commencing as of the date of my death, the trustee shall pay the income from the property retained in trust under the provisions of this Article, sometimes referred to as Trust B, **to my spouse so long as he/she shall live.** Any
All income to the surviving spouse.	unpaid or accrued income at the time of my spouse's death shall be paid to his/her estate. **In addition, the trustee shall pay to my spouse such amounts of principal as the trustee in its sole discretion may deem necessary for his/her health, education, support, and maintenance,** taking into
Principal to surviving spouse if needed.	consideration his/her income from this and other sources available therefor; provided, however, that no such payments shall be made unless Trust A shall have been exhausted to the extent that assets therein can be practicably converted into cash. Last sickness and funeral expenses of my spouse may be paid by the trustee.
Remaining principal to donor's children.	**Upon the death of the survivor of my spouse and me, the principal in Trust B, and any additions from Trust A or other additions at any time received, shall be administered and disposed of as hereinafter provided.** (Provisions for children then follow.)

8-18

Sheltering Assets and Deferring Estate Taxes

If the decedent's assets, after deducting debts and expenses, are less than the lifetime exemption amount at the time of his or her death, there is no federal estate tax. If the net assets exceed the lifetime exemption amount, there still is no federal estate tax if the additional assets are left either outright to the surviving spouse or to a Marital Trust (Power-of-Appointment or QTIP) for the surviving spouse. The estate tax is then deferred. The estate tax on the assets left outright or to a Marital Trust is levied *after* the death of the surviving spouse, but then only if they, together with the surviving spouse's other assets, exceed the lifetime exemption amount in effect when the surviving spouse dies.

Summary of Marital and Credit Shelter Trusts

The Credit Shelter Trust can be established at any amount up to the lifetime exemption amount. The lifetime exemption amount, under present law, is a moving target until 2011. The Marital Trust receives the excess not allocated to the Credit Shelter Trust. The Marital Trust can be a Power-of-Appointment Trust (giving power to the surviving spouse to withdraw or appoint property), or a

QTIP Trust (wherein the surviving spouse has no power to withdraw or appoint property), or partly each. The amount left to the Credit Shelter Trust (and its future appreciation in value) is exempt from estate tax. The amount left to the Marital Trust is not taxable in the donor's estate, but is subject to tax (if there is a tax) in the surviving spouse's estate.

Following are examples to show the variety of Marital Trust and Credit Shelter Trust allocations possible for different levels of assets owned by the donor at the time of death, assuming his or her death occurs in 2004 or 2005 (if death occurs between 2006 and 2008 the Credit Shelter Trust can be $2,000,000...in 2009, $3,500,000):

Donor's Assets	Marital Trust		Credit Shelter Trust
	QTIP	Power of Appointment	
$500,000	...	...	$500,000
$750,000	...	...	$750,000
$1,000,000	...	...	$1,000,000
$1,500,000	...	...	$1,500,000
$2,000,000	...	$500,000	$1,500,000
$2,500,000	$500,000	$500,000	$1,500,000
$3,000,000	$1,500,000	...	$1,500,000

8-19

Joint Trust

Another type of trust, the *Joint Trust*, is a living trust used to pool a couple's assets for their mutual benefit. The husband and wife are usually co-donors, co-trustees, and co-beneficiaries. Each person contributes his or her property to the trust (re-titles assets into the name of the trust), and the assets are invested and used by both as they agree. The trust is typically revocable and can be amended during the lifetime of both donors. If it is revoked, each donor can expect a return of the property that he or she contributed. (Unless the couple intends joint ownership, good records should be kept so that the assets can be traced.) Upon the death or incapacity of one, the trust can remain revocable (if the trust agreement so provides) and remain subject to amendment by the other, or it can become irrevocable. If it remains revocable, the surviving spouse can change the beneficiaries of the trust or remove property from the trust and make a new will or a new trust. That flexibility may be desirable in a first marriage, but not in a second or subsequent marriage. A Joint Trust that remains revocable after the death of the first spouse has the same fatal flaw in a second or subsequent marriage as a simple will or Power-of-Appointment Marital Trust: The surviving spouse can change the plan after the first spouse's death and leave all the couple's property to the survivor's own children.

If a Joint Trust is used in a second or subsequent marriage, it is recommended that it become irrevocable upon the death or incapacity of either spouse. A Joint Trust that becomes irrevocable upon the death or incapacity of one could have provisions for both spouses, and their children, as follows:

- Income payable to spouses (and the surviving spouse) for life;
- Principal payable to either spouse if needed for health, education, maintenance, or support; and

Upon the death of the surviving spouse:

- distribution of assets as previously agreed upon, e.g., 50-50 to his and her children, or some other split.

As with a joint will, a Joint Trust can present questions related to the property to be covered (e.g., property owned at the first death, or all property owned at the survivor's death), and a couple must make their intent clear to the drafting attorney. As with a joint will, a separate contract "not to amend or revoke" (if that is the intent) is recommended.

Provision may or may not be made in a Joint Trust for a successor co-trustee upon the death or incapacity of one spouse. An alternative is to have the ongoing spouse continue as sole trustee until his or her own incapacity or death. At that time, a predetermined successor trustee or co-trustees would assume the duties of trustee. One child might be designated from each family in a second or subsequent marriage to serve as co-trustees, with provision for arbitration in the event of a dispute.

A Joint Trust could be funded during the donor's lifetime or it could be funded via pour-over wills or with life insurance proceeds or other payable on death accounts. It could, upon the death of one, break into a Marital Trust and a Credit Shelter Trust (in which case expert tax planning is needed), or more typically, it could remain a single trust (in effect a Credit Shelter Trust), for the surviving spouse and, ultimately, the children.

A funded Joint Trust might be considered in either a first or subsequent marriage by a couple living in a community property state, or to house community property for a couple who formerly lived in a community property state but who now lives in a separate property state. The Joint Trust for community property would eliminate tracing problems.

A couple might also consider a Joint Trust in either a first or subsequent marriage if their combined assets are less than the lifetime exemption amount, i.e., $1,500,000 in 2004 and 2005, $2,000,000 from 2006 to 2008, $3,500,000 in

2009 (and not likely to grow), and if they want to provide for the surviving spouse but, at the same time, "lock-in" a planned distribution to children upon the survivor's death. If the couple's assets might exceed the lifetime exemption amount, separate Revocable Living Trusts that contain Marital and Credit Shelter Trust provisions are recommended for each spouse. In addition, separate trusts should be used in a second or subsequent marriage if there is likely to be discord among the children.

A critical portion of a *Joint Trust* might read as follows:

(In the preamble)

Summary:

Outlines donor's intent.

WHEREAS, it is the intent of each donor to create and fund a revocable living trust for the benefit of both donors during their joint lifetime, with such trust to become irrevocable upon the death of the first to die, or upon the permanent incapacity of either donor; and whereas it is further intended that the trust be for the lifetime benefit of the surviving donor, and then for the benefit of the lineal descendants of both donors, as specifically provided for herein, upon the death of the surviving donor;

8-21

(In the body of the agreement)

Both donors must agree to amend or revoke.

Subject to the following paragraph, **the donors together, while both are living and competent, may at any time, by written notice filed with the trustee, change any beneficiary hereunder, amend any provision hereof, or revoke this trust in whole or in part.**

Cannot be amended or revoked after death or incapacity of either spouse.

This trust shall become irrevocable upon the death of the first donor to die, or the permanent incapacity of either donor so as not to be able to handle his or her business affairs. Such permanent incapacity shall be determined by, and evidenced in a writing from, the incapacitated person's personal physician. **This Agreement may not be changed, amended or revoked after such death or permanent incapacity.**

Total Return Trust

A *Total Return Trust* is a trust that embraces the shift in investment philosophy from the historic Prudent Person Rule (emphasizing a conservative preservation of principal and generation of income strategy), to one incorporating Modern Portfolio Theory. This shift in standards is reflected in states adopting modern Uniform Prudent Investor Acts and Uniform Principal and Income Acts.

Total return investing will consider the long-term effects of inflation and loss of purchasing power: It will emphasize equity investments and a "portfolio approach" rather than an "asset by asset" approach to investing. A portfolio approach will diversify investments across various asset classes to balance the risk of loss against the total return desired. Total return will include income and capital appreciation, and total return investing will consider the needs of future beneficiaries as well as the current income beneficiary. Payments to the current income beneficiary (e.g., a surviving spouse) will be based upon a uniform percentage of the trust value, e.g., 3 to 5 percent, or adjusted cash flow (a trustee determined combination of income and harvested capital gains), rather than income alone.

The total return investment concept can be incorporated by the donor (while he or she is alive and competent) into a Testamentary Trust, a Revocable Living Trust (and within each of those, a Marital Trust and Credit Shelter Trust), a Joint Trust, and other trusts as appropriate.

8-22

A critical portion of a *Total Return Trust* might read as follows:

<u>Summary:</u>

Authorizes trustee to invest for total return, and to adjust payments to income beneficiary.

I hereby authorize and direct the trustee to invest trust assets for total return. In doing so I realize that the income received by my spouse as income beneficiary may be less than if the assets were invested for current income. Therefore, I **authorize the trustee to pay to my spouse, from the principal of the trust, such additional amounts as the trustee deems proper to provide a reasonable return for him/her considering among other things my intent to benefit both my spouse and my children with the total return of the trust.**

Irrevocable Life Insurance Trust

An *Irrevocable Life Insurance Trust* (ILIT) is designed to hold a life insurance policy that will provide liquidity upon the death of the insured spouse, or if it is a "second to die policy," upon the death of the surviving spouse. If the policy is issued on one life, it can provide financial security for the surviving spouse, the children, or both, or it can be used to concentrate assets in the hands of selected beneficiaries. If it is issued on the lives of both spouses, payable upon the death of the second to die, it is either intended to pay estate taxes upon the second death, or to replace the wealth that has been lost to estate taxes. Regardless of the type of policy used, the purpose of the insurance is to provide money when needed—money that is not itself subject to income tax or estate tax.

The dollars paid into the trust by the donor to pay premiums constitute a gift to the trust beneficiaries, typically the donor's children, and with planning, need not be subject to gift taxes or any use of the donor's $1,000,000 lifetime gift tax exemption. In community property states, the trust should be funded with the donor's separate property (transmuted by agreement from community property, if need be).

If an existing policy is transferred to the trust (instead of the trust acquiring a new policy) the donor must outlive the transfer by three years in order to avoid inclusion of the proceeds in his or her taxable estate for estate tax purposes. Under the 1990 Uniform Probate Code, the trust would need to be in place for at least two years before the donor's death in order to avoid inclusion of the policy proceeds in the surviving spouse's elective share calculation (see Chapter Nine). But, subject to those two timing rules, an ILIT can be used in a second or subsequent marriage in a variety of ways to benefit the donor's children from a prior marriage without having the proceeds be subject to estate taxes, probate, or claims of a surviving spouse. One such benefit may be to preserve a family business for them. (See Chapter Ten.)

8-23

Retained Interest Trust

A *Retained Interest Trust* involves an irrevocable gift of your property to a trust that pays you the income (or allows you use of the property) for a period of years or for your lifetime (or for the joint lifetime of you and your spouse), but then, upon your death(s), or the expiration of the period of years, transfers the property from the trust to a remainder beneficiary, e.g., to your children or to a charity.

The following are examples of Retained Interest Trusts:

- The Qualified Personal Residence Trust…a gift of your home to your children for their future sale or use, while in the meantime you continue to live in it for a period of years;

- A Grantor Retained Annuity Trust (GRAT)…a gift of assets, e.g., to children, whereby you retain a *fixed* annuity income for a period of years, or life, or joint-life;

- A Grantor Retained Unitrust (GRUT)…a gift of assets, e.g., to children, whereby you retain a *variable* annuity income for a period of years, or life, or joint-life;

- A Charitable Remainder Trust (CRT)…a gift of assets to charity whereby you retain a fixed annuity income (CRAT) or variable annuity income (CRUT) for a period of years, or life, or joint life. (The reverse of a CRT is the Charitable Lead Trust (CLT) where the income is paid to charity for a period of years or your lifetime, but the principal is retained for your designated beneficiary, e.g., your children.) There are current income tax benefits, as well as ultimate estate tax benefits, with a CRT or a CLT. A percentage of the gift is currently deductible from income, and the gifted assets are not subject to estate tax.

Medicaid Trust

A *Medicaid Trust* is designed to put assets beyond the reach of the state before one applies for Medicaid. A Medicaid Trust is, in essence, a gift of assets (typically to children) to impoverish oneself. In some cases, the donor might receive the income from the trust, and only make a gift of the remainder interest.

A Medicaid Trust might be attempted in a second or subsequent marriage if you want to preserve assets for your children regardless of the consequences to your spouse. To use a military analogy, we can say this: To use a Medicaid Trust is to call an air strike onto your spouse's asset position; you reserve your assets for your children, but your spouse's assets are put at risk to pay your nursing home costs. (*Note: Medicaid planning, with all its complexities, is a specialty, so a specialist must be engaged.*)

8-24

Generation Skipping Transfer Trust

A *Generation-Skipping Transfer Trust* (GST Trust) enables you to pass an amount equal to the lifetime exemption amount (currently $1,500,000) to your grandchildren, in trust, without the assets incurring an estate tax in your children's estates. The trust would typically arise out of a QTIP Trust and Credit Shelter Trust upon the death of the survivor of you and your spouse. Instead of distribution to your children at that time, the assets are retained in a GST Trust with income typically payable to your children for their lifetime, and with principal paid to them if needed for their health, maintenance, education, or support. The principal remaining upon your children's death is then paid to your grandchildren. With this technique, you, as a grandparent, are able to pass trust assets to your grandchildren without reduction for the estate taxes that may have been payable had those assets been included in your children's estates.

The future of the GST Trust as a tax saving device may depend upon the future of the estate tax itself. If the estate tax is repealed, the GST tax may also be repealed, or at least modified, and if that happens there may be no need, from a tax standpoint, for the GST Trust. A GST Trust might still be considered, however, in cases where your children are themselves in second or subsequent marriages. Such a trust could preserve your assets for the benefit of your children during their lifetime, and then be paid to your grandchildren.

Asset Protection Trust

An *Asset Protection Trust* (APT) is an irrevocable trust designed to shield assets from the claims of creditors…other than tax claims. The trust must be established *before there is a problem* in order to avoid claims of fraudulent transfer of assets. Creation and maintenance of an APT is expensive, and therefore it is more suitable (in conjunction with a corporation or limited liability company) for extra-large asset holdings that are potentially at risk from lawsuits. Although an APT might be considered in a given second or subsequent marriage, there are less expensive ways, in the ordinary case, to protect assets from spousal claims. If an APT is of interest, the states having modern APT statutes include Alaska, Delaware, Nevada, and Rhode Island. Offshore jurisdictions with modern APT laws include the Bahamas, the Cook Islands, Nevis, St. Kitts, and St. Lucia. British rule jurisdictions include England, the Isle of Man, and Jersey. Properly planned, the offshore APT will provide the best protection against creditor claims (including spousal claims) that money can buy. Needless to say, specialized legal counsel is needed.

Dynasty Trust

Finally, there is the *Dynasty Trust*, the ultimate GST Trust. A Dynasty Trust is **8-25** usually an Irrevocable Life Insurance Trust with special provisions that allow it to exist for generations, even perpetually. The trust is designed to protect assets from the claims of creditors while, hopefully, it increases in value and supports generation after generation of your descendants. Special consideration needs to be given to the following: applicable state law; the "rule against perpetuities"; income tax issues; generation-skipping transfer tax issues; investment and distribution issues; the "per stirpes" versus "per capita" issue; the issue of successor trustees; the trustee's powers; and the trustee's right to terminate the trust and distribute the property at some point in the future.

Despite its complexities, a Dynasty Trust can be considered if you have the financial ability to create a large life insurance trust and you wish to insulate the assets from your descendants' spouses and other creditors for generations to come.

Spendthrift Trust Provision

A footnote to the whole discussion of trusts is this: Every trust you create should contain a *spendthrift provision* to block beneficiaries and their creditors from encumbering or gaining access to trust assets before you intend the assets to be distributed. (A spendthrift provision will generally protect assets for your beneficiaries after your death, but will not protect assets in *your* Revocable Living Trust from *your* creditors during your lifetime. Where *your* creditors are the issue, a corporation, limited partnership, limited liability company, or Asset Protection Trust should be considered.)

Summary of Wills and Trusts

A basic understanding of wills and trusts is necessary for you to understand your options and to discuss them with an estate planning attorney.

Chapter Nine—Reading Notes

Probate, Spousal Elections, Will Contest, Trust Contest

Probate

When a person dies, why shouldn't the family come into the house and divide his or her things among themselves and be done with it? The division could be done according to the will, if there is a will, or as the family agrees, if there is no will. Such a process would be natural. Why should a branch of the state government be involved? Answer: Peace…and to be sure that debts and taxes are paid…and to be sure that beneficiaries get good title to their property.

Without an orderly, fair process, and a forum for resolution of disputes, there could be chaos. Therefore, in every county of every state there is a court designated to oversee the administration of estates in that county; it is known as the Probate Court (or Surrogate Court, Orphans Court, or District Court in some states), and an elected official, a Judge, is in charge of overseeing the probate process. The Probate Court that will have jurisdiction over your estate is the one where you live and have your domicile. (But your out-of-state real estate will be subject to the jurisdiction of the Probate Court where the real estate is located…unless the real estate is owned in trust or survivorship form.)

The role of the Probate Court, in essence, is to protect the rights of creditors, to see that the decedent's taxes get paid, to assure clear transfer of title to assets, and to assure the proper distribution of the decedent's net estate to beneficiaries (if there is a will), or to heirs according to the state's Statute of Descent and Distribution (if there is no will). Title to the decedent's probate assets vests immediately upon death: Beneficiaries or heirs own the decedent's probate assets from the start…subject, however, to the court appointed fiduciary's right to possess the assets for purposes of paying the decedent's debts, taxes, and estate expenses.

Although each state has its own statutes to govern the probate process in that state, and each Probate Court has its own rules of court to govern the mechanics of administration in that county, the following excerpt from an estate administration pamphlet prepared and issued as a public service by the Summit County, Ohio, Probate Court, is instructive. The court handles about 3,500 new estates each year.

What is estate administration?

When an individual dies, certain of his or her assets transfer or pass automatically by contract (i.e., joint and survivorship property); the remaining assets must be transferred through proceedings in Probate Court. It is the Court's responsibility to insure that those assets are collected, maintained, and fairly distributed among the decedent's heirs, beneficiaries, and/or creditors according to the directions of the decedent and/or the laws of Ohio. This transfer of probate assets is known as the administration of decedent's estate.

9-2

May funds be withdrawn from bank accounts?

Accounts in decedent's name alone may only be removed by a Court appointed fiduciary. Accounts in the decedent's name and other parties may have 75% of the amount removed by the survivor but the balance may only be removed, except in the case of a spouse, or if the amount is less than $25,000, upon presentation of a valid tax waiver.

What are the duties of the fiduciary?

Once the Court is notified of decedent's death, and receives a request to administer the estate, the court then appoints and issues letters of authority to a fiduciary (with a will, executor—without a will, administrator). It then becomes the responsibility of the fiduciary to administer the decedent's estate and to account to the Court for that administration. A fiduciary who fails to perform his or her duties is subject to removal by the Court. The fiduciary, who may be bonded, is appointed according to the decedent's will or by statutory guidelines.

What property must be appraised?

All property values which are not readily ascertainable, such as real estate, closely held corporation stock, and partnerships must be appraised. The Court will appoint an appraiser to value any real estate.

Does a fiduciary need an attorney?

Due to the complexity of the law and the legal problems that may be involved in estate administration, the Court strongly recommends that all fiduciaries seek legal counsel. Good legal advice and guidance can expedite probate, prevent costly errors, and insure that the fiduciary is not cited or sued for mistake or wrongdoing.

How long should the administration of an estate take?

Ordinarily, the average estate should be finalized within six (6) months of the date of appointment of the fiduciary. However, where litigation, federal or state tax returns, or creditor disputes exist, the estate may require a longer administration.

9-3

What are the steps of an estate administration?

A. Notice of death and application for authority to administer the estate (probate of will if one exists).
B. Appointment of fiduciary.
C. Gathering assets and filing Inventory (Inventory is due ninety (90) days after appointment).
D. Payment of creditors.
E. Filing and payment of estate taxes. While estate taxes are due within 9 months of decedent's death, there is available one 6-month automatic extension.
F. Distribution of assets to beneficiary(s) or heirs.
G. Closing the estate and filing a final account (Accounting is due six (6) months after appointment unless an extension is granted).

How is a problem with an estate brought to the attention of the court?

Estate problems are brought to the court's attention by the filing of pleadings which are set for hearing with notice to all interested parties.

What is a release from administration?

Where decedent's creditors will not be prejudiced, and the probate estate consists of property less than $35,000.00, the estate may be released from administration. An estate of $100,000.00 may be released from administration if all property passes to the surviving spouse of the decedent. A report of the distribution of assets is filed within sixty (60) days.

Must a will be probated?

The Last Will and Testament of a decedent must be presented to the court within three (3) years of the decedent's death. If a will is withheld intentionally, negligently, or without some reasonable cause, by any individual, such person may lose his right to inherit. An action may be filed in probate court at any time after death of the decedent to require the production of a will. Failure to produce a will upon court order may result in the holder being cited for contempt.

What if there is no will?

9-4

An estate where there is no will is generally administered in the same manner as if a will had been probated. However, the decedent's property is distributed according to the Ohio Descent and Distribution Law. If beneficiaries are unknown, the filing of a civil action to determine heirship may be required.

What if the will is unclear?

If the will is unclear, a civil action called a will construction must be filed in Probate Court.

What if there is an objection to the will?

Any interested party has the right to contest the validity of the will by the filing of a will contest in Probate Court within three (3) months after a certificate has been filed with the Court evidencing notice of probate to all parties.

Used with permission.

Court Appointed Fiduciary

The court appointed fiduciary is called an executor (executrix) if there is a will, or an administrator (administratrix) if there is no will. The Uniform Probate Code, and states that have adopted it, use the generic term "Personal Representative." The Personal Representative has the power of the court behind him or her, but must account to the court for actions taken. The Personal Representative will usually hire an attorney to handle the probate process, to prepare income and estate tax returns for the estate, and to represent the estate in all legal matters.

The Personal Representative appointed by the Probate Court in the usual case will be the person designated in the decedent's will. If there is no will, an application for authority to administer the estate is filed with the Probate Court by someone having an interest in the estate. In most estates, where there is no will, the surviving spouse is named the Personal Representative. An adult child could be named Personal Representative, but that does not usually happen when there is a surviving spouse.

Second or Subsequent Marriage Issues

In a second or subsequent marriage, three issues stand out in the administration of a deceased spouse/parent's estate. The first is *control*, the second is *discretion*, and the third is *compensation*.

As a practical necessity, the fiduciary must take control of the estate assets and be given a degree of discretion in handling the estate. Nevertheless, the Personal Representative is governed by a fiduciary duty to act with care, skill, and prudence in the interest of the estate (and the beneficiaries of the estate), and not in his or her own self-interest. To complicate that issue, however, the fiduciary will usually be a beneficiary of the estate. What protections do the other beneficiaries have should the Personal Representative breach his or her fiduciary duties? If warranted, the Personal Representative may be held liable for losses resulting from mismanagement, bad faith actions, or breach of fiduciary duty. In a given case, the Personal Representative may be removed by the Probate Court or denied compensation. He or she will not be punished, however, merely because there are disagreements or personality conflicts with beneficiaries.

Control

The *control* issue may first assert itself in the handling and distribution of the decedent's memorabilia, jewelry, furniture, works of art, and personal effects. The will may not be clear as to the testator's intent, or maybe there is no will. The will (or the Statute of Descent and Distribution if there is no will) may give priority, or discretion, to the surviving spouse. The surviving spouse (in the dual role of surviving spouse and Personal Representative) will have physical possession and legal control of the decedent's tangible personal property, i.e., all the property with family and emotional attachments. With that, when you add the emotions and changing family dynamics following the death of a spouse and parent, there is the potential for disagreement...especially when the surviving spouse is not otherwise related to the children. For many families, the relationships will have been good, and there will be no dispute, but in others the setting may be resent-ful, even volatile, with repressed feelings now coming to the surface. Hopefully, while living, the deceased spouse will have anticipated the emotional aspects of tangible personal property items, one way or another, and will have made specific provisions in his or her will or other written memorandum. (The making of gifts during one's lifetime may be the best strategy for some tangible property items.)

Control can also assert itself in a decision to sell or retain certain assets, in the allocation of certain assets among beneficiaries, and in the timing of distribu-tions. Such control might be exercised as if from the smooth hand of a master, or it might be used as if a blunt instrument, void of personal consideration.

Discretion

Discretion is the second issue. The Personal Representative, in the exercise of his or her fiduciary duties, is given latitude and discretion in valuing certain assets. Even where assets require an appraisal, the Personal Representative still has dis-cretion. An automobile may have a wholesale value, a retail value, or a value somewhere in between. Although subject to appraisal, the same can be said of boats, trains, planes, and jewelry. As to real estate, fair market value is somewhat in the eye of the beholder, and the best gauge is the actual selling price between an informed buyer and an informed seller, neither being under any compulsion to buy or sell. But, assuming the marital residence is not sold, a lower discretionary value for the residence may be negotiated between the surviving spouse, as Personal Representative, and the designated appraiser (if any). Unless the surviving spouse is receiving the entire estate, a lower value will favor the surviving spouse because the surviving spouse will normally receive the residence as part of his or her distribution from the estate. If the residence is "undervalued," additional assets will be apportioned to fulfill the surviving spouse's allotted portion of the total estate. In addition, if the residence is later sold, it will have built-in future profit potential for the surviving spouse.

The valuation of assets may also have income and estate tax ramifications that favor one beneficiary over another. For example, upon distribution of the estate (whether to an individual or to the trustee of a Marital Trust or Credit Shelter Trust), one beneficiary may receive an asset having a high tax-basis, e.g., a high value at date of death or alternate valuation date (and therefore low capital gains tax when sold), and another beneficiary may receive an asset of equal current value, but with a low valuation date tax-basis (and therefore high capital gains tax when sold). Although the assets are of equal face value, they are not of equal after-tax value.

9-6

Discretion is also involved in the investment of estate assets. The Personal Representative has a primary duty to preserve and protect estate assets, but not a duty to invest and make the assets productive. Clearly, it is only prudent to deposit estate funds into a bank account, but beyond that, the Personal Representative must look to the decedent's will or state statutes for guidance. If investments in stocks, bonds, mutual funds, etc., are allowable, there is obviously some latitude and discretion as to what the Personal Representative might choose to do. (A business owned by the decedent is a special investment problem. If the decedent had a business, is the business to be continued? For how long? Or should it be liquidated? The terms of the will and state statutes will have to be closely followed.)

Compensation

9-7 Finally, the Personal Representative is entitled to *compensation*, usually at a rate provided by statute. In many cases, the fiduciary's compensation is waived or reduced for family reasons, and because it constitutes taxable income to a recipient who might otherwise inherit the assets tax-free. Nevertheless, if the surviving spouse is not receiving the entire probate estate under the decedent's will (or if there is no will), the surviving spouse, as fiduciary, may take the fee as an additional source of revenue from the estate.

An Issue of Special Interest

Against this background, what stands out as the key issue in a second or subsequent marriage? Answer: The Inventory and Appraisal filed with the Probate Court, i.e., the listing and valuation of all the decedent's individual property interests. Both the surviving spouse and the children from a prior marriage should be especially interested in the Inventory and Appraisal. If the values or contents of the Inventory and Appraisal are not correct, they can be challenged, but the challenge must be done on a timely basis. Are all the decedent's probate assets listed? Are the values shown the actual fair market values of the assets? If there is a question, and if the amount involved justifies the expense, an interested party may want to retain an attorney, hire an appraiser, and challenge the Inventory and Appraisal in the Probate Court. When there is a challenge, however, the Personal Representative has two important advantages: First, the burden is on the challenger to prove the Inventory and Appraisal to be in error; and second, the expenses of the Personal Representative will be paid from the estate (although a Personal Representative acting in bad faith may be required to pay such expenses), whereas the challenger will have to pay his or her own attorney and appraisal fees...unless the Probate Court, upon application, allows such expenses to be paid from the estate (which could happen if the challenge is shown to have benefited the estate).

All of this begs the question: In a second or subsequent marriage, whom should you have as your Personal Representative? Your spouse? Your son or daughter? Your attorney? A bank or trust company?

Spousal Elections

Most married couples leave each other a good part of their estates. But some do not, especially in a second or subsequent marriage, and spousal elections are provided by law as a protection against disinheritance. An elective share, if taken by a surviving spouse, is taken instead of the share provided under the deceased spouse's will, i.e., the surviving spouse "elects against the will." If there is no will, the surviving spouse is entitled to an intestate share of the estate (see Chapter Eight).

9-8

Community Property States

In *community property states,* where each spouse owns one-half of the community property, the issue is simple relative to the community property: There is no spousal election. Because each spouse owns one-half of the community property at all times during the marriage, no protection is needed. Upon the death of one, the surviving spouse takes his or her half of the community property, and the decedent's half is distributed as he or she has provided for in estate planning instruments of transfer, e.g., by will, trust, survivorship accounts, beneficiary designations, etc., or if none, pursuant to the Statute of Descent and Distribution. In California, if no estate planning instrument of disposition has been used, the decedent's community property goes to the surviving spouse. In Texas, 50 percent goes to the surviving spouse and 50 percent goes to the decedent's children, unless they are also the children of the surviving spouse. In addition, Arizona, California, Idaho, New Mexico, and Washington have explicit rules for "quasi-community property," i.e., personal property acquired while married and domiciled in another state. For example, quasi-community property in California is treated as if it were community property, i.e., one-half is owned by the surviving spouse and the other one-half can be distributed according to the decedent's will or trust or other instruments of transfer. If there is no disposition, the quasi-community property also passes to the surviving spouse (Cal. Prob. Code § 6401 (b)).

Separate property in a community property state, e.g., property acquired before the marriage, property acquired by gift or inheritance during the marriage, or property acquired while domiciled in a non-community property state (except as deemed quasi-community property) is distributed pursuant to the decedent's will, trust, or other instruments of transfer, otherwise pursuant to the Statute of Descent and Distribution. The California and Texas statutes, as community property state examples, are summarized in Appendix H.

Separate Property (Common Law) States

In *separate property states* the surviving spouse is protected from disinheritance by spousal election statutes. Most separate property states have a "forced share statute," meaning the surviving spouse is entitled to a share of the decedent's probate estate regardless of the decedent's estate plan. The statute attempts to balance the idea of protection for a surviving spouse with the idea of freedom to transfer property. Depending upon the number of descendants, and whether any of them are also descendants of the surviving spouse, the forced share statutes generally provide an elective share to the surviving spouse of *one-third* to *one-half* the decedent's *net probate estate*. The net probate estate is the probate estate after debts and estate expenses, including the surviving spouse's claims for homestead, exempt property, family allowance, and specific monetary share (if any) and fiduciary fee (if any)...but *before* federal and/or state estate taxes.

The problem with the forced share concept is that it is easily bypassed in most forced share states by a spouse who is intent on disinheriting the other spouse. In those states, with planning, full expression can be given to the freedom to transfer property by making gifts during one's lifetime, and by the use of trusts, joint and survivor accounts, payable on death accounts, transfer on death designations, and beneficiary designations on IRAs, annuities, and life insurance policies. The surviving spouse can be left with an empty estate, an empty bag.

Uniform Probate Code States

The Uniform Probate Code (UPC) with its *augmented estate* concept was proposed as a fair solution to the problem. The UPC (a model code designed to improve the probate process) has been enacted at least in part by Alaska, Arizona, Colorado, Florida, Hawaii, Kansas, Idaho, Maine, Michigan, Minnesota, Montana, Nebraska, New Jersey, New Mexico, North Dakota, South Carolina, South Dakota, Utah, Virginia, and West Virginia. It also has had an influence on or been influenced by the statutes and case law in other states, e.g., the *Sullivan* case in Massachusetts, and statutes in New York and Pennsylvania. There are significant differences among the UPC states, however. For example, not all UPC states adopted the augmented estate concept.

The Augmented Estate Concept

The UPC augmented estate concept is a hypothetical estate made up of four segments of property attributed to a husband and wife. The 1969 version of the UPC provides the surviving spouse with a one-third share of the augmented estate. The 1990 version provides the surviving spouse with an accrued percentage of the augmented estate based upon the length of the marriage…Short-term marriages would benefit the surviving spouse little; long-term marriages would benefit the survivor as a 50-50 partner. Regardless of the length of the marriage, the 1990 UPC provides a minimum *Supplemental Amount* giving the surviving spouse a right to have his or her assets brought up to $50,000. Under both the 1969 and 1990 versions of the UPC, the augmented estate is in addition to the basic $43,000 protection for homestead, exempt property, and family allowance.

Under the 1990 Code, the accrual percentages are as follows:

9-10

UPC SECTION 2-202(a) ELECTIVE SHARE	
Length of Marriage	Elective-share percentage
Less than 1 year	Supplemental Amount Only.
1 year but less than 2 years	3% of the augmented estate.
2 year but less than 3 years	6% of the augmented estate.
3 year but less than 4 years	9% of the augmented estate.
4 year but less than 5 years	12% of the augmented estate.
5 year but less than 6 years	15% of the augmented estate.
6 year but less than 7 years	18% of the augmented estate.
7 year but less than 8 years	21% of the augmented estate.
8 year but less than 9 years	24% of the augmented estate.
9 year but less than 10 years	27% of the augmented estate.
10 year but less than 11 years	30% of the augmented estate.
11 year but less than 12 years	34% of the augmented estate.
12 year but less than 13 years	38% of the augmented estate.
13 year but less than 14 years	42% of the augmented estate.
14 year but less than 15 years	46% of the augmented estate.
15 years or more	50% of the augmented estate.

The Augmented Estate

The question then becomes, what makes up the "augmented estate"? In short, it is all the property owned or deemed to be controlled by the two spouses (their assets minus liabilities), plus the value of certain gifts previously made by either (valued as of when the gifts were made).

The augmented estate *includes all the couple's property*, not just property acquired with earnings during the marriage. Unlike community property, it includes each person's separate property acquired before the marriage and property acquired by gift or inheritance during the marriage. (Also note that, for valuation purposes, the value of installment payments to the surviving spouse from a trust, annuity, IRA, life insurance policy, etc., is the "present value," as determined by the Probate Court.)

The augmented estate has *four* distinct segments:

The First Segment of the Augmented Estate

Segment 1 is the deceased spouse's net probate estate after expenses and the $43,000 family allowances…but before estate or inheritance taxes.

The Second Segment of the Augmented Estate

Segment 2 is made up of the deceased spouse's non-probate transfers upon death to persons other than the decedent's estate or surviving spouse. The value included is the property value that passed to any person other than the decedent's estate or surviving spouse. It includes A, B, and C below:

A. Property owned by the decedent immediately before death that transferred outside probate at the decedent's death:

Examples:

A Revocable Living Trust.

1. Property over which the decedent alone had a presently exercisable general power of appointment, meaning that the decedent could have caused the property to be transferred to himself or herself, or to his or her estate, or to his or her creditors, or creditors of the estate.

A JTWROS account with a child.

2. The decedent's fractional interest in joint tenancy with right of survivorship property that passed upon decedent's death to someone other than the surviving spouse.

A P.O.D. account payable to a child.

3. The decedent's ownership interest in property or accounts held in P.O.D., T.O.D., or co-ownership form with right of survivorship to the extent that decedent's interest passed at death to or for the benefit of any person other than the decedent's estate or surviving spouse.

Life insurance payable to children.

4. The proceeds of life insurance, including accidental death benefits, on the decedent's life if the decedent, immediately before death, owned the policy or had a presently exercisable general power of appointment to control the policy or direct its proceeds.

B. Property transferred in any of the following forms by the decedent while married:

Examples:

A Retained Interest Trust (see Chapter Eight).

1. Any irrevocable transfer in which the decedent retained the right until death (or beyond) to the possession or enjoyment of, or to the income from, the property transferred.

A transfer of property to a "friendly trustee" for the decedent's benefit.

2. Any transfer in which the decedent created a power exercisable by the decedent alone, or with another, or by a non-adverse party, to or for the benefit of decedent or decedent's estate or the creditors of either. The value included in the augmented estate is the value of the property (or the value of the property producing the income) that passed at decedent's death to any person other than the decedent's estate or surviving spouse.

9-12

C. Property transferred by the decedent while married and within two years immediately preceding the decedent's death if:

Examples:

A Qualified Personal Residence Trust that terminates within 2 years of decedent's death (see Chapter Eight).

1. The property that passed did so as a result of the termination of a right, or interest in, or power over, property *that would have been included* in the augmented estate under paragraph A, 1, 2, or 3, or under paragraph B, above, but for the fact that the right, interest, or power had terminated before the decedent's death. The amount included in the augmented estate is the value of the property at the time of the termination to the extent that it passed to any person other than the decedent, the decedent's estate, spouse, or surviving spouse.

An Irrevocable Life Insurance Trust within 2 years of decedent's death.

2. Any transfer of or relating to an insurance policy on decedent's life if the proceeds would have been included under paragraph A, 4, above, if the transfer had not occurred.

A gift in excess of $10,000 made to a child of decedent within 2 years of death.

3. Transfers, not otherwise included in the augmented estate, to any person other than the surviving spouse to the extent the aggregate transfers to any one donee in either of the two years immediately before the decedent's death exceeded $10,000.

(See generally: *Uniform Trust and Estate Statutes, supra* at pages 44-45: *Uniform Probate Code* § 2.205.)

The Third Segment of the Augmented Estate

Segment 3 is all the decedent's non-probate Segment 2-type property that was received by the surviving spouse as a gift from the decedent, or as a result of the decedent's death, e.g., survivorship accounts, IRA or other retirement benefits, life insurance proceeds, etc., paid to the surviving spouse.

The Fourth Segment of the Augmented Estate

Segment 4 consists of all the surviving spouse's *own* individual property, and all the surviving spouse's *own* Segment 2 property that is not received by the surviving spouse from the decedent under Segment 1 or Segment 2. This calculation is made *as if* the surviving spouse had predeceased the deceased spouse. It includes property in the surviving spouse's own revocable living trust, and the surviving spouse's interest in joint and survivorship accounts, IRAs, etc., and property where the surviving spouse retains possession, enjoyment, or income from property that he or she irrevocably transferred to third persons, or where he or she relinquished such interest to third persons within 2 years of the decedent's death.

The Augmented Estate Can Be Modified

The couple themselves, by written contract, agreement, or waiver signed by the surviving spouse in prenuptial or postnuptial agreements (where permitted by state law), may waive their rights (including the right to an intestate share, homestead, exempt property, family allowance, and spousal elective share), or they may consent to third party transfers, or they may exclude assets from the augmented estate if they do so voluntarily, after fair disclosure, and if the exclusion is not deemed unconscionable by the Probate Court.

A waiver may be whole or partial, but a waiver of "all rights" is just that: All claims are forfeited. A waiver is not enforceable, however, if the surviving spouse proves that: The waiver was not signed voluntarily, or the waiver was unconscionable when it was signed and, before signing, the surviving spouse was: (1) not given a fair and reasonable disclosure of the property or financial obligations of the decedent; (2) did not voluntarily and expressly waive in writing any right to disclosure of the property or financial obligations of the decedent beyond the disclosure provided; and (3) did not have, or reasonably could not have had, an adequate knowledge of the property or financial obligations of the decedent. (See generally: *Uniform Trust and Estate Statutes*, *supra* at page 69: *Uniform Probate Code* § 2.213.)

Assets Can Be Excluded From the Augmented Estate

In addition to assets transferred to third parties (e.g., children) with the consent of the other spouse, assets transferred in exchange for consideration, i.e., in exchange for another asset or benefit, are excluded from the augmented estate. Automatically excluded from the augmented estate are assets that were placed in trust by third persons for the benefit of one of the spouses to the marriage…so long as the benefits conferred consist only of an income interest, e.g., payment of income for life, or if principal, only if payment is needed for the spouse's health, education, maintenance, or support, or if the principal payments are made with the consent of another person. This exclusion typically covers assets placed in trust by a parent of one of the spouses, and certain assets placed in trust by a *former spouse*, e.g., a deceased first spouse of one of the parties to a second marriage. Assets in a Credit Shelter Trust set up by a deceased first spouse would be excluded because the benefits are usually limited to income, with principal payments made only for health, education, maintenance, or support. Assets in a Power-of-Appointment Marital Trust would be included, however (because the surviving spouse has a general power of appointment over those assets), and assets in a typical QTIP Marital Trust would also be included, but only to the extent of the present value of the life income interest. The present value of the remainder interest would be excluded.

9-14

A Simple Example

Simply put, the augmented estate concept works like this: If one couple has been married for 10 years and another couple for 15 years, and in each case, their *combined resources* after debts, claims, and expenses, i.e., their augmented estates, equal $600,000, the surviving spouse of each couple is entitled to the following amount as an elective share of the augmented estate:

- $200,000, regardless of the length of the marriage if the state adopted the 1969 version of the UPC (1/3rd of $600,000);
- $180,000 for the 10-year marriage (30% of $600,000), and $300,000 for the 15-year marriage (50% of $600,000) if the state adopted the 1990 version of the UPC.

Allocation of Assets to Surviving Spouse

Where do the assets come from to fund the surviving spouse's share? The UPC describes three hypothetical funds used to satisfy the surviving spouse's share of the augmented estate. The first fund must be used up entirely before the second fund contributes, and the second fund must be exhausted before the third fund contributes.

The First Allocation Fund

Fund 1 consists of all property received by the surviving spouse from the decedent via Segment 1 and Segment 3 of the augmented estate, plus twice the elective share percentage times the Segment 4 property of the surviving spouse. (It should be noted that all of the surviving spouse's property owned at decedent's death or given away by the survivor during decedent's lifetime is presumed to have been received from the decedent, and the surviving spouse has the burden of proof to show that it was not a gift from the decedent. Good records will be needed.)

The Second Allocation Fund

If, after applying Fund 1, there remains an unfunded portion of the surviving spouse's elective share of the augmented estate, the beneficiaries of the second fund (Fund 2) must contribute proportionately to the deficiency. Fund 2 consists of all Segment 1 property passing to someone other than the surviving spouse, e.g., to a child or parent of the decedent, plus all Segment 2 property transfers to others except irrevocable transfers made within two years of the decedent's death (other than irrevocable life insurance transfers that are included in Fund 2).

9-15

The Third Allocation Fund

Fund 3 consists of all irrevocable transfers in Segment 2 made by the decedent within two years of his or her death, except life insurance proceeds already included in Fund 2.

Time of Election

In order to elect a share of the augmented estate, the surviving spouse must file a petition in the Probate Court within a time period prescribed by state law. The UPC provides a period of nine months from the decedent's date of death, but it could be six months after admission of the will to probate, if later. The Probate Court then determines the surviving spouse's elective share and its funding.

The Value of the Spousal Election Varies From State to State A Case Study

Following is the author's hypothetical calculation and funding of the elective share under the 1990 UPC, together, for comparison purposes, with the UPC states of Florida and Michigan. (Florida adopted the augmented estate concept but with significant modification. Michigan, despite its being a UPC state, did not adopt the augmented estate concept at all.) For further comparison, the surviving spouse's elective share is also shown as calculated under the forced share statutes of Illinois, New York, and Ohio. In the interest of comparison, assume residency in the various states shown, and assume that the husband dies after 15 years of a second marriage and leaves a 50-year-old wife and two adult children from a prior marriage. Further assume that his estate plan attempts to disinherit his wife; he leaves everything to his children from his prior marriage, and as a result, his wife elects to receive her statutory share. The couple's assets at the time of his death are as follows:

Assets	Husband	Wife	Total
Assets subject to will and probate [1]	$150,000	$100,000	$250,000
Assets in revocable living trust [2]	300,000	-0-	300,000
Assets in JTWROS bank account [3]	50,000	-0-	50,000
Assets in IRA account	-0-	50,000	50,000
Total assets	$500,000	$150,000	$650,000

9-16

(1) Assume the couple owned a $200,000 residence as tenants-in-common, and that the husband individually owned $50,000 of additional assets. Assume the husband's will leaves all his assets to his children.

(2) Assets representing non-probate transfers still under the husband's control at the time of his death. Assume the children are the designated trust beneficiaries. For Florida, assume the living trust was established after 1999.

(3) The husband's fractional interest in joint tenant with right of survivorship accounts that pass to a non-spouse joint tenant upon the husband's death. Assume the husband's children are the surviving joint-tenants.

The detailed comparison (incorporating the Spouses' Priority Claims from Appendix H) is shown in Appendix I. In summary, the wife's elective share of her deceased husband's property has been calculated as follows:

	Priority Claims	Elective Share of Husband's Property	Total To Wife
1990 UPC	$43,000	$135,000	$178,000
Florida	99,000	109,200	208,200
Illinois	18,000	31,667	49,667
Michigan	43,000	55,000	98,000
New York	44,000	139,667	183,667
Ohio	67,000	15,333	82,333

9-17

Florida, in adopting the UPC, adopted the augmented estate concept, but it uses a flat 30 percent of the augmented estate instead of an accrued percentage based on the length of the marriage. It also does not offset for assets owned, controlled, or previously given away by the surviving spouse. Michigan, in not adopting the augmented estate concept, can evaluate non-probate transfers on a case-by-case basis. In *Soltis v. First of Am. Bank Muskegon*, an Appellate Court stated that: "Settlor's retention of control over trust assets and reservation of a right to amend or revoke the trust during her lifetime did not render the trust illusory or transform it from an *inter vivos* trust into a testamentary trust which would be subject to a statutory spousal election." As authority, the case cited two previous Michigan Supreme Court decisions (*Goodrich v. City Nat'l Bank & Trust Co.* and *Rose v. Union Guardian Trust Co.*).

In Florida and Michigan, as well as Illinois, New York, and Ohio, the elective share does not depend upon the length of the marriage or when or how the property was acquired (assuming none of it was community property). New York, however, despite its status as a forced share state, has, by its statutes and case law (e.g., *Newman* and *Reynolds*), expanded the pool of assets subject to the surviving spouse's elective share. North Carolina and Pennsylvania have similar statutes. Illinois and Ohio, however, by statutes that are also supported by case law in each state (e.g., *Johnson* in Illinois; *Smythe* and *Dumas* in Ohio), would restrict the surviving spouse's elective share in this case to one-third of the deceased spouse's net probate estate.

Couples who live in forced share states like Illinois and Ohio, or UPC states like Michigan that do not employ the augmented estate concept, are able (at this writing) to plan their estates with an emphasis on freedom to transfer property, e.g., they can plan to leave their assets to their spouses, or they can plan to leave more to their children and less to their spouses if they so choose. Couples who live in the forced share states of New York, North Carolina, and Pennsylvania, however, will find that their freedom to transfer property is curtailed by statutes that expand the safety-net for a surviving spouse at the expense of other designated beneficiaries…ordinarily the deceased spouse's children from a prior marriage.

In short, the labels "UPC state" and "forced share state" can be misleading when it comes to describing a surviving spouse's elective share. The examples given show the crisscross patchwork pattern of treating revocable living trust assets, and other assets, as being subject to the spousal election in some states, but not in others. As stated, the *Uniform Probate Code* percentage of an augmented estate concept has not been adopted in all "UPC states." Other states, while not adopting the *Uniform Probate Code*, still, by statute or case law, provide broad spousal protection by subjecting living trust assets, and other assets, to a surviving spouse's elective share.

9-18

Summary

You can shop state by state for the best forum—if you are so disposed—and then decide where to own real estate, or where to reside as a final domicile. A community property state has strong spousal protection, yet there are differences among them. Texas, for instance, affords more spousal protection than California in our example (see Appendix H). The *1990 Uniform Probate Code* affords strong spousal protection in some cases, but not all. A surviving spouse of a short-term marriage, or a surviving spouse with substantial assets of his or her own, would find little protection. Finally, the separate property forced share states are not uniform. Some, like Illinois, emphasize freedom to transfer (which favors those wanting to protect their children), but others emphasize protection for the surviving spouse, e.g., New York.

If estate planning in a second or subsequent marriage is important to you, then an examination of state probate laws may be one more thing to consider when you choose a retirement location. The protection afforded a surviving spouse varies widely from state to state. (And, if you move to another state, they can change abruptly even after you move.)

Will Contest, Trust Contest

Litigation in the Probate Court might relate to a will or trust, or it might relate to probate administration, e.g., taking exception to the Inventory and Appraisal, or taking exception to an Accounting. A will contest is a lawsuit aimed at having a decedent's will modified or set aside. If the will (or a portion thereof) is set aside, the decedent will be deemed to have died intestate (or intestate as to that portion), and property will be distributed pursuant to the state's Statute of Descent and Distribution (unless a prior will of the decedent is admitted to probate as being the "last will"). A trust contest is a lawsuit aimed at having a decedent's trust suffer the same fate. The distribution of trust property would then be modified, or else distributed as if there were no trust. Will contests and trust contests stem from common soil, yet those who choose to till that soil may do so for different reasons.

A surviving spouse in a second or subsequent marriage ordinarily has little incentive to institute a will contest, and can be precluded from doing so unless he or she can show where a prior will would leave more than his or her intestate share of the estate (see Appendix H for examples of the intestate share.) The equivalent of an intestate share is generally available to a surviving spouse under the current will via the surviving spouse's elective share, i.e., by the surviving spouse electing to take against the will. That is not true, however, in all states, e.g., Ohio, where a specific monetary share is payable if there is no will (see Appendix H), but is not paid when a surviving spouse elects against the will. (A will contest could also benefit the surviving spouse if there are no descendants of the decedent because, with no descendants, the surviving spouse's intestate share is, in some states, 100 percent of the probate estate.)

Will Contest

Whereas a spouse's election against the will is simple and painless, a will contest is adversarial...A will contest means litigation, and litigation can be emotionally painful and financially expensive. A will contest can destroy relationships. Children from a prior marriage, nevertheless, may have strong incentive to initiate a will contest because the will may have left everything to the surviving spouse. If the children successfully contest the will, and if the decedent is then deemed to have died without a will, the children will be entitled to their intestate share...perhaps one-half or two-thirds of the net probate estate (depending upon the number of children and the state involved). The grounds for a will contest might include improper execution, fraud, forgery, mistake, lack of intent, prior revocation, lack of capacity, or undue influence.

State statutes require that a will contest be brought within a prescribed period of time—measured from when the will is admitted to probate. Will and trust contests require timely resolution because property ownership and title transfers must be made clear and final. Although the UPC allows up to three years to file the contest, many state statutes provide a much shorter period. In Ohio, for instance, a will contest must generally be commenced within three months of filing notice with the Probate Court that all interested parties have been notified, or waived notice, of the filing of the will. The "interested parties" are the persons named in the will and the heirs who would inherit if there were no will. (Other interested persons who might bring a will contest are persons who would have a direct interest that would be impaired or defeated if the will is admitted to probate. An example would be someone named in a prior will who is not named in the current will.)

Trust Contest

A trust contest based upon fraud, incapacity, or undue influence, on the other hand, is something that a surviving spouse might consider…especially in separate property forced share states such as Illinois and Ohio, or certain UPC states like Michigan. In those states, if a revocable living trust can be set aside, it will pour its assets into the probate estate as a waterslide pours its contents into a pool. The new pool of assets will then be subject to the surviving spouse's elective share. In UPC augmented estate states, and separate property forced share states like New York and Pennsylvania, however, where non-probate testamentary transfers are made subject to the spousal election, there would ordinarily be no reason for the surviving spouse to initiate a trust contest because the trust assets are treated as if they were part of the probate estate. They are automatically put into the spousal election pool by law.

9-20

The children of a prior marriage, in addition to contesting the will, may also have an incentive to contest the trust. The trust may give the surviving spouse a power to withdraw assets, or the power to control their disposition through the surviving spouse's will, e.g., the trust may be a Power-of-Appointment Marital Trust. If so, the surviving spouse can leave the decedent's trust assets to the survivor's children at the expense of the decedent's children. A successful trust contest by the decedent's children, therefore, could cause the trust assets to be re-distributed to them, or be made subject to the Statute of Descent and Distribution, i.e., the decedent's children could receive their intestate share, e.g., one-half or two-thirds, depending on the state and the number of children.

If filed, a trust contest will normally be filed in tandem with a will contest and, in many cases, for the same reason, e.g., lack of legal capacity, or undue influence. Nevertheless, the basis of a trust contest filed by a surviving spouse might be different: It might be to show that the trust was an attempt by the deceased spouse to circumvent the surviving spouse's elective share of the probate estate. In that case, the trust contest might be based upon an allegation of fraud (i.e., the deceased settlor intended to defeat the surviving spouse's right to an elective share), or an argument that the trust was illusory (i.e., the deceased settlor's retention of control over trust income and assets, or the retention of a power to revoke the trust, was tantamount to direct ownership).

Apart from a trust contest based upon fraud or illusion, the majority of trust contests, and will contests, will be based upon allegations of incapacity or undue influence, or a combination thereof.

Incapacity

Testamentary capacity was discussed in the Notes to Chapter Eight. Briefly stated, in making a will one need not have the same level of mental acuity required for the making of a business contract, but one must know that he or she is making a will. To paraphrase *Restatement (Third) of Property: Wills and* Other *Donative Transfers, supra,* § 8.1, the testator must understand his or her relationship to family members (the natural objects of his or her bounty…which can include stepchildren), must know generally the nature and extent of his or her property and the disposition being made of the property, and must be able to relate these elements one to another and coordinate them with an orderly plan of disposition.

Undue Influence

The issue of undue influence was also discussed in the Notes to Chapter Eight. Briefly stated, the will must express the "will" of the testator, not that of another person. Advisement to the testator, or attempts to persuade the testator, or even persistent and insistent requests are not enough, by themselves, to constitute undue influence. Taken alone, they do not represent the coercion needed to force one's will upon another. (However, such pressure, when exerted upon an elderly person who is dependent upon his or her caregivers, can give rise to a charge of undue influence. Nevertheless, the charge of undue influence must be proven.)

Proving the Allegation

The challenger in a lawsuit alleging incapacity or undue influence need not prove the allegation beyond a reasonable doubt, nor even by clear and convincing evidence, but only by a preponderance of the evidence—the scales of justice must have more weight…ever so slightly…a mere feather on the challenger's side—unless the one charged with undue influence rebuts the claim by a preponderance of the evidence, in which case the challenger must prove the charge by clear and convincing evidence. But how can the allegations of incapacity or undue influence be proved by a preponderance of the evidence, or by clear and convincing evidence? Incapacity might be shown through medical records, or the testimony of those who knew the testator at the time he or she made the will. Witnesses might arise from among the testator's family and friends, the testator's physician, and the witnesses to the will. The exertion of undue influence is more nebulous: It is not likely to be witnessed, or be the subject of expert medical opinion. It will have to be shown circumstantially as the product of the testator being susceptible, the other person (usually one who already has the bond of a trusting, confidential relationship with the testator) having an opportunity to exercise influence, an act on the part of that person to procure a new will or to modify an existing one, and a result that departs from a natural disposition of the testator's property, i.e., an unnatural disposition of property that benefits the person involved.

Restatement (Third) of Property: Wills and Other Donative Transfers, supra, § 8.3 states that a presumption of undue influence arises when suspicious circumstances accompany a transfer to one in a confidential relationship with the testator or donor. Suspicious circumstances can relate to the weakened condition of the donor, a change in the donor's attitude as a result of the relationship with the alleged wrongdoer, the alleged wrongdoer's role in preparing or procuring the will, trust, or other instrument of transfer, whether the instrument was prepared in haste or secrecy, whether independent legal or other advice was gotten, whether there was continuity of purpose or a decided change from prior plans, and whether a reasonable person would see the disposition as unnatural, unjust, or unfair.

Practical Steps to Protect Your Estate Plan

You may have good and rational reason (even late in life) to change your estate plan relative to your spouse and children. Should you be concerned that either might contest your will or trust? In practice, most wills and trusts are not contested, and among those that are, only a fraction of the contests are successful. The law presumes validity, and the burden of proof is on the contestant to show that the will or trust should be modified or set aside by a court. Yet, will and trust contests do occur, so the stage is set in a second or subsequent marriage where the following scenes could be played out:

- **Scene One**…You make a new pour-over will and establish a QTIP trust. The QTIP provides income to your surviving spouse, but the principal is preserved for ultimate distribution to your children from a prior marriage. The prior will, revoked by the new will, would have left a substantial portion of your estate outright (or in a Power-of-Appointment Marital Trust) to your surviving spouse. **Result**: Your surviving spouse files a will contest and trust contest alleging incapacity…and undue influence exerted by one of your children.

- **Scene Two**…You make a new will that leaves—substantially—all of your estate outright to your surviving spouse. The prior will, revoked by the new will, would have left a substantial part of your estate to your children (either directly via the will or indirectly via a pour-over will to a living trust). **Result:** Your children file a will contest alleging incapacity and undue influence exerted by your surviving spouse.

Neither scene is a pretty one…Both could involve vexatious litigation. So how can a will or trust contest be avoided, or at least discouraged? There are no guarantees, but the following approaches should be helpful:

- First, establish your estate plan while you are still in good mental and physical condition;
- Second, give copies of your will, trust, and other estate planning instruments to your spouse and to your children, either directly, indirectly via separate safe-deposit boxes, or through your attorney as custodian.
- Third, give your attorney, your spouse, and your children written instructions that the execution of any late-in-life change to your estate planning documents should be videotaped outside the presence of your spouse and children, but in the presence of at least two independent witnesses who know you. Your attorney should ask sufficient questions on the tape to establish that you can pass the "capacity test," and that this is in fact "your will."
- Fourth, secure an affidavit from your physician at the time you make the change stating that you are capable of understanding a business contract and capable of handling your business affairs at that time…a higher standard of mental capacity than is needed to make a will.
- Fifth, consider inserting a no-contest clause, a so-called *in terrorem* clause, into your will and trust to the effect that anyone contesting your will or trust will be denied, and their descendants will be denied, any share of your property. Enforcement of this provision varies from state to state; your attorney can advise you of the law in your state.

Chapter Ten—Reading Notes

Estate Planning

Estate planning begins with your plans for building an estate, however large or small, however humble or grand, however perceivably necessary or desirable to support yourself, your dependants, and your loved ones. In building your estate, you will be concerned with growth of your real net worth, the value of your assets minus liabilities after allowing for taxes and inflation. Your personal motivation, education, career, business contacts, marriage, family and school connections, savings, investments, and both material and genetic fortunes of birth will determine the size of your net worth and the type of estate that you build. Luck will also play a part.

10-1

Once you stop building your estate, whether by choice or due to life events, and usually well before that point, you will make plans for its *conservation and distribution*. Conservation and distribution planning is needed in the event of your incapacity, as well as death, and should be put in place at the start of your career, or at the start of your marriage and family. Your estate plan can then be maintained throughout your life, with adjustments made as times and circumstances change.

Ethics

Before discussing the basics of estate planning, and the elements of conservation and distribution planning, there is another issue for discussion, seldom seen, that veils the whole subject. That issue is ethics. Ethics is always an issue, but it is an acute issue in a second or subsequent marriage. We will discuss ethics in a legal context—an attorney-client estate planning context—but the issue of ethics also applies to the relationship you have with your financial planner.

If you and your spouse engage an attorney to advise you regarding estate planning, and to draft wills, trusts, and related instruments, who does the attorney represent? Who is the client…you, your spouse, the two of you as a couple?

To paraphrase part of the American Bar Association's Code of Professional Responsibility, an estate planning attorney should represent a client competently (zealously within the bounds of the law), should preserve the confidences and secrets of the client, and should avoid even the appearance of professional impropriety.

Estate planning for a husband and wife need not be (and usually is not) an adversarial engagement, but the question remains: Who is the client? It is common for a couple to meet together with the attorney. The couple may have differing interests, but they look to the attorney to advise them together. In most cases, the advice can be given and ethical issues can be discussed and resolved without either person having to go to a separate attorney.

In a second or subsequent marriage, the initial meeting with the attorney should involve a discussion of the couple's separate property, marital property, family, and goals, as well as attorney fees, and the potential conflict of interest the attorney may have. An agreement should be made at that meeting about the attorney's representation, and the agreement should be reduced to writing in the form of an engagement letter. The couple's essential choice of representation is this: Either the attorney will represent the husband and wife as a couple, or the representation will be separate. If it is separate, a corresponding choice must be made: Either the attorney will represent only one of the parties, or the attorney will represent the wife as an individual, and at the same time, will also represent the husband as an individual.

Joint Representation

If the attorney-client relationship relates to the couple, the couple will have agreed to common goals and do not anticipate a conflict with each other. With joint representation, the couple shares the attorney-client privilege: If there is litigation, each one can compel disclosure of information or prevent disclosure of information. (Not a pretty picture.) Apart from litigation, however, the attorney can and should (some would say "must") share communications received from one spouse with the other. Some would say that if the communication is intended to be confidential, or a secret, its disclosure will depend upon the agreement among the parties and the relevance of the disclosure to the engagement. Others would say that ethics override the agreement, and disclosure is required; there can be no secrets. In a given situation, the attorney may have to withdraw from representing either party.

Separate Representation

Separate representation for only one of the parties is ethically straightforward: That person is the attorney's client. If, however, there is separate representation for each of the parties by the same attorney, the attorney has two individual clients and can advise each client as to his and her separate interests without trying to reconcile the differences. In that case, the attorney-client privilege remains singular: Communications between the attorney and each client are confidential, and disclosure to the other cannot be compelled in litigation. Nevertheless, where there are secrets, the attorney has an ethical problem and may have to resign. The separate representation of each is not recommended.

Engagement Letter

The attorney-client engagement letter should cover the communication issue as part of the agreement distinguishing joint from separate representation. The letter should also outline the scope of the engagement and the objectives of the parties. In the absence of any agreement, e.g., no discussion is had of second or subsequent marriage issues, and there is no discussion of conflict of interest, attorney-client privilege, or confidential communications, it should be presumed that the engagement is a joint one: The client is the couple, as a couple.

10-3

The Basics of Estate Planning

Now, once you have established the parameters of your attorney-client relationship, and have an engagement letter, you can work with your attorney to develop your estate plan. The basic steps are as follows:

- Gather the facts relative to your spouse and yourself, both jointly and separately: What are the assets, where are they, what are the values, what is the ownership arrangement, what are the beneficiary designations on life insurance policies, annuities, 401(k)s, IRAs, etc.? (Note: You should name a primary and secondary beneficiary. Payment will be made to your estate if a named beneficiary is not living at the time of your death.)
- Write down what you want your estate plan to accomplish and then meet with your attorney to discuss your plans, your property, your family, the issues (including second or subsequent marriage issues), your options, probate, wills, trusts, powers-of-attorney, healthcare directives, estate and gift taxes, and legal fees.
- Confirm in writing your objectives and the work to be done.

- Have the attorney prepare estate planning documents and instruments that reflect your wishes. Make sure you understand what they say, and then walk through various scenarios with the attorney. Give your estate plan a "dry run." The documents and instruments can include wills, durable general (or financial) powers-of-attorney (the giving of authority to another to act as your agent in handling your financial affairs), advance healthcare directives (e.g., living wills and healthcare powers of attorney), living trusts with or without marital and credit shelter provisions, other trusts, beneficiary designations for life insurance, 401(k)s, IRAs, P.O.D. and T.O.D. accounts, etc., creation of corporations, partnerships, limited liability companies, corporate buy-sell agreements, partnership agreements, etc. (Note: In a second or subsequent marriage, there is an added issue when it comes to giving powers-of-attorney. Should your spouse have the authority, or should the power to make financial or healthcare decisions vest in an adult child?)

10-4

- After you sign your estate planning documents and instruments, store them in a safe place…with notice of their location given to your attorney and to your family. For example, you can keep your original will in a safe-deposit box (so long as state law allows its withdrawal if the box is sealed), in a fireproof box at home, or with your attorney. Your trust agreements can be signed in multiple originals…you keep one, give one to your trustee (or successor trustee), and one to your attorney. You can retain recorded deeds and powers of attorney in a safe-deposit box or fireproof box (with spouse or child having access to the box). Advance healthcare directives can be provided to your spouse, children, and physician. Copies of all should be retained by your attorney.

- Update your asset listing and valuations annually at year-end, or when you do your income taxes. Confirm asset ownership and beneficiary designations at the same time.

- Review your estate planning documents and instruments periodically (e.g., business agreements every year, wills, trusts, and other documents and instruments every 2-3 years).

- Meet with your estate planning attorney every 3-5 years for a review and another dry run with current data. Meet sooner if a change in plans is called for by changes in your family, your health, your life insurance, your net worth, your business, or the estate and gift tax laws.

Elements of Conservation and Distribution Planning

The goal of the estate planning process is to design and implement an efficient plan for the conservation and distribution of your estate. Under the heading of conservation and distribution, you will need to make decisions regarding *financial management, investment management, tax management,* and *personnel management.*

Financial Management

Inherent in planning for distribution of an estate and deciding who gets what, how, how much, and when, is the issue of financial management. With financial management, you plan, organize, and control your beneficiaries' use of your assets.

Financial management starts with the goals you have for each beneficiary, compares your goals with their individual needs and circumstances, and then considers each beneficiary's strengths and weaknesses. For example, can your spouse or child manage money? Are there special management needs as a result of disability or diminished capacity? Are there minor children? Is a spouse or child a spendthrift? Is any beneficiary financially naive? Should money be kept in trust? If so, for how long? What timeline should you use?

10-5

Absent special circumstances and regardless of whether a trust is used or not, planning for distribution of an estate usually involves a plan to treat beneficiaries who are in the same class as equals, e.g., "to my children equally, share and share alike." But planning can go beyond that: It can consider individual needs and other resources, as well as the resources available from your estate. What assets do your beneficiaries have now? What assets of yours will be available, and what will their values be after payment of debts and taxes? With financial management (if you choose to exercise it) you match your assets to individual beneficiaries based upon individual health, education, and support needs, individual business capabilities, individual time of need, and individual involvement with you and your business. For example, if your estate will include a business interest or investment real estate, is one child active in the business or involved with managing the real estate? If a child is actively involved, should that asset be distributed to that child, with other assets, e.g., securities or life insurance, distributed to other children...or should the business or real estate be sold with the proceeds distributed equally? If it is to be sold, is there an existing buy-sell agreement? Another example would be to consider the known propensities of your children, and—equally important—the propensities of their spouses. Would an inheritance be invested for retirement, education, or to produce income, or would it be spent on a stepped-up lifestyle, or to start a new business? In summary, financial management can help preserve your estate for the purposes you intend, e.g., to provide a base of security for your spouse and children, or to educate your grandchildren.

Investment Management

Investments were discussed in Chapter Five in the context of building an estate, and in Chapter Seven as they relate to retirement income. Whether you are young and accumulating assets, or retired and using them to provide a life income, your asset allocation and individual investment choices will take into consideration your current tolerance for risk and required rate of return. The same investment principles should be applied when you can no longer make those decisions yourself, e.g., upon your incapacity or death. The questions then become: Have adequate investments been provided to meet your needs during your incapacity, and to meet the needs of your beneficiaries after your death? (If not, see Chapter Six.) And, if you are not actively making investment decisions, who will manage and control the investments and make those decisions: a trustee, or you (still) through the terms of a trust, or your beneficiaries…either directly as recipients of your estate, or as trust advisors for assets retained in trust? Finally, what do the investments consist of, and what degree of expertise will be needed to manage them? For example, if you have a substantial brokerage account, a 70 percent stock, 30 percent fixed income portfolio may need to become an income producing 50-50 portfolio upon your incapacity, or a conservative 35 percent stock, 65 percent fixed income portfolio for a surviving spouse following your death. Who will decide what to sell and what to buy? In contrast to that, if your estate is primarily a life insurance estate, an investment portfolio will have to be designed from the start. Of course, different and specialized asset management will be needed if your investments are primarily in real estate or a closely-held business. But regardless of the type of assets you accumulate, you will want them to be conserved for their intended purpose, and investment management is critical to conservation.

Tax Management

Conservation also involves tax management. Investments may be in taxable or tax-free securities, and as shown in Chapters Five and Seven, the effect of income taxes must be considered when calculating a real rate of return for a beneficiary.

In planning for beneficiaries after your death, you can consider not only their income needs, but also the individual tax brackets of the beneficiaries when designing provisions for a Credit Shelter Trust. An independent trustee of a Credit Shelter Trust can, by design, sprinkle income among beneficiaries based upon need and individual tax brackets. All of the income can go to a surviving spouse, or it can go to the surviving spouse only if needed, with the rest spread among children or grandchildren as the trustee, in his/her (or its) discretion, decides.

Income tax planning is also an important part of planning for the distribution of tax-deferred investments such as annuities and IRA and 401(k) accounts. Those benefits are taxable to the recipient (at least in part) and after income taxes, the recipient may net less than sixty cents on the dollar. Will one beneficiary get one hundred-cent dollars (e.g., a distribution of cash or securities), but another only sixty-cent dollars (e.g., payments from an IRA account)? (You should discuss rollover and IRA stretch-out options with your tax advisor, and then coordinate those plans with your estate plan. Make sure your beneficiaries are advised to analyze and exercise their options on a timely basis; the loss to income taxes may be offset by tax-deferred earnings.)

Tax management also involves planning to minimize the effect of estate and gift taxes, and, through tax apportionment planning, which beneficiaries will bear the economic cost of those taxes. For example, will the estate tax be borne by the probate estate or by the residual beneficiaries of a trust or proportionately by all property recipients (which, in the last case, could mean that IRA and 401(k) beneficiaries might only receive thirty-cent dollars after both estate taxes and income taxes are paid)? Know your estate tax exposure, and if a tax will be payable, know how it will be paid.

10-7

Minimizing the effect of estate taxes is the driving force behind the Marital Trust, Credit Shelter Trust, Irrevocable Life Insurance Trust, Generation Skipping Transfer Trust, Dynasty Trust, and Charitable Trusts discussed in Chapter Eight. If your assets exceed the lifetime exemption amount, e.g., $1,500,000 in 2004-2005, $2,000,000 in 2006-2008, or $3,500,000 in 2009, the Marital Trust/Credit Shelter Trust combination with a Pour-Over Will is a basic estate tax saving strategy. If your assets are less than the lifetime exemption amount, and not likely to grow (meaning the federal estate tax is not an issue), you can nevertheless weigh the costs and benefits of such planning as it relates to state estate taxes (if your state has an estate tax). Apart from state estate taxes, if, after considering the Marital Trust/Credit Shelter Trust combination (including mirror-image husband-wife Marital Trust/Credit Shelter Trusts), the federal estate tax is still an issue, then the more sophisticated Irrevocable Life Insurance Trust, Charitable Trust, and Generation Skipping and Dynasty Trusts can be considered, as well as gifts, and special entities such as family limited partnerships (FLPs) and limited liability companies (LLCs) with their potential to discount the value of assets for estate tax purposes. We will discuss those tools in this chapter.

The annual gift exclusion (currently $11,000, or $22,000 with the consent of the donor's spouse; both to be adjusted periodically for inflation) is the driving force behind the annual gifting programs of many families: It is an effective way to reduce the size of any estate subject to estate taxes. Gifts that qualify for the annual exclusion (and their future growth in value) are removed from the donor's top estate tax bracket; they are transferred estate and gift tax free to the donee. A similar principle applies to the lifetime gift tax exemption amount of $1,000,000 (which is scheduled to stay at $1,000,000, even though the lifetime estate tax exemption will increase). The $1,000,000 lifetime gift tax exemption amount can be gifted in addition to the annual exclusion amount. It can be done in stages over a period of years, or all in one step. Note, however, that with each gift, the donee takes the donor's tax basis for income tax purposes (usually the property's cost with any required adjustments), and therefore, a capital gains tax may be payable upon the donee's sale of the gifted asset. For that reason, a "deathbed gift" of appreciated property may be poor tax planning because the asset would, if inherited instead of being received as a gift, have taken a "stepped-up" basis equal to its fair market value on date of death, or if so elected (and if it would result in a lower estate tax), on the alternate valuation date up to six months later. With a stepped-up basis, there may be little or no capital gains tax payable upon sale. To illustrate, if a property owner gives an asset having a cost of $200 but a value of $1,000 to his or her child, the child will have a tax cost basis of $200. If the child inherits the same asset upon the property owner's death, instead of receiving it as a gift, the asset will have a tax cost basis of $1,000. (Note: If the asset is a house, the numbers might be $20,000 and $100,000.)

The top federal estate tax rate is 48 percent in 2004, reducing 1 percent a year to 45 percent in 2007, 2008, and 2009…with total elimination in 2010, only to be reinstated to 50 percent again in 2011. Time, politics, and economics will tell if there will be a federal estate tax in the future, but a prudent planner will assume an ongoing estate tax. The gift tax rate, and rate reduction, is the same as the estate tax, but the gift tax is scheduled to remain in effect after 2009 at a rate equal to the highest individual income tax rate (projected to be 35 percent).

Personnel Management

Will your beneficiaries receive their inheritance directly or will you leave it in trust for their benefit? If there is to be a trust, you must evaluate potential trustees, and then successor trustees in the event of the death, resignation, or removal of the initial trustee. Will the trust have complicated tax or investment issues? Should the trustee be a bank or trust company, or should it be a member of your family or a trusted advisor? Which one would add the most value? Should the beneficiaries be able to change the trustee? Who should direct the investments…the beneficiaries or the trustee? How should control and flexibility be balanced between the trustee and the beneficiaries? How long will the trustee serve before the assets are distributed?

Estate Planning in a Second or Subsequent Marriage

With your goals in mind, and keeping in mind the tools available for use in estate conservation and distribution planning (See Chapter Two: Property Ownership and Transfer; Chapter Six: Insurance; and Chapter Eight: Wills and Trusts), we will now look at assumed joint representation and specific ways to *maximize* the benefits you leave to your spouse. We will then look at assumed separate representation and specific ways to *minimize* those benefits, while you *maximize* the benefits you leave to your children from a prior marriage. You will be taking a hard line with your children in the first instance, and with your spouse in the second. We will then look at ways to soften those approaches and achieve a reasonable balance.

Maximize Benefits to Spouse

There is a difference between conferring a benefit and giving control. Assuming you want the exclusive benefit of your estate (and here we mean estate in the broad sense of all the property you own or control, not just your probate estate) to go to your spouse (and children, if any, of this marriage), and you want no benefit to go to your children from a prior marriage, you can achieve your objective directly with gifts, JTWROS or P.O.D./T.O.D. accounts, a simple will, and beneficiary designations on your life insurance, IRAs, 401(k), etc. You can achieve the same objective indirectly with a trust. The issue is not the benefit; the issue is control.

10-9

Give Spouse Total Control

If your estate is not large, you will probably give all of your assets directly to your spouse via your will, a joint-tenant-with-right-of-survivorship deed, JTWROS and P.O.D./T.O.D. accounts, life insurance, a 401(k), and IRA beneficiary designations. Everything you own will go outright to your spouse. You can do the same thing (but may choose not to for estate tax reasons) even if your estate is large.

Reasons Not to Give Total Control

There may be good reasons, however, even apart from estate tax reasons, why your spouse should not have total control of your assets after you die. For example, he or she may have creditors (a former spouse?), your spouse may be a spendthrift, your spouse's children may have troubled lives or have too much influence over your spouse, or your spouse may have a sizeable estate even apart from yours (and to add to it would be to add to overall costs and estate taxes). There may be any number of reasons why you would not give your spouse control of your assets.

Withhold Control by Use of Trusts

If you want to separate the benefits for your spouse from legal title and control of your assets, you can do it (subject to your spouse's community property and spousal election rights) by placing your assets in trust for his or her benefit. A Credit Shelter Trust combined with a QTIP Marital Trust will afford your spouse the use of the assets without control of them, or if you wish, you can give a degree of control, even a large degree, without giving him or her complete control.

The Credit Shelter Trust can pay all of its income to your spouse. It can also pay principal if needed to maintain his or her present standard of living. In addition, you can provide your spouse with a right to withdraw the greater part of $5,000 or 5 percent of the principal balance each year. The QTIP Marital Trust will provide income and can provide principal, even liberal doses of principal if you wish, to afford your spouse a comfortable standard of living, assuming sufficient assets. The QTIP Trust/Credit Shelter Trust combination can also provide assurance that upon your spouse's death the assets remaining will go to a secondary beneficiary of your choice, e.g., your children from this or a prior marriage, or your favorite charity, but not to your spouse's children from a prior marriage, or to someone your spouse might marry after your death.

The degree of control you give your spouse can range from "no control," to control of the trustee's investment decisions (your spouse can be the "trust advisor"), to replacement of the trustee for good or specified reasons, to actually being the trustee himself or herself. To name your spouse as trustee is to express confidence in his or her abilities, as well as his or her willingness to be governed by the trust agreement (which is to assume that he or she will not distribute principal unless authorized by the trust). There is a danger, however, when you name your spouse as trustee of your QTIP or Credit Shelter Trust, that the terms of the trust may become blurred. One person's want is another person's need. If your spouse makes unauthorized withdrawals of principal from the Credit Shelter Trust, the estate tax shelter will be in jeopardy: The Internal Revenue Service could claim that the trust, in operation, was tantamount to full ownership by the spouse, and the additional estate taxes could range from 35 up to 45 percent or more of the trust. Unauthorized withdrawals from either the QTIP or Credit Shelter Trust will also distort your estate plan...The assets you had planned to leave to others will not be there.

Outright Distribution vs. Use of a Trust

In choosing to maximize benefits to your spouse, therefore, you will have concluded the following:

- If the distribution is outright to your spouse, i.e., your spouse is given title to the assets:
  - He or she can manage the investment of the assets and can manage his or her own finances: There is no need for anyone else, e.g., a trustee, to be involved;
  - Estate taxes are not a concern and income taxes are a secondary matter: All income will be received by your spouse;
- If the distribution is to a trust to be held for your spouse's benefit by an independent trustee, i.e., your spouse is the beneficial owner but another holds legal title to the assets:
  - Your spouse needs help with investments; or
  - You are concerned about your spouse's ability to manage his or her personal finances; or
  - Estate taxes are a concern; or
  - Your spouse may need your assets only in a supplemental way to his or her own; or
  - Any combination of the above. (If you name your spouse as trustee, you are not concerned about his or her ability to manage the investments or his or her management of personal finances; your concern is primarily to save estate taxes…and you believe your spouse will adhere to the standards of the trust.)

Other Powers for Spouse

As a complement to your plan to benefit your spouse, you can name him or her as Personal Representative under your will, i.e., as executor or executrix of your estate. You can also name your spouse as attorney-in-fact under a Durable General (or Financial) Power of Attorney. If desired, the power-of-attorney can specifically authorize your spouse (but only your spouse) to make gifts of your property to himself or herself, even very generous gifts. Your spouse can also be named a decision-maker in advance healthcare directives.

Protect Plan from Attack

Can your children from a prior marriage attack a plan to distribute all your property to your spouse? They can initiate a will contest and a trust contest (or they can contest a power-of-attorney), but as we saw in Chapter Nine, they will not succeed unless they overcome basic legal presumptions and prove lack of capacity, undue influence, or another invalidating reason such as fraud, improper execution, etc.

You can best protect your estate plan for your spouse by taking the five steps outlined at the end of Chapter Nine.

Summary

Subject to a successful attack, you can give your spouse all the benefits from your accumulated property, and you can give control that ranges from complete control to no control…apart from the control realized under priority claim or elective share statutes, or under community property law.

Maximize Benefits to Children of Prior Marriage

The law favors leaving property to your spouse rather than to children from a prior marriage. The law is based upon the duty of mutual support and the historic model of a single marriage. A plan to leave all your property to your children from a prior marriage, a plan to circumvent the bias in the law, will have to be mapped out like a military campaign. There may only be a light skirmish between the lawyer for your spouse and the lawyer for your children, but there could also be all-out war. You will have to study the legal terrain…It may be favorable terrain or it may be a minefield. You may even have to move to different terrain, move to another state to gain more favorable ground.

The first step, therefore, is to learn the law. Do you live in a community property state like California, a traditional separate property forced share state like Illinois, a Uniform Probate Code augmented estate state like Florida, or a traditional separate property forced share state like New York, which has adopted certain augmented estate concepts? What is your state's law of intestate succession, i.e., if you do not have a will, how is probate property distributed under the Statute of Descent and Distribution? Does your state have statutes or court decisions that will subject the assets in a living trust to the elective share of a surviving spouse? Would joint tenant with right of survivorship accounts with children be treated the same way? What is your state's position on *in terrorem* clauses; could your spouse contest your living trust without fear of loss?

The next phase of the campaign is to know your property, and to know your spouse's property. What do each of you own or control? What is its value? How is it titled? For contractual benefits like life insurance, IRAs, and P.O.D./T.O.D. accounts, who is the primary beneficiary? Is there a secondary beneficiary? Do either of you own a business or commercial real estate? If so, is there a buy-sell agreement? If not, what is the succession plan? Are there ERISA retirement plan benefits such as pension, profit-sharing, or 401(k) benefits that, by federal law, are payable to a surviving spouse unless the covered employee elects otherwise and the spouse consents?

The third step is to calculate your spouse's elective share of your overall probate and non-probate estate. The calculation should consider your present and estimated future assets, and your present and future state of domicile.

The fourth step is to develop a lawful strategy to leave all your property to your children.

This four-step process will require the help of at least one experienced estate planning attorney, and possibly a second in your future state of domicile. An estate planning attorney can advise you of statutes, case law, and proposed legislation in your state, and in the state where you plan to retire, if different. For ethical reasons, your attorney should not have represented your spouse in the past, and should not represent him or her in any phase of your current planning. Your representation needs to be separate. You alone are the client.

The Elements of Conservation and Distribution

Your plan should first be designed with state law in mind, and then should consider the issues of financial management, investment management, tax management, and personnel management. The issues of financial management and investment management are issues related to your children's abilities to manage money…and their lives. If either is questionable, consider leaving your assets in trust rather than outright. If a trust is needed, then personnel management is an issue, and you will need to select a suitable trustee and decide on specific trust provisions such as when and to whom distribution will be made. Tax management may or may not be needed; the federal estate tax will not present a hurdle if your taxable estate is less than your lifetime exemption, e.g., $1,500,000 in 2004-2005, $2,000,000 in 2006-2008, or $3,500,000 in 2009, but if estate taxes will be due, consider making gifts to your children (or grandchildren, e.g., Section 529 college saving plan contributions) to lessen the burden.

Seek Your Spouse's Cooperation

Once you have a plan, you have a choice: You can share your plan with your spouse or you can go it alone. With your spouse's cooperation, your plan can be a complete success; without it, you may only succeed in part…but it can be a large part.

With your spouse's cooperation, you can enter into post-nuptial agreements in states allowing them, e.g., community property states, and certain states having adopted that portion of the Uniform Probate Code. With a post-nuptial agreement, you can clarify and even augment the property to be deemed your separate property, or property in which your spouse disclaims any interest. Also, with your spouse's consent, you can name your children as beneficiary of your ERISA plan retirement benefits.

Community Property States

If you live in a community property state, you can leave all of your separate property, and one-half of all community property, to your children. With your spouse's consent, you can also transmute community property into your separate property, i.e., you can agree to skew your marital property so that upon your death it will go to your children. You can also agree with your spouse to make gifts of marital property to your children. (Within reasonable limits, you can also make gifts of marital property on your own…but so can your spouse.)

Finally, in a community property state, if you have (or can get) all of the marital property titled in your name only, you can transfer it to your Revocable Living Trust and leave it upon your death (together with your separate property) to a Credit Shelter Trust and a QTIP Trust for your spouse's lifetime benefit, with the remainder then left to your children. Under this arrangement, your children will inherit all your separate property and eventually all the community property…both yours and your spouse's. But that will only happen with your spouse's consent. Upon your death, your spouse will have a choice to either break into your trust and take out his or her one-half of the community property (and, by the terms of your trust, forfeit the lifetime income from your separate property and your half of the community property), or receive a lifetime income generated from your separate property and both halves of the community property (but forfeit the ability to leave his or her half of the community property to his or her own children, heirs, or other beneficiaries). If you leave part or all of your separate property and your community property in trust for your spouse, it could satisfy your spouse's need for more income, and that need may outweigh his or her desire to leave an estate. At the same time, your children may be willing to wait for their inheritance if the wait increases the size of the inheritance. (It should be noted that with this arrangement there are special income, estate, and gift tax issues to be considered.)

Separate Property Forced Share States

In a separate property forced share state that does not classify living trust assets (or joint-tenant-with-right-of-survivorship accounts with children) as assets subject to a spouse's elective share, the campaign is an easy one. Put your assets into a living trust with your children as beneficiaries, or put your assets into joint-tenants-with-right-of-survivorship accounts with your children as co-tenants. (For debtor-creditor reasons, JTWROS accounts with children are not recommended in large amounts). Then name your children as beneficiary for all your other death benefits, e.g., life insurance, IRA accounts, and P.O.D./T.O.D. accounts.

Leave nothing to be governed by your will or the Probate Court. With no probate estate there is no spousal election.

In addition to assets you can control directly, if you have ERISA retirement benefits, and if your spouse will not consent to naming your children as beneficiaries, establish a QTIP Marital Trust that meets certain technical requirements of Internal Revenue, and name the trust as beneficiary of your retirement plan. Your spouse may be willing to accept payments based upon his or her life expectancy, with any balance remaining upon your spouse's death payable to your children.

Augmented Estate States

The challenge remaining is the challenge presented by the states that totally or partially adopted the augmented estate concept. It may have been done via the Uniform Probate Code, or via state statutes and court decisions that include living trusts, retained interest trusts, and other assets such as survivorship accounts in the probate pool of assets subject to the spouse's elective share.

If you live in a state that has adopted the Uniform Probate Code augmented estate concept (Minnesota would be an example), you can calculate your spouse's elective share of your property. At a minimum, your spouse is entitled to the $43,000 priority claim for homestead, exempt property, and family allowance, and under the 1990 UPC, an amount up to the $50,000 Supplemental Amount, the minimum elective share. The elective share will be one-third of the augmented estate under the 1969 UPC or, if it will exceed $50,000, a percentage based upon the length of the marriage under the 1990 UPC. In either case, the elective share amount will depend upon the value of the respective assets you each own, control, or have given away. (See Chapter Nine.)

If your spouse owns, controls, or is charged with more separate assets than you, then your spouse will not receive an elective share from your assets. Also, if your spouse's assets are equal in value to yours, there is no elective share. Only if your assets exceed those of your spouse will he or she be entitled to an elective share. Under the 1990 UPC, your spouse's share of your assets in excess of his or her assets would be 50 percent after 15 years of marriage, and less for a short-term marriage (subject to the minimum Supplemental Amount).

In an UPC augmented estate state, if your assets exceed your spouse's assets, your first strategy will be to enter into a post-nuptial agreement where you both waive your claims against the other's estate. Such a waiver can include all claims (including priority claims), or only claims to certain designated assets. If a post-nuptial agreement cannot be negotiated, you can consider an annual exclusion gift program for your children and grandchildren (currently $11,000 per donee per year…a program that can be accelerated with Section 529 college saving plan contributions) to reduce your assets to the level of your spouse's assets…assuming sufficient assets would remain to meet your needs. In addition, you can irrevocably transfer additional gift amounts, e.g., an amount up to your lifetime gift tax exemption amount of $1,000,000, and have it excluded from your augmented estate so long as the gift is completed more than 2 years before your death and you retain no control or beneficial interest in the transferred assets. For example, the assets of an irrevocable trust for your children where you retain an income interest during your lifetime will *not* be excluded. An outright gift with no strings attached *will* be excluded—regardless of value—if made more than 2 years before your death.

If no post-nuptial agreement can be had, and no practical transfer of property can be made, you might consider an irrevocable life insurance trust, or as an alternative, outright ownership of a policy on your life by your children. If you decide to give your children a life insurance benefit, the question becomes: Should a trust be used to hold the policy proceeds upon your death, or should your children receive the proceeds directly? The answer hinges on your appraisal of your children's need for financial and investment management, and on the general stability of their lives. Regardless of the answer, you can use the $11,000 per child annual gift exclusion to leverage a large life insurance death benefit through gifts of premium dollars to your children, or to a trust for their benefit. (To satisfy trust and gift tax rules, the children would have—but probably not exercise—a right, for a limited period of time, to withdraw the annual gift you make to the trust.) If the trust approach is used, you must survive its date of execution by 2 years in order to avoid its inclusion in the elective share calculation.

If none of the above strategies is satisfactory, and if the goal to leave all of your property to your children is important enough, then, subject to the imperfect and sometimes expensive asset protection measures soon discussed, you will have to move from your augmented estate state to one that allows you more freedom to transfer property.

New York, North Carolina, and Pennsylvania

The final model to be considered is that represented by New York, North Carolina, and Pennsylvania…separate property forced share states that, despite not being Uniform Probate Code states, expressly provide for an augmented estate that includes living trust and certain other assets in the pool of assets subject to the surviving spouse's elective share. The approach taken by these states, and other states with case law evolving in this direction, is even more favorable to a surviving spouse than the Uniform Probate Code's augmented estate approach. Under the UPC, the assets of the surviving spouse will be taken into consideration, and if they equal or exceed those of the deceased spouse, or if the marriage is a short-term one, the surviving spouse may receive nothing beyond priority claims, and possibly an amount up to the $50,000 Supplemental Amount available under the 1990 UPC. In New York, North Carolina, and Pennsylvania, however, the surviving spouse is entitled to an elective share of all the assets the deceased spouse owned or controlled, including non-probate transfers (e.g., living trust assets, survivorship accounts, transfers with a retained interest) *even though the marriage may have been short-term or the surviving spouse may have assets of his or her own that equal or exceed the deceased spouse's assets, i.e., no credit is given for the surviving spouse's own assets.* For example, the value of the deceased spouse's assets may be $300,000, and those of the surviving spouse $3,000,000, but the surviving spouse is still entitled to an elective share of the decedent's $300,000.

If you live in New York, North Carolina, Pennsylvania, or any other separate property state that subjects living trust, retained interest trust, and survivorship account assets to a surviving spouse's elective share without considering the length of the marriage or the survivor's own assets, your campaign to leave all your assets to your children from a prior marriage will involve a post-nuptial agreement if allowable under state law (and if your spouse is agreeable), annual exclusion gifts, life insurance on your life owned by your children (or owned by them indirectly through an irrevocable trust), or else will lead to one of two alternatives: Give all of your assets irrevocably to your children well before your death, or move to another state. If neither alternative is practicable, and if the stakes warrant the expense, you can employ one or more of the asset protection vehicles outlined below.

10-17

Asset Protection Planning

Asset protection planning may be beneficial regardless of where you live, but it is most needed if you live in an augmented estate state and the value of your property far exceeds that of your spouse, or if you have very significant assets and live in a separate property forced share state that includes non-probate transfers in the pool of assets subject to the elective share of a surviving spouse.

Despite their appeal, however, sophisticated asset protection vehicles are costly, they do not come with a warranty, and they can be a challenge to drive…especially off-road, i.e., offshore. To use asset protection planning to disinherit a spouse is to leave the well traveled roads of tax law and debtor-creditor law in favor of roads less often traveled. There may still be income, estate, and gift tax savings to be had, and there may be insulation from creditors' claims, but you will not be immune from attack on either of those fronts, or from pursuit by your spouse's lawyer. Nevertheless, use of one or another asset protection vehicle may enable you to live where you want, live the way you want, and still leave all your property to your children. Specially designed asset protection vehicles can include:

- A closely-held corporation;
- A limited liability company;
- A limited partnership;
- An irrevocable life insurance trust;
- An asset protection trust;
- A combination of the above

Corporations, limited liability companies, and limited partnerships all share one common thread: They are formed for valid business purposes. If you own a business or commercial real estate, or even a portfolio of securities, there may be *valid business reasons* to gather those assets into a separate entity that will, as a natural byproduct, satisfy your need for asset protection.

Closely-Held Corporation

0-18 It is common practice to operate a business in corporate form. For income tax purposes, the corporation may be a "C" corporation (income is taxable to the corporation) or an "S" corporation (income is taxed proportionately to the shareholders). A corporation generally affords limited liability for its shareholders, allows transference of ownership (transference of shares of stock…subject to any corporate restrictions or shareholder agreement), provides for centralization of management, and provides for continuity of life, i.e., its continuance can be perpetual. In a second marriage where the goal is to prevent your spouse from being involved with or benefiting from your corporation after your death, the following steps can be considered for control and asset protection purposes (even though estate tax issues will remain):

- Creation of two classes of stock. Issue voting and non-voting shares of stock, with the corporate net worth weighted 98 or 99 percent to the non-voting stock. Retain the voting stock and gift the non-voting stock to your children from a prior marriage. The gift can be all at once or in annual stages; it can be outright or to an irrevocable trust for their benefit. You retain control of the corporation with the voting stock. (A variation would be to put the voting stock into a trust with you or your designee as trustee to vote the stock and control the corporation; voting control would pass to your children upon your death.)

- Have a restrictive shareholder agreement whereby upon your death your shares are sold to your children at fair market value. (If your ownership of the corporation is only 1 or 2 percent, the value of your shares will be relatively small…even if a "control premium" is part of the value.)

- Or, in lieu of creating two classes of stock, have only one class and gift it all to your children. (The stock can still be controlled through use of a voting trust.)
- Or, as an extra step with further insulation, contribute all of your corporate stock to a limited liability company (LLC), and gift 98 percent of the LLC's value to your children. Your remaining 2 percent and their 98 percent could then fund a family limited partnership (FLP) with you having 1 percent as a limited partner and 1 percent as the general partner. You could then indirectly control the corporation through your 1 percent interest as general partner of the FLP.
- Regardless of whether you use one or two classes of stock, and regardless of how the stock is owned, have a year-to-year employment or management agreement with the corporation whereby you are paid a reasonable salary and appropriate "perks" during your active years, and reasonable consulting fees after you retire. Upon your death, the compensation would cease.

If the size of your estate exceeds the lifetime exemption amount at the time of your death, the above corporate strategies may or may not result in estate tax savings, but they are ways to maintain an income during your lifetime, pass your business to your children, and leave little or no value upon death that will be subject to your spouse's elective share.

Limited Liability Company

A limited liability company is a type of entity that was created by state law several years ago. An LLC affords protection from creditors and is suitable for managing a business, for managing real estate investments, or for managing a portfolio of securities. As with a corporation, the rationale for forming an LLC should be profit-driven and rooted in a business purpose, e.g., centralization of management, easy transference of ownership, or continuity of life. An LLC is more flexible than a corporation, however, and it can have "pass-through" taxation, as if it were an "S" corporation, i.e., the net income of the LLC can be taxed to the owners.

The same ideas outlined for the closely-held corporation can be applied to the LLC, i.e., you can have voting and non-voting members, you can gift your ownership interest to your children, you can use a voting trust to control the business, you can have an employment or consulting agreement, and you can leave little that will be subject to a spouse's elective share.

Limited Partnership

A limited partnership is a proven way to fractionalize property ownership into small units with a discounted value suitable for annual gifting. It is typically designed to afford pass-through taxation and is therefore ideal for real estate investments. It can also be used to house a portfolio of securities. (Arguably, a more complex FLP or LLC is also a better way to own life insurance than an irrevocable life insurance trust: A FLP or LLC affords a flexibility that the trust cannot.)

A limited partnership protects its limited partners from personal liability but, by law, it must have a general (managing) partner who is personally liable for partnership obligations. The general partner can be an individual, or it can be a corporation or limited liability company so long as such entity has financial substance and is not an empty shell. The personal liability of the general partner is a drawback because creditors, e.g., real estate mortgage lenders, can look to the general partner for payment. Nevertheless, the personal risk of the general partner may be minimal if the partnership liabilities are less than the value of the mortgaged assets. If the partnership assets consist of a portfolio of securities, or fully paid-for real estate free of environmental problems, there is no extraordinary risk that cannot be covered by insurance.

The principles used to make gifts of a closely-held corporation or LLC interest can be applied to a FLP: You can irrevocably gift the bulk of your assets to your children in the form of limited partnership units all at once, or in annual stages, and you (or your designee) can maintain control as general partner (or co-general partner) with a 1 or 2 percent ownership interest. As general partner, you can pay yourself reasonable compensation through a management agreement for services rendered to the partnership. Upon death your compensation ceases, your general partnership interest passes to your children, and there is little value in your estate.

With a limited partnership, the value of assets is typically discounted for estate and gift tax purposes, and this is one of the reasons for its use. If the partnership assets consist of a portfolio of marketable securities, however, little or no discount might be had...Although the point can still be argued that a discount should be applied because the limited partner lacks control and lacks a market for the units owned. The lack of control and limitations on transferability of partnership units not only provide the basis for minority and marketability discounts, but they strengthen the protection against creditors, including those of a surviving spouse. The discounted value of limited partnership assets presents a smaller target (perhaps 30-40 percent smaller after allowable discounts), and a court judgment against a limited partner's interest in the partnership may be uncollectible, as a practical matter, because of the barrier presented by the usual partnership agreement. A judgment creditor of a limited partner (or of a limited liability company member) is typically given only a charging order, i.e., a court order entitling the creditor to distributions *if and when made*, but no right to make decisions, no right to require distributions, no right to require liquidation of the business, and no other rights as a partner or member. (There is also the possibility that the creditor holding a charging order will have pass-through taxable income to report even though no distribution of income is made. Given that picture, a creditor— including a surviving spouse—may be willing to sell at a reduced value.)

To be effective as an asset protection device, the limited partnership must be rooted in a valid business purpose with a profit motive, and it must be established before a problem with a creditor arises.

Irrevocable Life Insurance Trust

The Irrevocable Life Insurance Trust is also an asset protection device. With planning, its annual premiums can be funded by other asset protection devices, e.g., the ILIT can be a member of your LLC or FLP and receive its pro-rata portion of income distributions. It can then use those distributions to pay life insurance premiums.

The ILIT was discussed in Chapter Eight as a means to provide financial security for a spouse or children, and as a means to provide liquidity to pay estate taxes or to replace the wealth lost to estate taxes. It can also be used to preserve and protect a business or other assets for your children. For example, upon your death an ILIT can purchase the business, or your interest in a business, from your estate or living trust, or can purchase the entire business from a FLP or LLC, and can then distribute your interest, or the whole business, to your children from a prior marriage, or to a child who is active in the business.

Asset Protection Trust

For a price, an Asset Protection Trust (APT) affords the best protection against the claims of creditors that money can buy. An APT *cannot* be used to evade or fraudulently transfer assets from existing or foreseeable creditors, but it can be used to preserve and protect your property from possible future creditor claims. It needs to be established before a problem arises, and it needs to be designed and funded with the Uniform Fraudulent Transfer Act in mind. Nevertheless, substantial protection can be afforded for your surplus assets, i.e., those in excess of current and liberally estimated future creditor claims that exceed current and reasonably foreseeable future assets.

As stated in Chapter Eight, there are domestic APTs and offshore APTs. The offshore APTs offer the most protection because they are not subject to the U.S. Constitution, which provides full faith and credit to judgments gotten in one state and transferred to another for enforcement. For example, a Delaware or Alaska APT may be tested by a judgment obtained in New York and transferred to Delaware or Alaska for enforcement. If all your assets are in an offshore APT, however, your creditors, including your surviving spouse, will have to sue in the foreign jurisdiction and abide by its rules…rules which favor the APT, and rules which do not recognize judgments obtained in the U.S.A. Through a combination of a limited liability company (whether domestic or offshore) and an offshore APT with a domestic co-trustee who resigns at the first sign of trouble in favor of the offshore co-trustee, you can maintain control of your assets and have layers of protection that will financially discourage and legally intimidate creditors, including a surviving spouse.

A Balanced Approach

0-22

A balanced approach to estate planning in a second or subsequent marriage would be to provide adequately for your spouse (and children of this marriage, if any), yet satisfy a natural desire to leave an estate for your children from a prior marriage.

Start with the basic asset information developed earlier. What do you own and control? What does your spouse own and control? What are the needs of your spouse and your children? Analyze the needs of your spouse and children, consider your own goals and desires, and then design your estate plan around those factors.

Three Models for Consideration

As templates that you can use for comparison with your own analysis, consider three models that have been developed by experienced and intelligent people, models that are arguably fair to both your spouse and to your children from a prior marriage. The first is *community property law* as found in California, the second is the *augmented estate concept* as found in the *1990 Uniform Probate Code*, and the third is the *law of intestate succession* as found in your own state of domicile.

Note that each of the three models presupposes that a surviving spouse is first entitled to his or her priority claims against your estate for homestead, exempt property, and the family allowance. To that base is added the community property, UPC, or intestate succession model…a model you choose as *your* elective share for your spouse, and *your* allocation for your children from a prior marriage.

Consider the California Model

California law would credit you and your spouse with your separate property (property each of you owned before the marriage and property acquired by gift or inheritance during the marriage), and would split 50-50 all marital property (property acquired with the earnings or efforts of either during the marriage). With this approach, you would treat your marriage like a true partnership.

Consider the Uniform Probate Code Model

Using the 1990 UPC model, each of you would accrue a percentage of the total property owned or controlled by both of you as a couple. The percentage would be based upon the length of the marriage, with a 50-50 split achieved after 15 years. A minimum safety-net up to $50,000 would be provided. With this approach, however, you would not have a true partnership: A surviving spouse with less property than the deceased spouse would acquire a percentage of the deceased spouse's property, but a surviving spouse with more property than the deceased spouse would retain the excess. (Some would argue that this is fair and desirable because it would help the surviving spouse who had less separate property...See Chapter Nine for details.)

10-2

Consider the Intestate Succession Model

The third model embraces your state's Statute of Descent and Distribution, and then expands it to cover all your non-probate as well as probate property. For example, if your probate property would be split 33 1/3 percent to a surviving spouse and 66 2/3 percent to your children from a prior marriage (or 50-50 depending upon the number of children), you can arrange your life insurance proceeds, living trust benefits, P.O.D. accounts, IRA accounts, etc., the same way. With this approach, you do not consider partnership theories of marriage, and you do not consider the length of the marriage or the resources or needs of either your spouse or your children, you just divide all the property you own or control between your surviving spouse and your children from a prior marriage in an arguably fair way. It is arguably fair because your state legislature decided it was fair. You are just extending the idea to cover non-probate property (which can be done while still "avoiding probate").

Test the Three Models against Your Own Desires

The three models differ in approach, and the results can be viewed side-by-side to give you a range of possibilities. Your own reasons and emotions will control your final estate planning decisions (as they should) but this three-dimensional template can be a rational guide to a balanced estate plan in a second or subsequent marriage. For example, assuming payment of the priority claims, you can picture distribution of the balance of your property under each model and then compare the results with your separate analysis based upon your spouse's needs, your children's needs, and your own desires. Your final plan, a plan that may be the minimum required for your spouse under state law, or that may go far beyond the minimum, can then be put into place. Whether you supply the minimum or something much greater, your final plan will be based upon reasoned financial planning: It will be lawful, it will be a plan you consider to be fair, and it will be a plan you control.

Apply the Elements of Conservation and Distribution

Finally, having decided upon an overall financial plan for distribution of your property, you need to refine the plan to consider the investment management, tax management, personnel management, and asset protection ideas outlined in this chapter. Is outright distribution appropriate, or is a trust needed? Are estate taxes an issue? Will the estate be simple or complex? Is there a business or commercial real estate? Are there corporations or partnerships? Who should be the executor or trustee? Who should have a durable general (financial) power of attorney? Could a spousal election upset your plan? Is asset protection needed?

Summary

In considering the implementation of your estate plan, consider the tools available to you: post-nuptial agreements (where allowed), transmutation of community property, survivorship accounts, beneficiary designations on life insurance, annuities, IRAs, etc., contracts, buy-sell agreements, wills, QTIP, Credit Shelter, Irrevocable Life Insurance, and other trusts as outlined in Chapter Eight, and the corporations, limited partnerships, limited liability companies, and asset protection trusts outlined in this chapter. Your estate planning attorney can work through the options with you and can advise you on how to achieve the balanced plan you desire…no matter how large or small your estate. You can then share your estate plan with your spouse and negotiate a mutually agreeable plan that is fair and adequate for each of you—one designed to promote both present and future harmony. If disclosure is not advisable, or a harmonious mutual plan is not attainable, you can still be satisfied that you have an estate plan that you feel is right for you and your family, and one that will work after you are gone.

Estate Planning Attorney Web Sites

- WWW.ACTEC.ORG

  Home page for American College of Trust and Estate Counsel. Locate an ACTEC attorney by state, city, county, area code, zip code, or name. Such an attorney can refer you to someone in your locale who is conversant with second and subsequent marriage estate planning issues.

- WWW.MARTINDALE.COM

  Find an estate planning attorney in your locale.

OR...

- WWW.MONEYANDMARRIAGETWO.COM   Provides links to both sites.

10-2

Postscript

Millions of unmarried male-female and same-sex couples live together as domestic partners for significant periods of time. There may be implied or express oral or written cohabitation agreements between them, or their status may be that of a couple who share their lives together in a committed marriage-like relationship. There may be financial and legal tangles, however, when the relationship ends upon the death of one, or, as happens more often, when the couple breaks up. Children from this or a prior relationship may also have claims.

From state to state, case to case, and court to court, opposite-sex and same-sex domestic partner cohabitation agreements may or may not be enforceable. State law, the facts of the case, and public policy considerations will be determinative.

Of current national interest is the evolving law concerned with same-sex couples. Absent a U.S. Supreme Court decision or constitutional amendment, the law will evolve from state to state, e.g., Hawaii with its Reciprocal Beneficiaries Act (1997), granting many of the benefits of marriage, and Vermont with its civil union legislation (2000), granting domestic partners the same benefits and protections as spouses. In addition, same-sex marriage cases are pending in the courts of several states, and following the November 2003 Massachusetts Supreme Court decision, the issue is being debated in Congress and state legislatures across the country.

Against this background, in the meantime, domestic partners must rely on state-specific professional advice, carefully drafted cohabitation agreements, liberal employer policies, and wills, deeds, trusts, insurance, and other contracts such as payable on death and joint and survivor accounts to accomplish their financial, estate, and retirement planning goals.

Appendix A
Personal Balance Sheet
(Statement of Assets, Liabilities, and Net Worth)

		Ownership			
		You		Your Spouse	
	Joint &				
Assets	Survivorship	Pre-Tax	After-Tax	Pre-Tax	After-Tax
Cash Equivalents	$_____		_____		_____
Investments (Stocks, Bonds, Mutual Funds, Etc.)	$_____		_____		_____
Residence	$_____		_____		_____
Other Real Property	$_____		_____		_____
Closely-Held Business					
_____	$_____		_____		_____
_____	$_____		_____		_____
U.S. Savings Bonds	$_____	_____	_____	_____	_____
Annuities	$_____	_____	_____	_____	_____
ROTH IRAs			_____		_____
Traditional IRAs		_____	_____	_____	_____
SEP and R/O IRAs		_____		_____	
Employer Retirement Plans (401(k), Profit Sharing, Etc.)		_____		_____	
Life Insurance Cash Value (Face Amount $_____)			_____		_____
Tangible Personal Property	$_____		_____		_____
Other Assets:					
_____	$_____		_____		_____
_____	$_____		_____		_____
_____	$_____		_____		_____
Total Assets	$_____	$_____	$_____	$_____	$_____

<u>Liabilities</u>

Home Mortgage	$_____	_____	_____
Other Notes Payable	$_____	_____	_____
Credit Card Debt	$_____	_____	_____
Other Liabilities:			
_____	$_____	_____	_____
_____	$_____	_____	_____
_____	$_____	_____	_____
Total Liabilities	$_____	$_____	$_____
Net Worth	$_____ $_____	$_____ $_____	
(Assets—Liabilities)			
Total Net Worth	$_____	$_____	$_____

Appendix B
Personal Cash Management Statement
(Statement of Revenues and Expenses)

Revenues:	Mutual	You	Your Spouse
Salary, Wages, Commissions, Fees	$_____	_____	_____
Dividends, Interest	$_____	_____	_____
Business Profits	$_____	_____	_____
Sale of Assets	$_____	_____	_____
Rents, Royalties	$_____	_____	_____
Farm Income	$_____	_____	_____
IRA, Pension, Etc.	$_____	_____	_____
Social Security	$_____	_____	_____
Other Taxable Income	$_____	_____	_____
Gifts	$_____	_____	_____
Inheritance	$_____	_____	_____
Other:			
_____	$_____	_____	_____
_____	$_____	_____	_____
Total Revenue (#5)	$_____	$_____	$_____

| | (A) Fixed (Necessary) | | | (B) Variable (Discretionary) | | |
Expenses:	Mutual	You	Your Spouse	Mutual	You	Your Spouse
Food	$____	_____	_____	_____	_____	_____
Clothing	$____	_____	_____	_____	_____	_____
Mortgage/Rent	$____	_____	_____	_____	_____	_____
Auto	$____	_____	_____	_____	_____	_____
Insurance:						
Home/Auto	$____	_____	_____	_____	_____	_____
Hospital/ Medical	$____	_____	_____	_____	_____	_____
Disability	$____	_____	_____	_____	_____	_____
Life	$____	_____	_____	_____	_____	_____
Other	$____	_____	_____	_____	_____	_____
Repairs/Maintenance	$____	_____	_____	_____	_____	_____
Education	$____	_____	_____	_____	_____	_____
Entertainment	$____	_____	_____	_____	_____	_____
Vacation	$____	_____	_____	_____	_____	_____
Gifts & Charity	$____	_____	_____	_____	_____	_____
Appliances	$____	_____	_____	_____	_____	_____
Improvements	$____	_____	_____	_____	_____	_____
Income Taxes:						
Federal	$____	_____	_____	_____	_____	_____
State	$____	_____	_____	_____	_____	_____
Local	$____	_____	_____	_____	_____	_____
Other Expenses:						
_____	$____	_____	_____	_____	_____	_____
_____	$____	_____	_____	_____	_____	_____
Total Expenses **(#6)**	$____	$____	$_____	$____	$____	$_____

Net positive <negative>
Cash flow (#5–#6):

	Mutual	You	Your Spouse
Revenue (#5 above)	$_____	_____	_____
Less Fixed Expenses (A)	$_____	_____	_____
Margin Available	$_____	_____	_____
Less Variable Expenses (B)	$_____	_____	_____
Net Positive <Negative> Cash-Flow	$_____	$_____	$_____

Appendix C
Excerpt From Financial
Planning Questionnaire

Dear Financial Planning Client:

Congratulations on your decision to spend the time and the money to retain our firm to prepare your financial plan. Financial planning is no different than any other type of planning process.

- *First:* The Planner must gather the facts.
- *Second:* The Planner must analyze the facts and identify the issues.
- *Third:* The Planner must analyze the issues and the alternative ways of addressing each one.
- *Fourth:* The Planner must then prepare a written plan that presents the facts in a concise and organized way. The Planner will highlight the issues, make specific recommendations on how to address each issue, and lay out a plan to implement each recommendation.
- *Fifth:* The Planner must follow through with the client to implement those recommendations that are acceptable to the client.

The hardest part of the financial planning process is the fact gathering. This questionnaire might look a little intimidating at first, but don't let it scare you. Just set aside about 2 to 4 hours and do it. Please don't be delayed by any one question. Just skip the hard questions. We will help you answer them as your plan develops.

If two weeks have gone by and you have not completed and returned the questionnaire, please call our **Help Line** telephone number as shown on the front of this questionnaire. We will provide whatever professional assistance is needed to walk you through the process, including a meeting to help you with any questions.

Once you are done with the questionnaire, the hardest part of the financial planning process is over for you. Now we take over to develop your financial plan. We look forward to working with you.

337

Preliminary Information

The answers to the questions in this questionnaire are vital to the development of any meaningful Comprehensive Financial Plan. Your care in providing precise data will directly affect the ultimate accuracy of your plan.

In addition to the completion of the questionnaire, it will be necessary for you to gather the following information, data, and documents for our review:

- Federal, State, and Local tax returns for the last two years.
- Information relative to all insurance, such as the type of policy (i.e. life, disability, health, extended care, auto, homeowners, liability), policy numbers, face or benefit amounts, cash values, outstanding loan amounts, ownership and beneficiary designations, premium amounts, etc. The policies or copies of the policies would be most helpful.
- Copies of your most recent statements for all investment accounts. This would include all brokerage accounts, including all retirement and non-retirement accounts, as well as mutual fund statements and bank statements. Please furnish a list of any investment assets for which you do not receive statements. The list should include a description of the asset, current market value, annual income, and ownership.
- A list of liabilities including pertinent details such as date of loan, original amount borrowed, first payment date, terms of the loan, interest rate, monthly payment, balance as of December 31st of prior year, and current balance. This information can be included in the Annual Expenses section starting on page 31.
- All employee benefit statements and the most recent pay stub.
- Business documents such as corporate books, partnership agreements, buy-sell agreements, stock redemption agreements, salary continuation agreements, income tax returns, financial statements for the last two years, leases, and any other agreements or contracts.
- Copies of estate planning documents such as wills, trusts, powers of attorney, etc.
- Any other pertinent information you feel we need to know.

Based upon a Comprehensive Financial Planning Questionnaire prepared by Lifetime Planning Inc., Mansfield, Ohio. Used with permission.

Appendix D
Government Life Expectancy Table

Table I			
(Single Life Expectancy)*			
Age	Divisor	Age	Divisor
35	48.5	73	14.8
36	47.5	74	14.1
37	46.5	75	13.4
38	45.6	76	12.7
39	44.6	77	12.1
40	43.6	78	11.4
41	42.7	79	10.8
42	41.7	80	10.2
43	40.7	81	9.7
44	39.8	82	9.1
45	38.8	83	8.6
46	37.9	84	8.1
47	37.0	85	7.6
48	36.0	86	7.1
49	35.1	87	6.7
50	34.2	88	6.3
51	33.3	89	5.9
52	32.3	90	5.5
53	31.4	91	5.2
54	30.5	92	4.9
55	29.6	93	4.6
56	28.7	94	4.3
57	27.9	95	4.1
58	27.0	96	3.8
59	26.1	97	3.6
60	25.2	98	3.4
61	24.4	99	3.1
62	23.5	100	2.9
63	22.7	101	2.7
64	21.8	102	2.5
65	21.0	103	2.3
66	20.2	104	2.1
67	19.4	105	1.9
68	18.6	106	1.7
69	17.8	107	1.5
70	17.0	108	1.4
71	16.3	109	1.2
72	15.5	110	1.1

*From Internal Revenue Service Regulation § 1.401 (a) (9)—9 A-1

Table II
(Joint Life and Last Survivor Expectancy)*

Age Of Older Spouse	Younger Spouse Is Younger By Number Of Years										
	0	1	2	3	4	5	6	7	8	9	10
40	50.2	50.8	51.3	51.8	52.4	53.0	53.7	54.3	55.0	55.7	56.4
41	49.3	49.8	50.3	50.9	51.4	52.0	52.7	53.3	54.0	54.7	55.4
42	48.3	48.8	49.3	49.9	50.4	51.1	51.7	52.3	53.0	53.7	54.4
43	47.3	47.8	48.3	48.9	49.5	50.1	50.7	51.3	52.0	52.7	53.4
44	46.3	46.8	47.3	47.9	48.5	49.1	49.7	50.4	51.0	51.7	52.4
45	45.3	45.8	46.3	46.9	47.5	48.1	48.7	49.4	50.0	50.7	51.5
46	44.3	44.8	45.4	45.9	46.5	47.1	47.7	48.4	49.1	49.8	50.5
47	43.4	43.9	44.4	44.9	45.5	46.1	46.7	47.4	48.1	48.8	49.5
48	42.4	42.9	43.4	44.0	44.5	45.1	45.8	46.4	47.1	47.8	48.5
49	41.4	41.9	42.4	43.0	43.6	44.2	44.8	45.4	46.1	46.8	47.5
50	40.4	40.9	41.5	42.0	42.6	43.2	43.8	44.4	45.1	45.8	46.5
51	39.5	40.0	40.5	41.0	41.6	42.2	42.8	43.5	44.1	44.8	45.5
52	38.5	39.0	39.5	40.1	40.6	41.2	41.8	42.5	43.2	43.8	44.6
53	37.5	38.0	38.5	39.1	39.7	40.3	40.9	41.5	42.2	42.9	43.6
54	36.6	37.1	37.6	38.1	38.7	39.3	39.9	40.5	41.2	41.9	42.6
55	35.6	36.1	36.6	37.2	37.7	38.3	38.9	39.6	40.2	40.9	41.6
56	34.7	35.1	35.7	36.2	36.8	37.4	38.0	38.6	39.3	40.0	40.7
57	33.7	34.2	34.7	35.2	35.8	36.4	37.0	37.6	38.3	39.0	39.7
58	32.8	33.2	33.7	34.3	34.8	35.4	36.0	36.7	37.3	38.0	38.7
59	31.8	32.3	32.8	33.3	33.9	34.5	35.1	35.7	36.4	37.1	37.8
60	30.9	31.3	31.9	32.4	32.9	33.5	34.1	34.8	35.4	36.1	36.8
61	29.9	30.4	30.9	31.4	32.0	32.6	33.2	33.8	34.5	35.1	35.8
62	29.0	29.5	30.0	30.5	31.1	31.6	32.2	32.9	33.5	34.2	34.9
63	28.1	28.5	29.0	29.6	30.1	30.7	31.3	31.9	32.6	33.2	33.9
64	27.1	27.6	28.1	28.6	29.2	29.8	30.4	31.0	31.6	32.3	33.0
65	26.2	26.7	27.2	27.7	28.3	28.8	29.4	30.0	30.7	31.4	32.0
66	25.3	25.8	26.3	26.8	27.3	27.9	28.5	29.1	29.8	30.4	31.1
67	24.4	24.9	25.4	25.9	26.4	27.0	27.6	28.2	28.8	29.5	30.2
68	23.5	24.0	24.5	25.0	25.5	26.1	26.7	27.3	27.9	28.6	29.2
69	22.6	23.1	23.6	24.1	24.6	25.2	25.7	26.4	27.0	27.6	28.3
70	21.8	22.2	22.7	23.2	23.7	24.3	24.8	25.4	26.1	26.7	27.4
71	20.9	21.3	21.8	22.3	22.8	23.4	23.9	24.5	25.2	25.8	26.5
72	20.0	20.5	20.9	21.4	22.0	22.5	23.1	23.7	24.3	24.9	25.6
73	19.2	19.6	20.1	20.6	21.1	21.6	22.2	22.8	23.4	24.0	24.7
74	18.4	18.8	19.3	19.7	20.2	20.8	21.3	21.9	22.5	23.1	23.8
75	17.6	18.0	18.4	18.9	19.4	19.9	20.5	21.0	21.6	22.3	22.9
76	16.8	17.2	17.6	18.1	18.6	19.1	19.6	20.2	20.8	21.4	22.0
77	16.0	16.4	16.8	17.3	17.8	18.3	18.8	19.4	19.9	20.6	21.2
78	15.2	15.6	16.0	16.5	17.0	17.5	18.0	18.5	19.1	19.7	20.3
79	14.5	14.9	15.3	15.7	16.2	16.7	17.2	17.7	18.3	18.9	19.5
80	13.8	14.1	14.5	15.0	15.4	15.9	16.4	16.9	17.5	18.1	18.7
81	13.1	13.4	13.8	14.2	14.7	15.1	15.6	16.2	16.7	17.3	17.9
82	12.4	12.7	13.1	13.5	13.9	14.4	14.9	15.4	15.9	16.5	17.1
83	11.7	12.1	12.4	12.8	13.2	13.7	14.2	14.7	15.2	15.7	16.3
84	11.1	11.4	11.8	12.2	12.6	13.0	13.4	13.9	14.4	15.0	15.5
85	10.5	10.8	11.1	11.5	11.9	12.3	12.8	13.2	13.7	14.3	14.8

*From Internal Revenue Service Regulation § 1.401 (a) (9)—9 A-3

Appendix E
Inflation Table

78 Years of INFLATION					
1926–2003					
1926	-1.1%	1952	0.8%	1978	9.0%
1927	-2.3%	1953	0.7%	1979	13.3%
1928	-1.2%	1954	-0.7%	1980	12.5%
1929	.6%	1955	0.4%	1981	8.9%
1930	-6.4%	1956	3.0%	1982	3.8%
1931	-9.3%	1957	2.9%	1983	3.8%
1932	-10.3%	1958	1.8%	1984	3.9%
1933	.8%	1959	1.7%	1985	3.8%
1934	1.5%	1960	1.4%	1986	1.1%
1935	3.0%	1961	0.7%	1987	4.4%
1936	1.4%	1962	1.3%	1988	4.4%
1937	2.9%	1963	1.6%	1989	4.6%
1938	-2.8%	1964	1.0%	1990	6.1%
1939	0.0%	1965	1.9%	1991	3.1%
1940	.7%	1966	3.5%	1992	2.9%
1941	9.9%	1967	3.0%	1993	2.7%
1942	9.0%	1968	4.7%	1994	2.7%
1943	3.0%	1969	6.2%	1995	2.5%
1944	2.3%	1970	5.6%	1996	3.3%
1945	2.2%	1971	3.3%	1997	1.7%
1946	18.1%	1972	3.4%	1998	1.6%
1947	8.8%	1973	8.7%	1999	2.7%
1948	3.0%	1974	12.3%	2000	3.4%
1949	-2.1%	1975	6.9%	2001	1.6%
1950	5.9%	1976	4.9%	2002	2.4%
1951	6.0%	1977	6.7%	2003	1.9%

From Bureau of Labor Statistics—Consumer Price Index—All Urban Consumers—U.S. City Average—All Items 1982-84 = 100.

Appendix F
Minimum Required
Distributions from IRAs

Table for Determining Applicable Divisor for MDIB* (Minimum Distribution Incidental Benefit)

Age	Applicable Divisor	Age	Applicable Divisor
70	27.4	93	9.6
71	26.5	94	9.1
72	25.6	95	8.6
73	24.7	96	8.1
74	23.8	97	7.6
75	22.9	98	7.1
76	22.0	99	6.7
77	21.2	100	6.3
78	20.3	101	5.9
79	19.5	102	5.5
80	18.7	103	5.2
81	17.9	104	4.9
82	17.1	105	4.5
83	16.3	106	4.2
84	15.5	107	3.9
85	14.8	108	3.7
86	14.1	109	3.4
87	13.4	110	3.1
88	12.7	111	2.9
89	12.0	112	2.6
90	11.4	113	2.4
91	10.8	114	2.1
92	10.2	115 and older	1.9

*From Internal Revenue Service Regulation § 1.401 (a) (9)—9 A-2. Use this table unless your spouse is your beneficiary and your spouse is more than 10 years younger than you. If your spouse-beneficiary is more than 10 years younger than you, see Regulation § 1.401 (a) (9)—9 A-3.

Appendix G
Valuation Checklist for Shares of Closely-Held Corporation

1. List the stockholders with the number of shares of each class owned by each stockholder.
2. List the officers and directors.
3. Examine the Corporate Record Book.
4. Is the corporation in good standing with states where it does business?
5. What is the history of sales or gifts of shares, and the valuation of shares for deceased stockholders?
6. Are any Buy-Sell Agreement or other stock restrictions in effect?
7. Compensation of family members over last 5 years:
    *   Salaries
    *   Bonuses
    *   Employment contracts
    *   Deferred compensation agreements
    *   Perks (cars, club dues, expenses accounts)
8. Top management:
    *   Today?
    *   In 5 years?
    *   In 10 years?
9. Is there Key Man Insurance? On whom? How much? What type?
10. Is the corporation a likely acquisition target?
11. Who are the corporation's main competitors?
12. Does the corporation own patents, trademarks, or other intellectual property?
13. Prospective corporate earnings?
    *   One year?
    *   Five years?
    *   Ten years?
14. Describe expected volatility in earnings over next 5 years.
15. Are there product line budgets and profit and loss statements?

16. Who are the corporation's main suppliers?
    - Nature of the relationship?
    - Any fixed purchase agreements?
    - Reliability of supply?
17. Who are the corporation's main customers?
    - Nature of the relationship?
    - Any fixed sale agreements?
    - Expected stability/growth vs. risk of loss?
18. Regarding assets:
    - Land—book vs. fair market value: Any appraisal done?
    - Building—book vs. fair market value: Any appraisal done?
    - Equipment—book vs. fair market value: Any appraisal done?
    - Depreciation method—SL vs. DB (building/equipment)?
    - All assets titled in corporate name?
    - Any liens on assets?
    - Receivables—How good?
    - Inventory—How good?
    - Goodwill?
    - Unrecorded assets?
19. Regarding liabilities:
    - Any payments in arrears?
    - Any agreements in default?
    - All tax liabilities current?
    - Any contingent liabilities?
    - Unrecorded liabilities?
    - Long-term leases? (terms favorable/unfavorable?)
20. Any lawsuits pending or expected?
21. Product liability issues?
22. Other current or expected legal issues?
23. Is there adequate insurance?
    - Fire/casualty?
    - Public liability?
    - Product liability?

24. Nature of banking relationships:
    - Banks utilized?
    - Specific nature of relationship?
    - Line of credit—Amount used? Amount available? Terms?
25. Any extraordinary charges or credits to income or retained earnings within last 5 years?
26. Any change in accounting methods in last 5 years? Are statements audited? Examine reports.
27. Nature of the industry and history of the business (including product and market evolution)?
28. Condition of the industry—future outlook?
29. Niche within industry?
30. Any comparable company which has publicly traded stock?
31. Any foreign competition?
32. Any opportunities in foreign markets?
33. Expected effect—positive or negative—of changes in currency exchange rates?
34. Number of employees:
    - Union—Today?—In 5 years?
    - Non-union—Today?—In 5 years?
    - Salaried—Today?—In 5 years?
    - Hourly—Today?—In 5 years?
35. Key employees by department:
    - Sales
    - Marketing
    - Production
    - Finance
    - Administration
36. Is there a written Mission Statement? Written business plan?
37. What are the plans for future growth of the company?
    - Marketing?
    - Capital expansion?
    - Return on equity?
38. Is there a succession plan for key stockholders?
39. Obtain financial statements for last 5 years.
40. Obtain tax returns for last 5 years.

Appendix H
Examples of Intestate Succession Laws

Assumptions: $500,000 gross estate ($400,000 accumulated out of earnings during the marriage, including a $200,000 residence, and $100,000 acquired before the marriage or by gift or inheritance during the marriage), with decedent survived by a 50-year-old spouse and two adult children from a prior marriage, but no children of this marriage, and debts and estate expenses of $37,000. Assume the couple always lived in the state shown.

	California	Illinois	New York	Ohio	Texas
Separate property state or community property state?	Community	Separate	Separate	Separate	Community
Priority Claims Of Spouse					
Homestead allowance [1]	$ 0	$ 0	$ 1,333	$12,000	$71,000
Exempt property [2]	0	0	40,000	15,000	5,000
Family allowance [3]	24,000	18,000	2,667	40,000	24,000
Total Priority Claims (A)	$ 24,000	$18,000	$44,000	$67,000	$100,000
Estate Distribution					
Gross estate	$500,000	$500,000	$500,000	$500,000	$500,000
Deduct community property owned by surviving spouse (B)	(200,000)	0	0	0	(200,000)
Net probate estate	$300,000	$500,000	$500,000	$500,000	$300,000
Debts and expenses	(37,000)	(37,000)	(37,000)	(37,000)	(37,000)
Priority claims of spouse (A)	(24,000)	(18,000)	(44,000)	(67,000)	(100,000)
Net Distributable Estate (C)	$239,000	$445,000	$419,000	$396,000	$163,000
Distribution of Net Estate:					
To surviving spouse	*$79,666	*$222,500	*$234,500	*$145,333	*$61,000
To adult children of prior marriage	**159,334	**222,500	**184,500	**250,667	**102,000
Net Estate Distribution (C)	$239,000	$445,000	$419,000	$396,000	$163,000

Recapitulation

		(1)	(2)	(3)	(4)	(5)
Debts and expenses		$37,000	$37,000	$37,000	$37,000	$37,000
To surviving spouse:						
Community property (already owned by surviving spouse)	(B)	200,000	0	0	0	200,000
Priority claims	(A)	100,000	67,000	44,000	18,000	24,000
Specific monetary share [4]		0	*20,000	*50,000	0	0
Share of remaining estate [5]		*61,000	*125,333	*184,500	*222,500	*79,666
Subtotal		$361,000	$212,333	$278,500	$240,500	$303,666
To adult children of prior marriage:						
Share of remaining estate [5]		**102,000	**250,667	**184,500	**222,500	**159,334
Total		$500,000	$500,000	$500,000	$500,000	$500,000

(1) <u>Homestead allowance</u>—assuming decedent's interest in the residence is valued at $100,000:

California: No specific homestead allowance apart from the family allowance (Prob. C. 6540 et seq.).

Illinois: No specific homestead allowance apart from the family allowance (755/ILCS 5/15—1).

New York: Widow may remain in house for 40 days without liability for rent (R.P.L § 204). Assume a fair rental value of $1,000 per month for this half interest, or $1,333 for 40 days.

Ohio: Surviving spouse may remain in the homestead free of charge for one year, or receive fair rental value if it is sold within that year (RC 2106.15). Assume a fair rental value of $1,000 per month for this half interest, or $12,000 for one year.

Texas: The homestead shall descend and vest in like manner as other real property of the deceased and shall be governed by the same laws of descent and distribution, but shall not be partitioned during the lifetime of the surviving spouse so long as the surviving spouse elects to use it as a homestead (Texas Probate Code § 283; Texas Const. Art. XVI, § 52).

In this example, the decedent's 50% community property interest in the residence vests in the children, but in effect, the surviving spouse has a life estate as a homestead interest (Thompson v. Thompson (1951) 236 S.W. 2nd 779). For purposes of a dollar value comparison, the author has quantified the value of a life estate in the decedent's $100,000 community property interest in the residence to a 50-year-old surviving spouse by use of Internal Revenue Service Regulation § 20.2031-7 (d) (7) and a 5 percent interest assumption, with the result rounded to the nearest $1,000. On this basis, the present value of the homestead is $71,000. (The valuation would be higher for a younger person and lower for an older person. Arguably, the present value could be discounted further on the basis that the surviving spouse might not use the property as a homestead for the rest of his or her life.)

(2) <u>Exempt property</u>—assuming appraised value of decedent's share of household goods, etc., is $10,000, and that decedent owned one automobile valued at $15,000:

California: No specific exempt property allowance beyond family allowance (Prob. C. 6540 et seq.).

Illinois: No specific exempt property allowance beyond selection of personal property as part of family allowance (755/ILCS 5/15-1).

New York: Household goods, furniture, computers, books, personal effects, etc., up to $11,000; farm machinery, etc., up to $15,000; one motor vehicle up to $15,000; money or other personal property up to $15,000 (E.P.T.L. § 5-3.1). In this case, add $15,000 of "money" to the assumed $10,000 household goods, etc., and $15,000 automobile.

Ohio: Up to two automobiles having a total value not exceeding $40,000 (RC 2106.18), and one watercraft, one outboard motor, or one of each (RC 2106.19) shall pass to the surviving spouse. Household goods are distributed to the surviving spouse as part of the specific monetary share included in the net estate paid to the surviving spouse. Assume one $15,000 automobile and no watercraft.

Texas: The court shall, by order, set apart for the use and benefit of the surviving spouse, minor children, and unmarried children remaining with the family of the deceased, all such property of the estate as is exempt from execution or forced sale by the constitution and laws of the state (Texas Probate Code § 271). The exemption covers certain household goods, vehicles, tools, and apparatus of trade or profession, etc. (Texas Const. Art. XVI, § 49) Upon termination of estate administration, such property passes to the decedent's heirs or devises (Bolton v. Bolton (1998) 977 S.W. 2nd 157). Assume exempt property valued at $25,000, discounted to $5,000 for its temporary use by the surviving spouse during estate administration.

(3) Family allowance—assuming a surviving spouse and no minor children:

California: A reasonable allowance for maintenance may be granted by the Probate Court (Prob. C. 6540 et seq.). Assume an allowance of $2,000 per month for one year, or $24,000.

Illinois: A sum of money deemed reasonable by the Probate Court for the family's support for nine months. Consideration is given to the spouse's condition, the condition of the estate, and non-probate assets received by the spouse. Minimum award $10,000 (755/ILCS 5/15-1). Assume an allowance of $2,000 per month for nine months, or $18,000.

New York: Reasonable sustenance for 40 days is allowable (R.P.L. § 204). Assume $2,000 per month, or $2,667 for 40 days.

Ohio: $40,000 to the family (surviving spouse and minor children, if any) minus, if two automobiles pass to the surviving spouse as exempt property, the specified value of the automobile having the lower value (RC 2106.13).

Texas: The court shall fix a family allowance for the support of the surviving spouse and minor children of the deceased. The surviving spouse and minor children may, by application and affidavit disclosing their separate property, apply for an amount necessary for maintenance for one year (Texas Probate Code § 286). The application may be denied where adequate separate property exists (Noble v. Noble (1982) 636 S.W. 2nd 551). Assume an allowance of $2,000 per month for one year, or $24,000.

(4) Specific monetary share to surviving spouse:

California: No specific monetary share beyond the family allowance.

Illinois: No specific monetary share beyond the family allowance.

New York: $50,000 to surviving spouse if decedent is survived by spouse and one or more children (or descendents) of decedent (E.P.T.L. 4-1.4).

Ohio: The first $60,000 if the surviving spouse is the natural or adoptive parent of at least one of the decedent's children, or the first $20,000 if the surviving spouse is not the natural or adoptive parent of any of the decedent's children (R.C. 2105.06).

Texas: No specific monetary share beyond the family allowance.

(5) Share of decedent's remaining estate (as far as it relates to surviving spouse and children of decedent):

California: **RE: Decedent's one-half interest in community property and quasi-community property:**
- 100% to surviving spouse if decedent is not survived by a child (or descendants) or a parent (or descendants) (Prob. C. 100, 101, 6101[a] and [b]).
- 50% to surviving spouse if decedent is survived by one child (or descendants), or parent(s) (or descendants of parent(s)).
- 33 1/3% to surviving spouse if decedent is survived by more than one child (or their descendants) (Prob. C. 6401).

RE: Decedent's separate property:
- 100% to surviving spouse if no children (or descendants), or no parents (or descendants of parents) of decedent.

- 50% to surviving spouse if decedent is survived by one child (or descendants), or parent(s) (or descendants of parent(s)).
- 33 1/3% to surviving spouse if decedent is survived by more than one child (or their descendants) (Prob. C. 6401).

Illinois:

- 100% to surviving spouse if no children (or descendants) of decedent.
- 50% to surviving spouse and 50% to child or children (or descendants) of decedent if decedent had one or more children (755/ILCS 5/2—1).

New York:

- 100% to surviving spouse if no children (or descendants) of decedent.
- 50% to surviving spouse and 50% to child or children (or descendants) of decedent if decedent had one or more children (E.P.T.L. § 4-1.4).

Ohio:

- 100% to surviving spouse if no children (or descendants) or all children (or descendants) are children (or descendants) of decedent and surviving spouse.
- 100% to children (or descendants) if no surviving spouse.
- 50% to surviving spouse and 50% to child (or descendants) if there is one child of decedent, and surviving spouse is not the natural or adoptive parent.
- 33 1/3% to surviving spouse and 66 2/3% to children (or descendants) if there is more than one child (or descendants) of decedent, and surviving spouse is not the natural or adoptive parent (R.C. 2105.06).

Texas: **RE: Decedent's one-half interest in community property:**

- 100% to surviving spouse if no children (or descendants), or all children (or descendants) are children of decedent and surviving spouse.
- 50% to surviving spouse and 50% (subject to surviving spouse's life estate in the homestead) to child or children (or descendants) if there is one or more child/children of decedent, and surviving spouse is not the natural or adoptive parent thereof. (Prob. C. § 45).

RE: Decedent's separate property:

- Real property to children (or their descendants), subject to a 33 1/3% life estate for surviving spouse, and 33 1/3% of decedent's personal property absolutely to surviving spouse if decedent survived by a child or children (or their descendants), and 66 2/3% to children (or their descendants).

- 50% of real property and 100% of personal property to surviving spouse if decedent survived by no descendant, but survived by parent(s) or their descendants.

- 100% to surviving spouse if decedent is not survived by descendants, parents, or descendants of parent(s).

- 100% to children (or their descendants) if there is no surviving spouse (Prob. C. § 38 [b]).

Appendix I
Examples of Spousal Election Laws

<u>Assumptions</u>: Husband dies after 15 years in a second marriage leaving a 50 year old wife and two adult children from a prior marriage. His probate estate is $150,000, which includes his $100,000 interest in the residence as tenant-in-common. He also had $300,000 in a revocable living trust and $50,000 in a joint tenants with right of survivorship account. His will, trust, and joint account leave all his property to his two adult children. His wife elects to take her statutory share.

		Model 1990 UPC[1]	Florida[2]	Illinois	Michigan[3]	New York[4]	Ohio
Deceased husband's probate estate	(A)	**$150,000**	**$150,000**	**$150,000**	**$150,000**	**$150,000**	**$150,000**
Less assumed deductions:							
Debts and expenses	(B)	37,000	37,000	37,000	37,000	37,000	37,000
Priority claims of wife:							
Homestead) Also See		15,000	71,000	-0-	15,000	1,333	12,000
Exempt property) Appendix		10,000	10,000	-0-	10,000	40,000	15,000
Family allowance) H		18,000	18,000	18,000	18,000	2,667	40,000
Total Priority Claims	(C)	$43,000	$99,000	$18,000	$43,000	$44,000	$67,000
Total deductions (B + C)	(D)	$80,000	$136,000	$55,000	$80,000	$81,000	$104,000
Net probate estate (A - D)	(E)	**$70,000**	**$14,000**	**$95,000**	**$70,000**	**$69,000**	**$46,000**
Add decedent's non-probate testamentary substitutes:							
Revocable living trust		$300,000	$300,000	$0-	$0-	$300,000	$0-
JTWROS bank account		50,000	50,000	-0-	-0-	50,000	-0-
Total	(F)	$350,000	$350,000	$0-	$0-	$350,000	$0-
Add wife's UPC Segment 4 assets:							
Assets subject to probate		100,000	-0-	-0-	-0-	-0-	-0-
IRA		50,000	-0-	-0-	-0-	-0-	-0-
Total	(G)	150,000	-0-	-0-	-0-	-0-	-0-
Total amount subject to wife's elective share (E + F + G)	(H)	**$570,000**	**$364,000**	**$95,000**	**$70,000**	**$419,000**	**$46,000**
Calculation of elective share		50% of (H)	30% of (H)	33-1/3% of (H)	$50,000 + 25% of (H - $50,000)	33-1/3% of (H)	33-1/3% of (H)
Wife's elective share		**$285,000**	**$109,200**	**$31,667**	**$55,000**	**$139,667**	**$15,333**
Funding of elective share							
UPC Fund 1 (All of "G")		$150,000	-0-	From net probate estate ("E")	From net probate estate ("E")	From net probate estate ("E") and non-probate testamentary substitutes ("F")	From net probate estate ("E")
UPC Fund 2 [From "E" + "F"]		135,000	109,200				
UPC Fund 3 (None needed)		-0-	-0-				
Total		$285,000	$109,200				

(1) 1990 Uniform Probate Code with accrued percentage of augmented estate.

(2) Florida has adopted the Uniform Probate Code but has a life estate homestead exemption (quantified here by the author to a present value based upon Internal Revenue Service Regulation § 20.2031-7 (d) (7) and a 5 percent interest assumption).

(3) Michigan has adopted the Uniform Probate Code but has not adopted the augmented estate portion.

(4) New York has not adopted the Uniform Probate Code but by statute and case law includes non-probate testamentary substitutes in the calculation of a surviving spouse's elective share.

Appendix J
Table of Cases

Chapter Two—Property Ownership and Transfer:

Matter of Estate of Savage (1994)
259 ILL. App. 3rd 328
631 N.E. 2d 797

In re: Estate of Thompson (1981)
66 Ohio St. 2nd 433
423 N.E. 2d 90

Steinhauser v. Repko (1972)
30 Ohio St. 2nd 262
285 N.E. 2d 55

Wright v. Bloom (1994)
69 Ohio St. 3rd 596
635 N.E. 2d 31

Chapter Three—Prenuptial Agreements:

Dubin v. Wise (1976)
41 Ill. App. 3rd 132
354 N.E. 2d 403

Juhasz v. Juhasz (1938)
134 Ohio St. 257
16 N.E. 2d 328

Eule v. Eule (1974)
24 Ill. App. 3rd 83
320 N.E. 2d 506

Posner v. Posner (1970)
Memo: FL Court
233 So. 2d 381

Fletcher v. Fletcher (1994)
68 Ohio St. 3rd 464
628 N.E. 2d 1343

Troha v. Sneller (1959)
169 Ohio St. 397
159 N.E. 2d 899

Gross v. Gross (1984)
11 Ohio St. 3rd 99
464 N.E. 2d 500

Worthington v. Worthington (1986)
21 Ohio St. 3rd 73
488 N.E. 2d 150

Hook v. Hook (1982)
69 Ohio St. 2nd 234
431 N.E. 2d 667

Chapter Eight—Intestate Succession, Wills, Trusts:

Beresford v. Stanley (Ohio 1898)
9 Ohio Dec. 134
6 Ohio N.P. 38

In re: Reynolds (1996) **
NY A.P. CT.
664 N.E. 2d 1209

Doyle v. Schoot (1989)
65 Ohio App. 3d 92
582 N.E. 2d 1057

Smythe v. Cleveland Trust Co. (1961) **
172 Ohio St. 489
179 N.E. 2d 60

Dumas v. Estate of Dumas (1994) **
68 Ohio St. 3d 405
627 N.E. 2d 978

Sullivan v. Burkin (1984)
390 Mass. 864
460 N.E. 2d 572

Niemes v. Niemes (1918) **
97 Ohio St. 145
119 N.E. 503

Wallbrown v. Kent State Univ. (2001)
143 Ohio App 3rd 762
758 N.E. 2d 1213

Chapter Nine—Probate, Spousal Elections, Will Contest, Trust Contest:

Dunnewind v. Cook (1998)
Ind. Ct. App.
697 N.E. 2d 485

Newman v. Dore (1937)
275 N.Y. 371
9 N.E. 2d 966

Goodrich v. City National Bank
& Trust Co. (1935)
270 Mich. 222
258 N.W. 253

Rose v. Union Guardian Trust Co. (1942)

300 Mich. 73
1 N.W. 2d 458

In re: Estate of Henne (1981)
66 Ohio St. 2d 232
421 N.E. 2d 506

In re: Estate of Smith (1997)
120 Ohio App. 3d 480
698 N.E. 2d 455

Johnson v. LaGrange State Bank
Muskegon (1978)
73 Ill. 2d 342
383 N.E. 2d 185

Soltis v. First of America Bank-
(1994)
203 Mich. App. 435
513 N.W. 2d 148

Krischbaum v. Dillon (1991)
58 Ohio St. 58
567 N.E. 2d 1291

West v. Henry (1962) *
173 Ohio St. 498
184 N.E. 2d 200

*   Also cited in Chapter Eight
**   Also cited in Chapter Nine

0-595-31047-8